PLACE NAMES OF

WISCONSIN

Edward Callary

The University of Wisconsin Press

The University of Wisconsin Press
1930 Monroe Street, 3rd Floor
Madison, Wisconsin 53711-2059
uwpress.wisc.edu

3 Henrietta Street, Covent Garden
London WC2E 8LU, United Kingdom
eurospanbookstore.com

Printed in the United States of America

This book may be available in a digital edition.

Library of Congress Cataloging-in-Publication Data
        Names: Callary, Edward, author.
        Title: Place names of Wisconsin / Edward Callary.
        Description: Madison, Wisconsin: The University of Wisconsin Press, [2016]
            | Includes bibliographical references.
        Identifiers: LCCN 2016012949 | ISBN 9780299309640 (pbk.: alk. paper)
        Subjects: LCSH: Names, Geographical—Wisconsin. | Wisconsin—History.
        Classification: LCC F579 .C35 2016 | DDC 977.5—dc23
        LC record available at https://lccn.loc.gov/2016012949

For

William and **Kathryn**,

Namers of Tomorrow

A place is only space until it has a name

Contents

Acknowledgments

Many people and institutions contributed to the creation of this book, foremost among them the library of the Wisconsin Historical Society, a magnificent resource and one of Wisconsin's cultural treasures. In addition, I want to thank each of the following librarians, local historians, and informed citizens who responded willingly and patiently to my often tedious requests. Many of their names appear in the body of this book for providing personal communications. I thank them all and offer my sincere apologies to anyone I may have overlooked. I especially appreciate the comments of the three anonymous readers of the manuscript whose suggestions have made this a more readable and more reliable book.

Mike Abitz
Cindy Arbiture
Karen Baumgartner
Lorraine Beyersdorff
Carrie Bissen
Charlene Borghese
Beverly Brayton
Peggy Derrick
Beth Dippel
Pamela Ekholm
Kaylene Engel
Timothy L. Ericson
Matt Figi
Rick Hass
Nancy Hawkinson
Joe Hermolin

Nicholas J. Hoffman
Marion Howard
Julie Johnson
Cecil Kavajecz
Carol Krogan
Kathy Laakso
Don Lau
Helen Lena
Linda Levenhagen
James Linak
Bruce Lindgren
Glenda Lyons
Mike Maki
Maureen Malone
Carol March McLernon
Nanci A. Mertes

Amy Meyer
Melanie Meyer
Mara Munroe
Cynthia Nelson
Julie Nosgovitz
Dan Olson
Kent Peronto
William D. Petersen
Mary Quante
Randall E. Rohe
Jarrod Roll

Marilyn Rudrud
Heidi Rushmann
John Russell
Tom Schuller
Sharon Strieter
Denny Thompson
Eric Vanden Heuvel
Don Weggen
Kitty Werner
Nick Zuvich

 Introduction

The idea for this book came to me somewhat by chance more than a decade ago. On one of my many pleasure trips from northern Illinois to Wisconsin I was looking through the list of place names on the Wisconsin state highway map and it struck me: "You can find almost all of Europe in Wisconsin." I saw such names as Arland and Valders from Norway, Stockholm and Lund from Sweden, Paris and La Grange from France, Orihula and Cadiz from Spain, Bern and Helvetia from Switzerland, Alma and Sevastopol from Russia, Oulu and Ladoga from Finland, Dundee and Elcho from Scotland, Askeaton and Avoca from Ireland, Brussels and Rosiere from Belgium, and Crivitz, Schleswig, and several Berlins and Hamburgs from Germany, along with dozens of names from England and Wales. To judge from its place names, Wisconsin was the Europe of the West. This observation led me on a pleasant journey of several years searching for the origins of Wisconsin's place names, all the while being conscious of how the names reflected and embodied the peoples and cultures of the state over the nearly five hundred years of its recorded history. The place names of Wisconsin provide glimpses into the lives of its citizens, their origins, histories, and records of their concerns, their hopes, their ambitions, and their legacies to twenty-first-century Wisconsinites.

Place names are formally called *toponyms*—a word made up of Greek *topos* meaning 'place' and *nym* meaning 'name.' Toponyms include the names of landforms, such as mountains and rivers, and political divisions, such as counties and cities. How many toponyms are there in Wisconsin? No one can say for sure, but as of mid-2016 the U.S. Geographic Names Information System (GNIS), the nation's digital gazetteer, included more than forty thousand names for Wisconsin, ranging from the names of two levees (Whitman Dike in Buffalo County and Yellow Banks in Portage County) to the names of more than three thousand churches and five thousand lakes. It would be nice to know the origins of all of these names, but in order to keep this book to a manageable size and serve readers who are primarily interested in their home-towns and the places near them, I concentrated on the names of populated places and civil divisions rather than on natural features of the landscape. I began with a list of the 2,259 names of inhabited places found in DeLorme's *Wisconsin Atlas and Gazetteer*. To this number I added the names of Wisconsin's counties, the town names that did not duplicate community names, and the name of the state itself. This brought the number to nearly 3,500. Of these I was able to determine to my satisfaction the sources or most likely sources of the slightly more than two thousand names that are included in this book. To my great regret, among the missing thousand are some of Wisconsin's more intriguing names, such as Radspur, Weirgor, and Frog Station.

I have generally not included the names of landforms, such as islands, caves, and mountains (Timm's Hill, Wisconsin's highest peak, is mentioned because it provided the name of the Town of Hill in Price County); some rivers and lakes are mentioned when communities or towns took their names. While I have reluctantly omitted the names of such features as airports (but see Foscoro below), military bases, bridges, colleges, and universities, there is one name that simply cannot be omitted from any book claiming to deal with Wisconsin's names, and another, the name of the state itself, that deserves more consideration than an entry in the body of the book can provide. The first name, which has become synonymous with Wisconsin and its people, is of course Badger.

The badger (*Taxidea taxus*) appears on the Wisconsin state seal and on the state flag and since 1957 has been the official state animal. Although several origins of the relationship between creature and Wisconsinite have been proposed, Badger as a moniker most likely arose in the mid-1820s and originally referred to a small group of hardscrabble prospectors and lead miners of south-western Wisconsin who created primitive shelters for themselves by tunneling into the sides of hills or valleys, much as badgers hollowed out their dens. Wisconsinites have been known as Badgers since at least the early 1830s, when New York newspaper editor Charles Fenno Hoffman, after an extended visit to the Great Lakes, wrote of meeting "a long-haired 'hooshier' from Indiana, a couple of smart-looking 'suckers' from the southern part of Illinois, [and] a keen-eyed, leather-belted 'badger' from the mines of Ouisconsin." The name was disparaging at first, but by the Civil War it had become a badge of honor. Several Wisconsin regiments carried battle flags that featured a badger. The Third Independent Battery of Wisconsin Light Artillery was known as the Badger Battery, and Company F of the Wisconsin Twenty-Eighth Infantry was called the Badger Guard. (For an authoritative account of the name, see Karel D. Bicha's "From Where Come the Badgers?")

The origin and meaning of the name of the state have been objects of much speculation and controversy for nearly a century. Wisconsin takes its name from the Wisconsin River, which heads in Vilas County and flows south through central Wisconsin for nearly 450 miles, turning sharply west where it forms the boundary between Dane and Sauk Counties and emptying into the Mississippi River south of Prairie du Chien. It would take several pages merely to list the various recordings and meanings, both silly and serious, that have been proposed since 1673, when Jacques Marquette wrote in his journal, "The river on which we embarked is called Mescousing," and 1838, when Frederick Marryat, a British army officer, gave the first known account of the meaning of the name: "This river has been very appropriately named by the Indians the 'Stream of the Thousand Isles,' as it is studded with them" (Vogel, "Wisconsin's Name," 182). The problems with Wisconsin's name are two: the original and historical meaning of the name and the change of the initial consonant from *M* to *W*.

First, considering the source and meaning of the name, the following chronological selection is representative of the variety of suggestions that have been made since 1838. (See Vogel, "Wisconsin's Name," for background and criticism.) The only agreement is that Wisconsin is an adaptation of a Native American name for the Wisconsin River. Brunson's mid-nineteenth-century suggestion is the most widely known and has been adopted by a number of tourism and promotional bodies for its association of Wisconsin with untamed nature and raw beauty, associations more inviting than 'little muskrat house' or 'where it is cold.'

Alfred Brunson (1855), Ojibwa, 'gathering of the waters'
Frederic Baraga (1879), Ojibwa, 'beaver or muskrat lodge'
Benard Brisbois (1880), Ho-Chunk, 'gathering, having many tributaries'
Elijah Haines (1888), Indian, 'strong current'
Chrysostom Verwyst (1891), Ojibwa, 'muskrat house' (Verwyst added "doubtful")
Henry Gannett (1905), Sauk, 'holes in the banks of a stream in which birds nest'
Frederick Lawrence (1920), Sauk, 'wild rushing channel'
Alanson Skinner (1921), Menominee, 'little muskrat house'
John Herrington (1934), Ojibwa, 'grassy place'
Charles Hockett (1948), Potawatomi, 'toward where it is cold, to the north'
Phebe Nichols (1948), Menominee, 'a good place to live'
Virgil Vogel (1965), Mesquaki (Fox), 'red land'
Edward Taube (1967), Algonquian, 'at the great point'

Little more became known of the origin of Wisconsin's name until about 2005, when Michael McCafferty, a Native American language specialist at Indiana University, proposed the meaning 'it lies red,' from the now-extinct Miami-Illinois language and given to Marquette by one of his Miami-Illinois guides. According to McCafferty, "The 'red' in the Miami name of the Wisconsin River refers to the spectacular red sandstone walls through which the river flows at the Wisconsin Dells. Naming the Wisconsin River after its most striking geological features is consistent with Miami placenaming practices" (53). And indeed red sandstone is a conspicuous feature of the Wisconsin River shoreline through much of its length.

The second problem concerns the spelling of the name. The following chronological list is suggestive of recordings of the name, from Marquette's 1673 Miscousing to 1845, when Wisconsin became the official form. All are from maps—identified by cartographer or publisher, unless otherwise indicated. Extended summaries of these variants can be found in Vogel (*Indian Names*; "Wisconsin's Name"), Cassidy ("Miscousing—Wisconsin"), and McCafferty.

Marquette (1673), Miscousing
Jolliet? (1674), Misconsing
Franquelin (1681), Miscous
Thévenot (1681), Missiosing
La Salle (1682), Ouisconsing, or Misconsing
Hennepin (1683), Ouiscousin, Ouisconsin, Ouisconsing
Coronelli (1688), Miscousin
Franqueli (1688), Ouisconsing
Morden (London) (1688), Miscousin
Coronelli (1694), Ouisconsing
Delisle (1700), Ouisconsin
Lahontan (1703), Ouaricon-sint[1]
Nicholas de Fer (1705), Ouisconsing ou Misconsin Riv.
Guignas (1728), Ouiscousin

1. In 1944, George R. Stewart, the preeminent American names scholar of his time, argued that an early form of the name of what appears to be the Wisconsin River was altered into that of the state name Oregon. Stewart claimed that Ouaricon-sint (or Ouaricon-sink), which appears (hyphenated) on Lahontan's map of the Great Lakes, was modified first by Major Robert Rogers to Ouragon and Ourigan, and then by traveler Jonathan Carver to Oregon. This issue continues to be disputed, and it is far from clear that the names of both Wisconsin and Oregon derive from the same source.

Lewis Evans (Philadelphia) (1755), Wisconsing[2]
Sauk and Fox Treaty (1804), Ouisconsing
Thomas Forsyth (1812), Ouisconsin
Stephen H. Long (1822), Wisconsin[3]
Territorial Legislature (1845), Wisconsin[4]

The earliest recordings of Wisconsin are unanimous in writing the initial consonant as *W*; of this there is no dispute. Marquette and Jolliet clearly heard and recorded *W*. The question is why *M* was rewritten *Ou* by La Salle (and La Salle is inconsistent; in one report he writes the name with initial *M* and later in the same report with *Ou*). McCafferty has proposed an ingenious explanation, arguing that La Salle rewrote Jolliet's Misconsing with a French cursive capital *M* that he later mistook for *Ou*, the typical spelling for French phonetic [*w*]. La Salle's formidable presence in French exploration of North America and his influence with leading cartographers of the day both in Quebec and Europe not only provided for but guaranteed that the *Ou* spelling would prevail. The question then became when would the French *Ou* spelling of [*w*] be eclipsed by *W*, the English spelling of [*w*]. Lewis Evans, working in British rather than French North America, was the first cartographer to use the *W* spelling, in his General Map of the Middle British Colonies in America.

Origins of the Names

Most of Wisconsin's names come from the following sources or were created through the following naming processes.

Native American Names

Anyone who looks at a Wisconsin map or pages through a Wisconsin atlas or gazetteer will notice the large number of names that appear to be Native

2. This is the first known map to spell the name of the river with initial *W*.

3. James Finlayson, cartographer for Carey and Lea, Philadelphia publishers, credits Stephen H. Long, an engineer with the U.S. War Department, with establishing this form of the name, making it the first known recording with the present spelling.

4. By making the spelling Wisconsin official, the legislature rejected several other spellings, including Wiskonsan, which had been vigorously promoted by territorial governor James Duane Doty. The U.S. Congress had formally recognized the spelling Wisconsin a decade earlier when the Wisconsin Territory was organized in July 1836.

American. Indeed, the naming of Wisconsin owes a great deal to Native Americans, whose naming legacy began with the arrival of the first Paleoamericans some ten to twelve thousand years ago as the last North American ice sheet receded. We have no direct knowledge of the names they gave to the landscape, but many of their names were surely continued by their descendants, notably the Menominee and Ho-Chunk (Winnebago) peoples and later the Ojibwa and Potawatomi. Despite the different languages from which they came, however, Native American place names in Wisconsin share a number of characteristics. They were overwhelmingly descriptive, suggestive of the area's flora or fauna or human activity, names such as Ojibwa *sisibakwatokan* 'place where sugar is made' (today's Sugar Island), Ho-Chunk *tichora* 'green lake,' and Menominee *nepiaskon* 'cattails, rushes' (modern Nepeuskun). To say, however, that Native American naming was largely descriptive is not to suggest that it was in any sense simple or rudimentary; in fact, it was quite the opposite. Native American naming, in Wisconsin as in other parts of North America, was complex, sophisticated, and often poetic. Ojibwa *nijode* 'twin' was the name of the site where today's West Twin River merges with East Twin River (now the city of Two Rivers) before the conjoined streams flow into Lake Michigan, and long before French explorers reached the Mississippi River the Ho-Chunk knew the rock island in the river at Lake Pepin as *hay-nee-ah-chah* 'soaking mountain.' This name was translated into French as *la montagne que trempe à l'eau* 'the mountain that stands in the water,' which was shortened and taken into English as Trempealeau.

Most of what we think of as "Native American" names in Wisconsin are, in the strictest sense, not Native American at all; that is, they are not names that were used by Native Americans for purposes of geolocation or reference to features of the political or natural landscape. Rather, the scores of Wisconsin's "Native American" names were given by Europeans largely in the nineteenth century, often in a burst of nostalgia long after native influence in an area had ceased. This extensive European naming based upon the Native American word stock took several forms. First, Native American words, whether or not they were topographic, were altered in spelling or pronunciation as necessary to be brought into line with European language patterns and used as place names. Ojibwa *kinoji* 'pike' became Kenosha, Ho-Chunk *ne ce day-ra* 'water yellow lake' became Necedah, and Menominee *okahkoneh* 'where there are pike' became Kaukauna. Second, Native American words were frequently translated—Ojibwa *mitchikan* 'enclosure' became Fence, and Ho-Chunk *day-wau-sha-ra* 'lake of the fox' became Fox Lake. Third, a number of "Native American" names are pseudo-Indian; they were confected by Europeans from presumed words or parts of words from native languages. The nineteenth-century ethnologist and geographer Henry Rowe Schoolcraft was notorious for creating names such as Tuscobia and Algoma from bits and pieces of native languages, particularly from parts of Algonquian words he claimed he encountered during his travels and researches along the Great Lakes. Finally, a number of Wisconsin's "Native American" names come from a naming tradition foreign to Native Americans—commemorative naming or naming a feature in honor of a person. Native Americans rarely if ever named places after individuals. Today's Oshkosh, Shawano, Tomah, Black Wolf, Waukechon—all recognizing Native American leaders—were named by Europeans after European naming practices became common in the nineteenth century. (For readers interested in Native American and Native American–associated names in Wisconsin, a good place to start is Virgil J. Vogel's inclusive but now dated *Indian Names on Wisconsin's Map*, first published by the University of Wisconsin Press in 1991.)

French Names

The first European known to set foot on the soil of what is now Wisconsin was Jean Nicolet de Belleborne, a French interpreter from Quebec, Canada, who met a band of Ho-Chunk near present Green Bay in the summer of 1634. Nicolet National Forest is named in his honor. In the wake of Nicolet came scores of French Canadian traders, trappers, and explorers who adapted or translated existing Native American names and contributed numerous place names of their own, especially in the late seventeenth and early eighteenth centuries, including what is likely the first written Wisconsin name, *La Baye des Puants*, 'the bay of the Winnebagos' for Green Bay, recorded by French voyageurs by the early 1640s. French names were often translations of Native American names or of Native American general vocabulary and used as place names: Menominee *wapesihpen* was translated into French as *pomme de terre*, the name of a tuberous root often translated as 'earth apple,' which in turn was taken into English as part of the name of Apple River; Ojibwa *wissakode* 'burned forest' became *bois brulé* (the modern Town of Brule); and *wauswagaming* 'at the lake of torches' became *lac du flambeau*, which exists in this form today as well as in English translation as Torch River and Torch Lake.

Many geographic features, to our knowledge, were first named by early French traders and explorers, names such as La Crosse, for the game played with the 'hooked stick'; Prairie du Sac 'meadow of the Sauk'; and Fond du Lac 'foot' or 'bottom' of the lake, referring to Lake Winnebago. Two French names, while not confined to the Great Lakes region, are associated with the area and have created a great deal of confusion and misinterpretation among English speakers: Embarrass and Dells. The Embarrass River, after which the Village of Embarrass in Waupaca County was named, was given its name by French boatmen, for whom an *embarras(s)* was an obstruction in a waterway created by uprooted trees or other debris that interfered with navigation. The current and traditional pronunciation is [AM brah], as recognized in the spelling of Ambrough Slough in Crawford County. The name has nothing to do with current English *embarrass* 'cause to be uncomfortable,' although a local story told tongue in cheek claims that the name is appropriate because the stream is so clear "you can see its bottom." The second such name is *dells*, made famous by the Wisconsin Dells resorts, named from American French *dalles* 'paving stones, flag stones,' which came to refer to a river channel and subsequently to a narrow valley. Through popular etymology the unfamiliar French *dalles* was transformed into the familiar English *dells*, also meaning 'valleys.'

Native American and French naming practices were largely replaced by two immigrant groups who began to arrive in the early decades of the nineteenth century: European settlers and Americans from the northeastern United States, both of whom brought their names and their naming traditions with them.

Transfer Names

Naming a new place for an old place, connecting new names with old names, has a long history in the naming of the Americas—as the names New England, New France, New Bedford, and New Iberia attest—but while limited in older areas, in the nineteenth century the practice became one of the major features of naming in the Midwest, where it provided a means to maintain emotional if not physical connections with farms, families, and communities left behind and likely not to be seen again. Often the word New was added, with all its implications of a fresh start and a bright future—New Amsterdam, New Munster, New Denmark—but most often the original name was given to the new location without modification. Norwegians brought with them the names Bergen, Requa, and Drammen; Germans brought Kiel, Cassel, and Hochheim; Swedes brought Falun and Veedum; Scots brought Melrose and Argyle; Czechs brought Kodan, Melnik, and Pilsen; Poles brought Krakow, Lublin, and Peplin.

As substantial as the European naming influence was, by far the largest number of transfer names in Wisconsin is from the northeastern United States, particularly New England: Rutland, Montpelier, and Burlington from

Vermont; Altoona, Montrose, and Paoli from Pennsylvania; Orfordville, Dunbarton, and Merrimac from New Hampshire; Portland, Somerset, and Unity from Maine; Westboro, Worcester, and Boyleston from Massachusetts. The largest name donor of all was New York State, which contributed upwards of one hundred place names to Wisconsin, running the alphabet from *A* to *W*: Albany, Barneveld, Cazenovia, Darien, Ellington, Fredonia, Genesee, Hamilton, Ithaca, Jordan, Lima, Marcy, Naples, Ontario, Paris, Rome, Saratoga, Tioga, Utica, Verona, and Waterford. Settlers from New York were so numerous that they were referred to collectively as Yorkers.

Often a name originated in the Northeast and made its way step by step across the country. Wyoming, a classic example, was first a name of the Wyoming Valley in northeastern Pennsylvania, from the Delaware language meaning 'at the big river flat.' From that local beginning, with the help of the popular Thomas Campbell poem "Gertrude of Wyoming," the name was carried to New York and from there progressively transferred west to more than a dozen states, including Wisconsin and the state of Wyoming. Potosi was originally the name of a silver mine in Bolivia, established by the Spanish in the 1540s. The name came to be associated with mining and wealth and was brought by miners first to Mexico in the late sixteenth century; then to Washington County, Missouri, by Moses Austin (father of Stephen F. Austin, the namesake of Austin, Texas), who began mining operations about 1800; then to Grant County, Wisconsin, in the 1830s by lead miners from Missouri.

Commemorative Names

By the time the Wisconsin Territory was organized in 1836 the Revolutionary War and the War of 1812 had been won, the Winnebago War and the Black Hawk War were over, Native Americans had ceded much of Wisconsin to the United States, and the Midwest was open for settlement. The cheap land now available was eagerly sought both by European settlers and by Americans moving westward. And what better way to confirm Americans' identity and history and to demonstrate their presence in the world than to commemorate the nation's founders and heroes? Washington and Jefferson were honored, of course, along with Europeans who had played an important role in the nation's founding, such as the Marquis de La Fayette. Not only were individuals honored, commemorative naming often extended to artifacts associated with them as well; estate names in particular became popular place names: Mount Vernon, Monticello, La Grange. In addition to the nation's founders, other illustrious national, state, and local figures were honored. Twelve of the first twenty governors of Wisconsin are remembered in the names of counties, towns, or communities, from the first, Nelson Dewey in 1848, through Leonard J. Farwell, Alexander W. Randall, Lucius Fairchild, Cadwallader C. Washburn, William Robert Taylor, Harrison Ludington, Jeremiah Rusk, William D. Hoard, George W. Peck, and William H. Upham, to the twentieth, Robert M. La Follette in 1901. Commemorative naming became so common that the practice was expanded from honoring national and local personalities to less well-known citizens, especially those who laid off building lots on their land for an expected community that they named for themselves or for close family members. These hoped-for communities failed by the hundreds but many live on, often unrecognized, in the names they gave to roads, cemeteries, schools, airports, and other sites whose names now seem oddly unconnected with their locations. Current names suggestive of the many now vanished communities that once carried the dreams and hopes of their founders include:

- Shueyville Road, near Clarno in Green County, a reminder of Shuey-ville, south of Monroe, founded by miller and farmer John W. Shuey, who purchased the site early in 1847 and established the Shuey's Mills post office in June of 1854. The community prospered for a time, but when the railroad was built through Clarno, the decline of Shueyville was ensured.
- The Foscoro Airport, near the Door-Kewaunee county line, takes its name from the former community of Foscoro, founded in 1869 by businessman George Rowe and Port Washington lawyers Henry Coe and George Foster. So that no one would feel slighted, the three founders blended the names of Foster, Coe, and Rowe into Foscoro. Rowe established the Foscoro post office in August 1871; the office was discontinued five years later.
- Some five miles east of Albany on the way to Evansville, a short highway connecting West Finnernan Road and Wisconsin 59 bears the intriguing name North Croak Road, a name that is completely opaque unless we know that it led to the once-viable community of Croak(e), named for Jimmy Croak, who emigrated from Kilkenny, Ireland, about 1840. The community is now little more than a memory but its previous existence lives on in the name of North Croak Road.
- Suldal Road and the Suldal Cemetery are reminders of the once active but now vanished community of Suldal west of Mauston in the Town of Lindina in Juneau County. Suldal was a Norwegian community founded in the late 1850s and named by settlers from Suldal in southwestern Norway.

Other Names

Native American names, French names, transfer names, and commemorative names are major types of Wisconsin's names, but there are a number of minor and complementary naming sources. Wisconsin is well represented with names associated with religion (Calvary, Lebanon, Jericho) and names taken from mythology, largely Norse (Iduna, Ino), and literature, especially note-worthy being Sir Walter Scott's Scottish novels (Athelstane, Ettrick, Melrose) and Henry Wadsworth Longfellow's 1855 epic poem *The Song of Hiawatha* (Pukwana, Misha Mokwa). Then, too, there are the many names given by the railroads (officials of the Wisconsin Central were especially eager to see that stations and the communities that grew around them carried for perpetuity the names of railroad officials, financiers, and their former homes in the East) and the hundreds of post offices that grew like Wisconsin weeds in the middle decades of the nineteenth century, many of which carried the names of the first postmasters, their family members, or their personal whims.

Glossary and Abbreviations

Within the entries, the words *city*, *town*, and *village* are capi-
talized only when they are necessary parts of official names; otherwise, they are
lower case.

city	A city is an incorporated administrative unit usually but not always more populous than a village. Bayfield, a city with a population of under five hundred, is smaller than many villages. There are currently about 190 cities in Wisconsin.
community	As the term is used here, a community is an advanced settlement; that is, a community is an inhabited site that has developed from an original settlement.
p.c.	Personal communication. Used to acknowledge contributions from individuals rather than printed sources.
popular etymology	When the origin of a name is unknown, there is a tendency to invent a plausible story to explain it. Trimbelle in Pierce County is said to have been named for a pretty girl, a "trim belle." As used in this book, popular etymology also includes modifying non-English spellings and other anglicizing and Americanizing of foreign words and

names. The town and community of Gordon in Douglas County was named for French fur trader Antoine Guerdon, and the name Guerdon, being foreign to local English speakers, was replaced with the familiar English Gordon. In like manner, Swedish Bengtsson became American Benson, and German Kuhne became Keen.

ppl A geographer's term (a shortening of "populated place") that refers to an area of human habitation of indeterminate population or geographic size. As used here, a ppl is an unincorporated area with a population and a name but may be no more than a site with one or two families and perhaps a store or gas station. Unless identified as a city or village, a site is presumed to be a ppl.

settlement As used here, a settlement is a previously uninhabited site upon which one or more immigrants established a residence. With the arrival of more immigrants a settlement may become a community.

town In Wisconsin a town is different from a surveyor's township, and it does not mean "a small community." Strictly speaking, a town is a minor civil division, and all areas in Wisconsin that are not incorporated as cities or villages are parts of towns. Wisconsin towns are similar to townships in other states, and the terms are often used interchangeably, as they are here.

village A village is an incorporated administrative unit usually but not always less populous than a city. The Village of Menomonee Falls, for instance, with a population greater than thirty-five thousand, is larger than many cities. There are currently about four hundred villages in Wisconsin. For want of a better word, as used here, village may also refer to a more or less permanent location inhabited by Native Americans.

Structure of the Entries

Each entry contains up to seven fields: headword, pronunciation if uncertain or unexpected, the county or counties in which the headword referent is located, incorporation status (if any) and date(s) of incorporation (if any), discussion of the name, and references.

The headwords identify more than two thousand inhabited geographical locations in Wisconsin. These are locations listed in DeLorme's *Wisconsin Atlas and Gazetteer*, augmented by the addition of the names of Wisconsin's seventy-two counties and twelve hundred or more towns. For example:

Oulu [OO loo]. Bayfield. Town (1904) and ppl. Named from the Oulu post office, established in September 1903 by Andrew Lauri, who chose the name for his birthplace, Oulu, a province and city in central Finland on the Gulf of Bothnia. This is the only Oulu in the United States. (*Historical Sketches of the Town of Oulu*, 20)

This is to be read: Oulu is in Bayfield County and was organized as a town in 1904; Oulu is also an unincorporated community (ppl) in Bayfield County. Both the town and the community took their name from the Oulu post office, itself named from Oulu in Finland. The pamphlet *Historical Sketches of the Town of Oulu*, especially page 20, provided some of the information used to prepare this entry.

At times, different places may bear the same name:

Portland. Dodge. Town (1846) and ppl. Monroe. Town (1856) and ppl.

Portland is the name of a town, organized in 1846, and the name of an unincorporated community in Dodge County. Portland is also the name of a town, organized in 1856, and an unincorporated community in Monroe County.

When an entry is not identified as a county, a town, a city, or a village, it is assumed to be a populated place (ppl) as in

Reighmoor [RAY mor]. Winnebago. Reighmoor is a community of lakefront homes on Lake Butte des Morts. Named for Stephen Reigh, an official of the Globe Realty Company, which founded the community in the 1920s. (Munroe, p.c.)

The dates should be used with caution, since a town, city, or village may have taken its name from an existing post office that was established several years before incorporation. The Adell post office, for instance, was established in Sheboygan County in 1851, but it was not until 1918 that the Village of Adell, which took its name from the post office, was incorporated.

The more than five hundred references cited in this book are not definitive but are intended to provide a starting point for further research on the names. They must be approached with caution, however, since they differ widely in coverage and reliability. Many are excellent resources, well researched and critically evaluated, while others are less trustworthy and consist of little more than repeated popular etymologies and local folklore, unidentified as such. Frederic Cassidy's investigations of Wisconsin names, conducted over more than fifty years, is name research at its very best. His *Dane County Place-Names*, first published in 1947 and reissued in 2009, is rightly regarded as a model of research, organization, and presentation. Probably the most well-known book on Wisconsin's names, Robert Gard and L. G. Sorden's *Romance of Wisconsin Place Names*, first published in 1968, is an engaging book, and as the name implies it is a "romance" in the true sense of the word. It is filled with the legends, folk tales, and stories that surround Wisconsin names, but it does not pretend to be an authoritative source. It is best seen as a companion to rather than a competitor of this book.

Pronunciation Guide

I have included broad phonetic transcriptions for names where the pronunciation is not obvious from the spelling or where local pronunciation is different from what the spelling or usage elsewhere would suggest, for instance, *Gingles* [JING guhlz], *Waino* [WAY no]. The accented syllable is in capital letters.

The phonetic symbols are illustrated first by a common English word and then by a Wisconsin place name:

[a] as in cat, Ackley [AK lee]
[ay] as in able, Abrams [AY bruhmz]
[ah] as in hot, Wonewoc [WAHN uh wahk]
[e] as in pet, Esdaile [EZ dayl]
[ee] as in eat, Chelsea [CHEL see]
[i] as in fifteen, Binghamton [BING uhm tuhn]
[eye] as in mine, Bovina [bo VEYE nuh]
[o] as in know, Eau Pleine [o PLAYN]
[oo] as in rude, Oulu [OO loo]
[u] as in hook, Basswood [BAS WUD]
[uh] as in about, Bavaria [buh VEHR ee uh]
[yoo] as in cute, Bellevue [BEL vyoo]
[er] as in heard, Hustisford [HYOOS tis ferd]
[ehr] as in fair, Jericho [JEHR uh ko]
[ahr] as in far, Marcellon [mahr SEL uhn]

[or] as in four, Orienta [or ee EN tuh]
[ow] as in how, Outagamie [OWT uh gay me]
[aw] as in saw, Waukau [WAW kaw]
[oy] as in toy, Beloit [buh LOYT]
[ch] as in itch, Charme [CHAHRM]
[g] as in leg, Hegg [HEG]
[j] as in edge, Portage [PORT ij]
[k] as in clean, Couderay [KOO duh ray]
[kw] as in quick, Quincy [KWIN see]
[ng] as in sung, Koshkonong [KAHSH kuh nahng]
[sh] as in hush, Tisch Mills [TISH]
[th] as in teeth Heath Mills [HEETH]
[z] as in easy, Hiles [HEYELZ]
[zh] as in treasure, Winneboujou [win uh BOO zhoo]

Place Names of Wisconsin

Lake *Superior*

DOUGLAS
BAYFIELD
IRON
ASHLAND
VILAS
MICHIGAN
WASHBURN
BURNETT
SAWYER
FLORENCE
PRICE
ONEIDA
FOREST
POLK
BARRON
RUSK
MARINETTE
LINCOLN
LANGLADE
TAYLOR
ST. CROIX
DUNN
CHIPPEWA
MARATHON
MENOMINEE
OCONTO
PIERCE
EAU CLAIRE
CLARK
SHAWANO
PEPIN
PORTAGE
WAUPACA
BROWN
KEWAUNEE
BUFFALO
WOOD
OUTAGAMIE
JACKSON
TREMPEALEAU
WINNEBAGO
MANITOWOC
LA CROSSE
ADAMS
WAUSHARA
CALUMET
MINNESOTA
MONROE
MARQUETTE
JUNEAU
GREEN
LAKE
FOND
DU LAC
SHEBOYGAN
VERNON
COLUMBIA
DODGE
OZAUKEE
RICHLAND
SAUK
WASHINGTON
CRAWFORD
MILWAUKEE
IOWA
IOWA
DANE
JEFFERSON
WAUKESHA
GRANT
RACINE
GREEN
ROCK
WALWORTH
KENOSHA
LAFAYETTE
ILLINOIS

MINNESOTA

Lake *Michigan*

DOOR

0   50 miles

N

Abbotsford [AB uhts ferd]. Clark, Marathon. City (1965). Named from the Abbotsford post office, established in June 1880, itself named for Edwin H. Abbott, a Boston lawyer who relocated to Milwaukee in the mid-1870s. Abbott, Charles Colby, and Colgate Hoyt were trustees of the stock of the Wisconsin Central railroad, and all three named stations and communities after themselves. See Colby; see Hoyt. (R. Martin, 28)

Abells Corners [AY buhlz]. Walworth. Named for one or more Abell families. Benjamin Abell, a schoolteacher and farmer, emigrated from Perry, New York, about 1844. (*Commemorative Biographical Record of the Counties of Rock, Green*, 419)

Abrams [AY bruhmz]. Oconto. Town (1917) and ppl. Abrams was known as West Pensaukee until 1882 when it was formally established by the Milwaukee & Northern railroad. Named for William J. Abrams, who served in the Wisconsin Assembly and was mayor of Green Bay in the early 1880s. (Rucker, "Lumbering Makes Oconto County")

Ackerville. Washington. Named from the Ackerville post office, which was established as Station in April 1856. The name was changed from Station to Ackerville when Philip Acker, from Hesse, Germany, became postmaster in March 1870.

Ackley [AK lee]. Langlade. Town (1879). Named for William (aka Willard) L. Acly, from Coventry, Chenango County, New York, possibly born in England. Acly came to Wisconsin in the early 1850s, changed the spelling of his name to Ackley, established a logging camp near the confluence of the east and west branches of the Eau Claire River, and was instrumental in the organization and early development of the town that bears his name. (Mendl and Mendl, 72)

Adams. Adams County was organized in 1848 and named in honor of John Quincy Adams (1767–1848), sixth president of the United States (1825–29), who had died less than a month before. The choice of the name may have been influenced by the popularity of John Adams, second president of the United States and father of John Quincy Adams. The city of Adams was founded about 1910 when the tracks of the Chicago & North Western railroad were laid a mile south of Friendship. The community that grew around the station was first known as Lower Friendship or South Friendship and later renamed, apparently by the railroad, for its location in Adams County. See Friendship; see Quincy.

Addison [AD uh suhn]. Washington. Town (1846) and ppl. Probably named for Addison, Vermont, possibly for Addison, New York, both named for the eighteenth-century English essayist and politician Joseph Addison. The post office was established in February 1847 as Hamer; changed to Addison in February 1850.

Adell [uh DEL]. Sheboygan. Village (1918). About 1873, site owner Christian Gersmehl laid out the community of Sherman, apparently named from the Town of Sherman. The name was changed about 1890 for the Adell post office, established in December 1851, Eliada Baldwin, postmaster. The source of the name is unknown. (Buchen, 272)

Adrian [AY dree uhn]. Monroe. Town (1854). Adrian is an original Monroe County township, created in 1854 largely through the efforts of William Wallace Jackson, a judge prominent in county government, who proposed the name for his former home, Adrian, Michigan, itself apparently named for the Roman emperor Hadrian, misheard as Adrian. About 1854 Jackson laid out the community of Jacksonville southwest of Tomah, which he expected would thrive as a station on the Chicago, Milwaukee & St. Paul railroad, but when the railroad took a different route Jacksonville began to decline. (Richards, 474)

Aetna (Etna) [ET nuh]. Lafayette. Probably named after Mount Etna, the famous volcano in Sicily. Etna's spectacular eruption in 1852 was widely reported in American newspapers. A Lafayette County history quotes an area resident: "There was a limekiln near here and the smoke, flames and fumes belching up from it resembled a volcanic eruption. As they had heard about Mount Aetna on the island of Sicily, they called the village Aetna" (*Lafayette County Bicentennial Book*, 149). The post office was established as Etna in March 1857, Jonathan Hoffman, postmaster.

Afton [AF tuhn]. Rock. Formerly known as Middleton or Middledale, the name Afton was chosen in the 1850s by Robert Harris, an engineer for the Beloit & Madison railroad and later superintendent of the Chicago & North Western. Harris took the name from the Robert Burns poem "Flow Gently, Sweet Afton," which Burns named from the Afton River in Ayrshire, Scotland. Afton is a popular place name, occurring in about half the states. (Stennett, 35)

Agenda [uh JEN duh]. Ashland. Town (1903). Apparently named from the Agenda post office, established in February 1887 by Alfred S. Eaton. According to a local account the name arose when the heading on a list of items to be considered at an early organizational meeting (the "agenda") was taken as an appropriate name. This is one of two places in the United States named Agenda; the other is in Republic County, Kansas.

Ahnapee [A nuh pee]. Kewaunee. Town (organized as Wolf in 1853, named from the Wolf River; changed to Ahnapee in 1859). George W. Wing, editor of the *Ahnapee Record*, recorded what he claimed was the Potawatomi legend of Ah-Ne-Pe, the great gray wolf. The Ahnapee post office was established in September 1858 and changed to Algoma in October 1897. See Algoma. (Howell, Foshion, and Ackerman, 9)

Ainsworth [AYNZ werth]. Langlade. Town (1904). Named for Thomas "Uncle Tom" Ainsworth, from Dorchester, England, a civil engineer and supervisor for the Keshena Improvement Company during construction of the Wolf River dam in 1869. (Dessureau, 184)

Akan [AY kuhn]. Richland. Town (1855). Probably named for Robert Aiken, from Allegheny County, Pennsylvania, described in Butterfield's 1884 *History of Crawford and Richland Counties* as "a genial, pleasant fellow [and] very well liked by his neighbors" (824). Robert Aiken represented the district in the state assembly in 1856. The post office was established in June 1858 as Akan, a phonetic spelling of Aiken, Zenas W. Bovier, postmaster.

Alaska. Kewaunee. Named for the Alaska Territory, purchased from Russia by the United States in 1867. The Alaska post office was established in June 1870, Frank Kwapil, postmaster.

Alban [AL buhn]. Portage. Town (1877) and ppl. Named in honor of James S. Alban, who came to Plover from Ohio in the mid-1840s. Alban was a lawyer and a state senator in the early 1850s. He was commanding officer of the Eighteenth Wisconsin Volunteer regiment during the Civil War and was mortally wounded at the Battle of Shiloh (Pittsburg Landing), Tennessee, in 1862. (Rosholt, *Our County, Our Story*, 224)

Albany [AWL buh nee]. Green. Town (1849) and Village (1883). First known as Campbell's Ford. The community was founded in 1847 by Dr. James Nichols and Erastus O. Pond, the latter a former Great Lakes ship captain who was the first Albany postmaster in 1848. Named for one of the eastern Albanys, likely Albany, New York, or Albany, Vermont. (Butterfield, *History of Green County*, 677)

Albany. Pepin. Town (1858). Likely named by settlers from Albany, New York, itself named in 1664 in honor of the Duke of Albany, later king of England as James II. Albany is a popular place name, occurring in more than half the continental states. (*Pepin County History*, 6)

Albertville. Chippewa. The local account is that the community was named for Albert Halvorsen, an Eau Claire barber and shopkeeper. The post office was established in March 1892, Frank A. Johnson, postmaster. ("Communities Draw Names")

Albion [AL bee uhn]. Dane. Town (1846) and ppl. Albion is an ancient and poetic name for England (and for Scotland), modified and interpreted as Latin *albus* 'white,' probably named for the White Cliffs of Dover. More than half the states have at least one place named Albion. The first permanent settler in what is now the Town of Albion in Dane County was Freeborn Sweet, according to his obituary, "a man of kind and generous heart," who arrived in the summer of 1841. Sweet Cemetery is named for the Sweet family. Early settler Isaac Brown suggested the name Albion for his former home in Orleans County, New York. The town of Albion in Trempealeau County (1870) may have been named by Adam Umphrey Gibson, who founded the Gibson School west of Eleva and who had lived for a time near Albion, Ontario. The circumstances regarding the naming of the town of Albion in Jackson County (1849) are unknown. Albany (q.v.) is from the same etymological source. (Cassidy, *Dane County Place-Names*)

Alderley. Dodge. Likely named by early settlers for Alderley Edge, a communty and parish east of Liverpool, England. The post office was established in September 1856, Jence Jerensen, postmaster.

Algoma [al GO muh]. Kewaunee. City (1879). Winnebago. Town (1850). Algoma in Kewaunee County was earlier known as Wolf River Trading Post and also as Ahnapee. The name was formalized as Algoma in 1897. An article in the *Ahnapee Record* at that time (probably written by editor George W. Wing) called Algoma "a melodious Indian name." Several meanings have been proposed: 'rosy hill,' 'park of flowers,' 'sandy place,' and 'snowshoe.' *Algoma*, however, has no meaning and it is not a genuine Native American name. Rather, it was confected by the nineteenth-century naturalist and ethnologist Henry Rowe Schoolcraft. In addition to Algoma, Schoolcraft coined *Itasca* and several other pseudo-Indian names. School-craft gave several accounts of the origin of Algoma. On one occasion he said the name was a blend of *Al-* from *Algonquian* and *goma* 'collected waters,' and on another he claimed the meaning was 'sea of Algonquians.' Although it is without a traditional etymology, Algoma, as Vogel notes, is "one of the more picturesque of the coined names in Wisconsin" (*Indian Names*, 233). Algoma is a popular place name; it first appeared in Michigan and has spread to Wisconsin, Mississippi, Virginia, West Virginia, Idaho, and Oregon, and, as a variant, Algona, to several other states as well. See Ahnapee; see Itasca.

Allen. Eau Claire. Founded by Charles L. Allen, a lawyer and real estate developer, who was the organizer and president of the Allen Land Company in the late 1880s and the Cameron Meadows Land Company in the early 1910s. (Bailey, 465)

Allens Grove. Walworth. In 1844 brothers Pliny, Sidney, Asa, Harvey, and Philip Allen, along with their wives, their children, and their father—sixty people in all—traveled from Rochester, New York, to Racine, settling at Allens Grove, which they laid out in 1852. The post office was established in September 1849, Philip Allen, postmaster. (Beckwith, 395)

Allenton. Washington. Founded as Dekorra by the Wisconsin Central railroad in 1882. The name was changed the following year for Andrew A. Allen, superintendent of the railroad. (Reinders and Melberg, 55)

Allenville. Winnebago. Named for site owner Timothy Rush Allen Sr., who emigrated from Madison County, New York, about 1865. Allen provided part of his farm to secure a station on the Chicago & North Western railroad. The Allenville post office was established in January 1882, Russell T. Hopkins, postmaster. (Stennett, 36)

Allouez. Brown. Town (1873) and Village (1986). Also an unincorporated community in Douglas County. Named for Claude-Jean Allouez (1622–89), a French Jesuit priest who was posted to New France in 1658. Allouez was given responsibilty for bringing Christianity to Native Americans of the Great Lakes region, and in carrying out this charge he established a mission near present La Pointe on Madeline Island in Lake Superior in 1665 and several missions in the Green Bay area, including the Mission of St. Francis Xavier near present Oconto. Allouez was an astute observer of his physical and cultural surroundings, and the detailed geographic and ethnographic information that he recorded proved to be of great value to later explorers, cartographers, and settlers. The Allouez post office operated in Douglas County from May 1899 until July 1903. The pronunciation is generally [AL uh way]. (Cassidy, *Brown County*)

Alma [AL muh, AWL muh]. Buffalo. Town (1856) and City (1885). Before the arrival of the first permanent settlers in the late 1840s, the area was known to pilots on the Mississippi River as Twelve Mile Bluff for the prominent rock outcropping used as a landmark and navigational aide. By the end of January 1856 William Hamilton Gates, from New York State, had purchased the townsite, laid out the community, and established the Alma post office, which he named for the Alma River in Russia, the site of one of the first battles of the Crimean War in 1854, which was widely reported in the press of the day. Alma is a popular place name, appearing in some twenty states, and was one of the more popular names for girls born in the United States in the late nineteenth and early twentieth centuries. (Curtiss-Wedge, *Buffalo and Pepin Counties*, 84)

Alma. Jackson. Town (1855). Also Alma Center. Village (1902). Several writers have suggested the town was named for Alma, the Nephite prophet of *The Book of Mormon*, but more likely the name was taken from the Alma River in the Crimea (see Alma, Buffalo County, above). Alma Center was first known simply as the Corners, then as Athol, named by Elisha Stockwell for his family home, Athol, Massachusetts, itself named for the Duke of Athol (Scotland). The post office was established as Athol in 1869; changed to Alma Centre in 1874 and to Alma Center in 1893. (*Jackson County, a History*, 27)

Almena [al MEEN uh]. Barron. Town (1899) and Village (1945). Founded in 1887 by Albert H. Koehler and Stone W. Sparlin. According to Sparlin, the petition for a post office called for the name Lightning City, named from Lightning Creek. When the post office department found this name unacceptable, Sparlin created *Almena* by blending *Al* from Albert with *mena* from Wilhelmina, the name of Koehler's wife. (Gordon and Curtiss-Wedge, 1133)

Almond [AL muhn(d), AWL muhn(d)]. Portage. Town (1851) and Village (1905). The community that became the Village of Almond was founded about 1850 by Sheldon Doolittle, a Methodist Episcopal minister, who chose the name for his former home, Almond, Allegany County, New York. (Drewiske, 2)

Alpha [AL fuh]. Burnett. A number of early settlers in the late 1860s were from Småland in southern Sweden. The area became known as Smaland Prairie and this was the name on the first post office application, which was rejected by federal postal authorities. Guy E. Noyes, the first postmaster, then resubmitted the petition with the name Alpha, reportedly from Alpha de Laval, the brand name of the separator he had just bought for his creamery. (Landelius and Jarvi, 243)

Alto [AL to]. Fond du Lac. Town (1847) and ppl. Apparently named about 1844 by Silas Miller, a lay preacher of the Methodist Episcopal Church, who operated a sawmill on the Rock River. The reason for Miller's choice of the name is uncertain. Worthing, noting the strong Dutch presence in the area, suggests the source may be Dutch "Halte, meaning 'stop' or 'resting place.'" The post office was established in August 1850, William S. Gillet, postmaster.

Altoona [al TOO nuh]. Eau Claire. City (1887). Altoona was founded in 1881 as East Eau Claire by the Chicago, St. Paul, Minneapolis & Omaha railroad as a railyard with roundhouse and shop facilities. The following year the railroad changed the name of the station to Altoona, for Altoona, Pennsylvania, itself named for Allatoona, Georgia. Roadmaster W. E. Beal has been credited with proposing the name, but the evidence favors Thomas P. Gere, superintendent of the railroad at the time. The choice of the name may have been influenced by settlers from Altona, Hamburg, Germany. (Hagen, 1)

Alverno [al VER no]. Manitowoc. Alverno developed around the Silver Lake Convent for the Holy Family of the Franciscan Sisters of Charity, which was founded about 1874. The name was formalized about 1876 for Mount Alverno in Italy, where St. Francis of Assisi, while at prayer, reportedly received the stigmata. (Kientz, 40)

Alvin. Forest. Town (1911) and ppl. Named for Alvin Spencer, a Baptist minister from Powell County, Kentucky, who brought his wife, Ashah

Jane, and their fifteen children to the area about 1908. The post office, with Alvin Spencer as postmaster, was established the following year. Spencer's granddaughter Nelma Brooks is the namesake of Nelma, five miles north of Alvin. ("Memories of Forest Co.," 182)

Amberg [AM berg]. Marinette. Town (1891) and ppl. Named for William Amberg, who owned several stone quarries in the area that specialized in granite paving and building blocks. The post office was established in 1884 as Pike; changed to Amberg in 1890. (*History of Amberg*)

Amery [AYM (uh) ree]. Polk. City (1919). Named for William Amery, a carpenter who had emigrated from England to Stillwater, Minnesota, in 1861. Amery held several township offices and served as Polk County treasurer in the early 1870s. The name was changed from Big Dam when the post office was established in December 1887. (Ericson, 2)

Amherst [AM herst]. Portage. Town (1852) and Village (1899). Most accounts agree that the name was chosen by Gilbert Park and Adam Uline for Amherst, Nova Scotia, Uline's former home, although some have suggested Amherst, Massachusetts, or Amherst, New York, as immediate sources. Amhersts in North America are ultimately named for Jeffery Amherst, First Baron Amherst, a British commander during the French and Indian War. Amherst was held in high regard by many Americans for his refusal to accept a field command during the Revolutionary War, and largely for this reason a number of communities have been named in his honor. The Amherst post office was established in June 1858, William Loing, postmaster. (Rosholt, *Our County, Our Story*, 242)

Amnicon [AM ni kahn]. Douglas. Town (1910) and ppl. Also Amnicon Falls. Named from the Amnicon River. From Ojibwa *aminikon* 'spawning ground,' related to *amiwag* 'they spawn.' The name may have been in use by the Northern Pacific railroad by the early 1880s. This is the only Amnicon in the United States. (Vogel, *Indian Names*, 156)

Anacker [AN uh ker]. Columbia. Named for the Anacker family, especially William Erigfreund Anacker, born in Hesse, Germany. Anacker served with the Union forces during the Civil War and was instrumental in the development of the community. (J. Jones, 711)

Anderson. Burnett. Town (1903). Named for Canute Anderson, for several years in the 1850s the only settler in the area. Anderson became a leading local political figure, representing the district in the state assembly in the late 1870s and early 1880s. He established the first post office in February 1860, which he named Berdo, reportedly for his birthplace in Norway. See Grantsburg. (Ericson, 2)

Anderson. Iron. Town. Organized in March 1900 as Vogel. The name was changed to Anderson in 1903 for J. B. Anderson, the first chair of the Town of Vogel. (Techtmann, 118, 147)

Angelica [an JEL uh kuh]. Shawano. Town (1886) and ppl. Probably named about 1866 by the first postmaster, Horace H. Wescott, for Angelica, Allegany County, New York, itself named for Angelica (Schuyler) Church, daughter of General Philip Schuyler, a hero of the Revolutionary War. (Michael)

Angelo [AN juh lo]. Monroe. Town (1854) and ppl. Seth Angle established a sawmill on the La Crosse River in the early 1850s. Angle's mill was bought by Edward Canfield, who laid out the community as Athens, the name probably chosen to rival nearby Sparta. The post office was established in 1855 as Angelo, a name created by postmaster Ira S. Angle by altering the Angle family name and perhaps incorporating 'O' from the name of Seth Angle's nephew, Oscar. (*Monroe County*, 14)

Angus [ANG guhs]. Barron. Founded in the summer of 1906 with establishment of the Angus post office by postmaster Matthew B. Uren. Although area historian Ethel Elliott Chappelle (*Around the Four Corners*, 45) claims that the name was "apparently" taken from Uren's herd of Angus cattle, more likely the name honors Angus Cameron, a leading Wisconsin political figure in the last half of the nineteenth century. Cameron was a U.S. senator (1875–81) and the namesake of the Village of Cameron (q.v.).

Aniwa [AN uh wah, AN uh wuh]. Shawano. Town (1885) and Village (1899). Named from the Aniwa post office, established by Thomas Dunn in January 1881. The origin of the name is uncertain. Possibly from Menominee *aniw* 'more, farther, beyond,' or a transfer with shortening from Annawan, Henry County, Illinois, itself named from Annawan Rock in Bristol County, Massachusetts. It is unlikely—although possible—that missionary reports from Aniwa island in the South Pacific prompted the name. This is the only Aniwa in the United States. (Vogel, *Indian Names*, 134)

Annaton [AN uh tuhn]. Grant. In the late 1850s William Kraemer established a wagon factory and general store at a site that became known as Bagdad. Kraemer formally laid out the community about 1861 as Anna's Town, named for Susannah Loy, wife of the first site owner and local physician, William Loy. Anna's Town was soon shortened to Annaton. This is the only Annaton in the United States. (*Grant County History*, 232)

Anson [AN suhn]. Chippewa. Town and ppl. The town name was suggested by early settler Arthur Clark in honor of the statesman and diplomat Anson Burlingame. Burlingame was a U.S. representative from Massachusetts in the late 1850s and was appointed minister to the Qing court of China by President Abraham Lincoln. By the time the town was organized in 1859, Burlingham had given several important speeches in the House of Representatives, which were widely reported. Communities in California and Kansas are also named for Anson Burlingame. (Stennett, 167)

Anston [AN stuhn]. Brown. Formerly known as Buckman, named for early settler Allan T. Buckman. The name was changed about 1906 by the Chicago & North Western railroad, apparently for a local Anston family. (Stennett, 37)

Antigo [AN ti go]. Langlade. Town (1881) and City (1885). In 1849 Francis Augustine Deleglise, "the father of Antigo," emigrated from Switzerland to Wisconsin where he became a successful surveyor and land speculator. Deleglise laid out the community as Springbrook about 1877 and changed the name in 1879, claiming that Antigo was the Ojibwa name of Spring-brook Creek. *Antigo* is a shortening of a Native American name that has been recorded in a number of forms, including *neequic-antigo-sebi*, *nequi-antigo-seebah*, and *nikwi-antigo-sibi*. The final element is clearly Algonquian for 'river,' but the significance of *antigo* is unknown. Several writers have suggested the name means 'balsam' or 'evergreen.' This is the only Antigo in the United States. (Vogel, *Indian Names*, 159)

Apollonia [ap uh LON ee uh]. Rusk. About 1880 Frederick Weyerhaeuser located the headquarters of one of his lumber companies at Vernon Junction. The site was renamed about 1893 for Weyerhaeuser's daughter Apollonia. See Weyerhaeuser. (*Rusk County History*, 13)

Apple River. Polk. Town (1876). The town took its name from Apple River, a translation with shortening of French *pomme de terre*, literally 'apple of the earth,' itself a translation probably based upon Menominee *wapesihpen*, the name of a white tuber also known as "arrowhead" or "duck potato." The same Algonquian root is found in the name of the Wapsipinicon River in Minnesota and Iowa. The Apple River post office was established in September 1877, Richard Pearson, postmaster. (Bright)

Appleton [AP uhl tuhn]. Calumet, Outagamie, Winnebago. City (1857). Modern Appleton includes the communities of Lawesburg, founded by George Lawe(s), and Martin, founded by Morgan Martin, both in 1849, and Grand Chute, laid out about 1850. Reeder Smith, a Methodist minister of the Michigan circuit, was largely responsible for the creation of Appleton. Smith chose the name for the Appletons, a prominent Boston family, in particular Samuel Appleton, who endowed the Lawrence Institute library, and Sarah Elizabeth Appleton, wife of Amos Lawrence, a wealthy Boston merchant and financier who pledged a large sum toward founding the Lawrence Institute, now Lawrence University, chartered in 1847. ("Samuel Appleton")

Arbor Vitae [AHR ber VEYE tuh]. Vilas. Town (1893) and ppl. Arbor Vitae, Latin for 'tree of life,' was founded in the fall of 1893 when the Ross Lumber Company built a sawmill, planing mill, stores, and homes. Named from Big and Little Arbor Vitae lakes, which, according to a local account, were themselves named for the local stands of white cedar, the bark of which Native Americans brewed into a tea to promote general health and provide protection from scurvy. (*Vilas County*, 3)

Arcade [ahr KAYD]. Fond du Lac. According to Worthing, "The name was doubtless suggested by the leafy trees . . . creating shady walks similar to a covered mall or arcade" (8). More likely, however, the name is a transfer from the village and township of Arcade in Wyoming County, New York. The post office was established in Adams County in June 1864 as Vinjie, probably named for a Norwegian settler named Vinjie (Vinje); changed to Arcade in October 1865.

Arcadia [ahr KAYD ee uh]. Trempealeau. Town (1856) and City (1925). Formerly known as Bishop's Settlement for early settler Collins Bishop. The name Arcadia was proposed by Sarah Bishop, wife of David Bishop, reportedly at the suggestion of another early settler, Noah Comstock. Arcadia was a district in ancient Greece, which came to be seen as a land of peace and prosperity, a paradise on earth. Because of these positive associations Arcadia is a popular place name, occurring in about half the states. (Curtiss-Wedge and Pierce, 270)

Arena. Iowa. Town (1849) and Village (1923). Arena was originally laid out north of its present location in the late 1830s, probably by Moses M. Strong, a lawyer, land speculator, and associate of James Duane Doty, who engaged Strong to survey the new capital at Madison. When it became clear that the railroad would be built a mile or so to the south, Arena was reestablished, probably by George M. Ashmore and Ebenezer Brigham. By the time the first train came through in 1856, most of Old Arena had been moved to trackside. The source of the name is unknown; possibly a transfer from Arena, Delaware County, New York. (*History of Iowa County*, 784–85)

Argonne [AHR gahn]. Forest. Town and ppl. Argonne was founded as Vanzile in the late 1880s by site owner Abraham Vanzile (Van Zile). The name was changed to North Crandon about 1892. The town was organized as North Crandon in 1901 and, as the result of a contest, in 1921 the name was changed in honor of the 1918 Allied offensive in the Argonne Forest in France. See Crandon. ("Memories of Forest Co.," 183)

Argyle [AHR geyel]. Lafayette. Town (1849) and Village (1903). Argyle was founded in the mid-1840s by Allen Wright and named for his former home in Scotland. The area was earlier known as Albion, a poetic name for England. (*Lafayette County Bicentennial Book*, 34)

Arkansaw [AR kuhn saw]. Pepin. Arkansaw takes its name from Arkansaw Creek, itself named about 1852 by Willard Holbrook, from Massachusetts. Holbrook established a sawmill about 1853 and platted Arkansaw in 1857. The reason for his choosing the name is unknown. The spelling reflects the usual pronunciation of Arkansas. (*History of Northern Wisconsin*, 705)

Arland [ARE luhnd]. Barron. Town (1904). Probably named for Arland (or Aurland), Norway, by Ole Johnson, who kept a general store and was instrumental in the organization of the township. The post office was established in April 1896, Peter Howe, postmaster. (Gordon and Curtiss-Wedge, 901)

Arlington [AHR ling tuhn]. Columbia. Town (1855) and Village (1945). Both the community and the town were named from the Arlington post office, established largely through the efforts of early settler Jeremy Bradley in 1852. The reasons for Bradley's choice of the name are unknown. Arlington, the name of several English villages, was transferred to Virginia in the seventeenth century and was the name of Robert E. Lee's estate, part of which is now the site of Arlington National Cemetery. There are more than a hundred Arlingtons in the United States, making this one of the more popular American place names. Any of the Arlingtons in the eastern states, especially those in New York or Vermont, may have provided the inspiration for Arlington, Wisconsin. (Columbia County Historical Society, 35, 58)

Armenia [ahr MEE nee uh]. Juneau. Town (1856). Named for what is now the Republic of Armenia, east of modern Turkey, perhaps by Armenian settlers but more likely from news reports of conflicts between Armenia and the Ottoman Empire. The post office was established in June 1858 by Jesse D. Sarles, a Methodist minister from New York.

Armstrong. Fond du Lac. The post office was established as Armstrong's Corners in June 1862 and named for postmaster Asher Armstrong, who had arrived in the area in 1851. The name was changed to Armstrong in June 1883. (Worthing)

Armstrong Creek. Forest. Town and ppl. The origin of the name is uncertain. Several namesakes have been suggested: an army engineer named Armstrong; Benjamin Armstrong, an Ojibwa interpreter who met with President Lincoln; and an unidentified railroad official. The town was organized in July 1922 as La Follette, named for former Wisconsin governor and then current U.S. Senator Robert M. La Follette. The name was changed to Armstrong Creek four months later. The post office was established in December 1888, Loren D. Lovewell, postmaster. (Kobylarz, 5)

Arnold. Chippewa. Formerly known as Silhawn, a blend of the names of W. H. Sill and Ed Hawn, officers of the Minneapolis Lumber Company, which located at Ruby in 1901. With establishment of the post office in 1905, it was renamed for Arnold Deuel by his father, postmaster Newton Deuel. See Ruby. (Nagel and Deuel, 14)

Arnott [AHR naht]. Portage. Named about 1880 for William L. Arnot, local landowner and civic leader. Arnot was chair of the county board and a member of the state legislature in 1877. His efforts to attract a station on the Green Bay, Winona & St. Paul railroad resulted in the station and post office being named in his honor. The spelling has alternated between Arnot and Arnott. (*Commemorative Biographical Record of the Upper Wisconsin Counties*, 19)

Arpin [AHR puhn]. Wood. Town (1901) and Village (1978). John and Antoine Arpin came to the area from Quebec, Canada, in the early 1860s. John Arpin and his sons Daniel and Edmund organized the Arpin Lumber Company, which laid out the community a mile east of its present location in 1890. (Jones and McVean, *History of Wood County*, 236)

Arthur. Chippewa. Town (1885). Named for Chester A. Arthur (1829–86), twenty-first president of the United States, serving 1881–85.

Arthur. Grant. Apparently founded as Washburn, reportedly named from the Washburn post office, established in 1855, by the first postmaster, John Newman, for early settler Arthur Washburn. The office closed early in August 1883 and reopened later that month as Arthur, possibly again for Arthur Washburn but more likely for Chester A. Arthur, then president of the United States. (Holford, 278)

Ashford [ASH ferd]. Fond du Lac. Town (organized in 1849 as Chili; changed to Ashford in 1854) and ppl. The name was reportedly proposed by Dr. Seth G. Pickett for the local stands of ash trees. The community of Ashford was founded by Ulrich Legler, who established a milling complex on the west branch of the Milwaukee River about 1859. See Elmore. (Butterfield, *History of Fond du Lac County*, 734)

Ashippun [ASH uh puhn]. Dodge. Town (1846) and ppl. Samuel Marshall, one of the first settlers in the early 1840s, suggested the name from the Ashippun River, often called the Ashburn River by popular etymology. Ashippun was probably a Potawatomi or Menominee name for the river, from a general Algonquian word for 'raccoon.' This is the only Ashippun in the United States. (Vogel, *Indian Names*, 148)

Ashland [ASH luhnd]. County (1860), Town (1872), and City (1887). The community of Ashland, from which the county and town take their names, was platted in the summer of 1854 for site owners Asaph Whittlesey (the first postmaster), George Kilbourn, and Martin Beaser. Beaser, a land speculator from New York who owned three-fourths of the community plat, was a great admirer of Henry Clay and suggested that the site be named for Clay's estate, Ashland, in Lexington, Kentucky. The post office was established as Whittlesey in March 1855, and the name was changed to Ashland in July 1860. (*History of Northern Wisconsin*, 66)

Ashton, Ashton Corners. Dane. Named from the Ashton post office, established in September 1849, itself named for Thomas Ashton, president of the British Temperance Emigration Society, founded in 1843 to promote immigration to the United States. By 1850 more than six hundred colonists had immigrated, one of whom was Henry Gillett, the first Ashton postmaster, in 1849. (Cassidy, *Dane County Place-Names*)

Ashwaubenon [ash WAH buh nahn]. Brown. Town (1872) and Village (1977). Named from Ashwaubenon Creek, the name of which is of uncertain origin. The Franciscan priest Chrysostom Verwyst, who lived and worked among the Ojibwa from the 1880s through the 1910s and was fluent in Ojibwa, claims the source is *ashiwabiwining* 'the place where they post a lookout.' Other writers, including Deborah Martin followed by Frederic Cassidy, an impeccable scholar of Wisconsin names, suggest a Menominee leader whose name was recorded as *Ashwaubemie, Ash-wau-pe-may*, and *Ashwaubena*. What meaning the name may have had is unclear; *Ashwaubenon* may well mean nothing more than 'the site of Ashwaubemie's camp.' (Cassidy, *Brown County*; D. Martin, 325)

Askeaton [as KEET n]. Brown. Named from the Askeaton post office, established in October 1868 by Maurice Summers, who named the office for his ancestral home, Askeaton, County Limerick, Ireland. (Cassidy, *Brown County*)

Astico [AS ti ko]. Dodge. Astico is probably a transfer from Hancock County, Maine, where the spelling is Asticou. Likely from an Abenaki word or personal name of uncertain meaning. (Bright)

Athelstane [ATH uhl stayn]. Marinette. Town (1903) and ppl. The community was named from the Athelstane quarry operated by William Amberg, which reportedly produced the darkest gray granite of all the quarries in the area. The quarry was likely named from a Scottish legend or from Athelstane, the thane of Coningsburgh in Sir Walter Scott's novel *Ivanhoe*. Athelstane is literally 'noble stone.' See Amberg. (*Marinette County Centennial*, 3)

Athens [ATH uhnz]. Marathon. Village (1901). Athens was founded in 1879 as Black Creek Falls by Fred Rietbrock, of the Milwaukee law firm Rietbrock, Johnson and Halsey. Rietbrock had purchased some fifty thousand acres in the area and actively recruited settlers from Europe as well as from the eastern states. Confusion between Black Creek Falls and Black River Falls led to a name change in January 1890. Schoolteacher Ferdinand Strupp suggested the name Athens, apparently influenced by the classical association of Athens and its location in Marathon County. See Rietbrock. (Sjostrom, 7, 8)

Atkins. Forest. Most likely named for Hubbard C. Atkins, superintendent of the Prairie du Chien & La Crosse railroad in the 1880s.

Atlanta. Rusk. Town (1901). About 1900 the Arpin Hardwood Lumber Company established a series of logging camps in the area around present Atlanta. The town was formally named in 1902, likely for Atlanta, Georgia. The post office was established in January 1902 by Arthur Arpin, son of John Arpin, a founder of the lumber company. See Arpin.

Attica [AD uh kuh]. Green. Formerly known as Winneshiek, named for a Winnebago leader whose village was near Freeport, Illinois, and later known as Milford. The post office was established in 1849 as Attica, the name proposed by Jeptha Davis, from Attica, Wyoming County, New York, itself named for the district of ancient Greece that included Athens. (Butterfield, *History of Green County*, 727)

Atwater. Dodge. Founded by Edwin and Joseph Hillyer, who operated a general store in Waupun from the 1840s. The brothers Hillyer named the community for their former home, Atwater, Portage County, Ohio, itself named for early settler and site owner Caleb Atwater. The post office operated from July 1858 until November 1863.

Aubrey [AW bree]. Richland. Named in honor of early settler Auburn Cass. Aubrey is apparently an adaptation of Auburn and perhaps Cass's nickname. The Aubrey post office was established in August 1899, Alfred H. Dow, postmaster. (Scott)

Auburn [AW bern]. The towns of Auburn in Fond du Lac (1847) and Chippewa (1872) Counties are transfers from Auburn, Cayuga County, New York. The name was popularized by Oliver Goldsmith's 1770 poem *The Deserted Village*, which begins "Sweet Auburn, loveliest village of the plain." As a place name, Auburn first appeared in the United States in New York at the beginning of the nineteenth century; there are now Auburns in thirty-six states. The village of New Auburn in Chippewa County was founded in the late 1870s as Cartwright and named for David W. and David J. Cartwright, father and son from New York, who erected a steam sawmill and spoke factory at the site in 1875. The name was changed in 1902 to Auburn and in 1904 to New Auburn. (Forrester, 52; Worthing)

Auburndale. Wood. Town (1874) and Village (1881). Named from the Auburndale railroad station and the Auburndale post office established by John Connor in June 1874. John and Robert Connor, from Scotland by way of Ontario, Canada, built the first mills, stores, and hotels in the area in the early 1870s. The brothers founded Auburndale and both claimed that they chose the name in honor of their auburn-haired daughters. This may, however, be a post hoc explanation, and Auburndale may be a transfer from Auburn, Massachusetts, near Worcester. Charles Colby, president of the Wisconsin Central railroad, was instrumental in building the railroad line from Stevens Point to Marshfield. Colby named a number of stations along the route for places in Massachusetts, including Worcester and Dedham. (R. Rudolph; *History of Northern Wisconsin*, 1214)

Augusta [uh GUHS tuh]. Eau Claire. City (1885). In the summer of 1856 the first permanent settlers arrived in the area then known as Bridge Creek, reportedly so named because the stream was too deep to ford and had to be crossed by a bridge. One of the settlers was Charles Buckman, who, along with John F. Stone, established a gristmill at the site. Buckman and Sanford Bills formally laid out Augusta in 1857, named for Augusta, Maine, Buckman's former home. (*History of Augusta*, 1)

Aurora [uh ROR uh]. Towns in Florence (1917), Taylor (1897), and Waushara (organized as Waushara in 1851; changed to Sacramento in 1854; changed to Aurora in 1859) Counties. Also Auroraville. Aurora, Latin for 'dawn,' is a popular place name, occurring in some thirty states. Many, including those in Wisconsin, are transfers from Aurora in Cayuga or Erie County in western New York State. The community of Aurora in Florence County was formerly known as Burnsville and Schneiderville, named for early settlers. Auroraville in Waushara County was known as Willow Creek and as Daniels Mills, for site owner Eli Wareham Daniels, who laid out the community in the early 1850s. (*Heritage of Iron & Timber*, 63; Reetz, 99)

Avalanche [AV uh lanch]. Vernon. Laid out about 1854 by Cyrus F. Gillett, from Orange County, New York. Gillett kept a general store and operated a sawmill on the Kickapoo River. According to the 1884 *History of Vernon County*, "The village takes its name from the formation of the earth immediately east of the place, which resembles a gigantic landslide or avalanche suddenly stopped in its destructive course" (722). Of the sixty-some geographic features in the United States named Avalanche, this is the only community so named.

Avalon. Rock. Named from the Arthurian legend where Avalon is a place of hope and peace. The name became popular in the 1890s after publication of Tennyson's *Idylls of the King*. The circumstances surrounding the naming of Avalon, Wisconsin, are unknown. The post office was established in December 1901 by Charles W. Brooks.

Avoca [uh VO kuh]. Iowa. Village (1870). Named about 1856 with construction of the Milwaukee & Mississippi railroad. Avoca is the name of a valley and river in County Wicklow, Ireland, where the Avonbeg and Avonmore Rivers join. The name was popularized by Thomas Moore's early nineteenth-century poem *The Meeting of the Waters*, which contains the lines "Sweet vale of Avoca! How calm could I rest / In thy bosom of shade, with the friends I love best." Rufus King, editor of the *Milwaukee Sentinel*, may have suggested the name Avoca Vale for the railroad station. Avoca was also the name of a short-lived community near Oakfield in Fond du Lac County in the early 1850s. (G. Shepard, 58)

Avon. Rock. Town (1847) and ppl. Avon is probably a transfer, most likely from Avon, New York, or Avon, Massachusettts. The name may have been chosen by early settlers William and Ermina Crippen, natives of Egremont, Massachusetts, who farmed in New York State for a decade and moved to the Avon area in the late 1840s. The post office was established as Avon Centre in May 1867. (W. Brown, 679)

Aztalan [AZ tuh luhn]. Jefferson. Town (1840) and ppl. Aztalan, Wisconsin's best known archaeological site, was first reported by Nathaniel Hyer of Milwaukee in 1836. Hyer was taken by the extent and complexity of the ruins and concluded that this must be the work of an advanced civilization. He named the site Aztalan for the legendary home of the Aztecs of Mexico, claiming that he had found the name and the Aztec tradition of a northern origin in the travel writings of the German naturalist Alexander von Humboldt. Aztalan was not the original home of the Aztecs but of people known as the Mississippian Culture (Mound Builders), which flourished in the eleventh and twelfth centuries. (Swart, 165)

Babcock. Wood. Named for Joseph Weeks Babcock, who owned and operated a sawmill complex at Nekoosa. Ever the entrepreneur, about 1890 when Babcock learned that the Chicago, Milwaukee & St. Paul railroad was planning to build a line through Remington Township, he formed the Babcock Land Company, which bought the site and built a hotel, depot, and other facilities for travelers and railroad employees. (Jones and McVean, *History of Wood County*, 240)

Bagley. Grant. Village (1919). Laid out about 1885 by the St. Paul Land Company, probably acting as agent for the Chicago, Burlington & Northern railroad. Named for site owners Alfred and Mary Bagley, originally from Vermont. (*Bagley through the Years*, 2)

Bagley. Oconto. Town (1917). Named for Charles and Levi Bagley, brothers from Maine who had extensive lumber operations in the area. (Werner, p.c.)

Bagley Junction. Marinette. Named for John Bagley, a Chicago lumberman who organized the Wisconsin & Michigan railroad in 1893 and later built the Tacoma Eastern railroad in Washington State. ("Iron Range Route")

Baileys Harbor. Door. Town (1861) and ppl. Named for a Great Lakes ship captain named Bailey who was caught in an unexpected, violent storm in 1848 and sheltered in the cove that bears his name. Bailey was sailing in the service of Alanson Sweet, one of the early site owners who opened a stone quarry in 1849. The area was formerly known as Gibraltar. The Baileys Harbor post office was established in December 1860, Moses Kilgore, postmaster. (Holand, 166)

Bakerville. Wood. Founded in 1879 by site owner and first postmaster James H. Baker from New York. (R. Rudolph)

Baldwin. St. Croix. Town (1872) and Village (1875). The station on the West Wisconsin railroad was established as Clarkesville, named for general freight agent Frank B. Clarke. About 1871 Dana Reed Bailey, a lawyer and later a state senator, purchased the site, which he renamed for Daniel A. Baldwin, president of the Chicago, St. Paul, Minneapolis & Omaha railroad, which absorbed the West Wisconsin. The post office was established in January 1872, William H. Peabody, postmaster. (Stennett, 167)

Baldwins Mill. Waupaca. Named for the Baldwin family, especially Milton Rice Baldwin, who came to the area from Cherry Valley, New York, in 1847. Baldwin was a miller and local official. ("M. R. Baldwin Obituary")

Ballou [buh LOO]. Ashland. Established about 1890 by the Wisconsin Central railroad shortly after the line was constructed between Mellen and Hurley. Formerly Schull, the name was changed in the early 1900s for Miner H. Ballou, treasurer and general manager of the Menasha Paper Company and a director of the railroad. (*Journey into Mellen*, 597)

Balsam Lake [BAWL suhm]. Polk. Town (1870) and Village (1905). Named from Balsam Lake. Probably a translation of Ojibwa *nominigan* 'balsam' and *sagaigan* 'lake.' The Balsam Lake post office was established in December 1871, Joseph Rivett, postmaster.

Bancroft [BAN krawft]. Portage. Stennett attributes the name to nineteenth-century historian and secretary of the U.S. Navy George Bancroft, but a more likely source is Warren Gamaliel Bancroft, who served in the Forty-Second Wisconsin regiment during the Civil War and was later pastor of the Oshkosh Methodist Church. Bancroft was a great-uncle and the name-sake of Warren Gamaliel Bancroft Winnipeg Harding, better known as Warren G. Harding, twenty-ninth president of the United States. The Bancroft post office was established in May 1876, Edwin L. Rich, postmaster. (Rosholt, *Our County, Our Story*, 355)

Bangor [BANG gor]. La Crosse. Town (1856) and Village (1899). Named by John Wheldon for his birthplace, Bangor, Wales. Wheldon is regarded as the first settler in Bangor, where he established the post office in October 1855. (Butterfield, *History of La Crosse County*, 723)

Bannerman. Waushara. Founded about 1901 as Bannerman Junction, a stop on the Chicago & North Western railroad. Named for William and John Bannerman, from Inverary, Scotland, operators of a quarry company in Berlin. The Bannermans purchased land in the area and bought the Berlin Granite Company about 1889. See Redgranite. ("Redgranite")

Baraboo [BEHR uh boo]. Sauk. Town (organized as Brooklyn in 1849) and City (1882). As early as 1842 the town of Barnabois or Barabois was authorized by the state legislature but not formally organized. In 1846 site owner and county commissioner Prescott Brigham platted the community of Adams, named for the Adams family of Massachusetts, especially John Quincy Adams. Shortly thereafter and adjacent to Adams, George Brown laid out a site he called Baraboo. In January 1849, by action of the Sauk County commissioners, Adams and Baraboo were merged as Brooklyn. The name of the town was changed to Baraboo in 1852 and the name of the community was officially changed to Baraboo about 1866. The name and spelling is that of the Baraboo River. The source of the name of the river is in doubt. In 1912 Harry Cole devoted ten pages of his fifty-page book on Sauk County place names to a review of the origin of the name without reaching a conclusion. The Winnebago name of the river was apparently *Hocooch-ra* 'shoot fish.' Its first known English recordings, *Beribeau* and *Bonibau*, date from 1829 or 1830. By the late 1840s *Baraboo* had become the regular spelling. It is generally agreed that the namesake is a French fur trader who kept a post near the mouth of the Baraboo River in the early nineteenth century. The problem lies in the fact that two French traders appear in the historical record, either of whom may be the namesake. One, a Pierre (or Peter) Barbeau, had a trading base in the Sault Ste. Marie area; the other, Pierre Beribault, operated out of St. Louis. In the early 1950s historian Alice Smith assessed the available evidence and echoed Cole's conclusion of forty years earlier: "There are many conjectures and uncertainties surrounding the appellation and it is very doubtful if the mystery will even be cleared" (7). Although circumstantial, the evidence points to the St. Louis Beribault (or someone with a similar name) rather than Barbeau if for no other reason than the early recordings clearly indicate three syllables in the name rather than two. (Cole, *Baraboo*)

Barksdale. Bayfield. Town (1907) and ppl. Named by William G. Ramsay, chief engineer for the DuPont Chemical Company, for Hamilton M. Barksdale, vice president of DuPont, which established the community for its employees about 1904 when it built facilities for the production of explosives. DuPont claimed to be the world's leading producer of TNT during World War II. (Stennett, 167)

Barnes. Bayfield. Town (1903). Named for early settler George Sardis Barnes, who opened the first hotel, saloon, and store north of the Eau Claire lakes in the late 1880s. (Marple, 62)

Barneveld [BAR nuh veld]. Iowa. Village (1906). Formerly known as Simpsonville for site owner David Simpson. The community grew around the Chicago & North Western station erected about 1881. By one account the name was suggested by a Dutch surveyor for Barneveld in the Netherlands. More likely, however, the name is a transfer from Barneveld, Oneida County, New York, the only other Barneveld in the United States, itself named for Jan van Olden Barneveld, the statesman and champion of Dutch independence from Spain in the late sixteenth and early seventeenth centuries. (Stennett, 41; G. Shepard, 60)

Barnum [BAHRN uhm]. Crawford. Founded about 1892 by Edward Seth Barnum from Bristol, Ontario County, New York, who purchased land along the Kickapoo River in 1857. ("Barnum Family Genealogy")

Barre [BEHR ee]. La Crosse. Town (organized in 1852 as Pierce; changed to Barre in 1853) and Barre Mills. Among the first settlers in the early 1850s were Martin Bostwick and his sons, Jerome and John. The Bostwicks chose the name for Barre, Vermont, their former home, itself named for Barre, Massachusetts, itself named for Colonel Isaac Barre, an English supporter of American independence before the Revolutionary War. The Barre Mills post office was established in January 1867, Andrew Craik, postmaster. (Butterfield, *History of La Crosse County*, 709)

Barron [BEHR uhn]. County, Town (organized as Dallas in 1862; changed to Barron in 1869), and City (1887). Barron County was organized in March 1859 as Dallas County, named for George M. Dallas, the namesake of Dallas (q.v.). The name was changed in 1869 in honor of Henry Danforth Barron, one of the outstanding political figures of northwest Wisconsin in the 1860s and 1870s. Barron (1833–82), from Saratoga County, New York, was a circuit court judge, state assemblyman, state senator, president of the Wisconsin electoral college, and regent of the University of Wisconsin.

The city of Barron began as a lumber camp established about 1860 by Swiss immigrant John Quaderer—for whom Quaderer Creek is named—acting as agent for the Knapp, Stout Lumber Company. (Simenson, 1, 14)

Barronett [behr uh NET]. Washburn. Town (1905). Barron. ppl. The community of Barronett was founded in 1880 by the Northern Wisconsin railroad as Foster City, probably named for the Foster family of Fairchild. Nathaniel C. Foster, with his son Edward organized and directed several major lumber operations in the area. The name was changed to Bourne for William R. Bourne, vice president and general manager of the Barronett Lumber Company. In 1881 Bourne, then postmaster, was instrumental in having the name of both the post office and the community changed from Foster to Barronett, a name of his own devising based upon Barron County. (Stennett, 169)

Bartelme [BAHRT uhl mee]. Shawano. Town (1912). Named for Christian Frederick Bartelme, who emigrated from Pomerania in 1887. Bartleme was instrumental in the formation of the town and served in several local offices. (*Shawano County Centuarawno*)

Barton [BAHRT n]. Washington. Town and ppl. Barton was founded in 1847 as Salisbury's Mills, named for Barton Salisbury, who established a sawmill on the Milwaukee River about 1845. The Wisconsin Legislature officially named the settlement Newark when the Town of Newark was organized in 1848. The Washington County Board subsequently changed the name of both township and community to Barton in 1853. Barton consolidated with West Bend in 1961. See Newburg. (Driessel, 29–30)

Basco [BAS ko]. Dane. Named from the Basco post office, established in September 1889, itself named for Basco, Hancock County, Illinois. The source of the Illinois name is unknown. Also known as Paoli Station. See Paoli. (Cassidy, *Dane County Place-Names*)

Bashaw [BAY SHAW]. Washburn. Town (1877). Burnett. ppl. Chappelle suggests the name is for a logging camp superintendent named B. A. Shaw (*"Why of Names,"* 23), but more likely Bashaw is a shortening of *Wabasha* 'red hat' or 'red leaf,' one of several nineteenth-century Sioux leaders whose main village was in Trempealeau County and later near the Mississippi River in southwest Minnesota. Wabasha's Sioux sided with the United States during the Black Hawk War of 1832.

Bassett [BAS it]. Kenosha. Bassett was founded with establishment of the Kenosha & Rockford railroad station sometime in the last quarter of the nineteenth century. The station was named for Henry Bassett and his son Reuben, who arrived from Washington County, New York, in 1842. Reuben Bassett was a longtime station agent and postmaster at Wilmot in the 1880s. (*Commemorative Biographical Record of Racine and Kenosha Counties*, 582)

Basswood [BAS WUD]. Richland. Probably named from the Basswood school, itself apparently named about 1862 for the basswood lumber of which it was largely constructed. Also known as Lucas, for James Lucas, an early settler for whom the Lucas post office was named in 1869. (Butterfield, *History of Crawford and Richland Counties*, 1029)

Batavia [buh TAY vee uh]. Sheboygan. Probably named for Batavia, Genesee County, New York, itself named for Batavia in the Netherlands. The name was brought to New York by Dutch settlers in the seventeenth century. About a dozen states have one or more places named Batavia. (Buchen, 334)

Bateman [BAYT muhn]. Chippewa. Named for Mathew P. Bateman, the site owner. Bateman emigrated from Ireland in the early 1850s. His son, Alison (Alicon), was the first postmaster in 1883. ("Bateman-L Archives")

Bavaria [buh VEHR ee uh]. Langlade. Named by settlers from Bavaria in southern Germany. The post office was established in December 1905, Stephen Simon, postmaster. (Dessureau, 249)

Baxter. Dunn. Named for the Andrew C. Baxter family. In 1904 Baxter brought his family from Vernon County to Big Beaver Creek where he established the first general store in the area. (Dunn County Historical Society, 99)

Bay City. Pierce. Village (1909). Platted about 1855 by Abner C. Morton as Saratoga, probably named for Saratoga, New York. The following year Morton established the Bay City post office, named for the bay in the Mississippi River. The community fell into decay and most of the buildings were moved to Warrentown. Charles Tyler, a professional musician originally from Syracuse, New York, bought the site for back taxes about 1857 and renamed it for the Bay City post office, of which he was then postmaster. ("Charles Rollin Tyler")

Bayfield. County and Town. Bayfield County was organized in 1845 as La Pointe; the name was changed to Bayfield in 1866 for the Town of Bayfield, established a decade earlier largely through the efforts of Henry M. Rice of St. Paul, the first U.S. senator from the state of Minnesota. Rice chose the name for Henry W. Bayfield, an admiral in the Royal Navy, who surveyed the Lake Superior shoreline for the British government in the 1820s. See La Pointe. (*History of Northern Wisconsin*, 79)

Bay Settlement. Brown. Bay Settlement is one of the oldest communities in Wisconsin. Augustin de Langlade, for whom Langlade County is named, and other French settlers were established in the area by the late seventeenth century. 'Bay,' a shortening of 'the Bay,' is a translation of French *la Baie*, a former name of Green Bay. The post office was established in December 1867, Frank Van Stralen, postmaster. (Cassidy, *Brown County*)

Bayside. Milwaukee, Ozaukee. Village (1953). Named for one or more bays along Lake Michigan, especially Donges Bay.

Beachs Corners. Trempealeau. Named for the Beach family. Charles G. Beach emigrated from Chittenden County, Vermont, in the mid-1860s. His sons Joseph and Fred were owners and editors of the Whitehall *Times* and Blair *Banner* newspapers in the late nineteenth century.

Bear Creek. Outagamie. Village (1902). Welcome Hyde established a lumber camp about 1850 on Bear Creek. When the railroad came through in 1880, the station was called Bear Creek and Hyde platted a parcel of land west of the station as Bear Creek in 1885. The community was incorporated as Welcome, in honor of founder Welcome Hyde. The name was changed to Bear Creek several years later to agree with that of the railroad station. (Truttschel, 110)

Bear Valley. Richland. Founded as Petersburg by Peter Haskins, from Chautauqua County, New York, who established a sawmill, gristmill, and blacksmith shop about 1853. The community was renamed for the Bear Valley post office, established in March 1858 by Aaron Southard. (Scott)

Beaver. Marinette. Town (1902) and ppl. Originally known as Armstrong Dam, for Ferdinand Amesley "Pinochle" Armstrong, from Aroostook County, Maine, who settled in the area in the early 1870s. The community was renamed for Beaver Creek, a tributary of the Peshtigo River, about 1884 when the post office was established by postmaster Ferdinand Armstrong. (*Marinette County Centennial*)

Beaver Dam. Dodge. Town (1845) and City (1856). Beaver Dam is either a translation from Ojibwa based upon *okwanim* 'dam' or a compound from the Beaver River, shown on early maps as the Ahmic River. *Ahmic* (in several spellings) is a general Algonquian word for 'beaver.' The area was formerly known as Grubbville, explained in local accounts as chopping down brush and saplings as forage for cattle, called "grubbing it." (Butterfield, *History of Columbia County*, 509)

Beebe [BEE bee]. Douglas. Named for the Beebe family, especially Casper V. Beebe, who established a medical practice at Superior in the late 1870s. (Stennett, 168)

Beetown. Grant. Town (1849) and ppl. In pioneer times trees with honeycombs were known as "bee trees." By one account, in 1827, in the cavity left by a bee tree that had been blown over by a storm, settlers found deposits of lead, including one nugget reported to weigh more than four hundred pounds. The lode became known as the Bee Lead (Holford, 571), from which the township and community took their names.

Beldenville [BEL duhn vil]. Pierce. Named for David and Harvey Ozro Belden, brothers who emigrated from Trumbull County, Ohio, about 1855. The Beldenville post office was established in May 1858, James H. Collins, postmaster. (*Pierce County's Heritage*, 9:10)

Belgium [BEL juhm]. Ozaukee. Town (1853) and Village (1922). Nicolas "Nic" and John Watry, who emigrated from Messancy, Belgium, in the late 1840s, are generally credited with proposing the name for their former home. The Belgium post office was established in the spring of 1857, John Hirn, postmaster. (Eccles, 7)

Bell Center. Crawford. Village (1901). Platted in 1855 and named for site owners Caleb D. Bellville, Dennis Bell, and Elias Bell. (Butterfield, *History of Crawford and Richland Counties*, 615)

Belleville [BEL vil]. Dane, Green. Village (1892). Belleville grew around a sawmill and gristmill established by John Frederick in 1847. The following year Frederick, along with John Mitchell, laid out the community, which they named for Belleville, Ontario, Frederick's former home. While the name would appear to be French meaning 'beautiful village,' Belleville, Ontario, was in fact named by Francis Gore, lieutenant governor of Bermuda and later of Upper Canada, for his wife, Annabella (Bella) Gore. (*Belleville*, 15)

Bellevue [BEL vyoo]. Brown. The town was organized in July 1856 as Manitou, named from the Manitou or East River. *Manitou*, Algonquian for 'spirit' or 'deity,' is a popular name for geographic features, but, as with other words associated with the spirit world, is generally avoided as a community name. Manitou was changed in 1857 to Belleview, a half-French, half-English compound, later respelled as French *Bellevue* suggesting 'beautiful view.' The name may have been suggested by John Penn Arndt, a Green Bay merchant and delegate to the first Wisconsin Territorial Council in 1836. (Cassidy, *Brown County*)

Bellinger [BEL in jer]. Taylor. Named for early settler John Bellinger. (*History of Taylor County*, 19)

Belmont. Lafayette. Town and Village (1894). Old Belmont was located near present First Capital State Park, where the Wisconsin Territorial Legislature first met in 1836. Modern Belmont grew around the station established in 1867 by the Mineral Point railroad. With the arrival of the railroad Old Belmont began to decline and many of the homes and businesses were physically moved to trackside. By local accounts Belmont Mound served as a landmark for early French traders and trappers and was referred to as *Belle Monte* 'beautiful hill.' (*Lafayette County Bicentennial Book*, 41)

Belmont. Portage. Town (1856). The source of the name is uncertain. By local tradition Belmont was suggested as the township name in 1856 by the wife of Azron D. Freeman, the first postmaster. Mary Freeman, a Canadian by birth, may have chosen the name for one of the several Belmonts in Canada or it may be a transfer from an eastern state, perhaps New York or New Hampshire. (Rosholt, *Our County, Our Story*, 261)

Beloit [buh LOYT]. Rock. Town (1842) and City (1857). Joseph Thibault (Tebo), a French Canadian trader and hunter, established a post on Turtle Creek in the early 1830s. In 1836 Caleb Blodgett, from Orange County, Vermont, generally recognized as the first permanent settler and the founder of Beloit, purchased Tebo's claim and established a sawmill in what became known as Blodgett's Place and later as New Albany, named by Blodgett for one of the New England Albanys, probably Albany, Vermont. New Albany formally became Beloit in the fall of 1837. Throughout the 1840s and most of the 1850s—and without substantiation—the name Beloit was assumed to derive from—or claimed to derive from—a French source: proposed etyma included the proper name *bellot*, said to mean 'pretty,' or *belloeit* (a nonword but claimed to be French) meaning 'the meeting of waters.' Two substantial accounts regarding the naming of Beloit, both involving Major Charles Johnson, can be given serious consideration. By one, Johnson was "partial" to the name Detroit and sought something similar but unique. He experimented with modifications, such as Betroit, until settling on Beloit. By the other account, Johnson provided the model but the name itself was chosen by Lucius G. Fisher. Fisher never missed an opportunity to take credit for coining Beloit. In his own words, "[after a committee had been appointed] we proposed several [names] and finally agreed to place the alphabet in a hat and see if we could not get a combination of letters that would give us a name. . . . While proposing this, Mr. [Charles] Johnson undertook to sound a French word for handsome ground and in trying he spoke 'Bolotte,' and I said after him 'Beloit,' like Detroit in sound and pretty and original I think. All sounded it and liked it and . . . it was unanimously adopted" (274, 279). See Luebke's *Pioneer Beloit* for a comprehensive discussion of the naming of Beloit.

Benderville. Brown. Platted about 1896 as Kishkekwanteno, a name of unknown origin likely fabricated from real or imagined "Indian" parts.

Kishkekwanteno proved awkward and within a decade had been replaced with Benderville, for site owner Ellen Bender. (Cassidy, *Brown County*)

Bennett. Douglas. Town (organized as Nebagamon in 1886; changed to Bennett in 1908) and ppl. Named for Richard Bennett, hotelier, real estate agent, and community benefactor. Bennett established the first post office in 1892. (Pellman, 89)

Benoit [buh NOYT]. Bayfield. Named for a Benoit [ben WAH] family, probably that of Antoine Benoit, an early French settler. Toussaint Benoit was the first postmaster when the office was established as Benoitville in August 1887. The name of the post office was changed to Peck on Christmas Eve 1890, and the community of Peck, named for then Governor George W. Peck, was laid out shortly thereafter. The settlement and post office were renamed Benoit about 1895. See Peck. (Stennett, 168)

Benson. Burnett. Named for shopkeeper Sven Johan Bengtsson, born in Västergötland, Sweden. Bengtsson's name was later Americanized to Benson. The post office was established in February 1885 as Randall (q.v.), with Bengtsson, now Bengston, as postmaster. (Landelius and Jarvi, 243)

Benton. Lafayette. Town (1849) and Village (1892). Named for Thomas Hart Benton (1782–1858), U.S. senator from Missouri (1821–51) and great-uncle of the artist of the same name. Benton was a popular and long-serving senator, and several Midwest states have a community or township named in his honor. The post office was established in 1844 as Cottonwood Hill; changed to Benton in May 1845. (Stennett, 43)

Bergen [BER guhn]. Marathon. Town (1870). Named by Norwegian settlers for Bergen, Hordaland, on the southwest coast of Norway. Andreas Vik (whose name was quickly Americanized to Week) emigrated from Eidfjord, Norway, and set up a sawmill on the Big Eau Plaine River in the 1840s. ("Town of Bergen")

Bergen. Vernon. Town (1853). Also named for Bergen, Norway. Settlement began with the arrival of Halver Jorgenson and Andrew Emberson in 1852. (*History of Vernon County*, 479)

Bergen Beach. Fond du Lac. Founded by Henry Bergen, from Hanover, Germany, about 1870. (Worthing)

Berlin [BER luhn]. Green Lake, Waushara. Town (1849) and City (1857). Nathan Strong, a surveyor hired to locate a suitable crossing point for a bridge and public road over the Fox River, established Strongville or Strong's Landing in the summer of 1846. By the late 1840s the area had been settled largely by members of the Seventh Day Baptist Church of Petersburg, Rensselaer County, New York, who chose the name from the location of their home congregation in Berlin, New York. See New Berlin. (Reetz, 17)

Berlin. Marathon. Town (1859). Named for Berlin, Germany, by settlers in the mid-1850s.

Bern. Marathon. Town (1902). Named by Swiss settlers for Bern(e), the capital of Switzerland since 1848.

Berry. Dane. Town (1850). Probably named for early settler Berry Haney, who kept a tavern in the 1830s and was the first postmaster of the Cross Plains post office in 1838. The Berry post office was established in May 1851, Joseph Bowman, postmaster. (Cassidy, *Dane County Place-Names*)

Bethel [BETH uhl]. Wood. In the late 1890s the Wisconsin Conference of Seventh Day Adventists established the Woodland Industrial School "to give young people a broad symmetrical training for usefulness . . . in a rural section removed from the contaminating influence of city life." When the post office department rejected the name Woodland, the name of the school was changed to the Bethel Industrial Academy, likely at the request of William Covert, president of the conference. The post office and community took the name of the school about 1900. (Jones and McVean, *History of Wood County*, 242)

Bethesda [buh THEZ duh]. Waukesha. Named from Bethesda Park, a spa built around a medicinal spring developed by Richard Dunbar in the late 1860s. Dunbar called the spring Bethesda, which he said meant "house of mercy." The water was claimed to cure ailments ranging from Bright's disease to kidney failure to "nervous prostration." Bethesda became so popular as a resort for tourists with real or imagined ailments that it was known as the Saratoga of the West, recalling Saratoga Springs, the famous spa in upstate New York. (Krueger, 394–95)

Bevent [buh VENT]. Marathon. Town (organized as Pike Lake in 1886; changed to Bevent in 1917). The area around Bevent was settled largely by Polish colonists in the 1850s. In 1890 the petition for a post office was apparently submitted with the name Koscieszyna, for Kościerzyna, in northern Poland. When this name was rejected, the petition was resubmitted as Berent, the German name of Kościerzyna, which was misread as Bevent. The office was established in April 1891, Martin Cychosz, postmaster.

Big Bend. Rusk. The Town was organized in 1875 when the area was part of Chippewa County. Named from the sharp bend in the Chippewa River northeast of Island Lake. Perhaps a translation of an Ojibwa name.

Big Bend. Waukesha. Village (1928). Named from the big bend in the Fox River, probably named by the earliest settlers, John Dodge, Prucius Putnam, and brothers Curtis B. and Orien Haseltine, all from Vermont. The

Big Bend post office was established in March 1848, Aaron Putnam, postmaster. (Damaske, *Along the Right-of-Way to East Troy*, 23)

Big Falls. Rusk. Town (1915). Named for the rapids on the Flambeau River.

Big Falls. Waupaca. Village (1925). Named for the falls on the Little Wolf River where A. W. Whitcomb established a sawmill in the late 1880s. Platted in the fall of 1890 for Whitcomb and George H. Fox, the site owners. Fox was the first postmaster in 1890. (McDevitt, 272)

Big Flats. Adams. Town and ppl. Probably named for Big Flats, Chemung County, New York. The town was organized as Verona in 1857; the name was changed to Brownsville in 1858 and to Big Flats in 1861. The post office was established in August 1862, John W. Potter, postmaster.

Big Foot Prairie. Walworth. Named for a Potawatomi leader of the 1820s and 1830s, whose name appears on the 1828 Treaty of Green Bay as "Maun-gee-zit, or big foot" and whose main village was near Lake Geneva. His name was translated into French as *Gros pied*, and into English as Big Foot. The traditional account is that Big Foot was named for the large tracks left by his snowshoes when he was pursuing game. The Big Foot post office was established in August 1838, Andrew Ferguson, postmaster. See Lake Geneva. (Vogel, *Indian Names*, 47)

Bigpatch (Big Patch). Grant. Platted in 1856 as Kaysville, for early settler William Kay, who built a blast furnace to process the local lead ore and opened a general store in the 1840s. Renamed in the early 1860s for the Big Patch post office, itself named for the Big Patch mines. In nineteenth-century American English, a *patch* was a shantytown associated with a mine. Several patches have been reported in the lead-mining areas of southwest Wisconsin and northwest Illinois. This particular name is probably unrelated to Henry Patch, the namesake of Patch Grove (q.v.). (Holford, 736)

Billings Park. Douglas. Named for Frederick K. Billings, president of the Northern Pacific railroad, who had personal and financial interests in the Lake Superior area. He is the also the namesake of Billings County, North Dakota, and the city of Billings, Montana.

Binghamton [BING uhm tuhn]. Outagamie. Probably named for Tracy Bingham, a prominent member of the Bingham family, who settled there in the 1850s and was elected to several local offices. (Ryan, 1363)

Birch. Ashland. Probably so named from the presence of *Betula papyrifera*, or white birch. (Stennett, 44)

Birchwood. Washburn. Founded about 1900. Probably named for the local stands of white birch, either by Walter (or William) A. Scott, general manager of the Chicago, St. Paul, Minneapolis & Omaha railroad, or by

George M. Huss, vice president and chief engineer of the Rice Lake, Dallas & Menomonie railroad. The town was organized as Loomis in 1903, named for shopkeeper Wilbur Loomis, and renamed for the community and post office in 1912. (Stennett, 168)

Birnamwood [BERN uhm wud]. Marathon, Shawano. Town (1883) and Village (1895). Named about 1880, probably by an official of the Milwaukee, Lake Shore & Western railroad, for Birnam Wood in Shakespeare's *Macbeth*, in which Macbeth is warned that he is secure "until Great Birnam Wood to high Dunsinane Hill shall come against him." By a local popular etymology the name was prompted when a railroad officer saw piles of burning brush and heard an Indian exclaim, "Heap big burnem wood." (*Shawano County Centuarawno*)

Biron [BIHR uhn]. Wood. Village (1919). In the 1840s Francis X. Biron, a merchant from Galena, Illinois, opened a store in present Wisconsin Rapids and began to transport supplies upriver to trade with millers and lumbermen. On one excursion in 1846 Biron bought a sawmill operated by George Fay and Joshua Draper, which he further developed, then proceeded to lay out the community that became known as Biron's Mills. (*Reflections of 150 Years*)

Black Creek. Outagamie. Town (1861) and Village (1904). Founded as Middleburg by Thomas J. Burdick, who established a blacksmith shop and wagon manufactory in the mid-1860s. The Green Bay & Lake Pepin railroad station was established as Black Creek, named from the stream, about 1868; the community was renamed when the post office was opened in June 1872. (Truttschel, 113)

Black Earth. Dane. Town and Village. Named from Black Earth Creek, itself named by early settlers who were struck by the dark, rich soil of Black Earth Valley. The first settlers, Solomon Hayden and Charles Turk, arrived in 1843. The British Temperance Emigration Society sponsored a number of early colonists, who called the area Gorst, for one of the Temperance Society's leaders, Robert Gorst. In 1848 the legislature created the township of Farmersville from Dane. That name was changed to Black Earth in 1851 and to Mazomanie seven years later. The present town of Black Earth was organized in 1858 as Ray, named for early settler James Ray and renamed Black Earth in 1859. The village of Black Earth was platted in 1850 by James T. Peck and Orien B. Hazeltine, who later served as the first postmaster, also in 1850. (Ruff, 3, 4, 10–11)

Black Hawk. Sauk. Named for Black Hawk, the Sauk War chief who led his people through northwest Illinois and southeast Wisconsin in the summer of 1832 in a desperate attempt to escape federal troops and state militia commanded by Henry Dodge in what became known as the Black Hawk War. After an encounter at Wisconsin Heights, Black Hawk's band was overtaken and destroyed near present Victory, Wisconsin, itself named in remembrance of that event. The conflict was brief, lasting but four months, but notable for such participants as Abraham Lincoln, Zachary Taylor, Jefferson Davis, and a number of others who became important figures in American history. In the 1816 Treaty of St. Louis, Black Hawk's name appears as *Muchetamachekaka* 'Black Sparrow Hawk.' The Black Hawk post office operated from December 1866 until the end of January 1907.

Black River Falls. Jackson. City (1883). The community grew around a saw-mill established about 1839 by Jacob Spaulding. Named from the falls on the Black River, a translation from Ho-Chunk (Winnebago), apparently meaning 'black water, dark colored river.' The river was so named, according to Stennett, because of "the dark appearance of the water . . . caused by the decomposition of pine and hemlock bark and roots from the forests that lined its banks for many miles" (161, 169). (Vogel, *Indian Names*, 130)

Blackwell, Blackwell Junction. Forest. Town (1921) and ppl. Named from the Blackwell post office, established in May 1905 by postmaster Ralph E. McEldowney. The office was named for sawmill owner John Blackwell. (Stennett, 46)

Black Wolf, Black Wolf Point. Winnebago. Town (1850) and ppl. Named for *Shounk-tshunk-saip-kaw* 'black wolf,' the leader of a band of Ho-Chunk (Winnebago), whose main village was on the southwest shore of Lake Winnebago. His name appears on several treaties of the late 1820s. (Vogel, *Indian Names*, 57–58)

Blaine [BLAYN]. Burnett. Town (1902). Portage. ppl. Both the town of Blaine in Burnett County and the community in Portage County were named for James G. Blaine (1830–93), a national political figure in the second half of the nineteenth century. Blaine was a U.S. representative and senator from Maine and U.S. secretary of state serving under presidents Garfield, Arthur, and Benjamin Harrison. He was the Republican candidate for president in 1884. Blaine was especially popular in the western states because of his support for railroad construction and internal development projects. (Rosholt, *Our County, Our Story*, 262)

Blair. Trempealeau. City (1949). Laid out in 1873 as Porterville by Duke Porter, son of early settler Richard Porter. The name was changed for John Insley Blair (1802–99), the founder and namesake of Blairstown, New Jersey. Blair, a New York financier and philanthropist, was a prominent figure in the development of western railroads and a major investor in the

Green Bay & Western railroad, which established Blair Station in 1877. (Curtiss-Wedge and Pierce, 270)

Blanchard [BLANCH erd]. Lafayette. Town (1868). Also Blanchardville. Village (1890). Founded in the 1840s by a branch of the Church of Latter Day Saints led by James Jesse Strang as Zarahemla, a name that was revealed to LDS founder Joseph Smith and appears in *The Book of Mormon*. Renamed for Alvin Blanchard, who owned the community site, along with Cyrus Newkirk. Blanchard was largely responsible for attracting the post office in May 1858, which he served as first postmaster. (*Lafayette County Bicentennial Book*, 65, 71)

Blenker [BLENG ker]. Wood. Named from the Blenker post office, itself named for and by John Blenker, a shopkeeper and the first postmaster in 1886. (R. Rudolph)

Bloom, Bloom City. Richland. Bloom township, organized in 1855, was reportedly named for the blooms on apple trees whose seeds had been brought from Ohio by Isaac McMahan in the early 1850s. The area was formerly known as Bon, Spring Valley, and West Branch, named by early settler Isaac Pizer for the west branch of the Pine River. The West Branch post office was established in May 1885, changed to Bon in December 1881, and to Bloom City in July 1887. (Butterfield, *History of Crawford and Richland Counties*, 982–83; Scott)

Bloomer. Chippewa. Town and City (1920). Apparently in the late 1840s Jeremiah (Jacob) Bloomer, a merchant from Galena, Illinois, built a dam and sawmill on the Chippewa River. When his timber enterprise failed, Bloomer returned to Galena, to be heard from no more, but the name Bloomer's Prairie remained. The site stood vacant until the summer of 1855 when Sylvester Van Loon, William Priddy, and several others arrived from New York State. The township and post office were established as Bloomer Prairie in 1858; the names were changed to Bloomer in 1871. (Prueher, 2–3)

Bloomfield. Towns in Walworth (1844) and Waushara (1855) Counties. Naming details are unknown. There are more than eighty Bloomfields in the United States; several are transfers, others are from personal names, but most are "hopefully descriptive" of the landscape, where fields burst with flowers in bloom.

Bloomingdale. Vernon. Founded in the fall of 1857 by Charles A. Hunt, Evan Olson, and J. E. Palmer. Most likely a translation and popular etymology of Norwegian *Blome Dalen* 'valleys of flowers.' (*History of Vernon County*, 498)

Blooming Grove. Dane. Town. Named in 1850 by the Reverend John G. Miller. The local story is that Miller claimed "the town names itself" because there are "such fine groves and so many wild flowers." The village of Blooming Grove, platted in 1915, is now part of Monona. (Keyes, 320; Mundstock and Stoker, 12)

Bloomington. Grant. Town and Village (1880). The town of Bloomington was organized in November 1859 as Lander, probably named by Henry Patch, the namesake of Patch Grove, for landowner Isaac C. Lander. Lander was changed to Tafton in 1860 for Delos W. Taft, who erected a gristmill at the site in 1852. For unknown reasons the name was changed to Bloomington in 1867. Bloomington is a popular place name, occurring in several dozen states, and an eastern Bloomington may have been transferred to Wisconsin. The post office operated as Tafton from July 1855 until June 1867, when it was changed to Bloomington. (Butterfield, *History of Grant County*, 810)

Bloomville. Lincoln. Probably named for landowner Charles Bloom, who emigrated from Prussia in the 1830s. The post office was established in June 1884.

Blue Mounds. Dane. Town (1848) and Village (1912). First known as Moundville, founded in 1829 by Ebenezer Brigham, the first permanent settler in Dane County. In Keyes's graceful description, "The twin mounds are visible at a great distance in all directions and derive their name from the haze which envelops them. In the Indian tongue this was called the 'smoke of the great spirit' and there are legends of lost caves in the sides of the hill whence this smoke is supposed to have issued" (326). According to Keyes, in early times gambling in Blue Mounds was so prevalent that the community was known "far and wide" as Pokerville.

Blue River. Grant. Village (1916). Named from the Blue River, its name apparently a translation of French *Rivière Bleu*. The community was known as Minnehaha until the Milwaukee & Mississippi railroad established a flag station in the early 1860s. Dewitt C. Perigo, proprietor of the local general store and the first postmaster, laid out the community in 1864. (Holford, 776)

Bluff Siding. Buffalo. Also known as Atlanta Station, a stop on the Chicago & North Western railroad. According to Stennett, an official of the Chicago & North Western railroad, Bluff Siding is named from "the precipitous rocky 'bluffs'" (45) along the Mississippi River near the site.

Boardman. St. Croix. In the early 1850s Clinton Boardman, a blacksmith from Vermont, and Samuel Beebe, a carpenter from New York, arrived in the area known as Lone Tree. Boardman, who is credited with inventing the modern extension ladder, established a sawmill and gristmill on Tenmile Creek. Beebe was the first postmaster in 1862. (Weatherhead, 71)

Boaz [BO az]. Richland. Village (1939). Founded in the late 1850s by Reason (Rezin) Barnes, from Allegany County in western Maryland, who, along with his son James, established a mill and later kept a general store. The namesake is apparently the biblical Boaz, the husband of Ruth and father of Obed, the grandfather of David. (Butterfield, *History of Crawford and Richland Counties*, 1015)

Bohners Lake [BON erz, BAHN erz]. Racine. Named for Antony (Anthony) Bohner of Burlington, a French immigrant who established a resort community on Bohners Lake in the late nineteenth century.

Bolt. Kewaunee. Named for Charles Griswold Boalt [*sic*], a civil engineer and county judge who emigrated from Ohio to Mayfield in 1854. Boalt owned half of the plat of Ahnapee. (*Commemorative Biographical Record of the Counties of Brown, Kewaunee and Door*, 530)

Boltonville. Washington. In 1854 Harlow Bolton, Asa Varney, and William Willis established a gristmill on Stoney Creek. Bolton, from Chenango County, New York, laid out the community the following year. (Quickert, 40)

Bonduel [BAHN doo EL]. Shawano. Village (1916). Named for Florimond Bonduel (1799–1861), a Belgian Catholic missionary who ministered to the Menominee and was actively involved in tribal affairs, particularly in promoting understanding and cooperation between the Menominee and the U.S. government. Bonduel is best known for assisting Oshkosh in his attempt to abrogate the 1848 treaty that ceded all Menominee lands in Wisconsin to the United States. The Bonduel post office was established in April 1864 by Charles Sumnicht, who is generally credited with choosing the name. (Vogel, *Indian Names*, 38)

Bone Lake. Polk. Town (1888). The origin of the name is unknown. By one local legend the name derives from the bones left after a battle between the Sioux and Ojibwa on an island in the lake in the 1850s. (Ericson)

Bonneval [BAHN uh val]. Forest. Perhaps a transfer from Bonneval, France, southwest of Paris. This is the only Bonneval (so spelled) in the United States.

Borea. Douglas. Origin unknown. Perhaps named from an early settler named Borea; perhaps a transfer from Boreas, Essex County, New York. Boreas was the Greek god of the north wind and winter. The post office was established in August 1913, George B. Carlson, postmaster. Borea is also a personal name, largely Italian.

Borth [BORTH]. Waushara. Named in April 1892 with establishment of the post office by August Borth, the first postmaster and owner of a local cheese factory.

Boscobel [BAHS kuh bel]. Grant. Town (1859) and City (1873). The site of Boscobel was purchased in 1854 by Charles K. Dean, Edward H. Brodhead, and several others on news that the Milwaukee & Mississippi railroad would be extending its line through the area. According to Butterfield's 1881 *History of Grant County* (774) the name was chosen (or created) after a visit by Rufus King, editor of the *Milwaukee Sentinel* newspaper. King described the Milwaukee & Mississippi station "in the most flattering terms . . . speaking of it as Boscobel, the name being said to have its derivation from the words *bosc* 'wood,' and *belle* 'beautiful.'" Other origins of the name have been proposed; one of the more remarkable concerns a farmer who had a cow named Boss and another named Belle, which the farmer called from the fields with Co-boss, Co-belle, which evolved into Boscobel. Pure invention, of course, but colorful invention nonetheless.

Bosstown. Richland. Apparently named for shopkeeper and livestock dealer William Henry Dosch, familiarly known as "Boss" Dosch. (Scott)

Boulder Junction. Vilas. Town (1927) and ppl. Named from Boulder Lake by the Chicago, Milwaukee & St. Paul railroad in 1905. (*Historical/Architectural Resources Survey*, 18)

Bovina [bo VEYE nuh]. Outagamie. Town (1853). Probably a transfer from Bovina, Delaware County, New York, where the name was created from the Latin root for 'cow.'

Bowers [BOW erz]. Walworth. Named for Henry Bowers, who established the post office in 1892.

Bowler [BOL er]. Shawano. Village (1923). Laid out in 1905 with construction of the Chicago & North Western railroad. Reportedly named for John C. Bowler, an attorney for the railroad and a local property owner. (Stennett, 46)

Boyceville [BOYS vil]. Dunn. Village (1922). Formerly known as Barker for the Wisconsin Central railroad station named for general freight and passenger agent James Barker. The post office was established as Boysville in March 1879; the spelling was changed to Boyceville in May 1880. The namesake is William D. Boyce, a local businessman. (Clark, 14)

Boyd. Chippewa. Village (1891). Founded by site owner John Cirkel. When the Wisconsin Central railroad was built through in the early 1880s, many of the homes and business establishments in Edson were disassembled and moved to trackside. The namesake is probably Robert K. Boyd, who surveyed the railroad right-of-way, served in several local offices, and donated Boyd Park to the city of Eau Claire. The post office was established in December 1881, Francis F. Goodfellow, postmaster.

Boydtown. Crawford. Named by and for Robert Boyd, who laid out the community shortly after arriving from Missouri in 1844. Boyd had expected the railroad to be built through Boydtown, but it was not. In the words of Butterfield's 1884 *History of Crawford and Richland Counties*, "The place being left off the line of a railroad, rapid as had been its growth, the decline was still more marked. Mr. Boyd died in 1856, but lived to see his hopes vanish" (620).

Boylston, Boylston Junction. Douglas. Probably named by a railroad official for one of the Boylstons in Massachusetts. The Boylston post office was established in April 1907, William J. Hope, postmaster.

Brackett. Eau Claire. Named for James M. Brackett, newspaper editor and publisher, notably of the Eau Claire *Free Press* in the 1870s. (*History of Northern Wisconsin*, 316)

Bradford. Rock. Town (1846). Named by William C. Chase, one of the first settlers, who arrived about 1836, for Bradford, his birthplace in Orange County, Vermont. (*Portrait and Biographical Album of Rock County*, 193)

Bradley. Lincoln. Town (1903) and ppl. Surveyed in June 1887 by the Sault Ste. Marie Land and Improvement Company. Probably named for William H. Bradley, the founder of Tomahawk (q.v.) and probable founder of Jersey City (q.v.). (Jones and McVean, *History of Lincoln, Oneida and Vilas Counties*, 88)

Bradley. Marathon. Named from the Bradley post office, established by Jeremiah Bradley in June 1891.

Branch. Manitowoc. Formerly known as Zalesburg for a local Zale family and as Lenaville for Canadian Edward Lenaville, who settled in the area in the mid-1830s. The post office was established as Branch, named from Branch River in 1854, and Branch became the name of the community in the early 1870s with construction of the Milwaukee, Lake Shore & Western railroad. (Stennett, 46)

Brandon. Fond du Lac. Village (1881). Named with construction of the Milwaukee & Horicon railroad in 1856 by William Lockin and several others for their former home, Brandon, Rutland County, Vermont, itself named about 1760 for James Hamilton, Scottish Duke of Hamilton and Brandon. In its early years the community was known as Bunggo and Bungtown, names of unknown origin. The post office was established as Luzerne in August 1851 and changed to Brandon in February 1856. (McKenna, 264)

Branstad [BRAN stad]. Burnett. Named for Ole C. Branstad, born Ole Anderson in Norway about 1840. Anderson took the name Branstad, the name of his family farm, when he left Norway as a youth. Branstad was a Civil

War veteran and an official of Burnett County, serving as register of deeds and as county treasurer. The post office was established in December 1897, Canute C. Clementson, postmaster. (Selin)

Brazeau [brah ZO]. Oconto. Town (1892). Named for Francis X. "Frank" Brazeau, originally from Quebec, Canada. Brazeau, an Oconto merchant, kept a general store from the 1870s. ("Brazeau")

Breed. Oconto. Town (1901) and ppl. Named for the Breed brothers, George, Edward, and Arthur, sons of Dr. John Breed, who emigrated from Jefferson County, New York, to Wisconsin in the mid-1850s. George Breed was chair of the town of Waupee before the charter was vacated in 1896. Arthur Breed was the first chair of the town of Breed. The post office was established in October 1888, George Breed, postmaster. (*Local History, Suring School District*, 35)

Briarton. Shawano. Local sources claim the community was named for the briars of the raspberry and blackberry bushes that grew wild after the timber was cut. The post office was established in April 1883, Conrad J. Coon, postmaster. (Michael)

Brice Prairie. La Crosse. Named for early settler Alexander Brice, who moved from New England to Wisconsin in the 1840s.

Bridgeport. Crawford. Town (1872) and ppl. The local account is that Bridgeport was named for the bridge over the Wisconsin River that connects Crawford and Grant Counties, creating a "port" on both sides. (Butteris)

Briggsville. Marquette. Founded and named by Alexander Ellis Briggs, from New York by way of Shoreham, Vermont. In 1850 Briggs formed a partnership with Amplius Chamberlain and together they dammed Neenah Creek to provide power for their sawmill. Briggs platted the community in 1854; that same year the post office was established as McIntyre Creek by Charles McIntyre. The name of the office was changed to Briggsville in November 1856. (Lovesy, 5)

Brigham [BRIG uhm]. Iowa. Town (1890). Named for Ebenezer Brigham. Born in Massachusetts, Bigham is generally regarded as the first permanent settler in what is now Dane County. He was instrumental in the founding and growth of Fitchburg and Arena as well as the community named for him. (G. Shepard, 70)

Bright. Clark. Midway between Atwood and Longwood, Bright was founded by Halbert A. Bright on his vegetable farm in the early 1900s. Bright, who emigrated from Nova Scotia in 1840, was a noted lumberman and dairyman and served several terms as mayor of Black River Falls. The Bright post office operated from January 1902 through March 1913. ("Green Grove Township History")

Brill. Barron. Founded in 1901 by the Chicago, St. Paul, Minneapolis & Omaha railroad. Named by William A. Scott or Walter A. Scott (probably Walter, but both men were general managers of the railroad), in honor of Hascal R. Brill, district judge of Ramsey County, Minnesota. See Wascott. (Stennett, 169)

Brillion [BRIL yuhn]. Calumet. Town and City (1944). The Town of Brillion was organized in 1855 as Brandon and renamed in the spring of 1857 from the Brillion post office, established by Thomas N. West in October 1855. An oft-repeated account is that West submitted the post office petition with the name Pilleola, supposedly confected from the names of his two daughters. This name was apparently rejected by the post office department in Washington. The petition was then either returned to West with the name Brillion or resubmitted by West with that name. Brillion is most likely a popular etymology from Brilon, North Rhine-Westphalia, Germany, part of Prussia in the nineteenth century and an area from which a number of German settlers emigrated. This is the only Brillion in the United States. (Stennett, 46)

Bristol. Dane. Town (1848). The name was suggested by early settler David Wilder for his former home, Bristol, Ontario County, New York, itself named for Bristol, Connecticut, or Bristol, Massachusetts; ultimately from Bristol, England. (Keyes, 327)

Bristol. Kenosha. Town (1840) and ppl. Named from the Bristol post office, established by Andrew Jackson in July 1839. The office was apparently named for Ira and Lester Bristol, brothers from Genesee County, New York, who had taken up residence in the area in the mid-1830s. The community was laid out by site owner Alfred Giddings in the 1850s. The choice of the name may have been influenced by the presence of settlers from one or another of the Bristols in New England. (Stennett, 47)

British Hollow. Grant. Formerly known as Pleasant Valley. Because a number of early settlers were lead miners from England and Wales, the area became known as British Hollow. The post office was established by Joel Pedlar, from Cornwall, England, in May 1860. (*Grant County History*, 320)

Brockway. Jackson. Town (1890) and ppl. Named for Eustace Lafayette Brockway, who owned several sawmills in the area, operated a steamboat on the Mississippi River, and served in the state legislature in 1872. (*Jackson County, a History*, 27)

Brodhead [BRAWD hed, BRAHD hed]. Green. City (1891). Platted in 1856 by the Milwaukee & Mississippi railroad on the line under construction from Janesville. Named for Edward Hallock Brodhead, one of the site owners. Brodhead, a native of New York, came to Wisconsin in 1852 as a construction engineer for the Milwaukee & Mississippi railroad, of which he later became president. Although Brodhead never lived in the community that bears his name, he was an early promoter and benefactor. (Taylor, 14)

Brodtville [BRAHT vil]. Grant. Named from the Brodtville post office, established in May 1864 by the first postmaster, Joakim Brodt, from Chautauqua, New York.

Brokaw [BRO kaw]. Marathon. Village (1903). In the early 1880s the Wausau Boom Company built a dam on the Wisconsin River near the site of present Brokaw. A community began to develop in the early 1900s around the Wausau Paper Mills, founded by paper magnate and village namesake Norman Brokaw. (Durbin, 49)

Brookfield. Waukesha. Town (1839) and City (1954). Probably named from Brookfield Junction, the railroad station established in 1853 where the tracks of the Milwaukee & Mississippi railroad crossed those of the Milwaukee, Watertown & Baraboo Valley. The source of the name is unknown, but Brookfield is likely a transfer, perhaps from Brookfield, Massachusetts. Positive associations make Brookfield a popular place name; it occurs in about half of the states. (*History of Waukesha County*, 730)

Brooklyn [BRUK luhn]. Green. Town (1849) and ppl. Brooklyn was founded by the Chicago & North Western railroad, which proposed to name the station Capwell for site owner and station agent Hiram B. Capwell. Capwell, however, declined the honor and the name of the township was substituted. Stennett (47) credits John E. Blunt, chief engineer for the railroad, with the suggestion to name it for Brooklyn, New York, itself named in the seventeenth century for Breuklen, near Amsterdam in the Netherlands.

Brooks. Adams. Founded as Brookings. The name was shortened to Brooks, apparently at the request of the Chicago & North Western railroad, sometime before the post office was established in 1915. The namesake may be Wilmot W. Brookings, railroad executive, political figure, and the namesake of Brookings, South Dakota. ("Adams County, Wisconsin")

Brothertown. Calumet. Town (1857) and ppl. Brothertown (Brotherton) was the name of a Delaware Indian village in Burlington County, New Jersey. When that site was sold in the early 1800s, the Muncie, a Delaware subtribe (for whom Muncie, the seat of Delaware County, Indiana, would later be named), along with several other Algonquian groups, established themselves at Brothertown, Oneida County, New York. Along with the remnants of several small bands of Mohicans and others, and now known as Brothertons, they removed to Wisconsin in the 1820s and early 1830s, eventually settling at what is now Brothertown. The community was known for several years as Deansburg in honor of Thomas Dean, the respected government agent who coordinated the Brothertons' move to the Midwest. See Stockbridge. (Vogel, *Indian Names*, 26)

Brown. County. When Brown County was created by Michigan territorial governor Lewis Cass in 1818 it encompassed the eastern half of present Wisconsin. The county was named (as were several in the Midwest) for General Jacob Jennings Brown (1775–1828), whose distinguished military service in the Great Lakes area during the War of 1812 made him a national hero. A decade earlier Brownville, in Jefferson County, New York, had been named for the same Jacob Brown. (Kellogg, 220)

Brown Deer. Milwaukee. Village (1955). The suggested origins of Brown Deer consist largely of legends and popular etymologies. By one local story, a deer jumped through a saloon and broke up a card game; by another, a brown deer stuck its head through the window of a house (or a barn, depending on the story); and by still another the name is from a sign erected by a saloon keeper named Schweitzer that read *Braun Hirsch*, 'Brown Deer' in German. (Kittleson)

Browning. Taylor. Town (1885). Probably named for Edward F. Browning, a New York City financier and a director of the St. Paul Eastern Grand Trunk Railway. Browning reportedly owned some twenty-five thousand acres in the Medford area. (Latton, 33)

Brownsville. Dodge. Village (1952). Named for Alfred D. Brown, who emigrated from England in 1846. The post office was established in September 1879, Peter Netzinger, postmaster. (Hubbell, 396)

Browntown. Green. Village (1890). Laid out in March 1881 by site owner James Dale on news that the Chicago, Milwaukee & St. Paul railroad was to be extended from Monroe to Mineral Point. The station and community were named, apparently by the railroad, for early settler William G. Brown, who, along with Henson Irion and John Wood, dammed Skinner Creek and established a sawmill and "corn cracker" in 1847. Brown was a Green County commissioner in the 1840s and later chairman of the county board. (Butterfield, *History of Green County*, 749)

Bruce. Rusk. Village (1901). Founded in 1884 by the Sault Ste. Marie Land and Improvement Company. Named for Alanson C. Bruce, who operated a logging camp from the 1870s in what is now the Village of Bruce. (*History of Bruce*, 6)

Bruemmerville [BREM er vil]. Kewaunee. Named for the Bruemmer family, especially Henry Bruemmer, who bought a gristmill on Silver Creek in 1866 and established a brick manufacturing plant. (Dopke, 2)

Brule [BROOL]. Douglas. Town (1886) and ppl. Named from the Bois Brule River, which rises in central Douglas County and empties into Lake Superior near Brule Point. The river has had several names since it was first recorded by La Salle about 1683 in its Sioux form *Nemitsakouat*. In 1788 Jonathan Carver named the river Goddard in honor of James Stanley Goddard, the Montreal merchant who accompanied Carver on part of his expedition. From about 1800 the river was referred to as Brule, Misakoda, Wisacoda, Burnt Wood, and Bois Brulé. About 1880 Brule became the usual form, which lasted until the 1940s when it was replaced by the current Bois Brule. The name of the community was formalized as Brule when the post office was established in 1890. Several historians have claimed that the namesake is Etienne Brulé, the guide and interpreter for Champlain's expedition to the eastern Great Lakes in the early seventeenth century. However, as Jerrard notes, "[Brule] is a contraction of the earlier French name 'Bois Brulé,' meaning a burned woodland" (7, 40). *Bois Brulé* is in fact a French translation of Ojibwa *wissakode* 'burned forest.' (Stennett, 47)

Brunswick. Eau Claire. Town (1857). Probably named by settlers from Brunswick, Maine, possibly for New Brunswick, Canada. Originally the name of a city in north central Germany, Brunswick became associated with King George I, who was Elector of Brunswick-Lüneberg.

Brushville. Waushara. Founded about 1853. Named for early mill operators Herman and Eliphalet Brush, from Lamoille County, Vermont. (Heltemes, 8)

Brussels [BRUHS uhlz]. Door. Town (1858) and ppl. Named for Brussels, Belgium. Several groups of Belgian settlers arrived in the early and mid-1850s. The Brussels post office was established in November 1862, Jean F. Gilson, postmaster. (Hale, 15)

Bryant. Langlade. Platted about 1883 and named for Sherburne S. Bryant, a Milwaukee businessman and society leader who owned several large tracts of timberland in Langlade and Price Counties. (Dessureau, 238)

Buchanan [byoo KAN uhn]. Outagamie. Town (1858). Probably named for James Buchanan, who was elected president of the United States in 1856.

Buckbee [BUHK bee]. Waupaca. Although several others have been suggested as namesakes, the community was most likely named for Gilbert Buckbee, who brought his family from Oswego, New York, about 1848. Among other enterprises, the Buckbees established a sawmill and a factory for producing broom handles. The Chicago & North Western railroad established Buckbee Station in 1879 and George W. Jones laid out the community of Buckbee in the early 1880s. (McDevitt, 260–61)

Buckholz Corners. Jackson. Named for site owner Christopher Buckholz, who emigrated from Prussia probably in the 1850s.

Buckman. Brown. Named for the Buckman family. Fred N. Buckman was a banker in Denmark, Wisconsin, and the first postmaster at Buckman in 1900. (Cassidy, *Brown County*)

Budsin [BUHD suhn]. Marquette. Apparently named for Budzyń in west central Poland by Ludwig Gust, who emigrated from Prussia in the late 1880s. The post office was established in May 1900, Gustav Gust, postmaster. (Reetz, 60)

Buena Vista [BYOO nuh VIS tuh]. Portage. Town (1853). Richland. Town (1849). Grant and Waukesha. ppl. Buena Vista in Portage County reportedly took its name from the Buena Vista roadhouse, a hotel and tavern established about 1850 by Wellington Kollock and William Wigginton, who were supposedly familiar with another Buena Vista tavern in southern Wisconsin and chose that name for their own establishment. The township of Buena Vista in Richland County was reportedly named at the suggestion of Melissa Briggs, whose husband had participated in the Mexican War. Ultimately from Spanish for 'good view,' Buena Vista is a popular place name, occurring in about half the states, in most of which Buena Vista is a Mexican War name, commemorating the battle of Buena Vista, where American forces under the command of Zachary Taylor defeated Santa Anna's army in February 1847. (Butterfield, *History of Crawford and Richland Counties*, 992; Rosholt, *Our County, Our Story*, 268–69)

Buffalo. County (1853). Named from the Buffalo River, called by French explorers *Rivière des Boeufs*, literally 'river of oxen,' *boeuf* being a shortening of *boeuf sauvage*, referring to the American bison or buffalo. The name of the river is often attributed to the Franciscan Recollect priest Louis Hennepin, who explored the area in the 1680s. Phonetic and semantic similarity led to the Americanization of *boeuf* as *beef*; thus the early use of the name Beef River. Buffalo River and Beef River were used interchangeably until about 1930 when the U.S. Board on Geographic Names made Buffalo River official for federal government use.

Buffalo City. Buffalo. Buffalo City was one of several communities founded in the Midwest by the Swiss-German Colonization Society of Cincinnati in the middle of the nineteenth century. In 1856 Frederick Pfeffer, an organizer of the society, brought a group of settlers to the area, where they constructed a sawmill and laid out Buffalo City, named for its location in Buffalo County. (Curtiss-Wedge, *History of Buffalo and Pepin Counties*, 87)

Bull. A number of Wisconsin waterfalls and rapids were long known as "bulls," and "bull" became part of the names of several, including Bull Falls on the Pine River, Big Bull Falls and Little Bull Falls on the Popple River, and Grandfather Bull Falls and Grandmother Bull Falls on the Wisconsin River. Mosinee was formerly known as Little Bull Falls; an earlier name of Merrill was Jenny Bull Falls, and Wausau was Big Bull Falls. These and other rapids were called *Bulles* by early French voyageurs, literally 'bubbles,' a word related to French *bouillir* 'boil' and *bouillant* 'boiling, impetuous,' descriptive of water rushing through a narrow channel. French *bulle* was easily turned into English *bull* by popular etymology, and fanciful stories were created explaining the names as falling water sounding like the bellowing of bulls. For a more detailed discussion of the name and its sources, see Kronenwetter's *Wisconsin Heartland*, especially page 62.

Bundy. Lincoln. See Jeffris.

Bunker Hill. Richland. Founded about 1845. Named by Dr. Hiram Sargent, an early settler, or Horace J. Lord, who established the Bunker's Hill post office in 1852. Probably named for Bunker Hill, Massachusetts, where one of the first engagements of the Revolutionary War occurred in June 1775. (Holford, 630)

Bunyan [BUHN yuhn]. Polk. Origin uncertain. The community was named from the Bunyan post office, established in August 1880 by George P. Anderson, the namesake of Georgetown (q.v.). Unlikely named for Paul Bunyan, the iconic American lumberman; possibly named for John Bunyan, author of the seventeenth-century Christian allegory *Pilgrim's Progress*. (Ericson)

Burke. Dane. Town (1851) and ppl. Early settlers, many of whom were from Ireland, began arriving in the late 1830s. The township and subsequently the community were named for Edmund Burke, the Irish statesman who was a staunch defender of the American colonies in the years preceding the Revolutionary War. (Cassidy, *Dane County Place-Names*)

Burkhardt [BERK hahrt]. St. Croix. Named for Christian Burkhardt, born in Reichenbach, Germany. Burkhardt immigrated to the United States about 1854 and in 1868 established a mill complex on the Willow River that included a cooperage, warehouses, and living quarters for company employees. Apparently Burkhardt intended to call the community Willow River Falls, but Burkhardt became formalized with establishment of the Chicago, St. Paul, Minneapolis & Omaha railroad station. The post office opened in 1857 as Bonchea (Bouchea), reportedly named for Peter Bouchea (Bonchea), a French hunter and trader who is credited with founding the first settlement in St. Croix County in the late 1830s near present Hudson. (Weatherhead, 70)

Burlington [BER ling tuhn]. Racine. Town (1839) and City (1900). Burlington was laid out by Enoch D. Putnam for site owner Enoch Woodbridge in 1836. In Putnam's words, "I had not even thought of a name, but after a moment's thought I said that the State of Vermont, from which I came, had one town celebrated above all others for the beauty of its location and scenery. I would propose the name of that town—Burlington—as a name for this new town" (Tully and Vande Sand, 7).

Burnett [ber NET]. County (1856). Named for Thomas Pendleton Burnett (1800–1846). A Virginian by birth, Burnett spent his young adult life practicing law in Kentucky. He became Indian agent at Prairie du Chien in 1829 and served in the Wisconsin Territorial Legislature in the mid-1840s. At the time of his death he was a delegate to the first Wisconsin Constitutional Convention. Why someone with so few ties to the area would be honored by having a county named for him is unknown.

Burnett. Dodge. Town (1846) and ppl. Established with construction of the Chicago, Milwaukee & St. Paul railroad in 1860. Named for Ellsworth Burnett, who was shot and killed by Indians on Rock River near present Horicon in 1836. Burnett was working as a surveyor for the federal government at the time. See Clyman. (Stennett, 49)

Burns. La Crosse. Town (1853) and ppl. Named for Timothy Burns. Born in Dublin, Ireland, Burns was instrumental in developing and promoting La Crosse County and its communities. He served in the Wisconsin Assembly and was the third lieutenant governor of the state (1851–53), dying in office.

Burnside. Trempealeau. Town. Named for Ambrose E. Burnside (1824–81). In December 1863, when the town was organized, Ambrose Burnside was a well-known Union general in the Civil War. His chosen pattern of facial hair inspired the term *sideburns*.

Burton. Grant. Named from the Burton post office, established in 1871 by John Yager. The office was named for early settler Daniel R. Burt, who established a sawmill on the Grant River about 1850. Burt was active in local and state affairs, serving as a delegate from Grant County to the state constitutional convention of 1846. The community was quite modest. Holford's 1900 *History of Grant County* notes that Burton included "a post office, store, and blacksmith shop, with a few dwellings, but the place was hardly sufficient in size to be called a village" (710).

Busseyville [BUHS ee vil]. Jefferson. Named for Thomas Bussey, who emigrated from Yorkshire, England, in 1855, established a gristmill on

Koshkonong Creek, laid out a settlement, and offered free lots to anyone who would build a dwelling. The post office was established in May 1863, Henry C. Son, postmaster. (Swart, 208)

Butler. Clark. When the town of Butler was organized in 1915 the name was to be Cesnik, for Ignac Cesnick (Ignatz Ceznic), a Slovenian who in 1908 joined with the Foster Lumber Company to develop and promote the community of Willard. For unknown reasons, the name Butler was substituted in honor of George Butler, the first permanent settler in the township. (Curtiss-Wedge, *History of Clark County*, 427)

Butler. Waukesha. Village (1913). Probably named for William Butler, who emigrated from Yorkshire, England, in the mid-1840s. Butler owned substantial property in the area and was active in civic and religious organizations. The original Butler was established about 1848 south of the current location; present Butler grew around a Milwaukee, Sparta & North Western railroad yard built about 1910.

Butman Corners [BUHT muhn]. Trempealeau. Named for Stark and Hiram Butman, brothers who came to the area from Erie County, Ohio, in the early 1850s. (*Biographical History of La Crosse, Trempealeau and Buffalo Counties*, 663)

Butte des Morts [BYOO duh mor]. Winnebago. French for 'hill of the dead,' named from a mound described by Increase Lapham in 1851 as eight feet high and fifty feet in diameter. The mound was largely destroyed by railroad construction in the 1860s and 1870s. Several explanations of the name have been advanced, all having to do with the hill as a cemetery for Native Americans. By one account, local tribes used the mound simply as a burying place; by another, it became a general cemetery after clashes between rival groups; and by still another, scores of Fox warriors were piled at the site and covered with dirt after a particularly bloody battle with French forces about 1730. Each of these accounts may hold a germ of truth but the complete story of the name has yet to be told. The community of Butte des Morts grew around a trading post established by Augustin Grignon shortly before 1820. Grignon established the post office in June 1849. (Lawson, 238)

Butternut. Ashland. Village (1903). Named in the mid-1870s, probably by the Wisconsin Central railroad. The name is either a translation from Ojibwa *kitchi pakan* 'large nut' or an independent creation from the local butternut trees. In the late 1870s the area attracted a number of German settlers from Milwaukee and became known as the Butternut Colony. The community was formally platted in 1878, taking the name of the Butternut post office, established in February 1877 by Harvey C. Matthews. (*History of Northern Wisconsin*, 74)

Butts Corners. Rock. By 1860 John Butts had emigrated from Pennsylvania and established a farm and blacksmith shop.

Byrds Creek. Richland. Adam Byrd, from Ohio, built the first sawmill in Richwood township. Byrd was elected to several local offices and was a member of the county board in 1851. The post office was established in March 1890 as Bird's Creek and changed to Byrd's [*sic*] Creek two months later. (Butterfield, *History of Crawford and Richland Counties*, 1217)

Byron. Fond du Lac. Town (1846) and ppl. Settled in the early 1840s by the Reverend Isaac Vaughn and colonists from Genesee County, New York. Named from Byron, New York, itself named for the poet George Gordon, Lord Byron. (Worthing)

Byron. Monroe. Town (1863). Byron was proposed by Charles A. Crawford, a farmer from New England. The reason for his choice is unknown; perhaps a transfer from Byron, Oxford County, Maine, or Byron, Genesee County, New York. (*Monroe County*, 2)

Cable [KAY buhl]. Bayfield. Town (1904) and ppl. Founded about 1880 by the Chicago, St. Paul, Minneapolis & Omaha railroad. Named for Ransom Reed Cable, president of the Chicago, Rock Island & Pacific railroad. (Stennett, 170)

Cadiz [kah DIZ, KAY diz]. Green. Town (1849). About 1843 Abner Van Sant and his son-in-law, John Deniston, built a sawmill on Honey Creek and several years later laid out the community. Cadiz is a transfer name from Cattaraugus County, New York, or Harrison County, Ohio, themselves named for the city in southwestern Spain. (*Coloma Area Sesquicentennial*, 3)

Cadott [kuh DAHT]. Chippewa. Village (1895). Named for the Cadotte (Cadeau) family, Métis fur traders of Lake Superior. Cadotte is a Canadian French spelling reflecting the pronunciation of the formal form of the nickname *cadot* 'little dog.' According to a Cadott historical marker, Michel Cadotte operated a trading post on the Yellow River from the late 1780s. (The post, however, may have been established later and by one of his sons, Michel or Jean Baptiste.) Robert Marriner established the post office in June 1873 and founded the community of Cadotte shortly thereafter. The site was formerly known as Cadotte's Falls. (*Cadott Community Centennial*, 5)

Cady. St. Croix. Town (1870). Named from Cady Creek, itself named for early settler Jacob Cady, who brought his family to the area from Addison County, Vermont, about 1850 and established a sawmill on the stream that bears his name. (*Commemorative Biographical Record of the Upper Wisconsin Counties*, 166)

Cainville [KAYN vil]. Rock. Named for Seth J. Cain, from Schuyler, Herkimer County, New York, a local promoter who donated land for the Chicago & North Western railroad station and was instrumental in establishing the post office in the early 1860s. Also known as Magnolia Station. (W. Brown, 2:673)

Calamine [KAL uh meyen]. Lafayette. Named after calamine, the zinc ore formerly mined near Mineral Point and best known as the primary ingredient of calamine lotion, used to treat sunburn and insect stings. The community was laid out in anticipation of the railroad by Mineral Point lawyer and local politician Montgomery M. Cothren, in January 1856.

Calamus [KAL uh muhs]. Dodge. Town (1846). Named from Calamus Creek, itself named for the Calamus, or Sweet Flag, a semi-aquatic plant often found along streams.

Caldwell. Racine. Named for early settlers Joseph and Tyler Caldwell, brothers from Vermont, who arrived in the area about 1836. The post office was established as Caldwell Prairie in August 1848, Daniel J. Gleason, postmaster. (F. Stone, 163)

Caledonia [kal uh DON yuh]. Columbia. Town (1851). The name was probably suggested by John S. Richmond, a native of Glasgow, Scotland, who was instrumental in the organization of the township. Caledonia, a poetic name for Scotland, was the Latin name for northern Britain. In "The Lay of the Last Minstrel," Sir Walter Scott writes of "Caledonia! stern and wild." (*Memorial and Biographical Record . . . of Columbia, Sauk, and Adams Counties*, 605)

Caledonia. Trempealeau. Town (1857). Named by early Scottish settlers, especially brothers Alexander and Donald McGilvray, from Inverness, Scotland, who operated a ferry across the Black River from about 1852. In 1860 Alexander McGilvray was instrumental in establishing the post office as Scotia, an alternate name for Scotland and the source of the name Nova Scotia. (Curtiss-Wedge and Pierce, 270)

Calhoun [kal HOON]. Waukesha. Named for George E. Calhoun, owner of the site on which the Chicago & North Western railroad station was built in 1882. (Stennett, 50)

Callon [KAL uhn]. Marathon. Named for the Callon family of Wausau. William Callon emigrated from County Armagh, Ireland, in 1849 and became a prominent figure in the local logging and lumber industries from the late 1850s. (Stennett, 50)

Calumet [KAL yuh MET]. County. Organized in 1836, attached to Brown County in 1840, reorganized in 1842. The Calumet, French for 'reed, pipe,' was the ceremonial "peace pipe" associated with Native Americans of the

Great Lakes region. Calumet was apparently also the name of a Menominee village on Lake Winnebago. The Calumet County seal shows crossed peace pipes with the words "We extend the Calumet to all Mankind."

Calumet. Fond du Lac. Town (1839). Also Calumetville. The community was founded by George White, an agent for the Fond du Lac Land Company, in 1838. White, John Norton, and William Urmston were instrumental in the organization of the town of Calumet in 1842. See New Holstein.

Calvary [KAL vuh ree]. Fond du Lac. Founded by Silas M. Barrett, a railroad contractor and president of the Sheboygan & Fond du Lac railroad in the late 1860s. Named from Our Lady of Mount Carmel Convent, known as the Calvary Convent, established in 1852 and named for the biblical Calvary. (Stennett, 50)

Calvert. La Crosse. Named for Robert Calvert, originally from Scotland. Calvert was secretary of the La Crosse Board of Trade and surveyor of customs for the Port of La Crosse from the early 1880s. (Bryant, 262)

Cambria [KAM bree uh, KAYM bree uh]. Columbia. Village (1866). Cambria grew around a sawmill established by brothers John and Samuel Langdon about 1845. The sawmill and the gristmill that followed were foreclosed in 1848 by James Bell, who formally laid out the community as Belleville. Bell sold his interests in Belleville to Welsh settlers John Ap Jones and Evan Edwards, who changed the name to Cambria, the Latinized form of Cymru, the Welsh name of Wales. (*Ap* is Welsh for 'son of.') There are Cambrias in some twenty states; most were named by settlers (often miners) from Wales. (Butterfield, *History of Columbia County*, 715)

Cambridge. Dane, Jefferson. Village (1891). Founded about 1847 by site owner Alvin B. Carpenter. The local story is that Carpenter named the community for Cambridge, Washington County, New York, the home of his boyhood sweetheart. (Cassidy, *Dane County Place-Names*)

Cameron [KAM ruhn]. Barron. Village (1894). The original Cameron was founded about 1879 on news that the Chippewa Falls & Northern railroad would be extended through the area to Spooner. The site was platted by Lemuel C. Stanley, a Chippewa Falls lumberman and the namesake of Stanley (q.v.), when the station was established in 1882. When the tracks of the Soo Line were laid a mile to the north, many of the buildings in Cameron were loaded onto wagons or sleds and moved to the present site. The name Cameron was suggested either by Lemuel Stanley or by Colonel George W. Ginty in honor of Angus Cameron of La Crosse, U.S. senator from Wisconsin at the time. (Crotteau, 1, 3)

Cameron. Wood. Town (1903). Named for James W. Cameron, from Nova Scotia. Cameron joined Henry Sherry to form the Sherry-Cameron Lumber

Company of Vesper, Wisconsin, about 1880. Cameron died in 1902 and the town was named in his honor the following year. (R. Rudolph)

Camp Douglas. Juneau. Village (1893). Founded as Douglas Camp Junction, a lumber camp established in the mid-1860s by James Douglas. The name was probably suggested by Amplius "Amp" Chamberlain, Douglas's business associate. In 1888 Camp Douglas became the site of the Wisconsin Military Reservation, Camp Philip Reade; later renamed Camp Williams for the camp commander, Charles R. Williams. (*Juneau County*, 81)

Campbell [KAM buhl]. La Crosse. Town. Named for Erasmus D. Campbell, mayor of La Crosse when the town was organized in 1857. Campbell was lieutenant governor of Wisconsin, serving 1858–60.

Campbellsport [KAM buhlz port]. Fond du Lac. Village (1902). Formerly known as Crouchville for early settler Ludin Crouch, who, along with John Howell, erected a sawmill on the east fork of the Milwaukee River in the early 1840s. The mill was bought by Emil Brayman, who named the site New Cassel for Cassel, Germany. In the 1870s the Chicago & North Western's Air Line railroad was built a mile or so west of New Cassel and the station was named for site owner Stuart Campbell. The post office was established in May 1877, Platt Durand, postmaster. Cassel merged with Campbellsport in 1902. (Worthing)

Candy Corners. Eau Claire. Candy Corners apparently takes its name from the Candy Corners store, established and named by Jothan (or Jotham or Jonathan; the name was variously recorded) Garnett about 1888. The historical Candy Corners school was located a mile north of the present community.

Canton [KANT n]. Barron. The original Canton was several miles south of its present location, near Sumner. When the Minneapolis, St. Paul & Sault Ste. Marie railroad was built through the area in 1884, businesses relocated and buildings were disassembled and moved to trackside. As Gordon and Curtiss-Wedge's 1922 *History of Barron County* so aptly put it, "When the people of Sumner saw that the railroad was not coming to them, they resolved to go to the railroad" (1137). The site owner was Lemuel C. Stanley, the namesake of Stanley (q.v.). Ultimately from the city in southern China, Canton is a popular place name in the United States, and Canton, Wisconsin, is likely a transfer, perhaps from St. Lawrence County, New York, or Stark County, Ohio.

Canton. Buffalo. Canton was organized in January 1867 as the Town of Page (Paige), named for an early settler. Four months later the name was changed to Canton at the suggestion of town clerk and justice of the peace Thomas W. Glasspoole, for his former home, Canton, Illinois, itself so named because the site was thought to be directly opposite that of Canton (Guangzhou), China. (Kessinger, 628)

Carcajou [KAR kuh joo]. Jefferson. Apparently named from the Carcajou Club, a shooting fraternity formed on the north shore of Lake Koshkonong by a group of Janesville sportsmen about 1896. Carcajou is from Canadian French for 'wolverine,' taken from the Algonquian language Montagnais. This is the only community so named in the United States. (Bright; Swart, 331)

Carlsville. Door. Apparently named for one or more German settlers named Karl, anglicized to Carl.

Carlton. Kewaunee. Town (1856). Formerly known as Dean, for Elisha B. Dean from New York State, who established several commercial enterprises in the early 1850s, and also as Sandy Bay. Probably named for early settler James Carlton. (*Kewaunee, Wisconsin*)

Carnegie [KAHRN uh gee, kahr NE gee]. Douglas. Named for industrialist Andrew Carnegie, who founded the Carnegie Steel Company in Pittsburgh, Pennsylvania, in the 1870s. Carnegie was one of the leading philanthropists of his day and a number of states have at least one public library provided by Carnegie, many built around 1900.

Carnot [KAHR nuht]. Door. The name was most likely chosen by Belgian Walloon settlers in honor of Marie François Sadi Carnot (1837–94), the French statesman serving as fourth president of the Third French Republic when the Carnot post office was established in June 1891. (Hale, 18)

Caroline [KEHR uh leyen]. Shawano. Named for Caroline Koeppen, wife of August Koeppen, a Shawano County surveyor who was engaged by site owners Charles and Louise Netzel to plat the community in 1878. (McDevitt, 91)

Carrollville. Milwaukee. Formerly known as South Milwaukee Springs. The name was changed toward the end of the nineteenth century, probably for Patrick and John Francis Carroll, who founded the Lakeside Distillery, the area's first business, in 1893. The post office was established in November 1899 as Otjen, in honor of Theobald Otjen, at the time a U.S. representative from Wisconsin. (Cech, 55)

Carson. Portage. Town (1878). Probably named for Irish settler Samuel Carson, who immigrated to the Stevens Point area about 1872. (Rosholt, *Our County, Our Story*, 277)

Carter. Forest. Named for John Carter, who built the first house in what is now the community of Carter. The post office was established in August 1899, Wilbur H. Miner, postmaster. Miner and his brother, Henry, founded Minertown (Minertown-Oneva), south of Carter, in the late 1890s as headquarters for the Miner Lumber Company. (Stennett, 51)

Cary. Wood. Town (1901). Cary was originally a shipping point on the line of the Milwaukee, Dexterville & Northern railroad. The name was probably chosen by George Hiles, owner of the railroad, for John W. Cary, general solicitor for the Chicago, Milwaukee & St. Paul railroad in the late 1880s. (R. Rudolph)

Caryville. Dunn. Named for John W. Cary, the likely namesake of Cary in Wood County. In addition to his business associations with the Wisconsin, Pittsville & Superior railroad, Cary was president of the Milwaukee Land Company, which platted the site in the early 1890s. The Caryville post office was established in November 1882, Menzus R. Bump, postmaster. (Curtiss-Wedge and Jones, 202)

Cascade [kas KAYD]. Sheboygan. Village (1914). Founded by James Preston and Huntington Lyman about 1847. Named for the rapids on the north branch of the Milwaukee River. (Buchen, 268)

Casco [KAS ko]. Kewaunee. Town (1856) and Village (1920). Founded about 1854 and named by Edward Decker for his former home, Casco, Maine, itself named from Abenaki *gasko* 'heron.' Decker, "the most prominent personality in Kewaunee County's history" (Zurawski, 8), was a miller and banker, president of the Ahnapee & Western railroad, and state senator in the early 1860s. The post office was established in September 1858 by Decker's sister, Lucy.

Cashton [KASH tuhn]. Monroe. Village (1901). In 1879 William Henry Harrison Cash, a land speculator from New Lisbon, Wisconsin, built the Viroqua branch of the Chicago, Milwaukee & St. Paul railroad through the area and named the station for himself. The railroad brought on the demise of Hazen's Corner or Mt. Pisgah, founded several years earlier a mile or so south of present Cashton. The post office was originally established in April 1856 by postmaster Jonathan S. Hazen. (Richards, 399)

Casimir [KAZ uh mihr]. Portage. Named from the St. Casimir church, a Polish congregation established by the Reverend Joseph Dabrowski in 1871. The fifteenth-century St. Casimir is the patron saint of Poland. (Perret, 16)

Cassel [KAS uhl]. Marathon. Town (1891). Settled largely in the late 1850s by German colonists sponsored by the Pittsburg Settlers Club. Named for Cassel (Kassel) in central Germany. (Marchetti, 539)

Cassell [KAS uhl]. Iowa, Sauk. Named from Cassell Prairie, itself named for Dr. James N. Cassell, who arrived in the area in the late 1840s. Cassell was the first doctor and first druggist in Lone Rock. (Cole, *Baraboo*)

Cassian [KA shuhn]. Oneida. Town (1903). The origin of the name is uncertain. A station on the Chicago, Milwaukee & St. Paul railroad named Cassanova Junction was established in the late 1880s. According to a local account, Cassanova may have been shortened to Cassian, perhaps by Jens

P. Jensen, a stonemason who emigrated from Denmark about 1874. Jensen kept a general store and was the first postmaster in 1902. This is the only Cassian in the United States, although there are Cassias in Florida and Idaho. (Jones and McVean, *History of Lincoln, Oneida and Vilas Counties*, 141; Thompson, p.c.)

Cassville [KAS vil]. Grant. Town (1849) and Village (1882). In 1836, shortly before the organization of Wisconsin Territory, the site was purchased by Lucius Lyon; Garrett Visscher Denniston, an Albany, New York, lawyer; and several other eastern investors on a hunch that Cassville would become the territorial and subsequently the state capital of Wisconsin. The name was in use by at least 1828 when the Cassville post office was established by Allen Hill. The namesake is Lewis Cass (1782–1866), a major political figure in the early United States. Cass was governor of Michigan Territory (which included present Wisconsin) from 1813 until 1831. He later served as U.S. secretary of state and ambassador to France. There are several dozen communities, townships, or counties named for Lewis Cass, primarily in the Midwest. (Holford, 601)

Castle Rock. Grant. Town (organized as Blue River in 1856; changed to Castle Rock in 1876). An early settler was Daniel Sylvester, from the state of Maine, who established a sawmill on Blue River about 1854. The post office was established as Castle Rock in July 1857, so named, in Joseph Schafer's words, "from a gigantic pine covered 'castle,' eroded from the St. Peter formation, which is an arresting object in the picturesque surroundings" (37).

Caswell [KAZ wel]. Forest. Town (1901). Probably named for Lucien B. Caswell, who served in the Wisconsin Assembly and later for eight terms in the U.S. House of Representatives, 1875–91.

Cataract. Monroe. The first permanent settler in the area was James Rathbone, who emigrated from Rhode Island and built a sawmill and gristmill in the early 1850s. The community was probably named by Rathbone for the rapids on Rathbone Creek. (Koehler, *History of Cataract*, 5)

Catawba [kuh TAH buh, kuh TAW buh]. Price. Town (1901) and Village (1922). Probably a transfer, perhaps from New York or New Jersey. Catawba is the name of a Native American people of the eastern United States, a river in the Carolinas, and a variety of grape. There are places named Catawba in about a dozen states. The post office was established in January 1898, Charles B. Welter, postmaster.

Cato [KAY to]. Manitowoc. Town (1857) and ppl. Formerly known as Harrisville for site owner John E. Harris. Formally named about 1854 by Alanson Hickok, who was instrumental in the formation of the township, for his former home, Cato, Cayuga County, New York, itself named for the Roman statesman, Cato the Younger. (Falge, 322)

Cavour [kuh VOR]. Forest. Probably named for Camillo Benso, the Count of Cavour, instrumental in the unification of Italy. In 1861, Cavour became the first Italian prime minister. The Cavour post office was established in July 1888, John L. Riseland, postmaster. The Town of Cavour was organized in 1897; the name was changed to Wabeno in 1901.

Cayuga [keye OO guh]. Ashland. Founded about 1888 as Kingsbury, west of its present location. After the timber was cut, Kingsbury declined but was revitalized as Cornell Siding, named for Cornell University, which owned several thousand acres in the area. The Cayuga post office was established in 1906, named for Lake Cayuga, one of upstate New York's Finger Lakes and the site of Cornell University. The lake was named for the Cayuga, an Iroquoian tribe. See Cornell. (*Journey into Mellen*, 604)

Cazenovia [kaz uh NO vee uh]. Richland, Sauk. Village (1902). Laid out by Allen Perkins in 1855. Named for Perkins's former home, Cazenovia, Madison County, New York, itself named in the 1790s for Theophilus Cazenove, an agent for the Holland Land Company. (Butterfield, *History of Crawford and Richland Counties*, 1268)

Cecil [SEE suhl]. Shawano. Village (1905). The source of the name is unknown. Perhaps named for one Cecil Leavitt, described in early accounts simply as "a railroad man." Stennett, usually a reliable reporter, claims the community was "named for a daughter of one of the officers of the Milwaukee, Lake Shore & Western Railway, when it was constructed [about 1884]" (53).

Cedarburg. Ozaukee. Town (1849) and City (1885). Cedarburg was settled largely by Altlutheraner, the "old Lutherans" who refused to join the nineteenth-century Prussian Union of Churches and immigrated to the United States. Many of them settled at Freistadt (q.v.); others, including four of the Groth brothers, Johann, Martin, Ludwig, and Wilhelm, took up homesteads along Cedar Creek in the early 1840s. They were later joined by William Schroeder and Frederick Hilgen. Hilgen, Schroeder, and Ludwig Groth are generally considered the founders of Cedarburg, which was formally platted in late 1844. (Damaske, *Along the Right-of-Way to Sheboygan*, 1)

Cedar Falls. Dunn. Named for the rapids on the Red Cedar River. The post office was established in January 1864, Martin Maxwell, postmaster.

Cedar Grove. Sheboygan. Village (1899). Named from the Cedar Grove post office, established by postmaster Sweezy Burr in January 1849. About 1847 Gerthinderk Takolste purchased from the U.S. government some six hundred acres of what now includes Cedar Grove. At about the same time the Reverend Pieter Zonne led a group of colonists from Gelderland province in the Netherlands to the area, which became known as the Zonne settlement. Several years later Gilbert Smith from New York State laid out Amsterdam east of present Cedar Grove. Takolste's, Zonne's, and Smith's holdings competed for population and commerce through the 1860s, but when the Milwaukee, Lake Shore & Western railroad was built through in the early 1870s, the name Cedar Grove was assured and much of Amsterdam was disassembled and moved to trackside. Amsterdam Park and Amsterdam Road perpetuate the name. (Hildebrand, 76)

Center. Outagamie. Town (organized as Lansing in 1849; changed to Center in 1853). According to local sources, the name is a transfer from Center Township, Columbiana County, Ohio, the temporary home of a number of colonists before settling permanently in Wisconsin. The area around Center Valley came to be known as the Ohio Settlement and the settlers as "Irish Buckeyes." (Truttschel, 78)

Centerville. The Town of Centerville in Manitowoc County, organized in 1850, was apparently so named because it was presumed to be halfway between Manitowoc and Sheboygan. The community of Centerville in southwest Wisconsin was reportedly so named for its location on the Iowa-Grant county line, the "center" of the adjoining counties. (Falge, 331; *History of Iowa County*, 797)

Centuria [sen TOR ee uh]. Polk. Village (1904). Founded by Cyrus A. Campbell of Minneapolis, townsite agent for the Minneapolis, St. Paul & Sault Ste. Marie railroad, who reportedly chose the name Centuria because the community was founded at the turn of the century. The post office was established in December 1901, Frank E. Dresser, postmaster. (*Centuria's Fiftieth Anniversary*, 11)

Chaffey [CHAY fee, CHA fee]. Douglas. Named from the Chaffee post office, established by postmaster John Chaffey (Chaffee) in October 1899.

Champion. Brown. Named from the Champion post office, established in August 1892 by Melanie Delvaux. The office was probably named for the small town of Champion, Belgium, southeast of Brussels, near the birthplace of Delvaux's husband, Jule. A local account, however, claims that the name was taken from Champion reaping machines, the predecessors of today's combines, of which the Delvaux were the local dealers. Champion was founded adjacent to or near Robinson, named from the Robinson post office and for Charles D. Robinson, who founded the *Green Bay Advocate* newspaper in 1846. When that office was discontinued in April

1895, the community was formally named Champion. (Cassidy, *Brown County*)

Chapel Ridge. Brown. Named for a chapel, the Shrine of St. Anthony of Padua, built in 1925 on a ridge overlooking Green Bay by Joseph LeMieux in honor of his wife, Odile LaPlant LeMieux. LeMieux was a noted stonemason responsible for several lighthouses on the Great Lakes. (Cassidy, *Brown County*)

Chapultepee. Trempealeau. The name Chapultepee is evidently a mistranscription of Chapultepec, the site of the 1847 American victory over the Mexican army at Mexico City, which was defended by the citadel of Chapultepec. The community takes its name from the nearby hill, Chapultepec Peak, itself probably named about 1855 by Charles J. Cleveland, who claimed that his father had taken part in the war with Mexico. Charles reportedly saw a resemblance between the prominence and the citadel of Chapultepec as it was described by his father. Chapultepec is from an Aztec word meaning 'grasshopper hill.' The historical Chapultepec school was located about halfway between Ettrick and Blair. (Curtiss-Wedge and Pierce, 277)

Charlesburg. Calumet. Named from the St. Charles Catholic Church, itself named for Carlo (Charles) Borromeo, the sixteenth-century archbishop of Milan, Italy. A local account claims that *berg* was added to the name to honor Jacob Berg, who donated land for the church about 1866. The post office was established in June 1872 as Charlesburgh by Benedict Schwerzler. (O. Meyer, 6–7)

Charlestown. Calumet. Town. Organized about 1849 by Parley Waller, Moses Stanton, and others. Named from a Charlestown in New England, probably at the suggestion of one of the Native American groups who settled in the Calumet County area in the 1820s and 1830s. The post office was established in May 1849, William Roberts, postmaster. See Brothertown; see Hayton.

Charme [CHAHRM]. Crawford. Named from Du Charme Creek, itself named for one or another of the Ducharme traders and explorers from French Canada. By the mid-1750s Jean-Marie Ducharme was an established fur trader in the Michigan-Wisconsin area with a post near Green Bay.

Chase. Oconto. Town (1885) and ppl. Named from the Chase & Dixie sawmill, in operation on the Little Suamico River by the late 1860s. The post office was established as St. Nathans in 1873 and changed to Chase in the spring of 1890. (Rucker, "Lumbering Makes Oconto County")

Chaseburg. Vernon. Village (1922). Founded in 1866. Named for Henry Chase, from Vermont, who, along with George Little, established the

Coon River Mills in 1863. Chase represented the area in the Wisconsin Assembly in the late 1860s and early 1870s. (*History of Vernon County*, 552)

Chelsea [CHEL see]. Taylor. Town (1875) and ppl. Named about 1875 by the Wisconsin Central railroad for the Chelsea section of Boston, itself named for Chelsea, London, England. Chelsea is one of a number of names from the Boston area on the line of the Wisconsin Central chosen by Gardner Colby and his son Charles, both presidents of the railroad. See Colby. (Latton, 184)

Chenequa [shuh NEE kwuh]. Waukesha. Village (1928). Founded by Gustaf Unonius and a colony of Swedish settlers in 1841 as New Upsala, named for Upsala (the older spelling of Uppsala), Sweden, where Unonius had been a university student. In his memoirs Unonius wrote that the lake on which Chenequa lies was called "in the Indian language . . . Chenequa or Pine Lake." In fact, Chenequa is from Ojibwa *zhingwak* 'white pine.' (Stark, 47)

Cherneyville [CHER nee vil]. Kewaunee. Cherney is a phonetic spelling of Czech Černý 'black.' Named for one or more Cherney families. Tomas Cherney kept a local tavern in the 1870s. (Rucker, *History of Czech Settlements*, 6)

Cherokee. Marathon. Paul Umhoefer established a sawmill on the Eau Pleine River in the 1870s and became the first postmaster in 1891, naming the office for his former home, Cherokee, Iowa, itself named in the the 1850s for the Cherokee tribe of Native Americans. (*Town of Frankfort Centennial*, 30)

Chester. Dodge. Town (1846). Apparently named by settlers from Chester, Hampden County, Massachusetts, itself named for one of the Chesters in England. The post office was established in November 1847, Ebenezer K. Vaughn, postmaster. (Stennett, 55)

Chetek [shuh TEK]. Barron. Town (1874) and City (1891). Platted in the early fall of 1875 for the Knapp, Stout Lumber Company, which had recently established a camp at the site. Named from Lake Chetek, itself named from Ojibwa *zhede* (or *sha-da*) 'pelican.' The name of Chetac Lake in Sawyer County is from the same source. The post office was established in July 1872, as Shetek, a spelling that continued until 1883, when Chetek became official. (Gordon and Curtiss-Wedge, 1051)

Chicog [SHEYE kahg, shuh KAHG]. Washburn. Town (1902). Chicog is from Ojibwa *zhigag* 'skunk,' but it is unlikely the town was named directly for the animal, called by the French *bête puante* 'stinking animal' and *enfant de diable* 'child of the devil.' Perhaps a settler was impressed by the sound of the word, or perhaps Chicog was a local Ojibwa figure. The post office was established in December 1897 by Martha J. Nelson. This is the only Chicog in the United States. (Chappelle, *"Why of Names,"* 60)

Chili. Clark. The Chicago, St. Paul, Minneapolis & Omaha railroad founded Chili in the early 1890s and probably named it for Chile in South America, which was in the news at the time due to a brief civil war in 1891. The pronunciation is [CHIL ee], the way the name of the country is usually pronounced in American English. (Stennett, 170)

Chilton. Calumet. Town (organized in 1853 as Portland; changed to Chilton in 1856) and City (1877). Chilton was first known as Stantonville, founded about 1845 by Moses Stanton and his Native American wife, romantically claimed to be a direct descendant of the seventeenth-century Wampanoag leader Metacomet, better known as King Philip. The future Chilton was platted in 1852 by English land speculator John Marygold (Marigold). Apparently Marygold intended to name the community Chillington for one of the Chillingtons in England, but the name was erroneously entered as Chilton by the county recorder. (Minaghan and Vanderhoef, 20)

Chimney Rock. Trempealeau. Town (1881). Settled in the 1860s. Named from the summit called Chimney Rock, a weathered stone formation southwest of Strum.

Chippewa [CHIP uh wah]. County. Chippewa County was organized in 1845 and named from the Chippewa River, itself named for the Chippewa or Ojibwa, one of the tribes of the Three Fires, whose territory in northern Wisconsin stretched from the Upper Peninsula of Michigan into Minnesota. The first recorded name of the river was *Bon Secours*, 'River of Good Help.' Nicholas Perrot established Fort Bon Secours, a trading post at the mouth of the river, in 1685. The name Bon Secours was followed by Rivière des Sauteurs, the French name for the Chippewa of Sault Ste. Marie, 'people of the falls.' The name has been spelled in a number of ways, including Outchibous, Chippewyans, and Ojibwas (as names for the people). Bishop Frederic Baraga, who ministered to the Chippewa in the nineteenth century, wrote Otchipwe. The name is generally interpreted as 'puckered,' referring to stitching moccasins in such a way that they appeared crinkled or plaited. Today many Ojibwa refer to themselves as Anishinabe 'original people.'

Chittamo [CHID uh mo]. Washburn. From Ojibwa *atchitamo* 'squirrel,' a compound of *atchit* 'head first' and *amo* 'mouth.' Perhaps taken from the Longfellow poem in which Hiawatha addresses the squirrel: "Boys shall call you Adjidaumo, tail-in-the-air the boys shall call you." *Atchitamo* is the source of the English word 'chipmunk.' The post office was established in July 1908, Louise Grimes, postmaster. This is the only Chittamo in the United States. (Vogel, *Indian Names*, 143)

Choate [SHOT]. Langlade. Named for Leander Choate, from Maine, an Oshkosh lumberman, businessman and banker of the late nineteenth and early twentieth centuries. (Dessureau, 56)

Christiana [kris tee AN uh]. Christiana, the name of towns in Dane (1847) and Vernon (1855) Counties, is a slightly modified spelling of Christiania, the capital of Norway from the seventeenth century until 1925, when the traditional name, Oslo, was restored. In Dane County, Christiana was named from the post office, established in 1846. According to Norwegian historian Svein Nilsen, the prominent Norwegian settler Gunnell Olson Vindæg chose the name, "but as he was not particularly skilled in spelling, he unfortunately happened to write Christiana instead of Christiania, and this designation has since been retained" (Cassidy, *Dane County Place-Names*, 32).

Christie. Clark. Apparently named for and by Arminta (Minta) Christie, who established the post office in July 1875.

Cicero [SIS uh ro]. Outagamie. Town (1871) and ppl. Named by the first town chair, Stephen B. Salter, for his former home, Cicero, Onondaga County, New York, itself named for the Roman statesman, Marcus Tullius Cicero. (Balliet, 87)

City Point. Jackson. Town (organized in 1878 as Sullivan; changed to City Point in 1893) and ppl. Formally named from the City Point post office, established in January 1876. According to a local account, the name was changed at the suggeston of Fred Marcelin for his former home in in the city of Hopewell, Virginia. (Rogers, 49)

Clam Falls. Polk. Town (1876) and ppl. Named for the falls in the Clam River, which provided the name of the post office and the community that grew around a sawmill established by Dan Smith in 1872. Probably from Ojibwa, based upon *esag* 'clams.' The name of the river was recorded by Joseph Nicollet in 1837 as "Kayesikang or Shell River" (228).

Clark. County. Organized in July 1853. Clark County is named for George Rogers Clark (1752–1818), a hero of the Revolutionary War on the western frontier. Clark's capture of Kaskaskia and Vincennes in 1778 ensured that the Illinois Country would not be occupied by British troops. When the county was authorized, the name Clark was proposed by Lyman Draper, secretary of the Wisconsin Historical Society and a leading authority on the life and service of George Rogers Clark. Selection of the name may have been influenced by one or more local Clark families. Moses Clark surveyed much of Weston and was a township official in the early 1850s. (Curtiss-Wedge, *History of Clark County*, 79; Kellogg, 221)

Clarks Mills. Manitowoc. In the late 1840s Ira Clark established a sawmill and gristmill on the Manitowoc River. Clark and his business partner, Thomas Cunningham, built the first bridge over the river in 1847. (Falge, 322)

Clarno [KLAHR no]. Green. Town (1849) and ppl. Named for Andrew Clarno, an early settler from Sangamon County, Illinois, about 1830. The post office was established in June 1855, Leonard Ault, postmaster. (Butterfield, *History of Green County*, 767)

Clay Banks. Door. Town (1859). Clay Banks, a descriptive name that originated among Lake Michigan sailors, referred to the sharp, nearly perpendicular banks along the lake at this point, contrasting with the lower shoreline elsewhere. The banks became a point from which to reckon distance and provided a reference for navigation. The post office was established in December 1862, George H. Prescott, postmaster. (Holand, 443)

Clayton. Polk. Town (1875) and Village (1909). Named for Clayton Rodgers, an officer of Wisconsin volunteers during the Civil War and later foreman in David Humbird's lumber mill. An account written in the late 1870s characterized Rodgers as "the life of the town, a man who travels thirty miles every day, and does more mental and physical work than any other two men in Polk County." The name was probably chosen by David Humbird, who established the Clayton post office in 1876. David was the son of John Humbird, who named Cumberland and who was the nephew of Jacob Humbird, for whom Humbird was named. See Cumberland; see Humbird. (Almen)

Clayton. Winnebago. Town (1849). Named for John Middleton Clayton (1796–1856). At the time the town was organized, Clayton was U.S. secretary of state, newly appointed by President Zachary Taylor. He was later a U.S. senator from Delaware. (*History of Town of Clayton*, 27)

Cleghorn [KLEG horn]. Eau Claire. Named for the Cleghorn family. James Gilbert Cleghorn immigrated to the Midwest from New York State in 1854, first to Indiana, then to Minnesota, finally to Pleasant Valley, Wisconsin, in 1858. The post office was established in August 1900, Albert H. Zeitler, postmaster. (Bailey, 678)

Cleveland. The towns of Cleveland in Marathon (1884), Jackson (1885), and Chippewa (1885) Counties and the Village of Cleveland in Manitowoc County were named for Grover Cleveland (1837–1908), the twenty-second and twenty-fourth president of the United States, serving 1885–89 and 1893–97.

Cleveland. Taylor. Town (1896). Likely named for Samuel F. Cleveland, a prominent local landowner. (Nagel and Deuel, 127)

Clifton. Grant. Town (1850). Probably named for Bosman Clifton. Originally from Delaware, Clifton was a community and religious benefactor. (*Grant County History*, 232)

Clifton. Pierce. The Town of Clifton was organized in 1857, taking its name from the community of Clifton, now only a memory but a viable settlement during the middle years of the nineteenth century. Likely named from Clifton's Mills but the source of that name is uncertain. A Clifton may have been an early settler or miller, as Rohe suggests ("Names on the Land," 22), or, as Johnson and Wilmot suggest, the name may be a popular etymology compressed from an earlier Cliff Town (9). A local account is that the name was proposed for unknown reasons by Osborne Strahl, from Belmont County, Ohio. The Clifton Mills [*sic*] post office operated from May 1855 until October 1886.

Clinton. Rock. Town (1842) and Village (1882). Founded in April 1837 by settlers sponsored by the Jefferson Prairie Company of Jefferson County, New York, led by Deacon Chauncey Tuttle. Named in honor of DeWitt Clinton, governor of New York 1817–22. About 1856 the Chicago, St. Paul & Fond du Lac railroad established Ogden Station, probably named for William B. Ogden, president of the railroad. With arrival of the Racine & Mississippi railroad about 1857, the station was renamed Clinton Junction. The name officially became Clinton in 1864. (*Clinton Bicentennial*, 5)

Clintonville. Waupaca. City (1887). Named for the Norman Clinton family, from Ferrisburgh, Vermont, by way of Potsdam, New York. The local story is that Clinton set up a homestead at the site because his ox became sick and could go no farther. The area was known as Pigeon, named from the Pigeon River, until 1857 when the Clintonville post office was established with Urial Clinton, Norman's son, as postmaster. (Diedrich and Gehl, 193)

Clyde. Kewaunee. Named for Clyde Champion by his father, Seth, a director of the Kewaunee, Green Bay & Western railroad in the 1890s. ("Green Bay & Western Lines")

Clyman [KLEYE muhn]. Dodge. Town (1846), Village (1924), and ppl. The namesake is apparently a Colonel Joseph Clyman, about whom little is known. Stennett calls him "a noted Indian fighter, in the early days of Wisconsin" (55). Hubbell adds that Clyman "in personal appearance was said to have greatly resembled George Washington" (246). He may be the same person as James Clyman, reportedly the companion of Ellsworth

Burnett, who was killed by Indians in 1836. The post office was established in June 1849, Jonathan Finch, postmaster. See Burnett.

Cobb [KAHB]. Iowa. Village (1902). Previously known as Danville, Cross Plains, and Eden. The first settler in the area was Martin Ash, who operated a hotel he called the Bailey House from about 1850. The community was formally named in 1863 for Amasa Cobb, who represented Wisconsin for four terms in the U.S. Congress in the late 1860s. (G. Shepard, 61)

Cobban [KAHB uhn]. Chippewa. Named for Simon Cummings Frazer Cobban, born in Inverness, Quebec, the son of Scottish immigrants. After serving in the Civil War, Cobban moved to Chippewa Falls where he became a successful entrepreneuer and community benefactor, establishing the Chippewa Falls opera house about 1880 and organizing one of the first banks in the area. He owned much of the land upon which Cobban was sited. The Cobban post office was established in January 1904. (Gerber, *Memories of Cobban*, 5)

Cobb Town, Cobbtown. Waupaca. Also known as Sheridan Mills and as Sherman, from the Sherman post office. Cobbtown was reportedly named for the piles of corncobs generated by the flour mill established by Joseph and Samuel Leonard about 1860. (*"Ghost" Towns of Waupaca County*, 27)

Cochrane [KAHK ruhn]. Buffalo. Village (1910). Founded about 1840 by the St. Paul Land Company, agent for the Chicago, Burlington & Northern railroad. Named for Alexander Cochrane, a director of the railroad. Also known as Petersburgh, for Peter Schugg, considered by many to be the founder of Cochrane. (Curtiss-Wedge, *History of Buffalo and Pepin Counties*, 933)

Coddington. Portage. Named from the Coddington post office, established in July 1912 by postmaster Lewis A. Kyser and named for Wallace B. Coddington, who laid out the community as Pine Island in 1911. (Rosholt, *Our County, Our Story*, 274)

Colburn. Adams. Town (1890). Probably named for Sherman Colburn, originally from Vermont. Colburn immigrated to Wisconsin in 1855, fought in the Civil War, and became a successful farmer and a "public-spirited citizen." (*Memorial and Biographical Record . . . of Columbia, Sauk, and Adams Counties*, 676)

Colburn. Chippewa. Town (1886) and ppl. Named for Frank A. Colburn, born in Genesee County, New York. Colburn was sheriff of Chippewa Falls in the 1870s and chair of the Town of Sigel. The post office was established in May 1895, Angus Morrison, postmaster. (*History of Northern Wisconsin*, 206)

Colby [KOL bee]. Clark. Town (1873). Clark, Marathon. City (1891). Named for Gardner or Charles Colby, or both. Gardner Colby was a Boston financier whose Colby and Phillips Construction Company built a large portion of the Wisconsin Central railroad. He was president of the railroad in the 1870s and his son Charles, formerly vice president, succeeded him as president in 1889. Gardner Colby's endowment to Waterville College in Maine in 1865 allowed the school to remain open, and it was renamed Colby College in his honor in 1867. The Colbys are also the namesakes—although indirectly—of Colby cheese. The mild cheddar developed by Joseph Steinwand was named for Colby, Wisconsin, where it was first produced in the 1880s. (Scholtz; Marchetti, 224)

Coleman. Marinette. See Pound.

Colfax [KOL faks]. Dunn. Town (1868) and Village (1904). Named for Schuyler Colfax Jr. (1823–85), U.S. vice president under Ulysses Grant when the township was organized. Colfax was a popular Whig and later Republican politician, and several dozen places are named in his honor, especially in the midwestern states. (Dunn County Historical Society, 19)

Colgate [KOL gayt]. Waukesha, Washington. Founded about 1886 as Colgate Station. Named for one or more members of the Colgate family, related to James B. Colgate. The Colgates were New York financiers who invested heavily in midwestern and western railroads. The namesake is probably Colgate Hoyt, a director of the Wisconsin Central railroad in the late nineteenth century. See Abbotsford. (Keller)

Collins. Manitowoc. In March 1851 William Adams established the Collins post office, which was discontinued five months later. In 1896 the office was reestablished by postmaster Emil Taube. Both the second Collins post office and the present community are named for Sumner J. Collins, general superintendent of the Wisconsin Central railroad in the 1890s. The namesake of the first Collins post office is unknown. (Falge, 316)

Coloma [kuh LOM uh]. Waushara. Town (1853) and Village (1939). Named about 1855 by Charles White and Elias Follett, who had joined thousands of prospectors in the great California gold rush of the late 1840s. White and Follett brought the name to Wisconsin from Coloma, El Dorado County, California. Coloma was originally the name of a Maidu Indian village near Sutter's Mill, where the California gold rush began. (*Coloma Area Sesquicentennial*, 15)

Columbia. County. When Portage County was divided in 1846, two names for the new county were considered: York, proposed by settlers from New York State, and Columbia, proposed by James T. Lewis, a lawyer from the Columbus voting precinct, who would later be the ninth governor of

Wisconsin. According to Butterfield, author of the 1880 *History of Columbia County*, "The bill [calling for the name York] was about to pass, when [Lewis] succeeded in inducing the members to vote for an amendment striking out [York] and inserting [Columbia]" (376). Columbia, a Latinized form of Columbus, is a popular place name, occurring in some forty states.

Columbia. Clark. Founded in 1893 by the Columbia Improvement Company, itself named from the World's Columbian Exposition being held in Chicago at the time. (Curtiss-Wedge, *History of Clark County*, 662)

Columbus. Columbia. Town (1843) and City (1874). The first settler in what is now Columbus was Elbert Dickason, known as "Major" Dickason, in recognition of his service in the Black Hawk War. About 1839 Dickason built a sawmill and blacksmith shop and laid off a dozen building lots for a community he called Columbus. When Dickason's business enterprises failed, he moved ten miles northwest and established Wyocena (q.v.). See Columbia County. (Butterfield, *History of Columbia County*, 665)

Combined Locks. Outagamie. Village (1920). Formerly known as Garner's Landing for early settler Roland Garner. The community was named from the Combined Locks Paper Company, which began operations in the late 1880s. The company took its name from the upper and lower locks on the Fox River and the associated canals between Kaukauna and Little Chute. The post office was established in September 1892, Alexander Conkey, postmaster. (Kort, 50)

Comfort. Dunn. Named about 1900 for Comfort Starr, son of William J. Starr, an Eau Claire lumberman whose mill provided the nucleus for the village of Weston (q.v.). (Stennett, 171)

Commonwealth. Florence. Town (1882) and ppl. Laid out in March 1880. Named from the Commonwealth Iron Company, founded by Horace Tuttle of Cleveland, Ohio. The post office was established in April 1880. (*Heritage of Iron & Timber*, 28)

Como. See Lake Como.

Comstock [KAHM stahk]. Barron. Named for Henry S. Comstock, Barron County judge and editor of the *Cumberland Advocate* in the late 1880s. The post office was established in June 1878, Andrew P. Swanby, postmaster. (Stennett, 171)

Connorsville, Connersville. Dunn. Named from the Connorsville post office, established by David L. Connor in February 1874. Previously known as Bolan. (Dunn County Historical Society, 56)

Conover. Vilas. Town (1907) and ppl. Named for Seth Conover, a cheese merchant from Plymouth, Wisconsin. The local account is that Conover, an avid fisherman and outdoorsman, would take the train from Plymouth and have it stop and let him off so he could hunt or fish. He would flag the train at the same spot for his return trip. By the late 1800s the site was known as the Conover stop and this name became part of the Chicago & North Western timetable. (*Town of Conover*)

Conrath [KAHN rath]. Rusk. Village (1915). First known as Main Creek Siding, a switching site on the Wisconsin Central railroad, and the destination of the brothers Charles, Felix, Frank, Joe, and John Conrath, who established a logging camp and sawmill in 1904. The mill became the nucleus of a settlement named for the Conrath family. Several years later the community was formally organized by the Ben F. Faast Land and Colonization Company, which purchased some thirty thousand acres of cutover land in the Conrath and Sheldon areas. See Ojibwa. (Conrath and Terrill, 7, 15)

Cooks Valley. Chippewa. Town (1927). In the summer of 1858 Jacob Cook and Zerah Willis purchased adjacent properties in the valley that bears Cook's name. The post office was established in July 1870, William Miller, postmaster. (Forrester, 52)

Cooksville. Rock. Named for brothers John and Daniel Cook, who arrived with their families in the early 1840s and proceeded to establish a sawmill and lay out the community of Cooksville in 1842. Several years later and just east of Cooksville, Dr. John Porter laid out Waucoma, reportedly based on a Native American word meaning 'clear water.' Waucoma survived for several decades after the post office was named Cooksville in 1849. (Hartung)

Coomer [KOO mer]. Burnett. Apparently named for William Coomer, a merchant based in Taylors Falls, Minnesota. Who chose the name and the reason Coomer deserved the honor are unknown. The post office was established in March 1892, Orlando B. Smith, postmaster. (Ericson)

Coon. Vernon. Town (1857). Also Coon Valley. Village (1907). Earlier known as *Helgedalen* 'Helge's Valley' for Helge Gulbrandson, its first settler, from Norway. Renamed from Coon Valley, itself named for *Procyon lotor*, the common raccoon, by Henry Johnson, who established the first general store in the area and laid out Coon Valley in 1859. (*History of Vernon County*, 505)

Cooperstown. Manitowoc. Town (1856) and ppl. Named by Allen A. Cooper, the first postmaster in 1848. Named either for postmaster Cooper or for Cooperstown, New York. (Falge, 314)

Coppens Corner [KAH puhnz]. Brown. Named for Phil and Catherine Coppens, local landowners in the 1860s. Several Coppens families emigrated from Belgium in the nineteenth century. (Cassidy, *Brown County*)

Coral City. Trempealeau. Founded by Phineas and Benjamin Wright, who built a flouring mill in the summer of 1863. The local story is that Granville McFarland, as a practical joke, convinced Phineas Wright that some unusual rocks he had found while building the dam for the mill were coral. Wright, then in the process of laying out the community, thought that Coral City would be a good name. (Curtiss-Wedge and Pierce, 272)

Corinth. Marathon. The origin of the name is uncertain. Perhaps chosen for the city in ancient Greece, since Corinth fits with such classical names in the area as Marathon and Athens; perhaps a transfer from Corinth, Saratoga County, New York; perhaps named in honor of the 1862 Civil War Battle of Corinth, Mississippi, in which the Eighth Wisconsin Volunteers, carrying its regimental mascot, the bald eagle Old Abe, suffered severe casualties. The post office was established in October 1895, Otto Neumann, postmaster. See Eagle Point.

Cormier [KOR meer]. Brown. Named for a local Cormier family, who had significant landholdings in the area. George J. Cormier was a De Pere councilman in 1912.

Cornell. Chippewa. City (1956). Earlier known as Brunet Falls, named for Jean Brunet, who established an inn and trading post near the site in 1843. Named for Ezra Cornell and Cornell University. In the 1860s Ezra Cornell, one of the founders of Western Union, bought some hundred thousand acres of timberland in the vicinity. Upon Cornell's death in 1874, the land became part of the endowment of Cornell University, which Ezra Cornell had founded with Andrew Dickson White in Ithaca, New York, in 1865. The post office was established in August 1903, Miles G. Davis, postmaster. (Stennett, 171)

Cornucopia [korn uh KO pee uh]. Bayfield. From Latin for 'horn of plenty,' signifying abundance. Thomas J. Stevenson, an officer of the Cornucopia Land Company, is usually credited with proposing the name, claiming the area was "a veritable cornucopia of wilderness provender." However, according to Eric Larson, a chronicler of Cornucopia, the name may have existed before either the land company or the community and may have been suggested by the "horn of plenty" shape of the Siskiwit River where it empties into Lake Superior. Cornucopia, Wisconsin, is the only present community so named in the United States. The post office was established in May 1902, Albert Westcott, postmaster. (Larson)

Cottage Grove. Dane. Town (1847) and Village (1924). In the early 1840s Amos Beecher emigrated from New York State and established a tavern he called the Cottage Grove House. The tavern provided the name of the post office, established in 1841 by William C. Wells. The original location of Cottage Grove was at the site of present Vilas. When the Chicago & North Western station was located several miles to the southeast, many businesses and residents moved to the new site. (Cassidy, *Dane County Place-Names*)

Cottonville. Adams. Named for the Cotton family. An early settler with the remarkable name of Emulous Plutarch Cotton arrived in 1856. Emulous and his brother, Julius, built a dam and sawmill on Big Roche-a-Cri Creek, and the following year Julius Cotton laid out a community he called Roche-A-Cree; the name was later changed to Cottonville. ("Adams County, Wisconsin")

Couderay [KOO duh ray]. Sawyer. Town (1907) and Village (1922). Named from the Couderay post office, established in June 1903, itself named from the Couderay River. Couderay is a modification of *Courte Oreilles* 'short ears,' the name given by early French explorers to the Ottawa Indians who cut off the rims of their ears, making them appear short.

Council Bay. La Crosse. Apparently named from a mediating session on the Black River between a lumber company and a contingent of Ho-Chunk (Winnebago) in 1838. (Polleys, 21)

County Line. On the line separating Marinette and Oconto Counties.

Crandon. Forest. Town (1887) and City (1898). Previously known as Ayr, for Ayr, Scotland, birthplace of poet Robert Burns. Platted by the Chicago & North Western railroad as Crandon, named for Frank P. Crandon, tax commissioner for the railroad, who was instrumental in the organization of Forest County (q.v.). (Stennett, 17, 60)

Crane. Rusk. Named from the Crane post office, established in January 1910 by postmaster Lewis D. Crane.

Cranmoor [KRAN mor]. Wood. Town (1903) and ppl. Originally known as Bearss Marsh, platted in 1879 for Theodore Bearss and Philip Alexander. Cranmoor, a blend of cranberry and moor, was created by Julia Fitch and referred to the Fitch estate and to the Cranmoor Cranberry Company, organized by William H. Fitch in 1891. Post office established as Bears in 1890; changed to Bearss Marsh in 1893 and to Cranmoor in 1898. (D. Engel, 20, 43, 86, 128)

Crawford. County. Named from Fort Crawford, built in 1816 at Prairie du Chien and named for William Harris Crawford (1772–1834), U.S. senator from Georgia and secretary of both the War and Treasury Departments under President James Madison. When Crawford County was created in 1818 by Lewis Cass, governor of Michigan Territory, it encompassed the western half of the present state of Wisconsin. Crawford City, near

Lynxville, was a viable community for several years in the late 1850s. When the sawmill established by George Millet and Fenner Foster ceased operations, the settlement disappeared. (Butterfield, *History of Crawford and Richland Counties*, 721)

Crawford Crossing. Sauk. Named for James Crawford, who emigrated from Huron County, Ohio, and bought a farm south of Baraboo in 1847. (Cole, *Standard History*, 2:620)

Crivitz [KRIV its]. Marinette. Village (1974). Named by Frederick J. Bartels for Crivitz, his birthplace in northern Germany. Bartels and William Ellis, superintendent of the Peshtigo Lumber Company, laid out the community about 1883. The town of Crivitz was organized in 1897 and dissolved in 1927. This is the only Crivitz in the United States. (*Marinette County Centennial*, 3)

Cross Plains. Dane. Town (1847) and Village (1920). Named from the Cross Plains post office, established in May 1838 by Berry Haney, the probable namesake of Berry (q.v.). The origin of the name is uncertain. Local accounts suggest that Haney may have named the office for an existing Cross Plains, or for the site where the Military Road intersected another road between Madison and Arena. The present village of Cross Plains includes the communities of Christina, platted in 1855 by Peter L. Mohr and named for his wife; Foxville, platted by site owner Abijah Fox in 1857; and Baerville, platted in 1855 for site owners Johann and Juliana Baer. (Cassidy, *Dane County Place-Names*)

Cuba City. Grant, Lafayette. City (1925). Cuba City developed around a roadside inn known as the Western, established about 1850 by Stedman Davis to provide respite for travelers and merchants on the road from Mineral Point to Galena. Shortly after the railroad was built through the area in the mid-1870s, John Stephens, Solomon Craiglow, and Madison Johnson laid out the community as Yuba. Local folklore claims that when Stephens proposed the name Stephensville, Craiglow responded, "You b'damned we won't," to which Stephens replied, "That's it. We will call it Yuba." Apparently the name Yuba was insisted upon by Craiglow, who reportedly had been a miner on the Yuba River in California. The reason for the name change from Yuba to Cuba is unknown. The editors of Butterfield's 1881 *Grant County History* (833) claim that the name of the proposed Yuba City post office was changed to Cuba City because Wisconsin already had a Yuba post office (which I have not been able to verify). The post office was established as St. Rose in May 1856, changed to Cuba City in June 1875 (perhaps for the island of Cuba, which was prominent in news reports of the 1870s for a series of revolts against Spanish rule known as the Ten Years' War), and changed to Cuba in January 1895. See Yuba. (*Cuba City Centennial*)

Cudahy [KUHD uh hay]. Milwaukee. City (1906). Formerly known as Buckhorn. Renamed about 1892 when Patrick and John Cudahy transferred their meatpacking plant from Milwaukee. (Stennett, 61)

Cumberland [KUHM ber luhnd]. Barron. Town and City (1885). Norwegian settlers Ole Ritan and Gunder Dahlby are generally recognized as the founders of Cumberland. The town was organized in 1875 as Lakeland, and the Lakeland post office was established the following year. Both names were changed in 1879 with extension of the North Wisconsin Railway at the request of John A. Humbird, railroad president, for his former home, Cumberland, Maryland. (Gordon and Curtiss-Wedge, 1089)

Curran [KER uhn]. Jackson. Town (1889). Named for John and Betsy Curran, pioneers from Pennsylvania who arrived in the area in 1847. The post office was established in April 1890, Nicholas Murphy, postmaster. (*Jackson County, a History*, 29)

Curran. Kewaunee. Probably named, as historian James Linak suggests, by Irish settlers for Curran in County Derry, Ireland. There were, however, several Curran families in the area when the community was named. The post office was established in April 1870, Nicholas Murphy, postmaster. (Linak, p.c.)

Curtiss. Clark. Village (1917). In the winter of 1880 the Wisconsin Central railroad established Curtiss Station, named for civil engineer Charles Curtiss, who owned some two hundred acres in the area and oversaw much of the construction of the railroad between Abbotsford and Chippewa Falls. The post office was established in September 1881 by postmaster Gilbert Olson as Quar, reportedly named for the Olson family farm in Norway. (*Curtiss 75th Anniversary*, 2)

Cushing. Polk. Named for Caleb Cushing (1800–1879), an American diplomat and politician from Massachusetts who served with great distinction in the administrations of presidents Tyler, Pierce, Johnson, and Grant. Cushing was Envoy Extraordinary and Minister Plenipotentiary to China in the 1840s and to Spain in the 1870s. Locally, Cushing was instrumental in developing the natural resources of the St. Croix valley. He owned some forty-five thousand acres of land and was largely responsible for the founding of St. Croix Falls (q.v.). The post office was established in March 1870, James Smith, postmaster. (Ericson)

Custer. Portage. Formerly known as Dawson, named for a prominent Dawson family or families, landowners from the 1850s. Formally named with establishment of the post office in December 1876 for George Armstrong Custer, whose Seventh Cavalry had been destroyed at the Battle of the Little Bighorn in Montana six months earlier. (Perret, 15)

Cutler. Juneau. Town (organized as Cranberry Center in 1895; changed to Cutler in 1896) and ppl. Named in honor of Charles F. "Fred" Cutler, Juneau County clerk for more than three decades, beginning in 1857. (*Juneau County*, 43)

Cylon [SEYE luhn]. St. Croix. Town (1858) and ppl. The origin of the name is uncertain. The site was purchased by John B. Gibson in 1855. Gibson established the Cylon post office in July 1862. The local account is that Gibson wanted to name the post office for the island of Ceylon but changed the spelling when he discovered a community called Ceylon in southern Minnesota. This is the only Cylon in the United States. (Fouks and Fouks, *Marion Johnson*, 10)

Dacada [duh KAY duh]. Ozaukee, Sheboygan. Origin unknown. Possibly a variant of Dakota. The post office was established in April 1866, Peter Depiesse, postmaster. This is the only Dacada in the United States. (Eccles, 7)

Dahl [DAHL]. St. Croix. Probably named for one or more early settlers named Dahl. By 1880 several Dahl families were established in the area, one of which may also be the namesake of Dahl Lake in Polk County. The post office was established in March 1895, Sigur Johnson, postmaster.

Dakota. Waushara. Town (1851) and ppl. Platted for site owner and first postmaster Chapin M. Seeley, in 1853. Probably named for Dakota, the area of the Upper Midwest that would become Dakota Territory and later the states of North and South Dakota. Dakota was in the news in the 1850s, and several places were so named about that time. (Reetz, 195)

Daleyville. Dane. Daleyville grew around a store established about 1853 by Onun Bjornson Dahle, who emigrated from Telemark, Norway, in 1848. Dahle was active in the affairs of Perry Township, serving as clerk, treasurer, and justice of the peace. By popular etymology *Dahle* became *Daley*. (*Historic Perry*, 26)

Dallas [DAL uhs]. Barron. Town (1862) and Village (1903). Named for its location in Dallas County, as Barron County was called at the time. Named for George Mifflin Dallas (1792–1864), vice president of the United States under James K. Polk, serving 1845–49. Dallas was a popular political figure, and several dozen communities and townships in the United States are named for him, including Dallas, Texas. The settlement that became the village of Dallas grew around the Sylvan Spring post office, established in November 1872 by postmaster William Huffnail, and a sawmill operated by James A. Anderson from about 1878. See Mifflin. (*Dallas Centennial*)

Dalton. Green Lake. Named for the Dalton family. John Dalton emigrated from Belfast, Ireland, in the mid-1840s and with his family settled in what was then known as Pleasant Valley in the early 1850s. The name was formalized as Dalton about 1910 with construction of the Chicago & North Western railroad station, built on land formerly owned by John Dalton. (*Common Threads*, 77, 89)

Danbury [DAN buh ree]. Burnett. Danbury was founded by the Minneapolis, St. Paul & Sault Ste. Marie railroad when the line was extended to Superior in 1911–12. The source of the name is uncertain. Riis reports what he claims is the only written account of the naming of Danbury, in which Ed L. Peet, who was instrumental in establishing several communities in the area, based the name on that of one of the site owners, John Daniel Glass. Ericson and others suggest that the namesake may be Dan Springer, a contractor for the railroad. Another name proposed at the time was Blueberry (one daily train was known as the Blueberry Special), and Danbury may be a blend of *Dan* and *berry*. More likely a railroad official chose the name for Danbury, Connecticut. Many names in Wisconsin along the lines of the major railroads were imported from the East, especially from New England. (Riis and Koenen, 14)

Dancy. Marathon. Formerly known as Hutchinson, named for postmaster Samuel M. Hutchinson. The name was changed in the late 1880s, probably for Thornton Dancy, reportedly a section superintendent for the Chicago, Milwaukee & St. Paul railroad. ("Dancy, Wisconsin")

Dane. County. Created in December 1836. The name was chosen by James Duane Doty, governor of Wisconsin Territory in the early 1840s and an admirer of Nathan Dane of Massachusetts. Dane (1752–1835) was the architect of the Ordinance of 1787, one of the most underappreciated documents in American history. The ordinance created the Northwest Territory and established the framework for the governments of future states. The Town of Dane was organized as Clarkson in 1847 and changed to Dane in 1848.

Daniels. Burnett. Town (organized as Wood Lake in 1874; changed to Daniels in 1906). Named for Daniel Johnson, born in Grangärde Parish, Dalecarlia (Dalarna), Sweden, from where he emigrated in 1880. Johnson was active in local government and was an early township chair. (Landelius and Jarvi, 244)

Danville. Dodge. Named for and by site owner Daniel Bassett, from Montpelier, Vermont, who opened a general store about 1857. (*History of Dodge County*, 570)

Darboy [DAR boy]. Calumet, Outagamie. Settled originally by German farmers in the early 1840s, the area was known as Buchanan, named from Buchanan township, until the post office was established as Darboy in July 1877. The community grew around the Holy Angels Catholic Church (founded as St. Martin's of Manhattan Church in 1857). The namesake is Georges Darboy, activist archbishop of Paris, who was martyred by the Paris Commune in 1871 at the end of the Franco-Prussian War. This is the only Darboy in the United States. (Romenesko, 169)

Darien [DEHR ee uhn]. Walworth. Town (1840) and Village (1951). Founded by John Bruce, who purchased the site in February 1839. Known as Bruceville until the Turtle Creek post office was changed to Darien in 1840. Named for Darien, Genesee County, New York, itself named for the Isthmus of Darien, an alternate name for the Isthmus of Panama. (*History of the Settlement of Darien*, 1, 4)

Darlington. Lafayette. Town (organized as Centre in 1849; changed to Darlington in 1870) and City (1877). In 1847 Jamison Hamilton laid out the community of Avon, also known as Centre. The site was purchased by Joshua Darling of New York as an investment property in 1850. The Hamilton post office was changed to Darlington in 1851, and the name of Darlington became official about 1869. (Butterfield, *History of Lafayette County*, 527–28)

Davis Corners. Adams. Named for William A. Davis, who moved to Wisconsin from Utica, Michigan, in 1847. Davis established the post office in May 1855.

Day. Marathon. Town (1881). Origin unknown. Laessig (20–21) suggests that "Day" may have been a mishearing or misreading of the intended name, Daul, for Andrew Daul, the first township chair. Perhaps, but more likely the name honors a yet unidentified early settler named Day.

Dayton. Green. Laid out by mill owner Peolin P. Havens about 1847. The name was suggested by Amos D. Kirkpatrick, for his former home, Dayton, Ohio. Kirkpatrick represented the district in the Wisconsin Assembly in 1855. (Butterfield, *History of Green County*, 841)

Dayton. Richland. Town (1856). Probably named for Dayton, Cattaraugus County, New York, itself named for Jonathan Dayton, U.S. representative and senator from New Jersey in the late 1790s and the namesake of Dayton, Ohio. The historical community of Dayton Corners was laid out in the mid-1850s about four miles west of Richland Center by site owners Lorenzo Woodman and James Hofus. (Butterfield, *History of Crawford and Richland Counties*, 1016)

Dayton. Waupaca. Town (1852). Named for the Dayton family. Lyman Dayton, from Litchfield, Connecticut, arrived in the summer of 1850.

Dayton was a justice of the peace, a county sheriff, and the first postmaster at Nepawan in 1852. See Rural. (*Our Heritage*, 196)

Deansville (Deanville). Dane. Founded in 1860 by the first postmaster, Richard Dean, who emigrated from near Manchester, England, in the 1850s. (Cassidy, *Dane County Place-Names*)

Decatur [duh KAYT er]. Green. Town (1849). Named from the Decatur post office, itself named in 1842 by postmaster John Moore in honor of Stephen Decatur, naval hero of the War of 1812 and the second war against the Barbary pirates in 1815. A community named Decatur was laid out by hotelier William Jones in 1848. Jones subsequently sold the site to Isaac F. Mack, who called the site Flora, probably in honor of Flora Davenport, his daughter-in-law. The names contended for a time until 1852, when the state legislature made Decatur the official name of this now-vanished settlement. (Butterfield, *History of Green County*, 795)

Decker. Ozaukee. Named for the John Peter Decker family, which emigrated from Luxembourg in the late 1840s. ("Family Agnes-Walker")

Dedham [DED uhm]. Douglas. Named in the mid-1870s by Gardner Colby, then president of the Wisconsin Central railroad, for Dedham, Massachusetts. Colby owned several woolen mills in the southwest Boston suburb of Dedham, itself named for Dedham, England.

Deerbrook. Langlade. Deerbrook is a name that invites popular etymologies. Dessureau records one such, regarding a timber cruiser, who, "while camping near the Eau Claire river watched the deer 'drink his fill' each morning just as the sun peeped over the hills proclaiming a new day. Thus he called it 'Deerbrook'" (219).

Deer Park. St. Croix. Village (1913). Named for the deer herd established by George Otto Neitge and his brother Reinhardt, who emigrated from Prussia in 1850. The brothers periodically slaughtered part of their herd and sold the venison at Fort Snelling and St. Paul. The community was known as Willow River or Willow River Settlement until the arrival of the North Wisconsin Railway about 1874, when it took on the name of Deer Park. (Fouks and Fouks, *Deer Park*, 17–18)

DeForest. Dane. Village (1903). Laid out about 1856 by Isaac N. DeForest, who had arrived in the area from Albany, New York, several years before. The community was platted in 1874 by the Chicago, Milwaukee & St. Paul railroad. The post office was established as North Windsor, Isaac DeForest, postmaster, in May 1865. (Cassidy, *Dane County Place-Names*)

Dekorra [duh KOR uh]. Columbia. Town (organized as Dekorra voting precinct in 1846) and ppl. Named for one or more of the Winnebago leaders descended from Sabrevoir de Carrie, a French officer who died fighting at

Quebec in 1750, and his Winnebago wife, Hopokoekaw, often translated 'Glory of the Morning' (literally 'the false dawn preceeding sunrise'). The better known of their descendants included Waukon Decorah, for whom Decorah, Iowa, was named, and One Eye Decorra, signatory to a number of treaties in the first half of the nineteenth century and thought to have arranged the surrender of Black Hawk in 1832. Under several spellings, the Dekorras have provided place names in at least five states. (Vogel, *Indian Names,* 61)

Delafield [DEL uh feeld]. Waukesha. Town (organized as Nemahbin in 1843; changed to Delafield in 1844) and City (1959). One of Delafield's earlier names was Hayopolis, called by Theron Haight, publisher of the *Waukesha Freeman,* "a barbarous combination of Saxon and Greek." Hayopolis became known as Nemahbin, from the Nemahbin lakes, themselves named from Potawatomi or from Ojibwa *namebin* 'sucker fish.' About 1843 postmaster Nelson P. Hawks, an innkeeper from New York, proposed the name Delafield in honor of Charles Delafield, a Milwaukee businessman. See Namekagon. (Haight, 274; *History of Waukesha County,* 733)

Delavan [DEL uh vuhn]. Walworth. Town (1838) and City (1897). Founded in 1836 by Samuel and Henry Phoenix, from Perry, New York, as a colony dedicated to temperance, religion, and the abolition of slavery. Early property deeds contained clauses prohibiting the sale of liquor in all its forms, including wine and cider. Samuel Phoenix personally lobbied the Wisconsin Territorial Legislature to name the community Delavan in honor of Edward C. Delavan of New York, a founder of the American Temperance Union in 1836 and a widely known temperance leader. Phoenix was also successful in having the legislature name Walworth County for Reuben Walworth, a past president of the New York State Temperance Society. (Yadon)

Dell. Vernon. Founded about 1866 by Obediah Preston and first known as Prestonville. The name was formally Dell by August 1873 when the Dell post office was established by Dennis Adams. The office was discontinued early in 1905. Reasons for the name are unknown. (*History of Vernon County,* 498)

Dellona [duh LO nuh]. Sauk. Town (1850). Known as Sligo, for Sligo, Ireland, until about 1850 when the Dellona post office was established. Dellona is probably a coinage based upon "Dell." See Wisconsin Dells. (Krug, 297)

Dellwood. Adams. In the 1850s, when the Chicago, Milwaukee & St. Paul railroad was being built through Adams County, just north of present Dellwood, Christian C. Holm, recently arrived from Norway, laid out the community of Holmsville, which lasted until about 1920. In 1925 the

Badger State Development Company purchased the site and established a summer resort and entertainment center named Dellwood, hoping to trade on the popularity of the Wisconsin Dells. (Durbin, 109)

Delta. Bayfield. Town (organized as Mason in 1884; changed to Delta in 1924) and ppl. According to Meyer and Wuennecke (7) the Duluth, South Shore & Atlantic railroad chose the name when the station was established in the 1890s for the three branches of the White River, which configured in such a way as to form a rough outline of delta, the fourth letter of the Greek alphabet.

Delton, Lake Delton. Sauk. Previously known as Norris, for Edward Norris, who surveyed the area in 1849. Delton is a contraction of Dell Town, based upon Wisconsin Dells and Dell Creek. The name was changed to Mirror Lake in the mid-1920s and to Lake Delton in the late 1920s, when Chicago businessman William Newman built a vacation resort at the site. (Goc, *Many a Fine Harvest*, 161)

Denmark. Brown. Village (1915). Settled largely by Danish colonists beginning in the late 1840s. First known as Copenhagen, the name was apparently changed to Denmark when the Cooperstown post office was renamed Denmark in late 1857. See New Denmark.

Denzer. Sauk. Named for Heinrich William Denzer, who emigrated from Prussia in 1849. Denzer served in several local offices in the 1880s and was a community benefactor, donating land for a church and a school. (Derleth, 41)

De Pere [duh PEER]. Brown. City (1883). De Pere grew around the Mission of St. Francis Xavier, established in 1671 on the east side of the Fox River by the Jesuit priest Claude-Jean Allouez, for whom the village of Allouez is named. The site became known as *Rapides des Pères* 'rapids of the fathers,' subsequently shortened to De Peres, and then to De Pere. West De Pere, founded in 1850 by Dr. Louis Carabin of Green Bay, consolidated with De Pere in 1890. West De Pere was also known as Nicolet, for Jean Nicolet, the first European known to have entered present Wisconsin. The Town of De Pere was organized in 1839; in 1994 the name was changed to Ledgeview (q.v.). This is the only De Pere in the United States. (Cassidy, *Brown County*)

Deronda [duh RAHN duh]. Polk. According to Ericson, Lucina Sylvester, daughter of Abram and Julia Sylvester, chose the name for the hero of George Eliot's 1876 novel, *Daniel Deronda*. The post office was established in December 1887, Cary L. Otis, postmaster.

De Soto. Crawford, Vernon. Village (1886). Previously known as Winneshieks Landing, named for a Winnebago leader of the early nineteenth century who reportedly traded with French merchants near the site. De Soto was surveyed and platted in 1854 for three doctors, Simeon Powers, Euclid Houghton, and James Osgood. The ultimate source of the name is the Spanish explorer Hernando De Soto, reportedly the first European to see the Mississippi River in the late 1530s. Powers established the post office as Formora in February 1855. The name was changed to De Soto several months later. (Butterfield, *History of Crawford and Richland Counties*, 598)

Detroit Harbor. Door. Apparently named from Detroit Island, itself named from French *petite detroit* 'little strait,' for the strait known as East Channel between Detroit Island and Washington Island. (Hale, 29)

Dewey. The towns of Dewey in Portage (1898), Rusk (1898), and Burnett (1904) Counties and the community of Dewey in Douglas County were named in honor of Commodore George Dewey, commander of the U.S. Asiatic fleet. Dewey's destruction of the Spanish Pacific naval force at Manila Bay in the Philippines in 1898 made him a national hero.

Dewey Corners. Trempealeau. Named for the Dewey family, from Delaware County, New York. George D. Dewey purchased land from the government in the Town of Arcadia about 1856.

Dewhurst. Clark. Town (1901). Earlier known as Mound, the name was changed to honor Richard Dewhurst. Born in England, Dewhurst was the first county judge, founded the Neillsville bank, and served several terms in the Wisconsin Legislature in the 1860s and 1870s. (Scholtz)

Dexter. Wood. Town (first organized in 1858); also Dexterville. Named by George Hiles, who operated a sawmill at the site in the early 1850s and established the post office in the summer of 1858. Although a local legend claims that Hiles named Dexterville after Dexter, his trusty mule, the source of the name is unknown; perhaps it is a transfer from Dexter, Michigan, as Robert Rudolph suggests in *Wood County Place Names*.

Dheinsville. Washington. Named for the Philip Dhein (Johann Philipp Dhein) family, which emigrated from Germany in 1842. Dhein was instrumental in organizing the United Evangelical Protestant Christ Church (Evangelische Christus Kirche) in the 1850s. The post office was established in July 1855, Adam Staats, postmaster. (McBride, 61)

Diamond Bluff. Pierce. Town (1856) and ppl. According to local accounts, early French explorers named the landmark bluff on the Mississippi River *Monte Diamond* 'diamond mountain.' The site was purchased by Enoch Quimby, who laid out the community of Monte Diamond about 1854. Charles F. Hoyt established the Hoytstown post office in 1854, laid out the community of Diamond Bluff, and changed the name of the post office in 1855. (Ericson)

Dickeyville. Grant. Village (1947). Founded as Dickeysville by Charles Dickey, a Pennsylvanian who opened a general store in the early 1840s. Dickey was the first postmaster when the office opened in January 1849. (*Grant County History*, 109)

Diefenbach Corners. Washington. Named for the Peter Johann Diefenbach family who emigrated from Niederfischbach, Germany, east of Cologne, in 1853.

Dilly. Vernon. This is the only Dilly in the United States and the source of the name is unknown. Robert Kretche has a comprehensive account of the popular etymologies the name has generated and feels there may be some truth to the suggestion that Dilly resulted from a mishearing of Millie, the name of several local girls (59). The post office was established in May 1895, Anton Sebranek, postmaster.

Disco. Jackson. Named at the suggestion of Caroline Caves for Disco, Hancock County, Illinois, her former home. The post office was established as Marengo in August 1871, discontinued in December 1886, and reestablished as Disco in January 1892. The source of the Illinois name is uncertain, perhaps a transfer from Disco, Michigan, itself named for the Disco Academy, a high school founded about 1850 and named from Latin *disco* 'to learn.' (*History of Jackson*, 26)

Dobie [DO bee]. Douglas. Likely named for David Dobie, a contractor who operated a logging railroad for the Lake Superior Lumber Company in the 1890s. The post office was established in August 1909, Christian Swanson, postmaster. ("Douglas County")

Dodge. County. Created from Brown County in December 1836. Named for Henry Dodge (1782–1867), an early Wisconsin military and political leader. Dodge participated in the War of 1812, but it was the notoriety gained from his actions in the Black Hawk War of 1832 that led to his local and national political prominence. Dodge was the first governor of Wisconsin Territory (1836–41) and also the last (1845–48). He was territorial delegate to Congress (1841–45), and one of Wisconsin's first U.S. senators (1848–57). Dodge declined a likely nomination for the presidency on the Democratic ticket in 1844. Dodgeville in Iowa County is also named for Henry Dodge.

Dodge. Trempealeau. Town (1875) and ppl. Platted in February 1874 for site owner August Bambenek. Named for William E. Dodge (1805–83), a New York businessman and industrialist, cofounder of the Phelps-Dodge Mining Corporation in 1834. Dodge, a peace activist and philanthropist, was a cofounder of the Young Men's Christian Association (YMCA) in the 1840s and an associate of John I. Blair, for whom the city of Blair (q.v.)

is named. Dodge County, Georgia, is also named for William Dodge. (Curtiss-Wedge and Pierce, 270)

Dodgeville. Iowa. See Dodge County.

Doering [DIHR ing]. Lincoln. Surveyed in 1902 for site owners William and Therese Doering, who began farming in the area in 1897. The Doerings were instrumental in attracting the railroad to what became known as Doering station. The post office was established in April 1903, Frank Doering, postmaster. (Jones and McVean, *History of Lincoln, Oneida and Vilas Counties*, 89)

Donald. Taylor. Founded in 1903 by William J. Campbell, president of the Fountain-Campbell Lumber Company, and named for his son, Donald. Earlier known as Fountain. (Stennett, 173)

Door. County. Organized in February 1851, largely through the efforts of merchant and land speculator Alanson Sweet. Named from Death's Door Passage, the strait between Washington Island (Plum Island, actually) and the Door County mainland, connecting Lake Michigan and Green Bay. By longstanding tradition, the name originated when a Potawatomi raiding party sent from Washington Island against the Winnebago was caught by a sudden storm and all were drowned. An as yet unknown Winnebago or Potawatomi name for the site was translated by French explorers as *Porte des Morts*, in turn translated into English as 'door of the dead' or 'death's door.' The French name dates from at least the mid-1720s when the Recollect priest Emanuel Crespel wrote of rounding the *Cap a la Mort*, 'cape of the dead.' The name was rarely used until about 1817, when Samuel Storrow recorded "the southerly cape of Green Bay, Port des Morts." At about the same time Vermont traveler Willard Keyes noted in his diary "point 'De Mort' (or point of Death)." See Conan Bryant Eaton's *Death's Door* for a comprehensive account of the history and name of Death's Door.

Door Creek. Dane. Named from the Door Creek post office, established in February 1847, Orsemus McCray, postmaster. The office was named for the stream, Door Creek, the name of which is uncertain. Cassidy cautiously writes, "Possibly the 'door' refers to a narrow passage which Little Door Creek makes between high bluffs" (*Dane County Place-Names*). The naming of Door Creek is apparently unrelated to the naming of Door County.

Dorchester [DOR ches ter]. Clark. Village (1901). Founded by the Wisconsin Central railroad in July 1874. Named by Boston financier Gardner Colby, president of the railroad, or his son, Charles Colby, vice president, (or both) for Dorchester, Massachusetts, now a part of Boston, itself named for Dorchester, Dorset, England. (Curtiss-Wedge, *History of Clark County*, 659)

Doty [DO tee]. Both the Town of Doty (1922) in Oconto County and the community of Dotyville in Fond du Lac County are named for Judge James Duane Doty, the founder of Madison and of Fond du Lac. Doty (1799–1865) was the second governor of Wisconsin Territory (1841–44), represented Wisconsin in the U.S. House of Representatives (1849–53), and at the time of his death was governor of Utah Territory, having been appointed to that post by President Lincoln in 1863.

Douglas. County. Organized in February 1854. Named for Stephen A. Douglas (1813–61), U.S. senator from Illinois (1847–61). Douglas is best remembered for the Illinois senatorial campaign of 1858, which featured the famous Lincoln-Douglas debates and for his nomination for president by the Democratic Party in 1860. Douglas had substantial financial interests in northern Wisconsin and was one of the proprietors of Superior (q.v.). The town of Douglas in Marquette County, organized in 1858, was also named for Stephen A. Douglas.

Dousman [DOWS muhn]. Waukesha. Village (1917). Named from the Dousman post office, established in May 1856. The site owner was Talbot C. Dousman, brother of Hercules Dousman, a founder of Prairie du Chien, and son of Michael Dousman, a Great Lakes shipping magnate. The area was formerly known as Bull Frog Station. (Barquist and Barquist, 70)

Dover. Buffalo. Town. Organized in November 1870 at the request of William Henry Harrison Amidon and other settlers from New England. Named for one of the several Dovers in the northeast, perhaps Dover, Vermont, or Dover, New York. (Amidon, 15)

Dovre [DO ver]. Barron. Town (1879). Perhaps a transfer from Dovre, Minnesota, but more likely named directly for Dovre, Oppland, Norway.

Downing. Dunn. Village (1909). Named in 1884 by the Wisconsin Central railroad for James Downing, superintendent of local logging operations for the Knapp, Stout Lumber Company from the late 1860s. (Curtiss-Wedge and Jones, 181)

Downsville. Dunn. Named for Burrage B. Downs, who operated a sawmill on the Red Cedar River in the late 1850s. The post office was established in January 1865, Willis L. Downs, postmaster. (Dunn County Historical Society, 21)

Doyle. Barron. Town (1903). Named for John J. Doyle, a former township chair. Originally from Trumbull County, Ohio, Doyle established a farm near Rice Lake in the mid-1880s. ("John J. Doyle obit")

Doylestown [DOYLZ town]. Columbia. Village (1907). Founded in 1865 on the line of the Chicago, Milwaukee & St. Paul railroad by Lemuel Hastings Doyle, postmaster, justice of the peace, and member of the village board.

He was a member of the Doyle family for whom Doylestowns in Pennsylvania and Ohio, as well as Wisconsin, are named. (J. Jones, 375)

Drammen [DRAH muhn]. Eau Claire. Organized in November 1873 as the Town of Lant. Renamed in January 1877 for Drammen, Norway, southwest of Oslo.

Draper [DRAY per]. Sawyer. Town (organized in 1913; changed to Loretta in 1925; changed back to Draper in 1926) and ppl. Named in honor of Lyman Copeland Draper (1815–91), secretary of the Wisconsin Historical Society from 1854 until 1886. Draper devoted his working life to the collection and preservation of materials relating to American history. The post office was established in April 1906, John H. Lawrence, postmaster. (Stennett, 173)

Dresser. Polk. Village. Samuel Dresser arrived in the area from Buxton, Maine, in 1861 and was a member of the Wisconsin Legislature in 1870. According to a local account, when Dresser drew up the petition for a post office, he intentionally left the name blank. After the petitioners had all signed the document, Dresser wrote in the name Dresser Junction. When Cornelius Clark, Dresser's brother-in-law, complained, Dresser reportedly paid Clark a thousand dollars to withdraw his objection. Late in 1919 the village was incorporated as Valley City; by 1921 the name had reverted to Dresser Junction, which remained until May 1940 when Junction was dropped. (J. Ward, 23, 59, 78)

Druecker [DRUHK er]. Ozaukee. Probably named for Joseph and Johann Druecker, of Luxembourg descent. The Drucker brothers were lime merchants and in the 1880s received several patents for improved lime kilns. ("Luxembourgers in America")

Drummond. Bayfield. Town (1884) and ppl. Named by an officer of the Rust-Owen Lumber Company (probably William A. Rust) for Frank H. Drummond, vice president and general manager of Rust-Owen, which in 1882 contracted for some eighty thousand acres of timber in the area. Drummond had brought a construction crew to the site earlier that year to establish a base of operations. (Sorenson, 2, 5)

Duck Creek. Brown. A translation of French *Rivière aux Canards* 'river of ducks,' itself probably a translation of a Native American name. Also known as Eaton. (Stennett, 66)

Dudley. Lincoln. Founded in late 1886 by shopkeeper and hotelier Henry Dudley as a way station to support lumber operations between Wausau and the logging camps farther north. Named from the post office established by Dudley in August 1880. (Jones and McVean, *History of Lincoln, Oneida and Vilas Counties*, 88)

Dunbar. Marinette. Town (1889) and ppl. Modern Dunbar grew from the mill and lumber camp established by the Girard Lumber Company following completion of the Minneapolis, Sault Ste. Marie & Atlantic railroad in the late 1880s. Probably named for Warren Dunbar, an engineer for the railroad. The post office was established in January 1889, James W. Wells, postmaster. (*Dunbar Remembered*, 5, 31, 45)

Dunbarton. Lafayette. Dunbarton is most likely a transfer from Dunbarton, Merrimack County, New Hampshire, itself named for Dunbarton (Dumbarton), Scotland. The choice of the name may have been influenced by Samuel B. Dunbar, the site owner, who settled in the area about 1852. (*Lafayette County Bicentennial Book*, 117)

Dundas [DUHN duhs]. Calumet. Probably named by David W. Halsted, the first postmaster, for William H. Dundas. When the post office was established in May 1846, Dundas was chief clerk of the Post Office Department in Washington, D.C. He was later second assistant postmaster general of the United States.

Dundee. Fond du Lac. Named from the Dundee post office, established in 1862. The name was chosen by site owner Edward M. McIntosh and other settlers from Dundee, Scotland. (McKenna, 275)

Dunkirk. Dane. Town (1846) and ppl. Platted in December 1846 by Jonathon Parsons Jr. Probably named for Dunkirk, Chautauqua County, New York, itself named for Dunkirk, France. Two weeks after platting Dunkirk, Parsons laid out Dunkirk Falls in a horseshoe shape around Dunkirk. (Cassidy, *Dane County Place-Names*)

Dunn. County. Organized in February 1854. Named for Charles Dunn (1799–1872), a leading political figure in Wisconsin Territory and during the early years of Wisconsin statehood. Born in Bullitt's Lick, Kentucky, Dunn was appointed chief justice of the Wisconsin Territorial Court by President Andrew Jackson. When the county was created, Dunn was a state senator from Lafayette County. The Town of Dunn, organized in 1856, and the community of Dunnville were named for their location in Dunn County. Dunnville was formerly known as Colburn's Landing, named for early settler Amos Colburn, who established the Dunnville post office in July 1856. (Dunn County Historical Society, 21)

Dunn. Dane. Town (1848). The documents submitted in support of township creation apparently called for the name Door or possibly Dover, but the writing was unclear and the receiving clerk recorded Dunn, perhaps for Charles Dunn, the namesake of Dunn County, who was a delegate to the state constitutional convention at the time. The post office was established in February 1849, John Paine, postmaster. (Cassidy, *Dane County Place-Names*)

Duplainville. Waukesha. The area was first known as Remington Prairie, named for a prominent Remington family. The name was changed about 1856 when the Forest House post office was changed to Duplainville. The source of the name is uncertain and there are several possibilities. According to a 1958 article in the *Waukesha Freeman*, shopkeeper Tom Cook took the name from a map of France. Duplain is a French surname, found primarily in the Alsace-Lorraine area. A French place name or an early settler named Duplain may have been the source of the name or it may have been a transfer from Duplain, Michigan, itself named from French *Rivière du Plain*, translated into English as Maple River.

Durand [doo RAND]. Pepin. Town (organized as Bear Creek in 1856; changed to Durand in 1863) and City (1887). Durand was founded in the summer of 1856 by Miles Durand Prindle, from Derby, Connecticut, who chose the name for his mother's family, the Durands. Prindle kept the first general store in the area and in the early 1860s ran a steamboat, the *Idell Prindle*, named for his daughter, between Eau Claire and La Crosse. The post office was established as Chippewa in January 1857 and changed to Durand in 1858. (*Pepin County History*, 8)

Durham. Waukesha. The origin of the name is uncertain. According to local accounts, it is in honor of a herd of purebred shorthorn cattle brought to the area from England by John P. Roe in 1854. Durham is a popular place name, occurring in about half the states, and one of these may have contributed to the naming of Durham, Wisconsin. The original Durham is in northeast England, where the Durham shorthorn breed was developed. The post office was established as Durham Hill in February 1863, Samuel A. Tenny, postmaster. (Damaske, *Along the Right-of-Way to Burlington*, 13)

Durwards Glen. Columbia. Named for Bernard I. Durward, born in Montrose, Scotland. Durward brought his family to Milwaukee in 1845 and later to the glen that bears the family's name. Durward was an accomplished artist and poet and the author of *Wild Flowers of Wisconsin*, regarded as the first book of poems published in Wisconsin, in 1872. (Terry, xiii)

Duvall [doo VAHL]. Kewaunee. Named for Joseph Duvall, a prominent Kewaunee businessman and civic benefactor. The post office was established in July 1890, William Barrette, postmaster.

Duveneck [DOO vah nek]. Manitowoc. Named for one or more Duveneck families. Karl Friedrich Alexander Duveneck emigrated from Germany in 1872.

Dyckesville [DEYEKS vil]. Brown, Kewaunee. Louis Van Dycke, a former sea captain from Antwerp, Belgium, kept a general store, owned a sawmill and gristmill, was Kewaunee County's first district attorney, and established the post office, which he named for himself, in July 1858. (*Commemorative Biographical Record of the Fox River Valley Counties*, 2:948)

Eagle. Waukesha. Town (1841) and Village (1899). According to the 1880 *History of Waukesha County*, "[Eagle] received its name in a rather singular manner: In the year 1836, while Thomas Sugden, John Coats, and a Mr. Garton were prospecting, they came to a beautiful prairie about one and a half by two and a half miles in area. Here, hovering and curving over a large mound, near the residence of Ebenezer Thomas, was a monster bald-headed eagle. From this incident and time, the prairie and town were called Eagle" (735).

Eagle Point. Chippewa. Town (1855) and ppl. Apparently named for the nearby bluffs where Old Abe, surely the most famous Wisconsin eagle, was captured about 1860. Named for President Lincoln, Old Abe became the mascot of the Eighth Wisconsin Volunteers and was carried into a number of Civil War battles, including Corinth and Vicksburg.

Eagle River. Vilas. City (1937). Platted in 1885 by the Milwaukee, Lake Shore & Western railroad. Named from the Eagle River post office, established in August 1883 by Lyman J. Cook, itself named from Eagle River and Eagle Lake. A local story claims the river and lake were named in 1853 by explorers who observed an abundance of eagles. Alternatively, the name may be a translation from Ojibwa. Father Frederic Baraga recorded in his *Otchipwe Language* that the Ojibwa name of the river was *Migisiwisibi*, from *migisi* 'eagle' and *sibi* 'river.' Near the Eagle River Memorial Hospital is Aquila Court, a clever play on words; *aquila* is Latin for 'eagle.' (Stennett, 31, 66)

Earl. Washburn. Formerly known as Sinclair's Spur, named for H. L. Sinclair, agent for the Chicago, St. Paul, Minneapolis & Omaha railroad at Trego. Renamed in 1905 by John Whitney, the first postmaster, apparently for a relative, Earl McDill. (Stennett, 174)

Eastman. Crawford. Town (1855) and Village (1909). Formerly known as Batavia, probably named for Batavia, New York. Formally named from the Eastman post office, established in March 1854 by Philander Green, itself named for Ben C. Eastman, who represented the district in the U.S. House of Representatives for two terms in the early 1850s. (Butterfield, *History of Crawford and Richland Counties*, 590)

East Winona [wuh NO nuh]. Buffalo. Named for its location on the Mississippi River opposite Winona, Minnesota. Winona is a Lakota (Siouan) name given to first-born daughters. Wenona, in Illinois and Michigan, is a variant. In Longfellow's *Hiawatha*, Wenona, the daughter of Nokomis, is Hiawatha's mother.

Eaton. Brown. Town (1859). Reportedly named for Austin Eaton from Connecticut, an early settler. (J. Rudolph, 25)

Eaton. Clark. Town (1869). Named for early settlers Elijah and John Eaton, from New York State, who established a sawmill in the area about 1849. Elijah Eaton is the founder of Greenwood (q.v.). (Scholtz)

Eaton. Manitowoc. Town. Named in 1851 for lumberman Chauncy Eaton. The name was changed to Valders [*sic*] (Walders) for Valdres, Norway, in 1853 and back to Eaton the following year. (Falge, 338)

Eau Claire [o KLEHR]. County and City. Named from the Eau Claire River. *Eau Claire*, French for 'clear water,' is probably a translation of Ojibwa *wakami*, glossed by Baraga as "the water is clean, clear." On Joseph Nicollet's map from the early 1840s the stream is called the Wayokomig River, and in his journal Nicollet wrote "Clear Water River." The often-repeated story that the name originated in 1767 when a member of Jonathan Carver's expedition noticed the purity of the water and exclaimed "*L'eau claire*" 'the water is clear' has no basis in fact, nor does the story that Eau Claire is an English popular etymology of French *Rivière aux Clercs* 'river of the clerics.' In July 1855, what is now Eau Claire County was organized as the town of Clearwater in Chippewa County. Later that year land speculators Richard Wilson and William Gleason laid out a community they called Eau Claire rather than Clearwater, creating confusion between the name of the community and that of the town. The naming problem was not completely resolved until 1856 when the names of the town and post office, which had been established as Clear Water [*sic*] in 1849, were changed to Eau Claire. (Vogel, *Indian Names*, 190)

Eau Galle. Dunn. Town (1856) and ppl. St. Croix. Town (organized as Brockville in 1858; changed to Eau Galle later in 1858). Named from the Eau Galle River. Eau Galle is a translation with popular etymology of French *Rivière aux Galets* 'river of small stones' or 'river of gravel.' *Aux* was respelled as its homophone *eau*, so the name is now literally 'water stones.' The usual pronunciation is [o GAL ee], but [o GAL] and [o GAH lee] are also heard. The post office was established in September 1858, William Carson, postmaster. (Barland, 1)

Eau Pleine [o PLAYN]. The towns in Marathon (1884) and Portage (1858) Counties take their name from the Big and Little Eau Pleine Rivers. In American French, *pleine* (*plaine*) referred to maple trees in general and *eau pleine* more specifically to the 'water maple.' *Eau Pleine* is likely a translation from Potawatomi or Ojibwa; rendering the sap from maple trees was customary among many Native American groups. Des Plaines, Illinois, is a variant. The post office was established in April 1851, John B. Dubay, postmaster.

Eckers Lakeland. Calumet. Named for a local Ecker family, probably that of Peter Ecker, who served several terms as chair of the Town of Brothertown in the early twentieth century.

Eden. Fond du Lac. Town (1848) and Village (1912). Worthing tells the local story, a popular etymology but one that may hold several grains of truth: "By 1848 there were enough settlers to organize the town. A meeting was held and Adam Holliday arose, and with many puns on his name and that of Samuel Rand's wife, Eve, suggested the name of Eden after the garden where Adam and Eve dwelt and where there were many Holy Days (Hollidays). References were also made to the beauty of the fields and the abundance of fruits and flowers. Amid much gaiety the name was adopted" (27–28). Eden is a popular place name; there is at least one Eden in each of the continental states and one or more of these may have contributed to the naming of Eden, Wisconsin.

Edgar. Marathon. Village (1898). Established by the Milwaukee, Lake Shore & Western railroad in 1891. Named for William Edgar, who operated a sawmill near Wausau and was associated with the railroad, or for Charles Edgar, a partner in the Mortenson and Edgar Lumber company of Wausau, or both. (Stennett, 67; Huebsch and Huebsch, 11)

Edgerton [EJ er tuhn]. Rock. City (1883). Edgerton grew around Fulton Station, established by the Chicago, Milwaukee & St. Paul railroad in the early 1850s. Charles H. Dickinson, one of the area's leading citizens, met with Benjamin Edgerton, chief surveyor for the railroad, and asked permission to name the community after him. Edgerton is said to have replied, "Better wait until I am dead. I might do something in the meantime to discredit the name." His caution notwithstanding, the post office was established as Edgerton in July 1854. Edgerton, Kansas, was named for the same Benjamin Edgerton when he was chief engineer for the Kansas Southern railroad. (*Edgerton Story*, 38)

Edmund. Iowa. Named for the site owner, Edmund Baker, a native of Cornwall, England. Baker and his brother, John, settled in Iowa County in 1838. The Edmond post office was established in September 1881, Isaac P. Schooley, postmaster. (*Commemorative Biographical Record of the Counties of Rock, Green*, 298)

Edson. Chippewa. Town (1868) and ppl. Named for Edson Chubb, the first permanent settler, who arrived in 1857 from Vermont and erected the first sawmill in the area. About 1870 the Wisconsin Central railroad sought site donations from the landowners of Edson, and when they refused, the railroad routed through Boyd, at which time many of the homes and businesses in Edson were dismantled and moved to trackside. (Forrester, 61)

Egg Harbor. Door. Town (1861) and Village (1964). Several stories are told to explain the origin of this unusual name. By one, an early settler named the site from a nest of birds' eggs he happened upon; by another, friends on a boating excursion began good-naturedly tossing first biscuits, then eggs at people on other boats; and by still another, during the same or another excursion, one poor fellow, whose pockets were filled with eggs, was chased down and his clothing slapped until all the eggs were broken. There is one other Egg Harbor in the United States, in New Jersey, where the name is reported to be a translation of *eyen haven*, given to the area by seventeenth-century Dutch navigators for the clutches of wild birds' eggs they encountered. The Egg Harbor post office was established in August 1861. (Hale, 41–42)

Eidsvold [EYEDZ vold]. Clark. Probably named for Eidsvold (Eidsvoll), in southeastern Norway. The community grew around a mill built by Joseph Hadley in the early 1880s. The post office was established in March 1884, Jacob Bye, postmaster.

Eight Corners. Wood. According to Robert Rudolph, "At one time this was the only intersection along the Centralia-Vesper road where crossroads met forming at least eight corners; all others were 'T' intersections."

Eileen [eye LEEN]. Bayfield. The town was organized in 1904, largely through the efforts of community leader and state senator A. Pearce Tomkins, who suggested the name for his daughter, Eileen. (Stennett, 174)

Eisenstein [EYE zuhn steyen]. Price. Town (1902). Named in the early 1880s by settlers from Markt Eisenstein, then in German Bohemia on the border between Germany and the Czech Republic. (Goc, *100 Years on the Flambeau*, 23)

Eland [EE luhnd]. Shawano. Village (1905). Named about 1880 by Edward H. Rummele, chief engineer for the Milwaukee, Lake Shore & Western railroad. The reason for the name is unknown. Perhaps Rummele was inspired by the eland, the African antelope associated with the nineteenth-century explorer David Livingstone. (Stennett, 67)

Elba [EL buh]. Dodge. Town (1846). Elba is a popular place name, occurring in some twenty states. One of the several Elbas in New England may have been transferred to Wisconsin, or an early settler may have been fascinated by Napoleon's career, including his exile to the island of Elba in 1814. The local account is that Elba was chosen by George Rogers Clark Floyd, secretary of Wisconsin Territory in the 1840s, after local citizens could not agree on a name. The Elba post office operated from 1850 until 1857 when it was changed to Danville. (*History of Dodge County*, 403)

Elcho [EL ko]. Langlade. Town (1887) and ppl. Platted about 1887 by Benjamin

Franklin Dorr, Antigo city engineer and Langlade county surveyor. Named by Dorr for Elcho, southeast of Perth, Scotland. (Stennett, 67)

Elderon [EL duh rahn]. Marathon. Town (1887) and Village (1917). According to Stennett, the name is derived from the presence of elderberry bushes (called simply "elders") with "on" added. This is the only Elderon in the United States. The post office was established in June 1888, Calvin R. Day, postmaster. (Stennett, 67)

Eldorado [el duh RAY do]. Fond du Lac. Town (1848) and ppl. Named in early 1849 by the first postmaster, John O. Henning, who brought the name to Wisconsin from El Dorado County, California, where he had prospected for gold. Apparently the California county was the first to use the name in the United States. (Stennett, 67–68)

Eleva [uh LEE vuh]. Trempealeau. Village (1902). Previously known as New Chicago. Platted in September 1877 for the site owners, Elliott J. Carpenter, a gristmill operator, and Roswell P. Goddard, proprietor of the general store. Eleva is one of Wisconsin's mystery names. Several putative explanations of its origin have been proposed, but the actual source is unknown. It has been claimed that Eleva is a distortion of Indians' laments as they were forced to leave the area, "*I leave you* now"; teacher Lambert Merritt suggested the name for a place in Ireland; one of the Goddards had a daughter named Eva who died young and Eleva was named in her memory; and Goddard named the community for a village in France. The "explanation" most often repeated is a classic popular etymology, the "elevator origin," in which a grain elevator had been erected by the railroad tracks and only the first five letters had been painted before winter set in. Travelers assumed that "Eleva," the incomplete form of "elevator," was the name of the community, and the residents decided that Eleva was as good a name as any other. This is the only Eleva in the United States. (Fimreite)

Ella. Pepin. Origin unknown. Founded about 1871. Reportedly named for a daughter of settler Ed Roundy. The community was known informally as Shoo Fly because "a woman was seen waving her apron at a swarm of flies in her doorway" (*Pepin County History*, 20).

Ellenboro. Grant. Town (1852) and ppl. Named from the Ellenboro post office, established in August 1849, John H. Barnett, postmaster. The origin of the name is uncertain but the namesake is probably Ellen Rountree, daughter of John H. Rountree, the founder of Platteville (q.v.). (Holford, 749)

Ellington. Outagamie. Town (1850). Probably named by John R. Rynders, the first town chair, for his former home, Ellington, Chautauqua County, New York, itself named for Ellington, Connecticut. (Truttschel, 76)

Ellis. Portage. The area was formerly known as Poland Corners. Named with establishment of the post office in 1867 in honor of Albert Gallatin Ellis, mayor of Stevens Point at the time. Ellis, from Verona, New York, was a popular politician and newspaper publisher. He served in the territorial legislature and later as Wisconsin's surveyor general. See Polonia. (Rosholt, *Our County, Our Story*, 387)

Ellison Bay. Door. Ellison is an altered spelling of Eliason. About 1870 Johan (John) Eliason, probably from Denmark, built a pier and general store at the site and laid out building lots. Eliason was the first postmaster in 1873. (Thomas, 105)

Ellisville. Kewaunee. Named for early settler Lazarus W. Ellis, reportedly the father-in-law of Thomas Paddleford, who chose the name of the town of Montpelier (q.v.). The post office was established in December 1862, Levi M. Mack, postmaster. (*Kewaunee, Wisconsin*)

Ellsworth [ELZ werth]. Pierce. Town. Organized in 1857 as Perry, named for Oliver Hazard Perry, hero of the Battle of Lake Erie during the War of 1812. The name was changed in the 1860s to honor Elmer Ephraim Ellsworth, one of the first casualties of the Civil War, who was shot and killed as he was hauling down a huge Confederate flag in Alexandria, Virginia, which could be seen from the balcony of the White House. Ellsworth was Abraham Lincoln's friend and advisor when they lived in Springfield, Illinois. A dashing figure himself, Ellsworth raised a gaudily dressed Zouave unit at the outbreak of the Civil War. Augusta Ames, wife of Pierce County sheriff Henry Ames, is generally credited with suggesting the name. (Stennett, 175)

Elmhurst [ELM herst]. Langlade. Probably a transfer from Elmhurst, DuPage County, Illinois. The post office was established in December 1881, Frederick Spoehr, postmaster. (Stennett, 68)

Elmo. Grant. Elmo grew around the Junction House, an inn and tavern at the intersection of the roads to Galena and Mineral Point operated by Emanuel Whitham from about 1854. The Junction House was the sole structure at the site until the Galena & Southern Wisconsin railroad established a station and Whitham laid out the community in the mid-1870s. The name was changed from Junction about 1875 at the suggestion of Madison Y. Johnson, a founder of the railroad and one of the site owners of Cuba City. Johnson probably chose the name from the popular novel *St. Elmo*, by American author Augusta Evans Wilson, published in 1866. (Butterfield, *History of Grant County*, 832)

Elmore. Fond du Lac. First known as Leglerville, named for founder Ulrich Legler, the founder of Ashford (q.v.) who built a sawmill and gristmill in

1857. Renamed from the Elmore post office, itself named for Andrew Elmore, who represented the district in the Wisconsin Assembly in 1859 and 1860 and was known as the Sage of Mukwonago. (Worthing)

Elmwood. Pierce. Town (1902). Named from the Elmwood post office, established in January 1885 by postmaster Nathan Utter, who reportedly chose the name from the local elm trees. (Ericson)

Elo [EE lo]. Winnebago. Formerly known as Utica Center, named from Utica township. Renamed from the Elo post office, established in February 1869 by Richard Stiles. The local account is that Stiles found the name in a book, possibly a hymn book. However, the name may be of Finnish origin. Elo is a Finnish family name and can mean 'grain' or 'harvest.' August in Finnish is *Elokuu*, the month of the harvest. One other community in the United States is named Elo, in Houghton County, Michigan.

El Paso [el PA so]. Pierce. Town (1858) and ppl. The first permanent settler, George P. Walker, from Pennsylvania by way of Illinois, established the El Paso post office in July 1858, and Thomas McGee platted the community in the early 1860s. The name was probably chosen by Walker, but the source is unknown. In the best spirit of popular etymology, a local account has it that the name came from the fact that the community lies between two hills and an L-shaped road passes between them. This "L pass" became El Paso. The name may be a transfer from El Paso, Illinois, near Walker's home in the early 1850s. In its early years El Paso was informally known as Hard Scrabble. (Folsom and Edwards, 204–5; Johnson and Wilmot, 12)

Elroy [EL roy]. Juneau. City (1885). Founded by James Madison Brintnall and John Bennett in 1858. Brintnall intended to call the community LeRoy for his birthplace in Genesee County, New York, but when the post office department rejected the name, he spelled the first letter phonetically, creating Elroy. The post office was established as Fowlers Prairie in July 1857, Reuben Fowler, postmaster. ("Elroy")

Elton. Langlade. Named for Elton Larzelere, who was largely responsible for the organization of the town of Elton in 1886 (changed to Wolf River in 1925). Elton's father, Charles Larzelere, from Seneca Falls, New York, was instrumental in the formation of Langlade County and served as the first county chair in 1878. (Dessureau, 201)

Elvers. Dane. Formerly known as Elvers Mills. Named for Charles Elver. Born in Mecklenburg, Germany, Elver operated the family gristmill, kept the Elver House in Madison, and served in several local offices. The post office was established in July 1878, John Lohrs, postmaster. (Cassidy, *Dane County Place-Names*)

Embarrass [AM brah]. Waupaca. Village (1895). Named from the Embarrass River, itself named by early French explorers. In American French *embarras* referred to an obstruction in a waterway created by uprooted trees or accumulated debris that interfered with navigation and posed a danger to boatmen. The English equivalent for such a maritime obstruction was 'raft.' Not to be confused with English *embarrass* 'cause to be uncomfortable.' Embarrass also occurs in Minnesota and Illinois. The pronunciation is reflected in the name Ambrough (also spelled Ambro) Slough, a channel in Crawford County. (Stennett, 69)

Emerald. St. Croix. Town (1860) and ppl. Apparently named for Ireland, "the Emerald Isle," at the suggestion of William Fleming, from Fermanagh in Northern Ireland. Fleming immigrated first to Melbourne, Ontario, Canada, and then to St. Croix County, where he established a sawmill in 1858. (Weatherhead, 39)

Emerald Grove. Rock. Founded and named for unknown reasons by Dr. James Heath, who emigrated from Oxford County, Maine, in January 1836. The post office was established in August 1846, Erastus Dean, postmaster. (*History of Rock County*, 466)

Emery [EM (uh) ree]. Price. Town (1889). According to local accounts, when two new towns were organized, Charles H. Roser, chair of the Town of Worcester, suggested the names Emery and Hackett for two of his friends. Two of Roser's children were named Pearl Emery Roser and Charles Hackett Roser. See Hackett. ("Re: Embry Is a French Name")

Emmerich [EM uh rik]. Marathon. Named from the Emmerich post office, established in December 1890 and named for the first postmaster, Anton Emmerich. (Zamzow, 29)

Emmet [EM it]. Dodge, Marathon. The town of Emmet in Dodge County was organized in 1846 and named at the suggestion of Patrick Mahoney and other Irish settlers for Irish nationalist Robert Emmet, who led an unsuccessful rebellion against British rule for which he was hanged in 1803, at the age of twenty-five. The town of Emmet in Marathon County, formerly known as the Irish Settlement, was organized in 1888 and was also named for Robert Emmet. (Hubbell, 241; Marchetti, 572)

Empire. Fond du Lac. Town (1850). The name was suggested about 1850 by Alfred T. Germond, a businessman from New York City. Germond likely took the name from Empire State, by 1850 a well-established nickname for New York. The post office was established by Henry Giltner in 1846 as Owascus, which, according to Worthing, was pronounced [o AY suhs] and may have been a play on the phrase "oh ask us." Alternatively, *Owascus* may be an adaptation and shortening of Ojibwa *wawashkeshi* 'deer.'

Endeavor [en DEV er]. Marquette. Village (1946). Endeavor had its beginnings in 1890 in a revival meeting sponsored by the Home Missionary Society of the Wisconsin Congregational Church. Following the success of the meeting, a Christian Endeavor Society was formed, which led to the founding of the Christian Endeavor Academy, which gave its name to the community. The post office was established in October 1878 as Merritt's Landing, Cornelius Merritt, postmaster. (Reetz, 64)

Ephraim [EE fruhm]. Door. Village (1919). Founded in 1853 by Norwegian Moravians led by the Reverend Andreas (Andrew) Iverson. Iverson apparently suggested several biblical names, from which the congregation chose Ephraim, which appears in both the Old and New Testaments and has been associated with 'fruitful.' The parent Moravian settlement near Green Bay had been named Ephraim as well. (Burton and Burton, 37)

Erdman. Sheboygan. Named from the Erdman post office, established in May 1893 by tavern keeper William A. Erdman. (Buchen, 335)

Erin. St. Croix, Washington. Erin Corner in St. Croix County was named from Erin Prairie, settled largely by Irish families, beginning with John Casey in 1854. The Erin post office was established in June 1862, Richard Joyce, postmaster. In Washington County, Michael Lynch was one of the first settlers in the town of Erin, followed by Ryans, Quinns, Daleys, Firzgeralds, Donohues, and Murphys. The name was proposed by John Whelan, born in the Aran Islands on Ireland's west coast. Erin is a literary name for Ireland, especially popular with nineteenth-century Romantic poets. (Buchmeier and Stapleton, 13)

Esdaile [EZ dayl]. Pierce. Esdaile developed around a sawmill established by James Buckingham in the mid-1850s and was platted by subsequent mill owners Thomas and Mary Carney in 1870. Probably named for an Esdaile family. There is nothing to support the claim that the name was suggested by the *S* curve of Isabelle Creek as it wound through the "dale." The post office was established in January 1871, Hiram Patch, postmaster. This is the only Esdaile in the United States. (Krogstad and O'Keefe, 57)

Esofea [uh SOF ee uh]. Vernon. Named for the Esofea post office, established by Even Tomtengen in August 1868. Tomtengen emigrated from Biri, Norway, in 1850 and kept a general store from the mid-1860s. Local accounts are that Tomtengen created the name by combining the *E* from Even with a respelling of Sophia, reportedly the name of his wife or another family member. This is the only Esofea in the United States. (Vernon County Historical Society, p.c.)

Estella [e STEL uh]. Chippewa. Town (1921). Named for Laura Estella Flint, wife of Warren S. Flint, who came to Wisconsin from New Hampshire as a child in 1853. Flint operated a sawmill, general store, and blacksmith shop, established the post office in 1886, and laid out the now-vanished community of Estella. The Estella school was located east of Cornell. (Forrester, 528)

Ettrick [E trik]. Trempealeau. Town (1862) and Village (1948). In July 1860, the Armagh post office was established with John Cance, postmaster. Several months later Cance, from Glasgow, Scotland, changed the name of the office to Ettrick, for Ettrick Forest in Scotland, a royal hunting preserve and the scene of much of the action in Sir Walter Scott's narrative poem *Marmion*. (Curtiss-Wedge and Pierce, 81)

Eureka [yoo REE kuh]. Winnebago. The community was founded in the summer of 1850 by Lester Rounds, Walton Dickerson, and William Starr. The immediate origin of the name is uncertain. *Eureka* is Greek for 'I have found it' and the Wisconsin name is likely a transfer from Eureka, Humboldt County, California. By 1850 Eureka was not only the name of a California community but also the state motto. Eureka and Humboldt County were prominent in the news of the day because of the California gold rush. The Town of Eureka and Eureka Center in Polk County, Wisconsin, were reportedly named at the suggestion of Elias Hoover, but his inspiration is unknown. (Christiansen, 10–11; *History of Northern Wisconsin*, 1189)

Euren [YOOR uhn]. Kewaunee. Michel (Michael) Bottkuhl emigrated from Euren, adjacent to Trier, Germany, in the mid-1850s. The area was known as Bottkolville until about 1879 when Bottkuhl, now known as Bottkol, established the Euren post office. ("Bottkol-L Archives")

Evansville. Rock. City (1896). In 1846 Dr. John M. Evans, from Rutland, Vermont, arrived in what was known simply as the Grove, on Allen's Creek, and established a medical practice that extended into the twentieth century. The community was named for Evans when the post office was established by Curtis Bent in 1851. (Montgomery, 3, 14)

Evanswood. Waupaca. Named for early settler Evan Townsend, who operated a sawmill on Little River from 1848 and established the Evanswood post office in September 1854. (Ware, 157)

Excelsior [ek SEL see er]. Richland, Sauk. In 1855 William Coates and his business partner, Stephen Knowlton, purchased a gristmill, which provided the nucleus for the community of Excelsior in Richland County. Coates suggested the name, most likely from Longfellow's popular 1841 poem *Excelsior*. Excelsior, the town in Sauk County (1857) was founded by Stephen Van Rensselaer Ableman, a native of New York. *Excelsior*, Latin for 'higher,' is the motto of New York State. With its associations of advancement and progress, Excelsior occurs in more than a dozen states. See Rock Springs. (Butterfield, *History of Crawford and Richland Counties*; Cole, *Standard History*, 410)

Exeland [EKS uh luhnd]. Sawyer. Village (1920). Exeland was founded about 1907 when the Arpin Lumber Company built a logging railroad to the site and in so doing crossed the tracks of the Wisconsin Central. According to local accounts the *X* thus created led to the name Exeland. While this appears to be a popular etymology, I have found no better explanation. This is the only Exeland in the United States. (Chappelle, *Around the Four Corners*, 205)

Exeter. Green. Town (1849) and ppl. A transfer from either an Exeter in New England or directly from Exeter, Devon, England. The post office was established in July 1843, Thomas L. Summers, postmaster.

Exile. Pierce. Named from the Exile post office, established in December 1887, Hannah Ezard, postmaster. The source of the name is unknown. Local popular etymologies claim that the name arose because settlers felt exiled from their former homes as the area was remote from the civilizations they remembered. This is the only Exile in the United States, although an Exile existed in Uvalde, Texas, around the turn of the nineteenth century.

Fairchild. Eau Claire. Town (1874) and Village (1880). Named from the Fairchild post office, established in 1870 by postmaster William Reynolds. The office was named in honor of Lucius Fairchild, three-term governor of Wisconsin, 1866–72. Formerly known as Grubtown and later as Pedrick's Mill, a whistle stop on the Omaha railroad. (Stennett, 175)

Fairfield. Rock, Sauk, Walworth. The Town of Fairfield in Sauk County was organized as Flora in 1850, named, according to Cole, by Timothy Adams "for an old sweetheart." The name was changed to Fairfield in 1853. The community of Fairfield in Rock and Walworth Counties was formerly known as Maxsonville for Joseph Maxson and his son, Arthur, who settled on Turtle Prairie in the summer of 1837. The Maxsons, from Rhode Island by way of Centerville, New York, built the first sawmill in the area in 1841. Both Fairfields are likely transfers from Fairfields in New England. Fairfield is a popular place name, occurring in most states. (Cole, *Standard History*, 410; *History of the Settlement of Darien*)

Fair Play. Grant. Named from the Fair Play lead mine, which opened about 1841. Local histories claim the name arose from an incident regarding mine ownership in which rival claimants were headed toward a physical confrontation when someone in the crowd called for "fair play." Arbitration rather than fisticuffs followed. There are communities named Fair Play in five other states, all with similar naming stories. (Holford, 591)

Fairwater. Fond du Lac. Village (1921). The community was founded in the late 1840s and named from the Grand River, a reference to the waterpower it provided. The post office was established in 1846 as Mansfield, named for Eben F. Mansfield, from Maine, who built the first house in the area in 1844. The name was changed to Fairwater in 1848. (Worthing)

Fall Creek. Eau Claire. Village (1906). Fall Creek City, named for its location on Fall Creek, was laid out a mile or so north of present Fall Creek in about 1857. The post office was established in 1870 as Cousins, for Henry Cousins, an Eau Claire businessman, and changed to Fall Creek in July 1874. (Stennett, 176)

Fall Hall Glen. Jackson. In the late 1910s James B. Hall established a fishing and camping resort he named by combining 'falls' from the Black River falls with his name and adding 'glen,' which suggested the natural surroundings.

Fall River. Columbia. Village (1903). Founded in 1846 by Alfred Augustus Brayton, from Jefferson County, New York, who laid out the community, built a sawmill, kept a general store, and served as the first postmaster in 1849. Named from Fall River, itself probably named by Brayton for Fall River, Massachusetts. (J. Jones, 371)

Falls City. Dunn. Named from the falls on Red Cedar River. The post office was established in August 1858, Silas T. Wiggins postmaster. (Curtiss-Wedge and Jones, 214)

Falun [FA luhn, FAW luhn]. Burnett. Named for Falun (Fahlun), the capital of Dalecarlia (now Kopparberg) province, Sweden. The area around Falun attracted a large number of Swedish settlers, especially in the late 1860s and early 1870s. They included Claus Edward Johnson, the first postmaster in 1894. Falun is also the name of a community in Kansas and a township in Minnesota. (Landelius and Jarvi, 245)

Fancher [FAN cher]. Portage. Fancher, named by and for Orson Fancher, the first postmaster in 1891, grew around a siding built by the Green Bay & Western railroad to serve the local potato warehouses. Also known for a time as Smokie Spur, apparently from a tavern of that name. (Rosholt, *Our County, Our Story*, 398)

Fargo. Vernon. Named for the Fargo brothers, Enoch, Lyman, Lorenzo, and Robert, who emigrated from Colchester, Connecticut, in the mid-1840s and established several sawmills and gristmills. The Fargos were prominent community benefactors. The L. D. Fargo Library in Lake Mills is named in honor of Lorenzo Fargo. (Lawson, 700)

Farmington. There are or have been nearly a dozen Farmingtons in Wisconsin. A popular place name, it occurs in some forty states. Many were reportedly named for the superior quality of the soil, the excellent farms in the area, and the like. The claim in Butterfield's 1881 *History of La Crosse County* that the town of Farmington was so named because it "contains the finest farming lands in the county" (683) is typical. Other Farmingtons may be transfers from Farmingtons in eastern states.

Fayette. Lafayette. Town (1849) and ppl. Surveyed in June 1844 for site owner John Journey. Named from Lafayette County. The post office was established in August 1849, Martin W. Anderson, postmaster.

Fence. Florence. Town (1921) and ppl. The community was known informally as the Big Popple Settlement until the post office was established by Olous Anunson in 1899. At that time three names were considered: Podunk, for the Podunk dam, built by the Halvor Anunson Lumber Company; Big Popple, for Big Popple River; and Fence. According to one report, Fence "sounded more refined and not as crude" as "Popple" or "Podunk." Fence apparently refers to the Indian practice of constructing a wall of brush several miles long with sharpened sticks arrayed behind it. Deer were then driven toward the wall and when they jumped the brush fence they impaled themselves on the sticks. The name is apparently a translation of Ojibwa *mitchikan*, a fence or weir erected on a river to impede the transit of fish, which could then be captured. This is the source of the name of Fence Lake in Vilas and Marinette Counties. See Popple River. (*History of Fence*, 12, 47)

Fennimore [FEN i mor]. Grant. Town (1849) and City (1919). Little is known about John Gerard Fennimore, the presumed namesake of the city and town of Fennimore; the sesquicentennial history of Fennimore calls him "a real man of mystery." It is unclear why this particular name should have been chosen since there is no record of Fennimore's participation in local affairs or otherwise contributing to the community. Fennimore apparently took part in the Black Hawk War in 1832, but shortly thereafter he left the area, leaving no forwarding address. The community was laid out in April 1856 by the site owners, Dwight T. Parker, William W. Field, John G. Perkins, and George H. Cox, and named from the Fennimore post office, established by John McReynolds in May 1850. This is the only Fennimore in the United States, although there is a Fennimore Landing in Delaware and a Fenimore in New York State. (Cauffman, Finnegan, and Stauffacher, 6)

Fenwood. Marathon. Village (1904). Working through the Milwaukee, Lake Shore & Western railroad, which was extending its line to Marshfield, Wausau businessmen Cornelius Curtis and Judson Porter formed the Fenwood Lumber Company, which laid out Fenwood in the early 1890s. The reason for the choice of the name is unknown; it may simply be a promotional name based upon the positive associations of "fen" and "wood." This is the only Fenwood in the United States, although there is a Fenwood Heights in Maryland. (Stennett, 70)

Fern. Florence. Town and ppl. Formerly known as the Washburn Settlement. Formally named from the Fern post office when the town was organized in March 1917. One local source claims the name was chosen "because of the abundance of ferns in the area." (*Heritage of Iron & Timber*, 60)

Ferryville. Crawford. Village (1912). Informally known as Humble Bush, the name was formalized as Ferryville with establishment of the post office in 1857, itself reportedly named for the anticipated ferry service to Lansing, Iowa. The community was platted about 1858 for site owners William McCauley and Thomas W. Tower. (Butterfield, *History of Crawford and Richland Counties*, 603)

Fifield [FEYE feeld]. Price. Town (1879) and ppl. Founded by the Wisconsin Central railroad in 1876. Named for Samuel S. Fifield, who represented the district in the Wisconsin Assembly for much of the 1870s and was lieutenant governor of the state in the 1880s. (Lessard, 6)

Fillmore. Washington. Probably named for Millard Fillmore (1800–1874), vice president of the United States when Jonathan F. Danforth established the Fillmore post office in August 1849.

Finley. Juneau. Town and ppl. The 1898 petition for township formation called for the name Scandinavia, but for reasons that are unclear the name was changed by the Juneau County board to Finley, from the Finley post office, itself apparently named for Charleton H. Finley, the first permanent settler. (*Juneau County*, 44)

Fish Creek. Door. Named from the stream Fish Creek, itself named by Increase Claflin in the 1840s. The community was founded by Asa Thorp, from Oswego, New York, a cooper who specialized in building fish barrels. In the 1850s Thorp built a pier from which he supplied wood to passing steamboats. The post office was established in August 1858, Jacob St. Ores, postmaster. (Holand, 83, 179)

Fisk. Winnebago. Named for early settler Edwin B. Fisk, from New York State, who changed the name of the Hawley's Corners post office to Fisk's Corners when he became postmaster in 1850.

Fitchburg. Dane. Town and City (1983). The township was organized in 1847 as Greenfield. In 1853, to avoid confusion with Greenfield in Milwaukee County, the town was renamed for the Fitchburg post office, itself named in 1842 at the suggestion of Ebenezer Brigham, the first permanent settler in Dane County, for his birthplace, Fitchburg, Massachusetts. (*Fitchburg Bicentennial*, 10, 15)

Fitzgerald. Winnebago. Named for John Fitzgerald, an Oshkosh businessman and banker. Fitzgerald served in the Wisconsin Senate in 1856 and was mayor of Oshkosh in the early 1860s. (Harney, 296)

Flambeau [FLAM bo]. Towns in Price (1920) and Rusk (1875). Both townships are named from the Flambeau River. See Lac du Flambeau.

Flintville. Brown. In the early 1850s Richard Flint, from Maine, purchased a mill at the site, which became known as Flint's Mill and as Flintville when the post office was established in 1870. (Cassidy, *Brown County*)

Flora Fountain. Grant. Known as Slab Town in its early years when Flora Fountain was little more than a few rough dwellings around the Campbell, Herring & Campbell sawmill. Slab Town Road, which runs through Flora Fountain, is a reminder of the community's earlier name. The name Flora Fountain is credited to Mrs. William Beswick, reportedly for the local wildflowers and springs. The post office was established as Flora in 1891. (Holford, 581)

Florence. County (1882) and ppl. About 1875 Hiram D. Fisher opened the Spread Eagle iron mine, named from Spread Eagle Lake. Fisher laid out the community of Florence in 1880, named in honor of Florence Hulst, wife of Dr. Nelson P. Hulst of Milwaukee, who was one of the first to notice the deposits of iron ore along the Menominee River. (Kellogg, 223)

Folsom. Vernon. Apparently named for Frances Folsom, wife of President Grover Cleveland. When postmaster John T. O'Leary chose the name of the office in 1887 Cleveland was serving his first term as president. (Vernon County Historical Society, p.c.)

Fond du Lac [FAHN duh lak]. County (1836), Town (1838), and City (1852). French for 'foot of the lake.' The name was given by French fur traders in the eighteenth century and referred to the 'foot' or 'farthest point' of Lake Winnebago. The present city dates from 1835 when the site was platted for the Fond du Lac Land Company, founded in Green Bay by speculator James Duane Doty, the founder of Madison. The first permanent settlers, brothers Colwert and Edward Pier, arrived from New Haven, Vermont, the following year. Colwert Pier established the post office in September 1837. (Butterfield, *History of Fond du Lac County*, 335–36)

Fontana [fahn TAN uh]. Walworth. Founded in 1838 by Amos Bailey, Henry Clark, and Matthias Mohr. Perhaps inspired by local springs, Mohr chose the name Fontana, a poetic adaptation of 'fountain.' (Beckwith, 446)

Fontenoy [FAHNT noy]. Brown. Named from the Fontenoy post office, established in June 1870 by Diedrick Benecke. The local account is that Benecke did not propose a name for the post office but rather sought advice from the Post Office Department, where an official suggested Fontenoy.

The reason for the name is unknown. This is the only Fontenoy in the United States. (Cassidy, *Brown County*)

Footville [FUT vil]. Rock. Village (1918). Named about 1854 for and by Ezra A. Foot, the site owner. Foot was a prominent figure in the early years of Wisconsin statehood, serving in the state assembly and senate in the 1850s and 1860s. The post office was established as Bachelor's Grove, named for an early Bachelor family, in July 1846; changed to Footville in March 1855. (Stennett, 71)

Forest. County. Organized from Langlade and Oconto Counties in 1885 and apparently named for the forest that covered much of the county at the time. The county was created largely through the efforts of Samuel Shaw, operator of a local lumber mill and owner of the *Forest Republican* newspaper. Shaw was assisted by Frank P. Crandon, tax commissioner for the Chicago & North Western railroad and the namesake of Crandon, the seat of Forest County.

Forest Junction. Calumet. Early in 1873 the community of Forest was platted for site owner Charlotte A. Quentin. Shortly thereafter Baldwin, named for site owner and former state senator George Baldwin, was laid out next to Forest. Baldwin and Forest merged as Forest Junction when the post office was established in October 1873. The reason for the name Forest is unknown; Junction refers to the location where the tracks of the Milwaukee & Northern railroad crossed those of the Appleton & New London. (Haese, 4)

Fort Atkinson. Jefferson. City (1878). Named for military leader Henry Atkinson (1782–1842), commander of U.S. forces during the Black Hawk War of 1832. In July of that year Atkinson constructed a stockade known as Fort Coscong or Fort Koshkonong at the junction of the Rock and Bark Rivers. The community developed around the Fort Atkinson post office, established in 1839 by Dwight Foster, the first permanent settler. (Swart, 237)

Fort McCoy. Monroe. Established as the Sparta Maneuver Tract, a military training center, in 1909. Renamed in 1910 for Colonel Robert McCoy, who later commanded the Fourth Wisconsin Infantry regiment in World War I. McCoy was mayor of Sparta in the early 1920s.

Fort Winnebago. Columbia. Town (organized as Winnebago Portage in 1849; changed to Fort Winnebago in 1850). Named from Fort Winnebago, the military fortification built in 1828 to guard the strategic portage between the Fox and Wisconsin Rivers largely in response to the fears aroused by the Winnebago Uprising of 1827. The post office was established in September 1834, Henry Merrill, postmaster.

Forward. Dane. "Forward" has been the motto of the State of Wisconsin since 1851. The motto was apparently chosen by Nelson Dewey, the state's first governor, in a conversation with Edward Ryan, a Wisconsin Supreme Court justice, when they met in New York in the late 1840s. The Forward post office was established in March 1872, Christian Evenson, postmaster.

Fossland [FAWS luhnd]. Kenosha. Named for the Fossland family of Lake County, Illinois. Tobias Johanes Fossland emigrated from Flekkefjord in southern Norway to the Chicago area about 1910.

Foster. Clark. Town (1913). Named for Nathaniel Caldwell Foster. See Foster, Eau Claire. ("Foster Township")

Foster. Eau Claire. Founded about 1913 and named for Nathaniel Caldwell Foster, from Tioga County, New York. In 1891 Foster organized the N. C. Foster Lumber Company of Fairchild and later built the Fairchild & Northeastern, a logging railroad from Fairchild to Cleghorn. The area was formerly known as Emmet for Samuel Emmet Coon, who, with his brother Will, purchased the site in the late 1850s. (*Osseo Area Bicentennial Book*)

Foster Junction. Ashland. Named for George E. Foster, a Mellen lumber executive and businessman. Foster was a partner in the Foster-Lattimer Lumber Company and later the Mellen Lumber Company, which founded Foster Junction around 1910. When the community failed to prosper, many of the buildings were dismantled and moved to Mellen. (*Journey into Mellen*, 604)

Fountain City. Buffalo. City (1889). About 1839 Thomas A. Holmes of Milwaukee established a trading post near the mouth of Waumandee Creek. The site became known as Holmes Landing, a refueling stop for Mississippi River steamboats now generally recognized as the first permanent settlement in Buffalo County. The name was formalized as Fountain City, reportedly named for a large spring that provided much of the community's water, about 1854 when the Fountain City post office was established. (Johnson, 25)

Four Corners. Burnett. Four Corners, once a thriving community rivaling Trade Lake, was named for its location at the intersection of State Route 48 and County Road S. Locations such as this (Four Corners, Five Points, and the like) are popular locative place names.

Foxboro. Douglas. Probably named by a railroad official for Foxboro, Massachusetts, north of Boston. The post office was established in December 1895, John P. Kennedy, postmaster.

Fox Lake. Dodge. Town (1846) and City (1938). Named from Fox Lake, a translation of Ho-Chunk (Winnebago) *day-wau-sha-ra* 'lake of the fox.'

98

By the late 1830s the name had been shortened to *waushara* and in 1851 was given to the newly organized Waushara County (q.v.). The post office was established as Frankfort in July 1839, changed to Waushara in April 1840, and to Fox Lake in May 1856. (Vogel, *Indian Names*, 64)

Fox River. Kenosha. The community was named from the Fox River, which heads in Waukesha County near Colgate and flows south through Kenosha into Lake County, Illinois. The Potawatomi name for the river was apparently *Waukesha*, built upon *wekshi* 'fox.' See Waukesha County. (Vogel, *Indian Names*, 14)

Francis Creek. Manitowoc. Village (1960). Named from the stream Francis Creek, itself perhaps named for St. Francis of Assisi. The post office was established in June 1850, Joseph Lamirre, postmaster. (Stennett, 73)

Frankfort. Marathon. Town (1889). Named for his former home, Frankfurt, Germany, by Ed Protze, the first township chair. (Marchetti, 573)

Franklin. Sauk. Town (1854). Named for Benjamin Franklin. Most if not all of the other half dozen or so Franklin towns and communities in Wisconsin were named for Benjamin Franklin as well, but naming details for some are uncertain. (Goc, *Many a Fine Harvest*, 164)

Franzen [FRAN zuhn]. Marathon. Town (1901). Named for Christian Franzen, born in Holstein, Germany. Franzen served on the Marathon County Board and was elected to the Wisconsin Assembly in 1915. (Marchetti, 716)

Frazer Corners [FRAY zer]. Shawano. Named for early settler and civic leader George H. Frazer, the first chair of Town of Lessor, who also served as township assessor and treasurer. The post office was established in December 1881, Peter E. Blitchfeldt, postmaster. (*Commemorative Biographical Record of the Upper Wisconsin Counties*, 660)

Frederic. Polk. Village (1903). William J. Starr, a partner in the Eau Claire holding company of Davis and Starr, owned some ten thousand acres in the area, some of which he had surveyed in the fall of 1901 for the community he named for his son Frederic, then seven years old. (*Saga of Frederic*)

Fredonia [fruh DON yuh]. Ozaukee. Town (1847) and Village (1922). Probably a transfer from Fredonia, Chautauqua County, New York. Samuel L. Mitchell coined the New York name about 1800 and claimed it meant 'land of freedom.' Fredonia is a popular place name, occurring in about half the states. The post office was established in January 1850, William Bell, postmaster. (Eccles, 6)

Freedom. Outagamie. Town (1847) and ppl. When Freedom was organized in the summer of 1852, the first choice for a name was Jackson for James Jackson, an emancipated slave, generally recognized as the first permanent settler, who arrived in the vicinity about 1830. By local accounts, Jackson suggested the present name in recognition of his freedom from bondage. The area was formerly known as Sagole, an Oneida word meaning 'welcome, greetings.' A Sagole post office operated from March 1872 until February 1903. (Balliet, 77)

Freistadt [FREE stat]. Ozaukee. Freistadt is one of the oldest permanent German settlements in Wisconsin, established in 1839 by Lutherans fleeing Prussian religious persecution. Two Lutheran pastors are associated with the colony: Gustav Adolf Kindermann and Lebrecht Friedrich Krause, either of whom could have proposed the name from the northern German city of Freistatt 'free city.' (Eccles, 2)

Fremont [FREE mahnt]. Clark. Named for the famous western explorer John C. Fremont, one of the first U.S. senators from California and the first Republican candidate for president, nominated in 1856. The Town (1874) and Village (1882) of Fremont in Waupaca County were named from the Fremont post office, established in February 1851, itself named for John C. Fremont. (Scholtz)

Frenchville. Trempealeau. Named for its location on French Creek, itself named, according to tradition, for early French traders whose post was on the stream. The post office was established in August 1868, Ole Skauw, postmaster.

Friendship. Adams. Village (1907). The site of present Friendship was originally purchased by land speculator Henry Whitney. Developers Luther Stowell and William Burbank bought Whitney's property about 1857, laid out the community, and named it for Friendship, their former home in Allegany County, New York. (Goc, *From Past to Present*, 24, 32)

Friesland [FREEZ luhnd]. Columbia. Village (1946). Named by Dutch settlers from the province of Friesland in northern Netherlands. The spelling was often Freesland; the post office was established under this name in August 1915.

Frostville. Oconto. Named for Anders (Andrew) Christian Frost, who emigrated from Denmark in 1873, became master of the Maple Valley post office in 1878, and established a general store in Frostville about 1880. (Rucker, *From the McCauslin*, 78)

Fussville [FUHS vil]. Waukesha. Now part of Menomonee Falls. Named for landowner Henry Fuss, who emigrated from Germany in 1844. *Fuss* [foos] is German for 'foot.' The post office was established in July 1864, Frederick Ande, postmaster. ("Waukesha County, Online Genealogy")

Gagen [GAY juhn]. Oneida. Town (1881) and ppl. Named for pioneer settler and site owner Daniel Gagen, who emigrated from England in 1851 and laid out the community on Gagen Hill about 1865. (Jones and McVean, *History of Lincoln, Oneida and Vilas Counties*, 280)

Gale. Trempealeau. Town (1854); Galesville City (1942). Named for and by George Gale, an important figure in western Wisconsin during the early years of statehood. About 1841 Gale moved to Wisconsin from Vermont and established a law practice in Walworth County. He was a delegate to the state constitutional convention, a state senator in the early 1850s, and a circuit court judge. When La Crosse showed little interest in establishing an institution of higher learning, Gale purchased the site of Galesville and in 1854 received a state charter for Galesville University. The school closed in 1939. (*Galesville*, 5)

Galloway. Marathon. Named for landowner Charles A. Galloway, a partner in the Moore-Galloway Lumber Company of Fond du Lac. The post office was established in May 1904, Adolph J. Torgerson, postmaster. (Stennett, 75)

Gardner. Door. Town (1862). Named for local businessman Freeland B. Gardner, born in Onondaga County, New York. From about 1850 Gardner operated a shipyard, one of the first industries in Door County. The post office was established in October 1858 as Chickatoek (Chickatock) and changed to Gardner in 1866. (Hale, 23)

Garfield. The towns of Garfield in Jackson (1880) and Polk (1886) Counties were named for James A. Garfield (1831–81), twentieth president of the United States, who served the second-shortest term in presidential history, from March 4 until September 19, 1881. Garfield died from a gunshot wound inflicted by Charles Guiteau on July 2, 1881. Guiteau, often described as "a disgruntled office seeker," spent his early teen years in Ulao, Wisconsin, in the 1850s. The community of Garfield in Portage County was named for President Garfield in the early 1880s, probably by Sigvart T. Foxen, who established the Garfield post office in March 1884. (Christiansen, 12)

Garnet [gahr NET]. Fond du Lac. Origin unknown. Worthing suggests that Garnet may be a misreading of Gerner, from Philip Gerner, who established the post office in the spring of 1899.

Gaslyn [GAZ lin]. Burnett. Named for David C. Gaslin (Gaslyn), a logger on the St. Croix River from the 1860s. The post office operated from 1902 until 1919.

Gays Mills. Crawford. Village (1900). Named for James B. Gay, a civil engineer from Indiana who erected a sawmill on the Kickapoo River about 1848. James Gay's mill was complemented by a gristmill established by his brother John in the mid-1860s. (Butterfield, *History of Crawford and Richland Counties*, 738)

101

Genesee [JEN uh SEE]. Waukesha. Town (1839) and ppl. Formerly known as Jenkinsville for early settler Benjamin A. Jenkins, who established a mill and tavern about 1840. Named by Jenkins for his former home, Genesee County, in northwestern New York State, itself named from a Seneca word meaning 'pleasant valley.' The local story is that Jenkins refused to donate land for the Milwaukee & Mississippi railroad station, which then rerouted and founded Genesee Depot north of Jenkins's holdings. (*Waukesha County*)

Geneva [juh NEE vuh]. Walworth. Town (1838). See Lake Geneva.

Genoa [juh NO uh]. Vernon. Town (1861) and Village (1935). First known as Hastings Landing after David Hastings, the first known settler, who arrived in 1853. The community was laid out in 1854 by Hastings, Guiseppe "Joseph" Monti, and John Richards as Bad Axe City, named for its location in Bad Axe (now Vernon) County. The name was changed to Genoa in 1868. Of the several dozen Genoas in the United States, this is one of the few that was likely named directly for Genoa in northwestern Italy. The area was once known as Little Italy, and a large number of early settlers were Italian; in fact, Monti was looking for a site to relocate a group of largely Italian lead miners from Galena, Illinois, when Genoa was founded. (Jambois)

Genoa City. Walworth. Founded by James F. Dickerson, who dammed Nippersink Creek and established a sawmill in 1849. Probably named for Genoa, Cayuga County, New York, itself named for Genoa, Italy. The Genoa post office operated from December 1850 until June 1852 when it was changed to South Bloomfield. The Bloomfield post office was changed to Genoa Junction in January 1874. (Beckwith, 235)

Georgetown. Grant. Previously known as Smelser, for Jonas M. Smelser (Smeltzer), from Bourbon County, Kentucky. The post office was established in February 1850 as Smeltzer's Grove and changed to Georgetown in March 1870, for George Wineman, a prominent shopkeeper and the first Smeltzer's Grove postmaster. See Smelser.(Butterfield, *History of Grant County*, 824–25)

Georgetown. Polk. Town (1878). Named for George P. Anderson, a Civil War veteran from Ohio who settled in the area in the early 1870s and served as the first township treasurer. Anderson also established the post office at Bunyan (q.v.). (Ericson)

Germania [jer MAYN ee uh, jer MAYN yuh]. Marquette. Germania was founded about 1859 when Benjamin Hall, an unordained millennialist minister, brought a religious commune to the area from Massachusetts. Members lived under the same roof and took meals together, and all property was held in common. The commune dissolved shortly after Hall's death in 1879. The community took its name from the Germania post office, established late in 1855 by Philip E. Hase, who named the office for the large number of German settlers. (*Hase*, incidentally, is German for 'rabbit.') Germania, a Latinized form of Germany, is also the name of a community in Iron County and a township in Shawano. (Reetz, 68)

Germantown. Washington. Village (1927). Richland. ppl. Juneau. Town (1855). Washington. Town (1846). Named for or by German settlers. The oldest of the Germantown settlements is in Washington County, where the site owners, Garrett Vliet, Anton Wiesner, and Levi Ostrander, laid out the community about 1837. The earliest German settlers in Juneau County were Walter Gaige and Jacob Gundlach, who arrived in 1851. Gaige was the first township chair. (Blau and Gay, 7)

Gibbsville [GIBZ vil]. Sheboygan. Founded by brothers John, James, and Benjamin Gibbs, who emigrated from New York State about 1836. John Gibbs established the Gibbs post office in 1846. The short-lived Town of Gibbsville existed from January until May 1849. (Buchen, 336)

Gibraltar [juh BRAWL ter]. Door. Town (1857). The town was named from the community of Gibraltar (now Baileys Harbor), the seat of Door County at the time, at the suggestion of Solomon Beery, the first town clerk, presumably because "its general rough, rocky, and bluffy surface" reminded him of the Rock of Gibraltar. (C. Martin, 52)

Gibson. Manitowoc. Town (1858). Named by Darius Peck, who began farming in the area about 1856, for his former home, Gibson, Susquehanna County, Pennsylvania, itself named for early nineteenth-century politician and jurist John Bannister Gibson. (Falge, 334)

Gile [GEYEL]. Iron. Named for Gordon H. Gile of Oshkosh. Gile, along with Michael A. Hurley (the namesake of Hurley, Wisconsin) and several others, formed the Northern Chief Iron Company to exploit the ore deposits of the Penokee district in 1882. See Hurley. (Stennett, 77)

Gillett [GIL it, JIL it]. Oconto. Town (1867) and City (1944). Previously known as Gillett Center. Named for Rodney Gillett, from Albany, New York. Gillett brought his family to the area about 1858, established the Gillett post office in 1871, and with Uri Balcom laid out the community of Gillett on the line of the Wisconsin & Southern railroad in 1884. (Stennett, 77)

Gillingham [GIL ing ham]. Richland. Hugh Morrow, the first postmaster in 1880, apparently named the office for an eastern friend, John Gillingham, who had encouraged him to immigrate to Richland County. (Scott)

Gills Landing. Waupaca. Named for John Gill, who built a steamboat dock and landing at the confluence of the Wolf and Waupaca Rivers in the early

1850s. The post office was established in February 1859, William F. Water-house, postmaster. (Wakefield, 159)

Gills Rock. Door. Named for Elias Gill, who had extensive lumber interests in the area in the 1860s. Informally known as Hedgehog Harbor, reportedly for a sailor named Lovejoy who left his sloop on the beach over the winter of 1855–56. The vessel became home to a family of porcupines, which chewed through the hull. When Lovejoy launched his boat the following spring it took on water and quickly sank. The post office was established in April 1883 as Hedge Hog, Hans Tostensen, postmaster; changed to Gills Rock in 1902. (Thomas, 116)

Gilman. Pierce. Town. Organized in 1868 as Deerfield. The name was changed in 1869 to honor Benjamin Franklin Gilman, recognized as the first perma-nent resident, who settled in the area in 1859. The Gilman post office oper-ated from March 1874 until June 1900. (Ericson)

Gilman. Taylor. Village (1914). Named by Eau Claire businessman Delos R. Moon for the family of his wife, Sallie Gilman Moon, and their son, Lawrence Gilman Moon. The post office was established in March 1908. See Moon. (*History of Taylor County*)

Gilmanton [GIL muhn tuhn]. Buffalo. Town (1858) and ppl. Previously known as the Loomis Settlement for early settlers William, Dan, and Abijah Loomis, and also as Mann's Mill for Joel Mann, who established a sawmill at the site in 1859. Samuel Gilman and his four sons, Franklin, Edson, Andrew, and Daniel, emigrated from Vermont and settled in what became known as Gilman Valley in the 1850s. The Gilmantown (later Gilmanton) post office was established in May 1858, William Loomis, postmaster. (Curtiss-Wedge, *History of Buffalo and Pepin Counties*, 92)

Gingles [JING guhlz]. Ashland. Town (1924). Named for Alexander Gingles, a pioneer settler of Ashland County, who emigrated from Ireland in the 1890s.

Glandon. Marathon. William C. Landon, a prominent Wausau businessman in the late nineteenth and early twentieth centuries, established the post office in late 1908 which he named Glandon (G Landon), for either his father or his son, both named George. (Marchetti, 636–37)

Gleason. Lincoln. Founded in the early 1900s with construction of the Chi-cago, Milwaukee & St. Paul railroad. Named for Salem Gleason, one of the site owners. The post office was established in May 1902, William T. Bradley, postmaster. (Jones and McVean, *History of Lincoln, Oneida and Vilas Counties*, 85)

Glenbeulah [GLEN BYOO luh]. Sheboygan. Village (1913). Founded in the late 1850s for the Sheboygan & Mississippi railroad. Investors in the railroad included Edward Appleton, of the Boston Appletons, who gave their name to Appleton, Wisconsin. Appleton chose the name in honor of his mother, Beulah, prefixed with *glen*, the name thus taken to mean 'Beulah's valley.' (Buchen, 258)

Glencoe [GLEN ko]. Buffalo. Town (organized as Cold Springs in 1857; changed to Glencoe in 1858). The name was suggested by George Cowie, who arrived in the area in the mid-1850s and established the Glencoe post office in 1858. Cowie was from Edinburgh, Scotland, and proposed the name for Glencoe, Scotland, the ancestral home of his mother's clan, the McDonalds. Glencoe is a popular place name, occurring in about half of the states. (Curtiss-Wedge, *History of Buffalo and Pepin Counties*, 128)

Glendale. Milwaukee. City (1950). The community was known as Riverside until 1949, when a naming contest produced Cloverdale, Crestview, Glendale, Riverside, Riverview, River Front, Silver Bend, River Forest, and Wood Dale as semifinalists. The winning entry was submitted by the Glendale Advancement Association, itself named from West Glendale Avenue. (Morris, 50)

Glen Flora. Rusk. Village (1915). Formerly known as Miller's Siding, for Frank Miller, who built the first sawmill on Deertail Creek in the early 1880s. The name formally became Glen Flora with establishment of the post office in December 1887. The source of the name is unknown. Several popular etymologies have arisen. By one, Addie Otis coined Glen Flora by combining Glen, supposedly the name of the engineer who drove the first train through the area, with that of his daughter, Flora. By another, the same Addie Otis first proposed Flowery Glen, which, after some discussion, became Glen Flora, suggesting the flourishing of wildflowers each spring. (Wymore and Nelson)

Glen Haven. Grant. Town (1859) and ppl. First known as Stump Town and later as Ray's Landing for the steamboat landing established on the Mississippi River in the late 1830s by site owners Newton and Richard Ray. The community was laid out in the late 1850s by George Burroughs, who reportedly claimed that the hills and valleys of the area reminded him of the landscape of his native Scotland. Thus, Glen Haven was an appropriate name. (*Early History of Grant County*)

Glenmore. Brown. Town (1856) and ppl. The first permanent settler in the area was Samuel Harrison in 1846. When the township was set off from De Pere in 1856, John Dolland, a Brown County supervisor, suggested the name for Glenmore, Kilkenny, Ireland, near his birthplace. (Cassidy, *Brown County*)

Glenwood. St. Croix. Town (1885) and Glenwood City. Named from the Glenwood Manufacturing Company, formerly the Webster-Glover Manufacturing Company of Hudson. John Glover, a partner in the latter company, is generally credited with coining the name. His reasons for the choice are unknown but Glenwood, Minnesota, may have provided an inspiration.

Glidden. Ashland. Formerly known as Chippewa Crossing. Glidden was established by the Wisconsin Central railroad about 1876 and named for Charles R. Glidden, a prominent lumberman and railroad official. (R. Martin, 41)

Glover. St. Croix. Established as Glover Station, a spur on the Chicago, St. Paul, Minneapolis & Omaha railroad. Named for site owner John E. Glover, a partner in the Webster-Glover Manufacturing Company of Hudson. Glover may also have proposed the name of Glenwood (q.v.). (Ericson)

Goerkes Corner [GER keez]. Waukesha. First known as Storyville, named for early settler Augustus Story, who arrived in the area about 1837, and as Blodgett for Chester A. Blodgett. Frederick Goerke, keeper of an inn and tavern called the Junction House, was the first postmaster of the Blodgett post office, which operated from May 1885 until April 1895. ("Land Divisions within Waukesha County")

Goetz [GETS]. Chippewa. Town (1913). Named for Henry Goetz, Chippewa County treasurer in the late 1890s and treasurer of Sigel township. (*Chippewa County, Wisconsin: Past and Present*, 2:105)

Goodman. Marinette. Town (organized as Dunbar in 1899; changed to Goodman in 1915) and ppl. Founded in the late 1800s as a company town for employees of the Goodman Lumber Company of Marinette, established in 1879 by brothers James B. and William O. Goodman. (*Marinette County Centennial*, 5)

Goodnow [GUD no]. Oneida. Named for Edward A. Goodnough, rector of the Hobart Episcopal Church on the Oneida reservation from 1854 until 1890. ("Obituary of Edward A. Goodnough")

Gordon. Ashland, Douglas. The Town (1899) in Ashland County and the Town (1887) and community in Douglas are apparently named for Antoine Guerdon (Gaudin), a fur trader from La Pointe who had established a post at the junction of the Eau Claire and St. Croix Rivers by 1860. Over time, by popular etymology French *Guerdon* became English *Gordon*. The community in Douglas County was formally organized and named with construction of the Chicago & North Western railroad in 1882. The area was formerly known as Amik, general Algonquian for 'beaver.' (Sorenson)

Gotham [GO thuhm]. Richland. Richland City, named from Richland County, was founded in the late 1840s by Isaac Wallace, recently arrived from Vermont, and land speculator Garwood Greene. The community became an important commercial center and prospered for a decade until it was bypassed by the Chicago, Milwaukee & St. Paul railroad. William McNurlen, station agent for the railroad, founded a community upstream from Richland City, which he named Gotham, from the Gotham post office, established in 1882 by Myron W. Gotham, a Great Lakes ship captain. The Richland City post office was established in 1850, discontinued in 1887, and reestablished later that year. (Scott)

Grafton. Ozaukee. Town (1846) and Village (1896). Established about 1844 as Hamburgh, for Hamburg, Germany. The name was changed in 1846, probably by postmaster Phineas M. Johnson, for one of the Graftons in New England, themselves named directly or indirectly for Henry or Charles FitzRoy, eighteenth-century dukes of Grafton, England. (Eccles, 5)

Graham Corners. Fond du Lac. Named for Allen N. Graham, who established the Graham post office in October 1900.

Grand Chute [GRAN SHOOT]. Outagamie. Town (1849). Named for the greater of the falls on the Fox River. See Little Chute.

Grand Marsh. Adams. Named from the Grand Marsh post office, established in September 1850 and named for the local wetlands. The town of Grand Marsh was organized in 1853 and renamed Lincoln with the election of Abraham Lincoln in 1860.

Grand Rapids. Wood. Town (1850). See Wisconsin Rapids.

Grant. County. Organized in 1836. Named from the Grant River. The traditional account is that the river takes it name from an early trader or trapper named Grant, about whom little is known. The Wisconsin historian Louise Phelps Kellogg identifies a James Grant, "a prominent Montreal merchant" (112), who traded along the river in the last half of the eighteenth century. Cauffman, Finnegan, and Stauffacher mention an apparently different Grant, in their words "a strange loner" (4), who operated out of Fort Crawford at Prairie du Chien in the 1820s. This Grant reportedly traveled with only his trading stock and cooking gear, the latter including an iron pot which for convenience he wore on his head.

Grant. The several Grant townships in Wisconsin were named for Ulysses Grant, Commanding General of the Union Army in the last years of the Civil War and eighteenth president of the United States (1869–77). Most of the towns were named in the mid- or late 1860s when Grant's fame as a military leader was at its height.

Granton. Clark. Village (1816). Granton is named from its location in the Town of Grant with an additional syllable. The name was suggested by Edwin E. Woodman, former state senator and secretary of the Chicago, St. Paul, Minneapolis & Omaha railroad when the station was completed about 1890. In 1860 tavern owner Nelson Marsh applied for the post office of Maple Woods, which, through clerical error, was approved as Maple Works. That office was discontinued and reestablished as Granton in 1892. (Stennett, 177)

Grantsburg. Burnett. Town (organized as Burnett in 1864; changed to Grants-burg in 1866) and Village (1887). Founded by Canute Anderson, who emi-grated from Norway in 1851. By the late 1860s Anderson had built a saw-mill on Wood River, opened a tavern and general store, and laid out the community of Anderson. At about the same time Nimrod Hickerson established a "stopping place" for travelers that became known as Hicker-sonville and later as Wood River, several miles southwest of Anderson's store. With completion of the railroad in the mid-1880s Anderson's survival was ensured as was Wood River's demise. Anderson became known as Grantsburg at some point during the Civil War, for Union general Ulysses Grant. The name was officially changed from Anderson by the Wisconsin Legislature in April 1866. The Wood River post office, of which Nimrod Hickerson was the first postmaster, was changed to Grantsburgh in April 1867 and the spelling was modified in September 1893. Wood River, inci-dently, is a shortening of Ojibwa *wigobimij* 'tree or bark of the basswood.' The name was recorded by Nicollet in the 1830s as "Whitewood or Bass-wood River" (143, 241). (Crownhart, 13–15)

Granville. Milwaukee. Named by landowner Charles C. Everts for his fam-ily home, Granville, Washington County, New York, itself named for eighteenth-century British statesman John Carteret, the Second Earl Granville. (Stennett, 79)

Gratiot [GRASH uht]. Lafayette. Town and Village (1891). Named for Henry Gratiot [GRAY sho], French American pioneer, trader, and Indian agent, and his brother Jean Pierre, who operated a mining and smelting complex in the 1820s. The Gratiot's Grove post office was established in July 1834, Fortunatus Berry, postmaster. (*Lafayette County Bicentennial Book*, 115)

Gravesville. Calumet. Founded by Leroy Graves, who cleared land and built a sawmill about 1850. Graves represented the district in the Wisconsin Assembly in 1861. The post office was established in October 1860, Stephen H. Duley, postmaster. (Minaghan and Vanderhoef, 17)

Graytown. Barron, Dunn. Founded by Aaron B. Gray, from Steuben County, New York. Gray managed a hotel and kept a tavern in New Richmond from the mid-1870s. (Curtiss-Wedge and Jones, 214)

Green. County. Organized in December 1836. The name was proposed by William Boyles (Boyls), the Iowa County representative to the Wisconsin Territorial Legislature at the time. Boyles first suggested the name Rich-land. When this was rejected as "too plain," he offered Green, giving no reasons. Henry Gannett and others claim the namesake is Nathanael (Nathaniel) Greene, a hero of the Revolutionary War for whom several dozen counties and townships, especially in the Midwest, are named. Gannett's suggestion is supported by the spelling Greene, which was common for several years. However, Boyles may have chosen the name for his birthplace, Greene County, Pennsylvania, itself named for Nathanael Greene. (Butterfield, *History of Green County*, 257; Hamilton, 7)

Green Bay. Brown. The city of Green Bay (incorporated in 1854) is named from the large bay that separates Door County from the Wisconsin mainland. Native Americans surely had names for the bay, but what they were and what they meant is unclear. In his *Dictionary of the Otchipwe Language*, Bishop Frederic Baraga lists but does not gloss Ojibwa *Bodjwikwed* as the name of Green Bay. *Wikwed* is 'bay' but any relation of *bodj* to 'green' is unknown. Cassidy suggests the possible meaning 'shallow bay.' It is unknown if this name predates the French name *La Baye des Puants* 'the bay of the Winnebagoes,' which was in general use by the mid-1640s. (This name, literally 'the bay of the stinkers,' resulted from a misapplication of the Algonquian name Winnebago from a place to a people. See Winnebago.) With British occupation of the area in the 1760s the name Green Bay became common and existed beside French *La Baye Verte* 'the green bay.' Either the French or the English is the original and the other is a translation, but which is which is unclear. Also unclear is the source of "green." Jonathan Carver, who explored the area in 1766, suggests that Green Bay was an appropriate name because trees and flowers bloomed earlier there than at Mackinac. Nearly a century later, the naturalist Increase Lapham, Wisconsin's first notable scientist, gave the obvious (but not necessarily correct) explanation, stating that the name was derived from the unusually deep green color of the water in the bay. Stennett suggests that "green" may be a misinterpretation or misunderstanding of French *grande* 'big.' (*La Grande Baie* was occasionally found in eighteenth- and nineteenth-century writings.) In 1827 James Duane Doty referred to the bay as Grand Bay and to the community as Green Bay. The present city of Green Bay is a result of the 1838 merger of Navarino, platted in 1829 and named by site owner Daniel Whitney for the Greek seaport on Navarino Bay (modern Pylos) where a decisive naval battle establishing Greek independence was fought in 1827, and Astor, adjacent to Navarino, named for John Jacob Astor, owner of the American Fur Company. Tanktown, founded by Otto Tank, a Norwegian missionary, became part of the metropolitan area in 1850. See Ephraim; see Navarino. (Cassidy, *Brown County*; Cassidy, "Names of Green Bay," 168–78)

Greenbush. Sheboygan. Town (1849) and ppl. Founded by Sylvanus Wade, from Massachusetts by way of Pennsylvania and Illinois. Wade established a blacksmith shop and hotel that he called the Half Way House, presumed to be halfway between Sheboygan and Fond du Lac, about 1844. The following year the present name was suggested by Charles H. Robinson, most likely for Greenbush, Massachusetts, or possibly for Greenbush, Vermont. Wade established the post office in July 1846. (Buchen, 256)

Greendale. Milwaukee. Village (1939). Greendale is one of three experimental American communities founded by the Resettlement Administration of the U.S. Department of Agriculture in the 1930s to relocate struggling families from failing farms to planned communities. Fred L. Naumer, regional coordinator for the Resettlement Administration, designed and laid out Greendale in 1936. Greendale is in keeping with the names of two other resettlement communities, Greenbelt, Maryland, and Greenhills, Ohio. (Prey, 13)

Greenfield. Greenfield is a popular place name, occurring at least once in more than forty states. Wisconsin currently has one city and three townships named Greenfield. The Town of Greenfield in Milwaukee County was organized in 1839 as Kinnickinnic (q.v.), named from the Kinnickinnic River, and renamed early in 1841 from the Greenfield post office, established by Olney Harrington in the summer of 1839. Greenfield in Sauk County was named in 1853 by Nathan Dennison for his former home, Greenfield, Massachusetts. (Cole, *Standard History*, 411)

Green Grove. Clark. Town (1886). Named from the Green Grove post office, established in July 1878 by William Zassenhaus, itself perhaps named from the local scenery.

Green Lake. County. Green Lake is apparently an English translation of French *Lac Vert*, itself a translation of Ho-Chunk (Winnebago) *Tichora* 'green lake,' presumably named from the color of its water. Several members of the Dart family arrived about 1830 and the area became known as Dart's Ford or Dartford. In 1844 Anson Dart established the Green Lake post office, and in 1847 his son, Putnam, was the first postmaster at Dartford. Both offices were then in Marquette County. About 1870 the name of the Chicago & North Western station was formalized as Green Lake. (Reetz, 27)

Greenleaf. Brown. Named for Emery B. Greenleaf, general manager of the Milwaukee & Northern railroad. Formally platted in 1873 with establishment of the Greenleaf post office. (Cassidy, *Brown County*)

Greenstreet. Manitowoc. Joseph Zelenka (Josef Zelinka) emigrated from Czechoslovakia and opened a combination store, dance hall, and tavern, probably in the 1850s. Apparently Zelenka named the road in front of his establishment Green Street, for himself, Zelenka being derived from Czech *zeleny* 'green.' This became the name of the community when the post office began operating in 1875, with Zelenka as postmaster. (Manitowoc County Archives)

Greenville. Outagamie. Town (1850) and ppl. Named by Seymour Howe, the first postmaster, who was instrumental in organizing the township in 1850. Howe's reasons for choosing the name are unknown. (Stennett, 80)

Greenwood. Clark. City (1891). Founded by Elijah Eaton from Cherry Valley, New York. Eaton located in what became known as Eatontown in 1848. He served in the Wisconsin Assembly in the 1850s and platted Greenwood in 1871. The name was proposed by Mary Honeywell Miller, daughter of early settlers. In *History of Clark County* Curtiss-Wedge says the name was "befitting the beauty of the natural surroundings" (633).

Gregorville [GREG er vil]. Kewaunee. Named for a local Gregor family, perhaps that of Frank Gregor, a farmer born in Bohemia. Until he died in 1937, Gregor was Wisconsin's next-to-last surviving Civil War veteran. The post office was established in January 1899, Wenzel Zlab, postmaster.

Grellton. Jefferson. Named for the Grell family, especially John Frederick Grell, who emigrated from Mecklenburg, Germany, in 1855. Grell became a successful farmer and merchant, specializing in the production and sale of butter and eggs. The post office was established in November 1898, Henry C. Baurichter, postmaster. (Ott, 2:233)

Gresham [GRESH uhm]. Shawano. Village (1908). The community took its name from the Gresham post office, established in December 1883 and named by postmaster August Schmidt for Walter Quinton Gresham, at the time U.S. postmaster general under President Chester A. Arthur. Later Gresham served as secretary of the treasury and secretary of state under President Grover Cleveland. (Schmidt and Schmidt)

Grimms. Manitowoc. Probably named for Jacob Grimm. Born in Bavaria, Grimm was prominent in local affairs and a member of the county board in the 1860s. The post office was established in November 1874, Peter Mulholland, postmaster. (Falge, 317)

Grow. Rusk. Town (1905). Named by Frank Coggins and Howard Woodbury for their former home, Grow township (now Andover) in Anoka County, Minnesota, itself named for Galusha A. Grow, U.S. representative from Pennsylvania in the 1850s and Speaker of the House in the early 1860s. (*Rusk County History*, 22)

Guenther [GUHN ther]. Marathon. Town (1921). Named for one or more Guenther families. Leonhard Guenther emigrated from Germany and kept a tavern known as the Knowlton House from the 1850s. His family also operated several sawmills in the area. (Marchetti, 541)

Gurney. Iron. Town (1913) and ppl. The name was apparently chosen in the late 1890s by the first postmaster, Chauncey J. Medberry, for his business partner, James Theodore Gurney of Boston. Medberry and Gurney were inventors who held several patents for ice boxes, the refrigerators of their day. Medberry was president of the Gurney Refrigerator Company of Fond du Lac.

Guthrie [GUHTH ree]. Waukesha. Named by Charles R. Guthrie, the first postmaster, who established the office in January 1896.

Hackett. Price. Town (1887). The name was proposed by Charles H. Roser, an official of Worcester township, for his friend and business associate, Ephraim L. Hackett. Roser and Hackett had extensive lumber interests in the area. See Emery. (*Town of Emery Centennial*, 6)

Hager City. Pierce. The source of the name is uncertain. The community was most likely named for one or more Hager families. John Hager, from Germany, was established northeast of Maiden Rock by 1880. The post office was established in March 1887, John Schutte, postmaster.

Halder. Marathon. Named for George Halder, from Pittsburgh, Pennsylvania. Halder was a Wausau alderman and a Marathon County deputy sheriff. The post office was established by Josephine Heissel in July 1887. (Marchetti, 863)

Hale. Trempealeau. Town (1864) and ppl. Named for George Hale, who emigrated from Glastonbury, Connecticut, in 1858. Hale is generally considered the first settler in the township. (Curtiss-Wedge and Pierce, 92)

Hale Corner. Eau Claire. Named for the first known settler, Charles H. Hale, who arrived from Oxford County, Maine, in May 1856. (*Osseo Area Bicentennial Book*)

Hales Corners. Milwaukee. Village (1952). About 1836 Ebenezer Hale and his sons, Seneca and William, emigrated from Pompey, New York. The community was known as Hale's Corners by 1854 when the Muskego post office was relocated and renamed. The apostrophe was dropped in the late 1890s. (Shepherd and Weiler, 3)

Hallie [HAL ee]. Chippewa. Town (1915) and Lake Hallie. Reportedly named for Hallie Sherman, daughter of an officer of a local Civil War volunteer regiment. (Stennett, 177)

Halsey [HAWL zee]. Marathon. Town (1883). Named for lawyer and landowner Pierson Halsey, son of Lawrence Halsey, a partner in the Milwaukee law firm of Rietbrock, Halsey and Johnson, which founded Athens. See Rietbrock; see Johnson. (Marchetti, 969)

Hamburg [HAM berg]. Marathon. Town (1876) and ppl. Named for Hamburg, Germany, by German settlers, many from Pomerania. The spelling was changed from Hamburgh in 1893. Hamburg in Vernon County is also named for Hamburg, Germany. (Marchetti, 555)

Hamilton. Fond du Lac. Hamilton was founded in the 1880s as Ketcham, named from the Ketcham post office, established in August 1883 and named for James Ketcham. The names of the community, post office, and railroad station were changed in 1894 when Irenus K. Hamilton bought the local stone quarries. Hamilton and his brother, Woodman, emigrated from Lyme, New Hampshire, in 1855 and set up several sawmills near Fond du Lac. (Worthing)

Hamilton. La Crosse. The area of the present town of Hamilton was organized in November 1852 as Neshonoc, named from Neshonoc Creek, itself named from a general Algonquian word for 'two streams.' In March 1867 Neshonoc was vacated and reorganized as Hamilton, proposed by John M. Coburn for his birthplace in Madison County, New York, itself named for colonial patriot Alexander Hamilton. (Butterfield, *History of La Crosse County*, 821)

Hamilton. Ozaukee. Known as New Dublin, named by Irish settlers, until 1847 when the name was changed by site owner Edward H. Janssen, Wisconsin state treasurer in the 1850s, who probably chose the name in honor of William S. Hamilton, son of U.S. Founding Father Alexander Hamilton. William had business and political interests in Wisconsin, served in the Wisconsin Territorial Assembly in the early 1840s, and contributed significantly to the development of the lead mines around Wiota. (Eccles, 2)

Hammond. St. Croix. Town (1856) and Village (1880). Named by and for Rensselaer B. Hammond, a partner in the Mann, Hammond Land Company of Waukesha, which founded the community about 1856. (Stennett, 177)

Hampden. Columbia. Town (1849). Either a transfer from New England or from one of the Hampdens in Buckinghamshire, England. Town clerk Thomas B. Haslam has been credited with proposing the name. The Hampden post office was established in March 1850, Nelson B. Lloyd, postmaster. (J. Jones, 437)

Hancock. Waushara. The town was organized in 1855 as Sylvester, for William Sylvester, who kept a hotel called the Sylvester House from about 1850. It was renamed the following year from the Hancock post office, established in September 1854 by Benjamin Chamberlin, probably for Hancock, Addison County, Vermont. The community was formally platted in 1877 for site owner James F. Wiley, who represented the district in the state senate in the early 1880s. (Reetz, 113)

Hanerville [HAY ner vil]. Dane. Named from the Hanerville post office, established in October 1865 and named for James Haner, who emigrated from Easton, New York, in 1844. (Cassidy, *Dane County Place-Names*)

Haney [HAY nee]. Crawford. Town (1858). Named for John Haney, reportedly the first settler in the mid-1840s. About 1849 Haney crossed the Mississippi River and founded Lansing, Iowa. The Haney Valley post office operated from December 1862 until December 1867 and was reestablished as Haney in August 1883. (Butterfield, *History of Crawford and Richland Counties*, 611)

Hannibal. Taylor. Founded in 1903 by the Northwestern Lumber Company and named by its president, James T. Barber, for his former home, Hannibal, Missouri, itself named for Hannibal, the Carthaginian general who famously crossed the Alps into Roman territory in the second century BC. (Stennett, 177)

Hanover [HAN o ver]. Rock. Founded about 1844 by Joseph Hohensheldt and formerly known as Bass Creek. The name was formally changed about 1859 by site owner John Higgins for Hanover, Germany, and Hanover, Pennsylvania, itself named for Hanover, Germany. (Ehrlinger, 20)

Hansen. Wood. Town (organized as New Vesper in February 1901; changed to Hansen in May 1901). The area was originally known as Forest City, named from the Forest City post office, which operated from November 1867 until July 1869. In the mid-1880s Martin R. Hansen built a sawmill, laid out the community of Hansen, and established the Hansen post office. According to local sources, Hansen kept an informal bank at the mill and absconded with the millhands' deposits. See Vesper. (Jones and McVean, *History of Wood County*, 279)

Harding. Lincoln. Town. Named for Warren Gamaliel Harding, the recently elected twenty-ninth president of the United States when the town was organized in 1921. See Bancroft.

Harmony. Price, Vernon. Harmony is a popular place name, occurring in more than thirty states. In Vernon County the Town of Harmony was organized in 1855 and named from the Harmony post office, itself apparently named by postmaster and state assemblyman John McLees. In 1907, during discussions of a name for a new township in Price County, one Albert Soetebeer is said to have remarked, "If everyone wants to get along in harmony why not call it Harmony?" (*History of Vernon County*, 558; Hladish, Wudel, and Hladish, 11)

Harris. Marquette. The town was organized as Harris in 1853. The name was changed to Sharon in 1856 and back to Harris in 1857. Named from the Harrisville post office, established in March 1851 by postmaster James Harris. The community of Harrisville was platted in 1856 for site owners Joseph Farrington and William Stebbins. (Reetz, 69)

Harrison. The towns of Harrison in Lincoln (1889), Marathon (1888), and Waupaca (1890) Counties were named for Benjamin Harrison (1833–1901), twenty-third president of the United States, serving 1889–93.

Harrison. Grant. Town (1849). Named for William Henry Harrison (1773–1841), American military hero and political leader. Harrison is best remembered for his defeat of the Prophet and a force of Shawnee and Potawatomi warriors at the Battle of Tippecanoe in Indiana in 1811. Harrison was the first governor of Indiana Territory and ninth president of the United States, serving one month before dying in office in April 1841.

Harrisville. Marquette. Named for James Harris, who established the post office in March 1851.

Harshaw. Oneida. Named for Henry B. Harshaw, from Argyle, New York. Harshaw was postmaster at Oshkosh and in June 1891, when Charles Norway established the Harshaw post office in Oneida County, Harshaw was treasurer of Wisconsin.

Hartford. Washington. The area was first known as Rubicon, from the Rubicon River. When the town was organized in 1846 several names were considered, including Wayne and Benton, but Wright, for Silas Wright, then governor of New York, was eventually chosen. That name appealed to few and a year later it was changed to Hartford. By one account, Hartford was suggested by a settler from Hartford, Connecticut, who proposed the name after winning a coin toss. By another, Hartford is a blend of *heart*, supposed to be a native name derived from the shape of Pike Lake, and *ford*, where the Rubicon could easily be crossed. Most likely the name is a transfer from New England; Hartfords in New York and Vermont, as well as Connecticut, are possible sources. The post office was established in December 1847, Lewis E. Peck, postmaster. (*Heritage of Hartford*, 11)

Hatchville. Dunn, St. Croix, Pierce. Named for Frank and Ed Hatch, brothers who owned and operated a combination store and community center. Frank established the post office in November 1889. (Dunn County Historical Society, 81)

Hatfield. Jackson. Founded as Black River Station about 1873. Renamed for Edwin F. Hatfield of New York City, secretary of the Marquette,

Houghton & Ontonagon railroad and president of the Green Bay & Minnesota railroad in the 1880s. (*Historic Hatfield*, 8)

Hatley. Marathon. Village (1912). Probably named by Harvey Wadleigh for his former home, Hatley, Quebec, Canada. Wadleigh, who immigrated to Stevens Point in 1858 at the age of thirteen, became a successful businessman by providing ties to the railroads in the 1870s. The post office was established in December 1881, Thomas L. Moody, postmaster. (Pickering and Pickering, 10)

Hauer [HOW er]. Sawyer. Origin uncertain. According to a local account, Hauer is a misspelling or misunderstanding of Howard, the family name of Claude Howard, a local shopkeeper in the early decades of the twentieth century. (Lofgren, 22–23)

Haugen [HAW guhn]. Barron. Village (1918). Founded about 1886 and named for Nils Pederson Haugen, born in Norway in 1849. Haugen was a local lawyer and politician, serving in the state assembly and in the U.S. Congress from 1887 until 1895. (Stennett, 178)

Haven. Sheboygan. The source of the name is uncertain. Most likely Haven is an Americanization of the Dutch or German family name Hayen. Several Hayen families located in Wisconsin in the latter half of the nineteenth century, and a community called Hayen was reported east of Haven. The Haven post office was established in July 1897, Frederick W. Franzmeier, postmaster.

Hawkins. Rusk. Town (1903) and Village (1922). Probably named by the Minneapolis, St. Paul & Sault Ste. Marie railroad for Marsh P. Hawkins, secretary and treasurer of the Minneapolis & St. Louis branch of the railroad in the 1880s. The post office was established in October 1888 by Herbert W. True, namesake of the Town of True (q.v.).

Hawthorne. Douglas. Town (1907) and ppl. The community developed around the Chicago, Minneapolis, St. Paul & Omaha railroad station established in the early 1880s. The name was chosen by David E. Roberts, a Superior attorney and county judge, for W. B. Hawthorne, who operated the first logging camp in the area. (Pellman, 91)

Hayes. Oconto. By a local account, Hayes was named from Hayes Creek, itself named for an early lumberman named Hayes, who gave his name to the stream and then left the area. Another, and perhaps more likely, possibility is that the community was named from the Hayes post office, established in March 1879, by Julius Suring, the namesake of Suring (q.v.), itself likely named for then President Rutherford B. Hayes. ("Hayes, Oconto County")

Hayton. Calumet. Hayton was founded in the 1850s by Henry Modlin, who chose the name for his birthplace, Hayton, Cumberland, England.

Previously known as Wallerville, for early settler Parley Waller and also as Charlestown, named from the Charlestown post office, established in 1849 by William Roberts. (Minaghan and Vanderhoef)

Hayward. Sawyer. Town (1883) and City (1915). Named for Anthony Judson Hayward, a business associate of Philatus Sawyer, the namesake of Sawyer County. Hayward formed the North Wisconsin Lumber Company in 1880 and became a wealthy man. Unfortunately, he lost most of his money during the Alaska gold rush and on ill-advised investments in the Gogebic iron mines. (Marple, 74–75)

Hazel Green. Grant. Town (1849) and Village (1867). For unknown reasons Captain Charles McCoy, a veteran of the Black Hawk War, suggested the name Hazel Green when the post office was established in 1837. The community was informally known as Hardscrabble, a name given to any locale where it was difficult to eke out an existence. (Holford, 544)

Hazelhurst. Oneida. Town (1890) and ppl. Hazelhurst grew around the mills of the Yawkey-Lee Lumber Company, established by Cyrus C. Yawkey, his uncle William, and George W. Lee in 1888. The local account is that Cyrus's wife, Alice, chose the name for the hazel bushes growing along the railroad tracks. Cyrus Yawkey established the post office in August 1889. (Doucette et al., 12, 88)

Hazen Corners [HAY zuhn]. Crawford. Named for the Hazen family, especially Aaron Hazen, who emigrated from New York or New Jersey in the early 1840s. (Butteris)

Heafford Junction [HEF erd]. Lincoln. Named for George H. Heafford, General Passenger Agent for the Chicago, Milwaukee & St. Paul railroad, which built through the area in the early 1890s. The post office was established in March 1898, Warren Slater, postmaster.

Heath Mills [HEETH]. Jefferson. In the mid-1840s John Heath built a sawmill and a gristmill on Bark River. The community that grew around the mills became known as Heath's Mill or Heathsburg, but was platted as Sullivan, presumably named for Sullivan township, in 1856, and later renamed Heath Mills. The post office was established as Erfurt, named for Erfurt, Germany, in September 1861, Christian Vinz, postmaster. (Gnacinski and Longley, 91)

Hebels Corners [HEB uhlz]. Brown. Named for landowner Joseph Hebel, who emigrated from Germany about 1866. The Hebel post office operated from May 1899 until the end of 1907. (*Commemorative Biographical Record of the West Shore of Green Bay*, 180)

Hebron [HEE bruhn]. Jefferson. Town (1847) and ppl. The area was first known as Bark River, where a group of land speculators from Milwaukee, organized as the Rock River Claiming Company, dammed the river and built a sawmill in the 1830s. According to Swart, "The name of Hebron was decided by the participants of a 'sing' held at the Munro School, with everyone agreeing that the title of the hymn 'Hebron,' would be a good name for the new town" (77). While this account of the naming of Hebron may be correct, it is not unique to Wisconsin. Several other communities named Hebron, including Hebron in McHenry County, Illinois, have similar naming stories.

Heffron [HEF ruhn]. Portage, Waushara. Founded by John J. Heffron, a real estate developer from Stevens Point. The post office was established in January 1901 by Frank Wiora. (Rosholt, *Our County, Our Story*, 264)

Hegg [HEG]. Trempealeau. Probably named in honor of Hans Christian Heg, born in Buskerud, Norway. Heg, an outspoken antislavery activist, led the Fifteenth Wisconsin Volunteers, known as the Scandinavian Regiment, in the Civil War. He was mortally wounded at Chickamauga in September 1863. The post office was established in August 1871, Knud K. Hallenger, postmaster. (Curtiss-Wedge and Pierce, 82)

Helena [huh LEE nuh]. Iowa. Henry Dodge, for whom Dodge County is named, established the original Helena in 1828 to expedite the mining of lead ore in the Mineral Point area. A second Helena grew around the shot tower at what is now Tower Hill State Park. Helena's present location is some four miles northeast of the shot tower. Dodge likely chose the name for his daughter Christiana Helen. The post office was established in May 1836. (Folkedahl, 288, 292)

Helenville. Jefferson. Named from the Helenville post office, established in February 1851 by the remarkably named site owner and postmaster Ortgies Bullwinkel, who probably chose the name for his wife, Helen Bullwinkel. (Stennett, 83)

Helvetia [hel VEE shuh]. Waupaca. Helvetia is the Latin name of Switzerland. John H. Leuthold, who was born in Zurich, Switzerland, and immigrated to Waupaca County about 1857, suggested the name when the town was organized in 1860. Leuthold held several local offices, including township chair and justice of the peace. (*Commemorative Biographical Record of the Upper Wisconsin Counties*, 519)

Hematite [HEE muh teyet]. Florence. Named for the local deposits of hematite (iron oxide). (Stennett, 83)

Hemlock. Clark. Reportedly named for its location near a grove of hemlock trees. The post office was established in October 1883. (Curtiss-Wedge, *History of Clark County*, 664)

Hendren [HEN druhn]. Clark. Town (1910). Named for the Reverend William T. Hendren, who came to Neillsville in 1872 and was instrumental in establishing Presbyterian churches in Neillsvlle and Greenwood. (Scholtz)

Henrietta. Richland. Town (1855). Named for Henrietta Laws, daughter of James Laws, an early settler who operated a ferry across the Wisconsin River near Avoca. (Butterfield, *History of Crawford and Richland Counties*, 1140)

Henrysville. Brown. Named from the Henryville post office, established in May 1879 by postmaster John Henry Osterloh. (Cassidy, *Brown County*)

Herbster [HERB ster]. Bayfield. Reportedly named for Billy Herbster, camp cook for the Cranberry Lumber Company. The post office was established in November 1895, Walter A. Gould, postmaster. (Rohe, "Place-names," 127)

Herman. Shawano, Sheboygan. Herman in Sheboygan County was organized in 1850 as Howard, named for Hugh B. Howard, the namesake of Howards Grove (q.v.). The name was changed in 1851 at the request of German settlers for the Order of the Sons of Herman, a charitable and beneficent society formed in 1840 in New York City to foster German language and culture. The society took its name from the Germanic warrior who defeated a Roman army in the first decade of the first century. Known in Latin as Arminius, he was nicknamed Herman the German. The fraternal Sons of Herman was especially active in Wisconsin in the middle of the nineteenth century. The Town of Herman in Shawano County is likely named for the Sons of Herman as well. (Buchen, 336; McDevitt, 143)

Herold. Buffalo. Named for Wilhelm (William) Herold, born in Thuringia in central Germany. By 1860 Herold had settled on a farm near Alma. He established the post office, which he named for himself, in April 1891. (Pattison, 105)

Herrington. La Crosse. Named for Frank C. Herrington, yardmaster for the Chicago, Burlington & Northern railroad from the late 1880s. (*Biographical History of La Crosse*, 185)

Hersey [HER see]. St. Croix. Named in 1873 by the first postmaster, Sarles T. Adams, for Samuel F. Hersey, a partner in the lumber firm of Hersey and Staples of Stillwater, Minnesota. The community was organized along patriotic lines; the first streets included Liberty, Red White and Blue, Eagle, Independence, State, and Union. (Petranovich, 3)

Hertel [HERT uhl]. Burnett. Named from the Hertel post office, established in July 1898 by shopkeeper and postmaster Otto Hertel.

Hewett. Clark. Town (1875). Named for James Hewett, from Minerva, New York. Hewett was a lumberman, farmer, first mayor of Neillsville, and founder of Hewettville, a now-vanished community west of Neillsville. The post office was established as Hewettsville in October 1871, Sheldon B. Hewett, postmaster. (Curtiss-Wedge, *History of Clark County*, 570)

Hewitt. Marathon. Town (1894). Named for William Hewitt, a member of the Marathon county board and first president of the Village of Rothschild. (*Town of Hewitt: 1776 Bicentennial 1976*, 2)

Hewitt. Wood. Village (1973). In the late 1880s Frank Cramer established a blacksmith shop, and Robert Braasch opened a general store on the line of the Wisconsin Central railroad at a point known as 28, presumed to be twenty-eight miles from Stevens Point. Henry Hewitt, a lumberman from Menasha, established a side track that became known as Hewitt Switch. The name was formalized as Hewitt about 1882. The post office was established as Kreuser in May 1882 and changed to Hewitt the following year. (Jones and McVean, *History of Wood County*, 263–64)

High Bridge. Ashland. Named for the bridge some ninety feet above Silver Creek, built by the Wisconsin Central railroad in 1873. The area was formerly known as Silver Creek, a translation of Ojibwa *joniia sibi* 'silver river.'

Hilbert. Calumet. Village (1898). Established by the Milwaukee & Northern railroad in 1872 on land owned by Horatio Smith, president of the railroad, and Guido Pfister, a major stockholder. Named for Heliodore J. Hilbert, who was born in Luxembourg and immigrated to the U.S. in 1849. Hilbert, called by historians DeRozier and Halbach "one of Wisconsin's most notable early engineers" (13), was chief engineer for both the Winona & St. Peter and the Milwaukee & Northern railroads, and later Milwaukee city engineer. (DeRozier and Halbach)

Hiles [HEYELZ]. Forest. Town (1903) and ppl. Founded by Franklin P. Hiles of Milwaukee about 1902. Several years later Hiles sold the site and his lumber interests to the Foster Mueller Lumber Company of Milwaukee. ("Memories of Forest Co.," 188)

Hiles. Wood. Town (1901). Named for George Hiles, one of the wealthiest and most influential businessmen in central Wisconsin in the second half of the nineteenth century. Hiles was a successful sawmill operator and distributor of wood products but is best known for building the railroad to Dexter and to Merrillan. (Hiles and Hiles, 12)

Hill. Price. Town (1892). Probably named from Timm's Hill, Wisconsin's highest summit at just over 1,950 feet. The peak was apparently first known as Ostergren kulle 'ostergren hill' in honor of Knute Ostergren and renamed for Timothy Gahan, who operated a logging camp on Timm's Lake. ("Rib Lake Historical Society Newspaper Notes")

Hill Point. Sauk. Formerly known as Tuckerville, named for William Tucker. Renamed for one or another local prominences. (Cole, *A Standard History of Sauk County*, 417)

Hillsboro. Vernon. Town (1855) and City (1885). Named for the Hill brothers—William, Alonzo, Valentia, and Icabod—early settlers from Vermont. Valentia (Valencia) Hill filed one of the first land claims in the area about 1850. He previously had kept a general store and operated a sawmill on the Baraboo River. (*Commemorative Biographical Record of the Upper Lake Region*, 176)

Hillsdale. Barron. Originally known as Mooney's Mill for the sawmill and post office established by William Mooney in the 1870s. The Lee and Dickinson Lumber Company brought a second mill to the area a decade later. William Smith, lawyer for Lee and Dickinson, is generally credited with suggesting the name Hillsdale about 1884 but the reason is unknown. (Gordon and Curtiss-Wedge, 1139)

Hines. Douglas. Formerly known as Holmes, the community was formally named about 1902 for Edward Hines, founder of the Chicago-based Edward Hines Lumber Company, which had extensive timber interests in northern Wisconsin. The post office was established in January 1903, Donald McDonald, postmaster. (Stennett, 178)

Hingham [HING uhm]. Sheboygan. When the community was founded about 1850, several names were considered, including Hobartville for Edward Hobart, the site owner, and Tibbittsville, for postmaster Lemuel Tibbitts. Charles Rogers, a local merchant, suggested Hingham for his former home in Massachusetts, itself named for Hingham, Norfolk, England. (Buchen, 265)

Hintz. Oconto. Named in 1898 by the first postmaster, Robert Hintz. Hintz, born in Germany, held several local offices and represented the district in the Wisconsin Assembly in 1910.

Hixon. Clark. Town (1873). Named for Gideon Cooley Hixon, from Vermont, characterized by Scholtz as "a wealthy lumberman of La Crosse."

Hixton. Jackson. Town (1856) and Village (1920). Hixton is a compression with respelling of Hicks Town, named for early settler John L. Hicks, who emigrated from Oneida County, New York, about 1846. The community was platted as Williamsport about 1865 and renamed for the town about 1870. The post office was established as Pole Grove in 1856 and changed to Hixton in August 1874. (*Jackson County, a History*, 19)

Hoard. Clark. Town (1889). Named for William Dempster Hoard (1836–1918), governor of Wisconsin, 1889–91. Governor Hoard is generally considered the father of the Wisconsin dairy industry. (Scholtz)

Hobart [HO bahrt]. Brown. Town (1903). Named for John Henry Hobart, Episcopal Bishop of New York, who was instrumental in settling Native Americans on the Oneida reservation in the 1820s. Hobart founded Geneva

College in Geneva, New York, later named Hobart College in his honor. (Cassidy, *Brown County*)

Hochheim [HAHK heyem]. Dodge. Named by settlers from Hochheim, Hesse, in western Germany. The post office was established in February 1900, Adolph G. Schwanke, postmaster.

Hoepkers Corners [HEP kerz]. Dane. Named for the Hoepker family. John Heinrich Hoepker emigrated from Germany about 1846 and became a prominent livestock and pig farmer. (Cassidy, *Dane County Place-Names*)

Hofa Park [HAH fuh]. Shawano. Named for John J. Hof(f), who founded the J. J. Hof Land Company in the 1880s, primarily for the purpose of establishing Polish settlements in the area. See Pulaski.

Hoffman Corners. Monroe. Named from the Hoffman's Corners post office, established in 1857 by postmaster Gilbert Hoffman.

Hogarty. Marathon. Named for John Crump Hogarty, who emigrated from what is now West Virginia about 1845. Hogarty established a trading post about 1850, founded the post office in 1881, and served as the first chair of the Town of Harrison in 1888. (Marchetti, 571)

Holcombe [HOL kuhm]. Chippewa. Town (1905) (now Lake Holcombe) and ppl. Founded about 1902. Reportedly named for a Milwaukee friend by William (or Walter) A. Scott, general manager of the Chicago, St. Paul, Minneapolis & Omaha railroad. (Stennett, 178)

Holland. Brown. Town (1853) and ppl. First known as Franciscus Bosch for the St. Franciscus Bosch ('St. Francis Bush') Catholic Church, organized in 1848 by Dutch settlers from the parent community at Little Chute. The name was formalized as Holland with establishment of the post office in November 1860 by postmaster Bertus Vandenberg. (Cassidy, *Brown County*)

Holland. La Crosse. Town (1857). Named for or by Dutch colonists who followed early Norwegian settlers from the mid-1850s. (Bryant, 227)

Holland. Sheboygan. Town (1849). Named for the Netherlands (Holland). The first Dutch settlers in the mid-1840s included Jan Zeeveld and Leunis DeVos, followed by several families led by the Reverend Peter Zonne. See Cedar Grove.

Hollandale. Iowa. Village (1910). Named for Bjorn Haaland, who emigrated from Elne, Norway, in the spring of 1846. Haaland, his name Angelicized to Ben Holland, laid out the community of Benville in 1887 and gave his name to the post office, established as Holindale in 1888, changed to Hollindale in 1889, and to Hollandale in 1890. Holland was the first president of Hollandale and served in the Wisconsin Legislature, 1898–1903. (Lauper, Thompson, and Thompson, 5)

Hollister. Langlade. Named for Seymour W. Hollister, an Oshkosh business-man who was a partner with Leander Choate in the Choate-Hollister Furniture Company and founder of the Hollister and Jewell Lumber Company. See Choate.

Holmen. La Crosse. Village (1946). Earlier known as Frederickstown for Frederick Anderson, the community blacksmith. Formally named by the first postmaster, Charles A. Sjolander, with establishment of the post office in September 1875. The origin of the name is uncertain but the namesake is likely William Steele Holman [*sic*], U.S. representative from Indiana, who served in sixteen congresses from the 1850s through the 1890s. He was in office when the post office was named. (Uhls and Gullickson, 8)

Holt. Marathon. Named about 1900 by postmaster Adolph J. Torgerson, probably for Holt, Sørlandet, Norway, Torgerson's ancestral home.

Holton. Marathon. Town (1875). Named for George Holeton [*sic*], a carpenter from Poland, Ohio. Holton served in several local offices, including town chair. By about 1896 Holeton had become Holton through popular etymology. (*Holton's Heritage*)

Holway [HAHL way]. Taylor. Town (1889). Named for Nymphus B. Holway, from Maine, who was one of Wisconsin's richest lumbermen in the late nineteenth century. (*Footsteps of La Crosse*, 2)

Holy Cross. Ozaukee. Probably named from the Holy Cross Catholic Church, established by settlers from Luxembourg and Belgium in the late 1840s. The post office operated from December 1866 through July 1904.

Homestead. Florence. Town (1894). The origin of the name is uncertain but the town was likely named in commemoration of the Homestead Act of 1862, which allowed thousands of settlers to acquire government land. The post office operated from June 1896 through July 1900. The first postmaster was Eli Grimord.

Honey Creek. Sauk. Town (1849). The Honey Creek settlement was founded in 1842 by Bartholomew Ragatz and his sons, Christian and Thomas, from Canton Graubuenden, Switzerland. Named from Honey Creek, probably the location of a number of "bee trees," the source of honey, the primary sweetener of early settlers. Possibly a translation of Ho-Chunk (Winnebago) *Naumatonan*. (Derleth, 18)

Hoopers Mill. Jefferson. Named for the George Hooper family, which emigrated from Cornwall, England, in 1845. After failing to find the wealth they sought in the California gold fields, Richard Hooper and his brother, Thomas, established a sawmill on Rock Creek about 1853, around which the community of Hoopers Mill developed. (Ott, 1:244, 2:316)

Hopokoekau Beach [ho puh KEE kow]. Fond du Lac. Named for Hopo-koekau, the Winnebago wife of Sabrevoir de Carrie, a French Canadian army officer of the mid-eighteenth century. De Carrie and Hopokoekau established a line of distinguished nineteenth-century Winnebago leaders named Decorra. Hopokoekau is the heroine of Wisconsin poet William Ellery Leonard's 1912 poetic drama, "Glory of the Morning." See Dekorra. (Worthing)

Horicon [HOR uh kan, HOR uh kuhn]. Dodge. City (1897). Until the mid-1840s the area around Horicon Marsh was known variously as Elk Village, Indian Ford, Great Marsh of the Winnebagos, or Hubbard's Rapids, the last for landowner Henry Hubbard, governor of New Hampshire in the early 1840s and the namesake of the Town of Hubbard (q.v.). In 1846 William Larabee, from Whitehall, New York, purchased part of Hubbard's holdings, established a general store, and laid out the community of Horicon, which he named from the novel *The Last of the Mohicans* by James Fenimore Cooper. Cooper had taken Horicon to be an indigenous name for Lake George in upstate New York, near which lived a tribe of Native Americans called by the French "Les Horicons," with *horicon* taken to mean 'silvery water.' (Vogel, *Indian Names*, 88)

Horns Corners. Ozaukee. Named for Cedarburg lawyer Frederick W. Horn, the site owner and a prominent political figure. Horn served eight terms in the state assembly in the 1850s and 1860s. The post office was established in January 1857, Ernst Frankenberg, postmaster. (Eccles, 3)

Horseman. Barron. Apparently named for John Edward Horsman [*sic*], from Guelph, Ontario, Canada. Horsman was a hardware salesman who was elected Barron County treasurer in 1890. The post office (with adjusted spelling) was established in July 1893, Joel Ackerman, postmaster. This is the only community named Horseman in the United States. (Forrester, 497)

Hortonia [hor TON ee uh]. Outagamie. Both the town of Hortonia (1849) and the village of Hortonville (1894) are named for Alonzo Erastus Horton, who came to Wisconsin from Connecticut in the 1830s and established a sawmill on Black Otter Creek. He bought the site of Hortonville in 1848 and laid out the community the following year. Horton left Wisconsin for California, where he was instrumental in the organization and development of San Diego in the 1860s. (Balliet, 74)

Houlton [HOLT uhn]. St. Croix. Named in 1880 by Thomas Haggerty, the first postmaster, for Houlton, Maine, his birthplace in Aroostook County. (Ericson)

How. Oconto. Town (1875). Named for Calvin F. How Jr., a businessman, banker, and insurance executive of Wisconsin and Minnesota. ("Oconto County, Wisconsin: Town of How")

Howard. Brown. Town (1835) and Village (1959). Named from Fort Howard, the military post constructed by American forces in 1816 at Green Bay and named for Benjamin Howard, U.S. congressman from Kentucky, governor of Louisiana Territory, and brigadier general in the War of 1812. (Cassidy, *Brown County*)

Howards Grove. Sheboygan. Village (1967). The Howard's Grove post office was established in the summer of 1849 by postmaster Hugh B. Howard. About the same time Henry G. Mueller laid out Mueller Villa, known as Millersville, Miller being the approximate English pronunciation of the German name Mueller. In 1967 the two communities merged as Howards Grove-Millersville. This awkward name was shortened to Howards Grove in 1971. The area was also known as Pitchville, a name derived from German *pech* 'wax,' especially 'cobbler's wax' for the local shoemakers (several of whom were appropriately named Schumacher). See Herman. (Buchen, 337; Hildebrand, 79–80)

Hoyt. Iron. Named for New York banker and financier Colgate Hoyt, a trustee of the Wisconsin Central railroad in the 1880s. See Abbotsford. (R. Martin, 71)

Hub City. Richland. Hub City grew around a collection of gristmills and sawmills first erected in the early 1850s by Michael and James Ghormley. The mills were purchased in 1881 by Targe G. Mandt, a Stoughton wagonmaker originally from Norway. The first post office application in 1882 called for the name Mandtville. When this name was rejected the office was established as Stalwart and subsequently changed to Hub City. The name is most likely in honor of Hubbard C. "Hub" Atkins, an officer of several railroads, including the Chicago, Milwaukee & St. Paul. (Scott)

Hubbard. Dodge. Town (1846). Named for Henry Hubbard, governor of New Hampshire in the early 1840s, who had extensive land holdings in the area. See Horicon. (Hubbell, 70)

Hubbard. Rusk. Town (1911). Probably named for Minneapolis businessman Arthur O. Hubbard, who, along with Herbert and George Puffer, established the Puffer-Hubbard manufacturing company about 1901. (Morrissey and Moore, 29)

Hubbleton. Jefferson. Probably named for landowner Levi Hubbell (1808–76), state assemblyman, circuit court judge, and an ex officio justice of the Wisconsin Supreme Court. Charges of corruption led to Hubble's impeachment in the early 1850s and kept him from becoming a major political figure in the early years of Wisconsin statehood. The post office was established in July 1850, Lemuel Griggs, postmaster. Also known as Hubbleville. (Swart, 198)

Hubertus [hyoo BERT uhs]. Washington. Named from the St. Hubertus Catholic Congregation, established about 1846, itself named for St. Hubert or Hubertus, the first Bishop of Liège in the early eighth century. Hubert is the patron saint of dogs, hunters, mathematicians, metal workers, and opticians. This is the only Hubertus in the United States.

Hudson. St. Croix. Town (organized as Willow River in 1851; changed to Hudson in 1852) and City (1858). From 1848 the area was known as Buena Vista in recognition of the 1847 Battle of Buena Vista during the Mexican War. The following year, John Henning laid out the community of Willow River and Philip Aldrich established the Willow River post office. The names of the post office, community, and township were changed to Hudson in 1852 at the suggestion of Alfred Day for his former home in the Hudson River valley. North Hudson was laid out some years later by Daniel A. and Abram H. Baldwin, officers of the West Wisconsin railroad. The post office was established in July 1876. See Baldwin. (Easton, 843)

Hughey [HYOO ee]. Taylor. Named for Elmer K. Hughey, president of the Yellow River Lumber Company of Stillwater, Minnesota, and partner in the lumber firm of Dorchester and Hughey, which managed several lumbering operations in the last years of the nineteenth century. (Easton, 258)

Huilsburg [HILZ berg]. Dodge. Named for John and Samuel Huels, brothers who emigrated from Bavaria in 1847. The community of Huelsburgh grew around a store and brewery operated by John Huels. The post office was established as Huilsburgh [*sic*] in May 1873, August Thielke, postmaster. (*History of Washington and Ozaukee Counties*, 584)

Hull. Marathon. Town (1873). Named for David B. Hull, an early settler and the first township chair. (Marchetti, 552)

Hull. Portage. Town (1858). The origin of the name is uncertain. Rosholt suggests that the town was named by English settlers for Hull, Yorkshire, England. The post office was established in March 1884, Frank W. Muzzy, postmaster. (Rosholt, *Our County, Our Story*, 306)

Hulls Crossing. Sheboygan. Reportedly named for J. D. Hull, who donated land for the Chicago & North Western railroad station. (Stennett, 85)

Humbird. Clark. Founded in 1869 by the West Wisconsin railroad. Named for Jacob Humbird, who, along with Daniel A. Baldwin of New York, financed and built the West Wisconsin line. Jacob and John Humbird were leaders in railroad construction in Wisconsin in the middle years of the nineteenth century. See Baldwin. (Curtiss-Wedge, *History of Clark County*, 556)

Humboldt [HUHM bolt]. Brown. Town and ppl. The town was organized in November 1859 and named for the German explorer, geographer, geologist, and natural scientist Friedrich Wilhelm Karl Heinrich Alexander von Humboldt, who had died six months earlier. Humboldt was well known in the middle of the nineteenth century, and several dozen U.S. communities and townships were named in his honor. (J. Rudolph, 25)

Hunting. Shawano. According to Stennett, the community "was so named because there was much game in the vicinity, that allowed successful 'hunting' hereabouts. It also happened that a nearby landowner had this name, and hence the place had two reasons for its name" (85). The post office was established in June 1880, Lucius A. Bessey, postmaster.

Huntington. St. Croix. The earlier spelling Huntingdon suggests the name is a transfer, probably from Huntingdon, Quebec, Canada, the former home of postmaster John Bowron, who established the office in 1858. (Ericson)

Hurley. Iron. City (1918). Founded as Glen Hurley by the Milwaukee, Lake Shore & Western railroad in 1885. Named for Michael Angelo Hurley, a Wausau lawyer who apparently argued and won a lawsuit on behalf of the Northern Chief Mining Company, of which he was part owner, and in lieu of a fee asked that the community be named for him. (Lewis, 6)

Huron. Chippewa. The ultimate source of the name is the Huron (Wyandot) Native Americans, an Iroquoian people. Possibly a transfer from Michigan or New York, the Wisconsin name is more likely a transfer by settlers from Huron, Ontario, perhaps at the suggestion of Duncan H. McElmurry, the first postmaster in 1888, himself a native of Ontario.

Hurricane. Grant. Formerly known as Hurricane Corners. Probably named from a particularly bad storm. The Hurricane post office was established in September 1838 by John Wise. (*Grant County History*, 327)

Husher. Racine. Origin unknown. Local accounts suggest that Husher may be a mishearing or misrecording of Hoosier, from nearby Hoosier Creek. Indeed, Husher has long been reported as a variant of Hoosier, a nickname for anyone associated with Indiana. The post office was established in April 1891, Charles S. Meissner from Saxony, Germany, postmaster. (Weber, 30)

Hustisford [HYOOS tis ferd]. Dodge. Town (1845) and Village (1870). Named for and by John Hustis. After graduating from Yale University and practicing law in Mount Carmel, New York, Hustis went west in the fall of 1835. He became active in the cultural and civic affairs of Milwaukee, serving for a time as editor of the Milwaukee *Sentinel* newspaper. Hustis purchased several thousand acres on the Rock River at a site known simply as "the rapids," where he laid out Hustisford in the late 1830s. (*Celebrating Hustisford's 150 Year Heritage*, 12)

Hustler [HUHS ler]. Juneau. Village (1914). Hustler grew around a freight platform built by the West Wisconsin railroad in the early 1870s. The community was platted about 1896 for site owner Harmon Ranney and named from the Hustler post office, established by Ezra Jewel in 1891. Details are unclear but the name was likely chosen to suggest that the citizens of the area were "hustlers," that is, energetic and resourceful. It is one of a half dozen places so named in the United States. (*Juneau County*, 85)

Hutchins. Shawano. Town (organized as Hutchinson in 1878; changed to Hutchins in 1880). Named for the Hutchins family. Lyman Hutchins was an early settler from Rutland, Vermont. (*Shawano County Centuarawno*)

Hyde [HEYED]. Iowa. Named for William Hyde, who emigrated from New York and established a sawmill and gristmill on Mill Creek in 1856. The post office was established as Hyde's Mills in March 1864, Lorenzo D. Billington, postmaster. (Phillips, 10)

Idlewild. Door. Idlewild grew around a resort hotel built by Jarvis T. Wright in 1879. The source of the name is unclear. Idlewild is an attractive place name, evoking leisure amid unspoiled nature, as the earlier spelling Idyll-wild suggests. A native of New York, Wright may have chosen the name for one of the several Idlewilds near Manhattan, or Idlewild may have been proposed by Charles Henrotin, a Chicago financier, real estate developer, and diplomat. Idlewild was the name of several clubs, business ventures, and apartment buildings in Chicago when Wright built the Idlewild hotel. (Holand, 172)

Iduna [eye DOO nuh]. Trempealeau. In Norse mythology, Iduna tends the tree of shining apples, the source of eternal youth and vitality. The local account is that Iduna was proposed by A. H. Anderson when the post office was established in April 1900. However, John O. Hovre, the first postmaster, was of Norwegian ancestry and may have chosen the name himself. It is the only Iduna in the United States. (Curtiss-Wedge and Pierce, 274)

Imalone [eye muh LON]. Rusk. The source of this colorful, intriguing, and unique name is unknown. Several origins, all popular etymologies, have been proposed. By one, a service station owner with the equally colorful name of "Snowball" Anderson left his gas station in the hands of one Bill Granger. A salesman stopped by and asked Granger the name of the place;

he shrugged and said, "I'm alone," which the salesman dutifully wrote on his invoice. By another, Anderson named the station Imalone "because he was." (Stingl)

Independence. Trempealeau. City (1942). Independence was founded in the spring of 1876 when the Green Bay & Lake Pepin railroad station was established. The name was chosen in honor of the centennial year of the signing of the Declaration of Independence, either by Giles Cripps, the postmaster at Elk Creek, or by site owner and general manager of the railroad, David M. Kelly. (Gamroth, 15)

Indianford. Rock. Named from the site where Native Americans forded (or were thought to have forded) the Rock River. The post office was established in February 1863, Lovell M. Kellogg, postmaster. (Becker, 47)

Ingram [ING gruhm]. Rusk. Village (1907). Ingram grew around a railroad siding established about 1887 and named for Orrin Henry Ingram, a major figure in the lumber industry of the Chippewa Valley in the last half of the nineteenth century. Ingram was a logging and milling innovator and a community benefactor. (*Rusk County History*, 25)

Inlet. Walworth. Named for the inlet, the narrow passage connecting Delavan Lake with its northern neck.

Ino [EYE no]. Bayfield. Origin unknown. Possibly named for Princess Ino, in Greek mythology the daughter of Cadmus and Hermione and wife of Athamas, king of Boetia. Hera turned Athamas mad and he pursued Ino and her son, Melicertes, to a precipice from which she and Melicertes leaped to their deaths. Zeus then turned Ino into the sea deity Leucotha. Why this story would inspire the naming of a settlement in Wisconsin is unknown. It is unlikely a transfer name although there are at least two other Inos in the United States, in Alabama and in Virginia; the names of both are of unknown origin. The Ino post office was established in July 1908, Edward Thiels, postmaster.

Institute. Door. Institute takes its name from the St. Aloysius Institute, a Catholic boarding school, later known as SS Peter and Paul, founded in 1892 by Benedictine nuns from New Jersey. The post office was established in December 1892 by Sister Clementine Braunroth. (Hale, 94)

Interwald [IN ter wawld]. Taylor. Reportedly named from German *interwald* 'in the woods.' The post office was established in May 1887, Henry Voss, postmaster. This is the only Interwald in the United States. (*History of Taylor County*)

Iola [eye O luh]. Waupaca. Town (1854) and Village (1892). Although the usual legends such as "Iola was a beautiful Indian princess" have been advanced, the origin of the name is unknown. Iola is possibly from a woman's given name; possibly an adaptation of Eola; possibly a transfer. As a place name, Iola occurs in about a dozen states.

Iowa [EYE uh wuh]. County. Organized in October 1829. Named from the Iowa River, itself named from the Iowa, a Siouan people who lived in the area. The name may be from a Siouan language meaning 'sleepy' or 'drowsy ones,' perhaps given in jest, or from Miami-Illinois. (Bright)

Ipswich [IPS wich]. Lafayette. Founded about 1886. Probably named jointly by Charles C. Wheeler, general superintendent of the Chicago & North Western railroad, and John Patterson, the first postmaster, for Ipswich, Massachusetts, the first Ipswich in the United States, itself named for Ipswich, England. (Stennett, 86)

Iron. County. Organized in March 1893. Named for the extensive deposits of iron ore.

Iron River. Bayfield. Town (1892) and ppl. Named from the Iron River, recorded by Joseph Nicollet in 1836 as *Piwabiku Sibi* 'Iron River,' built upon Ojibwa *biwabik* 'metal, iron' (152). The name of the present town and community, however, arose in the 1880s when engineers for the Northern Pacific railroad noticed rust-colored water seeping from the riverbank, which they took as an indication of the presence of iron ore. The stream was thus named Iron River and the railroad construction camp became known as the Iron River Camp. The community grew around John A. Pettingill's trading post and the Iron River post office, established in the summer of 1888 by George T. McElroy. (*Iron River*, 4)

Ironton. Sauk. Town (1859) and Village (1914). In 1854, soon after the discovery of iron ore in Sauk County, Jonas Tower, a mining and smelting operator from Poughkeepsie, New York, purchased several thousand acres in the area and established a blast furnace, gristmill, and sawmill. About 1855 Tower laid out the community of Ironton, which he named for the local ore deposits. The post office was changed from Marston in 1856. (Bohn, 310–11)

Irvine [er VEYEN]. Chippewa. Named for William Irvine, manager of Frederick Weyerhaeuser's Chippewa Lumber and Boom Company from the 1880s. Irvine Park in Chippewa Falls, which Irvine donated to the city, is named in his honor. ("William Irvine")

Irving. Jackson. Town (organized in 1855 as Price; changed to Irving in 1856) and ppl. The first land claims in the area were filed by James Davis and Jonathan Nichols in the 1840s. Davis, the first postmaster, apparently proposed the name for his former home, Irving, Michigan, itself named for American writer Washington Irving. (*Jackson County, a History*, 33)

Irvington. Dunn. Possibly named for an Irvine [*sic*] family. George K. Irvine operated a sawmill on the Red Cedar River from about 1854. The post office was established in December 1896, Frank B. Lockwood, postmaster. (Curtiss-Wedge and Jones, 215)

Isaar [EYE zer]. Outagamie. Named for the Isar [*sic*] River in Austria and Germany. Several German Catholic families settled in the Isaar area in the late 1860s. This is the only Isaar in the United States. ("Isaar")

Isabelle. Pierce. Town (originally organized 1885). Named from Isabelle Creek, which flows into the Mississippi River southeast of Bay City. The stream was probably named, for reasons unknown, by agents surveying the area for the U.S. government about 1850. (Ericson)

Itasca [eye TAS kuh]. Douglas. Apparently the community was named from Itasca Street in Superior by Arthur W. Trenholm, vice president of the Chicago, St. Paul, Minneapolis & Omaha railroad in the early twentieth century. Itasca, a name found in a half dozen states, was coined by Henry Rowe Schoolcraft, one of the leading ethnologists of the nineteenth century. Several accounts claim that Schoolcraft derived Itasca from Ojibwa *totosh* 'woman's breast,' but this is in error. About 1832, Schoolcraft and the Reverend William Thurston Boutwell followed the course of the Mississippi River to its source in a lake in Clearwater County, Minnesota, southwest of Bemidji. Boutwell, being familiar with Latin, named the lake *veritas caput* 'true head.' Schoolcraft then created *Itasca* by combining the final syllables of *veritas* with the initial syllable of *caput*. The post office was established in February 1895, John Haney, postmaster. Occasionally spelled Itaska. (Weatherhead, 23; Stennett, 179)

Ithaca [ITH uh kuh]. Richland. Town (1855) and ppl. Named by William Cratsenberg, who emigrated from New York State about 1851, for Ithaca, Tompkins County, New York, itself probably named for its association with the town of Ulysses, New York, just as ancient Ithaca in Greece was associated with Ulysses, the hero of the *Odyssey*. Ithaca, New York, is the home of Cornell University, which owned several thousand acres of forest land in Wisconsin. See Cornell. (Butterfield, *History of Crawford and Richland Counties*, 1060)

Ives, Ives Grove [EYEVZ]. Racine. Likely named for Stephen Ives, a Racine merchant, who arrived from Massachusetts in the mid-1830s. The Mount Pleasant post office was changed to Ives Grove in December 1839. (Stennett, 87)

Ixonia [ik SON ee uh, ig ZON ee uh]. Jefferson. Town (1838) and ppl. According to local accounts, when the township was organized in 1846, there was no agreement on what the name should be, so letters of the alphabet were written on slips of paper and tossed into a hat. Mary Piper, young daughter of Benjamin Piper, the postmaster at Pipersville, then drew letters until a pronounceable word was formed. This is the only Ixonia in the United States. (*Ixonia*, 4; Jaeger et al., 2)

Jackson. County. Organized in 1853. Named for Andrew Jackson (1767–1845), military leader and seventh president of the United States, serving 1829–37.

Jackson. Burnett. Town (1902). The origin of the name is uncertain. The oft-repeated local story is that George L. Miller, a Prairie du Chien attorney with significant real estate holdings in Burnett County, chose the name for Civil War general Thomas "Stonewall" Jackson. If this is true, as Ericson notes, Jackson Township would be one of the rare Wisconsin names honoring a Confederate leader.

Jackson. Washington. Town (1846) and Village (1912). Probably named for Andrew Jackson. Formerly known as Riceville, for site owner Franz Reis, from Argenthal, Germany in the 1840s. Reis donated land for a station when the railroad was built from Milwaukee to Fond du Lac. The community grew around the combination general store and tavern built by Reis in 1873. (Quickert, 73)

Jacksonport. Door. Town (1869) and ppl. Founded in the late 1860s by a logging company established by Charles L. Harris of Green Bay, John Reynolds of Madison, and Andrew Jackson of Menasha. The choices for the name of the community were, naturally, Harrisport, Reynoldsport, or Jacksonport. Jackson had the strongest claim since it was his idea to establish a a community at the site. (Holand, 405)

Jacksonville. Monroe. Named for and by William W. Jackson, from Ontario County, New York, who established the post office in March 1856. See Adrian.

Jamestown. Grant. Town (1849) and ppl. Jamestown, in an area known as the Menomonee Diggings, grew around the first lead mine in the region, opened by James Boyce about 1827. Jamestown was named for early settler James Gilmore, who emigrated from Vermont in the late 1820s. The short-lived community of South Jamestown, also known as Puckerville, was laid out southwest of Jamestown about 1850. The Jamestown post office was established in September 1837, David B. Patterson, postmaster. (Holford, 584)

Janesville [JAYNZ vil]. Rock. Town (1842) and City (1853). Janesville grew around a tavern and a ferry operated by Henry F. Janes from about 1837.

Janes himself told the story of the naming of Janesville in the 1872 *Wisconsin Historical Collections*: "I had first given [the site] the name of Black Hawk, it having been one of the old warrior's camping grounds, and sent up a petition to the Post Office Department for a post office of that name, and recommended myself as Postmaster. Amos Kendall, at that time Postmaster General, refused to establish an office by that name, as there was one already bearing that name . . . and gave the name of Janesville to the post office" (433).

Jefferson. Jefferson County, as well as the towns of Jefferson in Green, Jefferson, Monroe, and Vernon Counties, were named directly or indirectly for Thomas Jefferson (1743–1826), American polymath, author of the Declaration of Independence, and president of the United States (1801–9). Jefferson County was organized in 1839 and named at the request of the Rogan brothers, James, Peter, and Patrick; Nathaniel Hyer; and several others, most of whom were from Jefferson County in upstate New York, itself established in 1805 and named for Thomas Jefferson. (Ott, 76)

Jeffris (Jeffries). Lincoln. Jeffris grew along a spur of the Chicago & North Western railroad built about 1891 to a sawmill operated by David K. Jeffris. Jeffris claimed that he named the site for his brother, James K. Jeffris, of Janesville. (Jones and McVean, *History of Lincoln, Oneida and Vilas Counties*, 88)

Jenkinsville. Lafayette. Named for early miner and farmer Jacob Jenkins, who arrived in the area about 1837. Also known as Meeker's Grove, for Dr. Moses Meeker, originally from New Jersey, who settled in the area in the 1820s and established the Meeker's Grove post office in 1857. Also spelled Jenkynsville. (Butterfield, *History of Lafayette County*, 562)

Jennings. Oneida. Named from the Jennings post office, established in April 1899 by John Mecikalski, and named for site owner David Vincent Jennings Sr. The Chicago & North Western station was named Lenox, for Lenox, Massachusetts. See Lennox. (*Commemorative Biographical Record of the Upper Wisconsin Counties*, 145; Stennett, 93)

Jericho [JEHR uh ko]. Waukesha. In 1836 brothers Jerry, Jonathan, and Lamas Parsons emigrated from Cattaraugus County, New York. Jerry Parsons built the Jericho tavern, from which the community took its name. The tavern was named for the biblical city, or for one of the Jerichos in New England. (Haight, 305)

Jersey City. Lincoln. Reportedly named by William H. Bradley, the founder of Tomahawk (q.v.), in recognition of the line of pureblood Jersey cattle introduced to the area by Robert Tweety in the early 1900s. (Durbin, 30; "Historic Dates, Places, and People of Tomahawk")

Jewett [JYOO it]. St. Croix. Named for the Jewett family, especially Samuel A. Jewett, from the state of Maine, who operated sawmills on the St. Croix and Chippewa Rivers from about 1850. Frank Jewett was the first master of the Jewett Mills post office in 1865.

Jim Falls. Chippewa. Named for James Ermatinger, who joined John Jacob Astor's American Fur Company about 1830 and opened a trading post on the western shore of the Chippewa River at what was then known as Vermillion Falls, a French translation of a Native American word for 'red,' for the color of the clay along the river banks. Ermatinger was active in local affairs and the community that developed on the opposite side of the river became known as Ermatinger Falls, later as James Falls, and finally as Jim Falls. (Gerber, *Making of Jim's Falls*, 15)

Jimtown. Richland. Named for two local landowners: Jim Burns and Jim Bachtenkircher, a shopowner who was active in civic affairs. (Scott)

Joel. Polk. Joel is probably named for Joel Richardson, of the Richardson family that moved to the area from Maine in the 1870s. Joel's brother Stephen founded Turtle Lake (q.v.), and the community of Richardson was named for the Richardson family. The post office was established as Joel in February 1889; the name was changed to Gregory in June 1890 and back to Joel in February 1891.

Johannesburg [jo HAN is berg]. St. Croix. Named for site owner Johannes S. Johnson, from Nestrand, southern Norway, who immigrated to Wisconsin in the early 1870s. (Ericson)

Johnsburg. Fond du Lac. Named from St. John the Baptist Church, itself a partial translation of *St. Johannes Gemeinde* 'St. Johns congregation,' established by settlers from Trier, Germany, in 1841. The post office was established as Hinesberg in August 1855, Jacob Heimerman, postmaster. (Worthing)

Johnson. Marathon. Town (1883). Named by Fred Rietbrock, the namesake of Rietbrock (q.v.), for his law partner and business associate Daniel H. Johnson. Johnson served as a justice of the circuit court from 1888 until his death in 1900. (Nowicki and Kolpack, 8)

Johnson Creek. Jefferson. Village (1903). Known as Belleville for the first postmaster, Charles J. Bell, who established the office as Johnson's Creek in 1848. The community was formally named in the 1870s for Timothy Johnson, generally recognized as the first permanent settler in the area. In the late 1830s Johnson built a sawmill on the stream that bears his name. (Swart, 156)

Johnsonville. Sheboygan. Formerly known as Schnapsville or Whiskeyville because at one time the community supported more taverns than stores.

Formally named with establishment of the post office in October 1866 for Andrew Johnson, who had ascended to the presidency upon the death of Abraham Lincoln in April 1865. (Hildebrand, 3)

Johnstown. Polk. Town (1889). Most likely named for John Pawling, chair of the Town of Georgetown in the late 1880s. (Christiansen, 12)

Johnstown. Rock. Town (1843) and ppl. Named from the Johnstown post office, established in August 1839 and named for John A. Fletcher, the first postmaster. (*History of Rock County*, 345)

Jonesdale. Iowa. Named for Griffith Jones, who emigrated from Wales in 1845. The Reverend Jones was instrumental in establishing the Welsh Calvinistic Methodist Church in Dodgeville township in the early 1850s. The community has had three names, all based on "Jones." Griffith Jones laid out a portion of the site on the line of the Illinois Central railroad early in 1888 as Jonesburg; in August 1888 he established the post office as Jonesville, and the following month he changed the name to Jonesdale. (Gempler et al., 3)

Jordan. Green. Town (1848) and Jordan Center. The first permanent settlers arrived in the late 1830s. The source of the name is uncertain but may have been chosen by Ora Satterlee, who established the Jordan post office in September 1851, for Jordan, New York, near his birthplace in Onondoga County, itself named for the biblical Jordan River.

Juda. Green. Origin uncertain. Juda may be a popular etymology of Jehu. Jehu Chadwick brought his family from Pennsylvania in 1837. He owned considerable property in the area and was an influential local figure. (Bingham, 171)

Jump River. Taylor. Town (1823) and ppl. Jump River is reportedly the translation of a Native American name meaning 'jumping river' for the stretch of rapids where the water "jumped" over the rocks. The post office was established as Broederville in March 1895 by postmaster Bernard Broeder and changed to Jump River in September 1909. (P. Nagel, 3)

Junction City. Portage. Village (1911). Named for the junction of the Wisconsin Valley and Wisconsin Central railroads. The post office was established in July 1874, George E. Oster, postmaster. (Rosholt, *Our County, Our Story*, 312)

Juneau [JOO no]. County (1857) and City (1887). The city of Juneau in Dodge County was platted late in 1845 by Martin Rich as Victory, reportedly because the community was "victorious" in having been chosen as the county seat rather than Fox Lake. In 1848 Victory was replatted and re-named Dodge Center for its location near the center of the county. The name was changed again in 1848 in honor of Solomon Juneau, who was living at Theresa at the time. Juneau, a French-Canadian trader from Quebec and recognized as the founder of Milwaukee, established a post on the Milwaukee River in 1818. Juneau's nephew Joseph is the namesake of Juneau, Alaska. See Theresa. (*History of Dodge County*, 538)

Kalinke [kuh LING kee]. Marathon. Named for the Kalinke family, who emigrated from Germany and were established farmers by the 1880s. The community was established on a part of Gottlieb Kalinke's farm about 1905. (*Town of Hewitt Bicentennial*, 39)

Kansasville. Racine. Founded about 1837 by John T. Trowbridge, a retired sea captain who managed a Great Lakes shipping firm. Trowbridge served in the Wisconsin Territorial Legislature in the early 1840s and established the Trowbridge post office in 1852. First known as Brighton, the name became Kansasville about 1855 in recognition of the violent confrontations in Kansas at the time, referred to as Bleeding Kansas, between proponents and opponents of slavery. The troubles in Kansas were widely reported in newspapers of the time. ("History of Racine, Wisconsin")

Kaukauna [kuh KAW nuh]. Outagamie. Town (organized as Kaukalin in 1839; changed to Kaukauna in 1851) and City (1885). From Menominee *okahkoneh* 'place where there are pike,' built upon *okaw* 'pike.' The name was first recorded in 1670 as Kakalin by the Jesuit missionary Claude Jean Allouez. Over the next two hundred years the name was recorded in various forms, including Kockaloc (apparently pronounced [KAHK uh lo]), Cau Caulin, and Cackalin. (The Grand Cackalin post office was established in Brown County in July 1835, discontinued in January 1839, and reestablished in 1840 as Kankalan.) Variant spellings persisted until the state legislature made Kaukauna official in 1851. That same year George Lawe, "the Father of Kaukauna," made the first community plat. Present Kaukauna includes Ledyard, a community established by the Kaukauna Water Power Company and named for A. Ledyard Smith of Appleton, an investor and promoter of hydroelectric power. (Truttschel, 99–100; Vogel, *Indian Names*, 154)

Keene. Portage. Named for a local Keene family, perhaps descendants of Valentin(e) and Kate Keene, who emigrated from Poland (probably Silesia) in the 1860s. Keene is an Americanized spelling of German Kuhne. The Keene post office operated from April 1870 until April 1904.

Keenville. Winnebago. Named for the Keene family, local landowners. John Kin emigrated from Prussia and purchased the site in 1854. By popular etymology Kin became the more familiar Keene. (Munroe, p.c.)

Kegonsa [kuh GAHN suh]. Dane. The community is named from Lake Kegonsa, the first of the four lakes connected by the Yahara River and known as First Lake from at least 1833 until 1855 when Lake Kegonsa was made official. The name was proposed in 1854 by Lyman C. Draper, secretary of the Wisconsin Historical Society. From Ojibwa *gigons* 'little fish.' (Cassidy, *Dane County Place-Names*)

Kekoskee [kee KAHS kee]. Dodge. Village (1958). Founded in 1856 by William Cady and Horace Connitt. The origin of the name, although undoubtedly from a Native American language, is unknown. Kekoskee (or a variant thereof) has been reported to be the name of a Winnebago village. There is no support for the local story that *Kekoskee* means 'the land of pleasant fishing.' This is the only Kekoskee in the United States. (Barker and Tennies, 38; Bright)

Kellner. Both the community of Kellner in Portage County and the Village of Kellnersville in Manitowoc County are named for the Joseph Kellner family, originally from Germany. The Kellners were feed and flour merchants in Kellnersville from the mid-1850 and in Manitowoc from the mid-1880s. Michael Kellner was the postmaster at Francis Creek in the late 1850s. That office was changed to Prag in 1866 and to Kellnersville in 1872. (Falge, 71)

Kelly. Marathon. Named for Nathaniel Kelly, a Wausau businessman originally from Ithaca, New York, who owned extensive lumber interests on the Eau Claire River. The post office was established in December 1881. (Stennett, 89)

Kempster. Langlade. Named for Dr. Walter Kempster, born in London, England. Kempster was a leading figure in the medical profession in Wisconsin in the last half of the nineteenth century, serving as health commissioner of Milwaukee, superintendent of what was then the Northern State Hospital for the Insane, and resident at the Winnebago State Hospital where Kempster Hall is named in his honor. The post office was established in January 1882, James Doran, postmaster. (Stennett, 89)

Kendall. Lafayette. Town (1849). Named for James Kindle, the first permanent settler. At the time the town was named, the Lafayette County commissioners changed the spelling to Kendall, "as it would be more easily written and spoken, Kindle being a very uncommon name" (Butterfield, *History of Lafayette County*, 624).

Kendall. Monroe. Village (1894). Named by site owner W. D. Medbury for Levi G. Kendall, assistant superintendent of construction for the Chicago & North Western railroad, then building the line from Madison to Baraboo. It was completed to Kendall in the early 1870s. (Richards, 401)

Kennan. Price. Town (1889) and Village (1903). Named for Kent K. Kennan, land commissioner for the Wisconsin Central railroad. In 1880 Kennan was appointed European agent for the Wisconsin Board of Immigration and reportedly was responsible for settling more than five thousand Europeans in the area between Stevens Point and Ashland. (Hudson, 212)

Kennedy. Price. Established as a station on the Chicago, St. Paul, Minneapolis & Omaha railroad about 1908. Named for Patrick Kennedy, a tavern keeper and one of the early settlers of Fifield. (Goc, *100 Years on the Flambeau*, 310)

Kenosha [kuh NO shuh]. County and City. From Ojibwa *kinoji* 'pike' (the fish). Kenosha was founded by the Western Emigration Company, organized by John Bullen in Hannibal, New York, in 1834. Settlers began arriving at what was then known as Pike Creek in the summer of 1835. The community was formally organized as Southport the following year. The present spelling became official and replaced earlier Kenozia, Kenosia, Kenozha, and several other forms in 1850 when the name of the South Port [*sic*] post office was changed to Kenosha, Kenosha County was organized, and the city of Kenosha was incorporated. (Stein, 8)

Keowns [KOW uhnz]. Washington. Probably named for Patrick Keown, who emigrated from County Down, Ireland, about 1845. The post office was established in December 1897, Sebastian N. Casper, postmaster. (Quickert, 258)

Keshena, Keshena Falls [kuh SHEE nuh]. Menominee. Named for Keshena 'swift flying,' a Menominee leader of the mid-nineteenth century, who was named from a vision in which his father, Josette, saw a cast of hawks in flight. The Keshena post office was established in March 1855, John Wiley, postmaster. (Vogel, *Indian Names*, 39)

Kewaskum [kee WAS kuhm]. Washington. Town (1849) and Village (1895). Named for Kewaskum, a Potawatomi leader of the 1840s whose main village was in the Pine Lake area. The meaning of Kewaskum (also recorded as Kewasum and Ke-Wah-Goosh-Kum) is uncertain, but has to do with 'turning' or 'retracing one's steps.' The name was probably proposed by Jesse Meyer(s), an early settler and the site owner. (Vogel, *Indian Names*, 48)

Kewaunee [kee WAH nee]. County and City. The county was organized in 1852 and named from the Kewaunee River, previously known as Wood's River for an early trader or trapper named Wood. Joshua Hathaway, who surveyed much of the area for the federal government, was among the first to use the Native American name for the river on his field maps of the 1830s. *Kewaunee* has been claimed to mean 'go around,' 'river of the lost,' 'I am lost,' and 'I cross a point of land by boat,' but it was correctly glossed by Hathaway as 'prairie chicken.' Kewaunee is from an Algonquian language or from a Potawatomi leader known as Prairie Chicken whose name appears as Kewaune, Kee-waw-nay, and Kee-waw-nee on treaties of the

138

1820s and 1830s. Kewanee, Illinois, and Kewanna, Indiana, are variants. West Kewaunee was formerly known as Coryville, for Abner Cory, an early settler and the first Kewaunee County judge, and also as Krok (q.v.). The Kewaunee post office was established in July 1852, John Volk, postmaster. (*Kewaunee, Wisconsin*; Vogel, *Indian Names*, 151)

Keyesville [KEEZ vil]. Richland. Known as St. Mary's until the post office was established in May 1873. Elisha Keyes suggested the name Jamesville for Norman L. James, who, at the time, represented the district in the state assembly. James returned the favor and proposed Keyesville, which met with general approval. Keyes was a multiterm mayor of Madison in the 1860s and author of the 1906 *History of Dane County*. (Scott)

Keystone. Bayfield. Town (1918). Possibly named by settlers from Pennsylvania, the Keystone State, for its location at the center of the original American colonies.

Kickapoo, Kickapoo Center [KIK uh poo]. Vernon. Town (1853). Named from the Kickapoo River, itself named for the Kickapoo, an Algonquian people who were first encountered by Europeans near the Wisconsin-Fox river portage in the late 1660s. The name was recorded in the 1690s as Quincapou and as kekapou. Kickapoo is generally taken to mean 'moves about, first here, then there,' in other words 'wanders.' The Kickapoo post office was established in June 1854 by Robert Wilson, who kept the Jackson House, an inn named for Andrew Jackson. (Vogel, *Indian Names*, 17)

Kiel [KEEL]. Manitowoc. City (1920). Founded by Henry F. Belitz in 1854. Belitz was born in Prussia, took part in the German uprisings of 1848, immigrated to the United States, and was an officer in the Union army during the Civil War. Gretchen Lindemann, matriarch of one of the first families to settle in the area, is generally given credit for choosing the name, for Kiel in northern Germany. The Schleswig post office, established in October 1860, August Krieger, postmaster, was changed to Kiel in September 1861. (Falge, 342)

Kieler [KEEL er]. Grant. Named for the Kieler family. Johannes (John) Kieler and his family emigrated from Prussia and established a general store and bootery at the site about 1855. John Kieler's son George was the first postmaster in 1883. (*Grant County History*, 262)

Kilbournville [KIL bern vil]. Racine. Named for land speculator Byron Kilbourne. The post office was established in February 1890, John Goebe Jr., postmaster. See Milwaukee.

Kildare. Juneau. Town. Organized in 1851 as the Town of Dells, named from the dells of the Wisconsin River. The name was changed to Kildare for County Kildare, Ireland, in 1852, changed to Lindon [*sic*] for Lyndon,

New Hampshire, in 1854 and back to Kildare in 1857. See Lyndon. (*Juneau County*, 45)

Kimball. Iron. Town (1913) and ppl. Named for Alanson M. Kimball, U.S. congressman in the mid-1870s. Kimball and his business partner, Charles R. Clark, established the Kimball-Clark Lumber Company in the 1880s. Clark was the first postmaster, in June 1889. (Stennett, 90)

Kimberly. Outagamie. Village (1910). Formerly known as Smithfield, the area was settled primarily by members of the Stockbridge and Brotherton parties in the early 1830s. The name was changed in the late 1880s when the Kimberly-Clark company purchased the site and established a paper and pulp mill. See Brothertown; see Stockbridge. (Truttschel, 104)

King. Waupaca. Named in 1941 in honor of Brigadier General Charles King, whose long military career extended from the Civil War through World War I. The Wisconsin Veterans Home is located at King. ("History of the Wisconsin Veterans Home at King")

Kingsley Corners. Dane. Named for Saxton P. Kingsley, from Massachusetts, who began farming in the area in 1856. (Cassidy, *Dane County Place-Names*)

Kingston. Green Lake. Town (1850) and Village (1923). Kingston was laid out about 1846 as Hewettsville by Charles Hewett, who operated a flour mill with his business partner, Josiah Drummond. The circumstances surrounding the renaming are uncertain. Kingston may be the name of a relative of one of the founders, or a transfer from a Kingston in New England or Canada, perhaps the former home of an early settler. The post office was established in April 1846 as Tahneehoodah, an unusual name of unknown origin; it was changed to Hart Lake in July 1846, changed to Hewitt's [*sic*] Mills in August 1847, and to Kingston in July 1848. (Reetz, 31)

Kingston. Juneau. Town (1876). Named for John T. Kingston of Necedah, an early settler and a state senator in the 1850s and 1860s. (*Juneau County*, 46)

Kinnickinnic [KIN uh ki nik]. St. Croix. Town (organized in 1856 as Dayton, probably named for Dayton, Ohio; changed to Malone in 1857; changed to Kinnickinnic in 1864). Named from the Kinnickinnic River. Kinnickinnic is a general term for the mixture of floral ingredients (including tobacco when available) used as smoking materials by some Native Americans. Kinnickinnic occurs in a number of Algonquian languages; the Ojibwa form is *kiniginige* 'he mixes.' The post office was established in December 1854 as Kinnick Kinnick.

Kirby. Monroe. Apparently named for a local shopkeeper about whom little is known. As the editors of the *Monroe County* so plainly put it, "Sometime during the mid-1800s a butcher named Kirby settled in this northern section. In due time, he departed, leaving behind his name for the settlement." The post office was established in June 1886, William Randall, postmaster.

Kirchhayn [KERK heyen]. Washington. From German 'church woods.' Probably a transfer from Kirchhain, Germany. The name was proposed by the Reverend Gustav Adolf Kindermann, the first pastor of David's Star Lutheran Church, who led a congregation of Altlutheraner (Old Lutherans) from Pomerania to the area in the early 1840s. The post office was established in October 1858, as Kirchhain, William Grosskoff, postmaster. (*History of Jackson*, 11)

Klevenville [KLEV uhn vil]. Dane. Formerly known as Bluff or Pine Bluff. When the Chicago & North Western railroad was built through the area in the 1880s the name was changed to Kleven for Iver K. Kleven, from Norway, who established a hardware store, operated a lumberyard, and was a community promoter and benefactor. The post office was established as Bluff in May 1882 and changed to Klevenville in April 1891. (Cassidy, *Dane County Place-Names*)

Klondike. Oconto. Informally known as Timme, named from the Timme post office established by postmaster John A. Borden in May 1891 and named for Ernst G. Timme, Wisconsin secretary of state in the 1880s. Formally named for the Klondike, Alaska, gold rush of the 1890s. Klondike in Kenosha County is probably named for the Alaska Klondike as well. A Klondike post office operated in Milwaukee County from May 1898 through September 1901.

Kloten [KLOT n]. Calumet. Probably named for Kloten, a municipality in the canton of Zürich, Switzerland, the former home of a group of early settlers. The Kloten post office was established in July 1872, John Mayer, postmaster.

Knapp. Dunn. Village (1905). Knapp grew around a station established by the West Wisconsin railroad about 1871. The station was named for John Holly Knapp, a partner in the Knapp, Stout Lumber Company of Menomonie, reported to be the largest lumbering operation in the world at the time. See Stout. (Dunn County Historical Society, 72)

Knapp. Jackson. Town (1889). Named for John Holly Knapp, a founder in the 1840s of what became the Knapp, Stout Lumber Company. See Prairie Farm; see Menominee.

Kneeland. Racine. Named for James and Moses Kneeland, from LeRoy, New York. The Kneelands were Milwaukee businessmen who actively promoted the formation and extension of Wisconsin railroads, especially the Milwaukee & Mississippi railroad, in which the Kneelands had substantial business interests. The post office was established in January 1889, Chris Hansen, postmaster.

Knellsville [NELZ vil]. Ozaukee. Named for Mathias Knell, a native of Luxembourg. Knell was the site owner and a public official, serving as township treasurer in the early 1860s. (Eccles, 11)

Knight. Iron. Town (1889 in Ashland County). Probably named for John H. Knight, Civil War veteran, Indian agent, and the first mayor of Ashland in 1887. (Techtmann, 128)

Knowles [NOLZ]. Dodge. Named for George P. Knowles, secretary and later solicitor for the Fond du Lac, Amboy & Peoria railroad in the 1870s. (Frederick, *When Iron Was King*, 173, 175)

Knowlton [NOLT uhn]. Marathon. Town (1859) and ppl. Named by Jacob X. Brands for his birthplace, Knowlton, New Jersey. In the mid-1850s Brands established the Twin Island hotel, also known as the Half-Way House on the trail between Wausau and Stevens Point. (Durbin, 68)

Knox. Price. Town (1895). Named for William and Samuel Knox, who built a sawmill early in the 1880s. The brothers later laid out the now-historical community of Knox some ten miles east of Prentice. The Knox Mills post office was established in August 1891, Hiram Knox, postmaster. (Bant, 1–3, 7)

Kodan [KOD uhn]. Kewaunee. Kodan is a mistranscription of Kodau, a city now in the Czech Republic. According to a local account, about 1893 postmaster Wenzel (or Wengle) Ullsperger requested a cancellation stamp reading "Kodau," but when the stamp was delivered it read "Kodan." Ullsperger decided it would be easier to change the name of the office than to argue with the Post Office Department.

Koepenick [KOP uh nik]. Langlade. Named for Edward S. Koepenick, early settler, sawmill owner, and first postmaster in August 1890. (Stennett, 90)

Kohler [KO ler]. Ozaukee. Kohler is an Americanized spelling of Koehler. Peter Koehler (at times misspelled Kaehler) purchased the site and began operating a mill about 1850. The post office was established in March 1888, Moretz Stelzer, postmaster. (Boettcher)

Kohler [KOL er]. Sheboygan. Village (1912). Founded by site owner Nic J. Balkins as Riverside in 1899. The name was changed when the Kohler Company, manufacturers of ceramic and plumbing fixtures, moved to the site from Sheboygan in 1912. About 1888 Kohler developed a drinking fountain called the Bubbler, and that trademark has become the generic name for drinking fountains in much of Wisconsin. The son and grandson of John Kohler, the founder of the Kohler Company, both named Walter Jodok Kohler, were twentieth-century governors of Wisconsin. (Buchen, 273)

Kohlsville [KOLZ vil]. Washington. Named for the Kohl family. Frederick Kohl purchased land in the area in the mid-1840s. His son, Andrew, had the site platted as Kohlville in 1869 and established the post office as Kohlsville the following year. (*Winding through the Town of Wayne*, 51, 53)

Kolb. Brown. Named from the Kolb post office, established at Kolb's Corners in May 1887 by Peter Kolb, who emigrated from Bruttig, Germany, in 1852. (Cassidy, *Brown County*)

Kolberg. Door. Possibly a direct borrowing of Kolberg, the German form of Kołbrzeg, a city in northern Poland. Possibly named for a Kolberg family. Kolberg (Colberg) is also a German (as well as Norwegian and Swedish) family name. The name may have been chosen by Conrad Guth, who established the Kolberg post office in 1895. (Hale, 102)

Koll. Chippewa. Named for C. J. Koll, dispatcher for the Chicago & North Western railroad. (Stennett, 180)

Komensky [kuh MEN skee]. Jackson. Town (1914). Probably named by members of the Czech community in honor of Jan Amos Komensky (anglicized as John Amos Comenius), the seventeenth-century Czech teacher and writer who advocated universal education and whose ideas contributed significantly to modern educational practices. (*Jackson County, a History*, 34)

Koro. Winnebago. Named from the Koro post office, established by James H. Foster in August 1850. The reasons for Foster's choice of the name are unknown. Perhaps in reading he had come across Koro, a volcanic island in the Fijian group. As a place name, Koro is unique to Wisconsin.

Koshkonong [KAHSH kuh nahng]. Dane, Jefferson. The name was first recorded about 1820 as Kus-kou-o-nog, the name of a Winnebago village on the Rock River. Other early recordings included Goosh-we-hawn, Coshconong, and Kushkawenong. The current spelling was apparently first used by James Duane Doty in the mid-1840s. A number of meanings have been proposed, including 'the lake we live on,' 'place of the gulls,' and 'where there are hogs.' Cassidy correctly traces the origin to Ojibwa *kackawanung* 'where there is heavy fog,' 'place closed in by fog.' The town was organized as Finch in 1838 and changed to Koshkonong in 1842. (Cassidy, *Koshkonong*; Vogel, *Indian Names*, 145)

Kossuth [kuh SOOTH, KAHS uhth]. Manitowoc. Town (1851). Named for Lajos Kossuth, a leader in the Hungarian revolution of 1848. Kossuth was president of Hungary in 1849, became a political refugee, and immigrated to the United States where he addressed a joint session of Congress in 1851. A dozen or so places were named in honor of Kossuth in the 1850s, including three townships in Wisconsin, two of which have been renamed. The post office was established in December 1849, Robert Noxon, postmaster. (Falge, 344)

Krakow [KRAH ko]. Oconto, Shawano. Named for the province and city of Kraków in southern Poland. Krakow was founded and probably named by John J. Hof(f) in the late nineteenth century and promoted largely to Polish settlers. About 1895 Hof donated building lots to Theophil Krygier for the construction of a general store. The post office was established in August 1895, Teofil Kryger, postmaster, and discontinued in April 1904. A second Krakow post office opened in Rock County in May 1910. See Pulaski. ("Pulaski Centennial")

Kroghville [KRO vil]. Jefferson. Named for Casper Krogh (Krough), who emigrated from Norway, dammed Koshkonong Creek, and established a sawmill in the mid-1840s. (Swart, 184)

Krok [KRAHK]. Kewaunee. Probably named for Krok (Cracus), seventh-century Duke of Bohemia, by Wojta Stransky, the first postmaster, who established the office in January 1875.

Kronenwetter [KRON in wet er]. Marathon. Town (1886). Named for Sebastian Kronenwetter, a prominent businessman and local official, originally from Wertemberg, Germany. Kronenwetter was the first town president and represented the district in the Wisconsin Assembly in 1885. (Marchetti, 565)

Kunesh [KOO nish]. Brown. Named from the Kunesh post office, established in March 1894 by George Kunesh, whose parents emigrated from Bohemia about 1860.

Lac du Flambeau [LAK duh flam BO]. Vilas. Town (1907) and ppl. A French translation of Ojibwa *wauswagaming* 'at the lake of torches.' Several of the native peoples of the Great Lakes area speared fish at night by the light of pine knot torches. The post office was established in January 1890, Jerry J. Sullivan, postmaster. Flambeau Lake in Vilas County and Flambeau River in Rusk County are from the same source, as are Torch River in Sawyer County and Torch Lake in Vilas County. (Vogel, *Indian Names*, 191)

La Crosse [luh KRAWS]. County and City. The area around modern La Crosse was known to the Ho-Chunk (Winnebago) as *He-nook-was-ra* 'woman's breast' and the river was *Enookwasaneenah* 'river of the woman's breasts,' named for a pair of sloping bluffs at the mouth of the La Crosse River. For French traders and explorers from at least the middle of the eighteenth century, the area was the Prairie la Crosse, the plain where Native Americans gathered to play a game in which a stick with a bag on one end was used to catch and throw a ball. The prairie was named from this "hooked stick," reminiscent of a crosier, the staff carried by a bishop as a symbol of pastoral office. The game is often called baggataway, from

144

Ojibwa *pagaadowe*, which Baraga glosses 'I play with crosier and ball.' The first permanent settlers were Nathan Myrick, from Westport, New York, and his business partner Eben Weld, who established a trading post on the mainland or on Barron Island in 1841. Myrick established the post office as La Crosse in 1843. The Town of La Crosse was organized in 1851; the name was changed to Greenfield in 1856. (Butterfield, *History of La Crosse County*, 330; Vogel, *Indian Names*, 191)

Ladoga [luh DO guh]. Fond du Lac. Named for the European Lake Ladoga, formerly shared by Finland and Russia, now in Russia. The Ladoga post office was established in July 1851, Marcus Brown, postmaster. (Worthing)

Ladysmith. Rusk. City (1905). Ladysmith was founded as Flambeau Falls in 1885 by the Flambeau Town Company, acting for the Minneapolis, St. Paul & Sault Ste. Marie railroad. The station was established as Warner, likely named for Eli Warner, secretary of the Minnesota Railroad Commission. Adding to the name confusion, the post office was established as Corbett in November 1887 by postmaster Robert Corbett and changed to Warner in 1890. The name Ladysmith became official when the Warner post office was renamed Ladysmith in May 1900. The primary source of the name is Ladysmith, KwaZulu-Natal, South Africa, named for Juana Maria de los Dolores de León Smith, Spanish wife of General Sir Harry Smith, governor of the Cape Colony. When Ladysmith, Wisconsin, was named, a British garrison at Ladysmith, South Africa, was under siege by Dutch forces during the Boer War, from early November 1899 through February 1900. The military action in South Africa was widely reported in American newspapers and provided the background and impetus for the naming of Ladysmith, Wisconsin, and several other Ladysmiths in the United States. A local story is that the namesake is Isabel Smith, wife of Charles Smith, president of the Menasha Wooden Ware Company. However, Isabel Smith was more the recipient of the onomastic honor than its inspiration. It was her good fortune to be locally prominent when the name Ladysmith was part of a worldwide news story. See Terrill's *Ladysmith Lore* (69–71) for a comprehensive account of the naming of Ladysmith.

La Farge (Lafarge) [luh FAHRJ]. Vernon. Village (1899). The origin of the name is uncertain. According to the local account, postmaster Samuel W. Green chose the name when the office was established in May 1863. Green claimed that he had been taken by this name after finding it in a book he was reading. La Farge is a French variant of Forge, a surname for someone who lived near a forge or who was a blacksmith. This is the only La Farge in the United States, although there is a La Forge in Missouri and a La

Fargeville in Jefferson County, New York, named for site owner John LaFarge. ("LaFarge, Wisconsin")

Lafayette [lah fee ET]. Lafayette County (1846) and the towns of Lafayette in Chippewa (organized as French Town in March 1857; changed to Lafayette in November 1857), Monroe (1856), and Walworth (1843) Counties were named for the Marquis de Lafayette, the French noble who served with great distinction during the Revolutionary War. Lafayette returned to the United States on several occasions, including a triumphal tour in 1824. Lafayette is a popular place name; there are some two hundred communities, townships, and counties named Fayette or Lafayette.

La Follette [luh FAHL it]. Burnett. Town (1901). Named for Robert M. La Follette, governor of Wisconsin, 1901–6, and U.S. senator, 1906–25.

La Grange [luh GRAYNJ]. Walworth. Town (1843) and ppl. Early settlers included Charles P. Ellis, his brothers-in-law, Caleb and Levi Harris, Cyrus Huton (Hutton), and Moses Rand, one of whom probably proposed the name about 1840 for a La Grange in New England. La Grange 'the barn' was the name of the Marquis de Lafayette's manor near Paris. Americans held Lafayette in such regard that even his estate became a popular place name; La Grange occurs in about twenty states. (Beckwith, 822)

Lake Church. Ozaukee. Named from St. Mary of the Lake Catholic Church, whose congregation was established in 1848. The church itself was built in 1881 and overlooks Lake Michigan near Harrington Beach. The post office was established in January 1894, Adolph Antoine, postmaster. (Paprock and Paprock, 41)

Lake Como [KO mo]. Walworth. Formerly known as Duck Lake. The name was changed about 1839 by Thomas McKaig, the Walworth County surveyor who also platted Lake Geneva (q.v.). Although McKaig gave no reason for his choice of the name, one cannot overlook the likely influence of the famous Lake Como in northern Italy. (Beckwith, 453)

Lake Five. Waukesha. Named from Lake Five in Washington County. According to historian Fred Keller, the lake was named for its location in section five of Lisbon Township. The post office was established in May 1855, Patrick McGovern, postmaster. ("Community of Lake Five")

Lake Geneva [juh NEE vuh]. Walworth. City (1883). Formerly known as Big Foot Lake; named for Maw-geh-set, a Potawatomi leader of the 1820s and 1830s whose village was near Lake Geneva. *Maw-geh-set* was translated into French as 'gros pied' and into English as 'big foot.' The traditional account is that Big Foot received his name from the remarkably large tracks left by his snowshoes as he pursued game around the lake. Lake Geneva was named for Geneva, New York, by John Brink when he was surveying southeastern Wisconsin for the U.S. government in the mid-1830s. The post office was established as Big Foot in August 1838 and changed to Geneva in April 1839 and to Lake Geneva in December 1882. See Big Foot Prairie. (Beckwith, 317)

Lake Mills. Jefferson. Town (1845) and City (1905). In 1836 Joseph Keyes left Northfield, Vermont, and proceeded to build several mills on the shores of Rock Lake. Keyes established the post office in 1844, choosing the name Lake Mills because "here is the lake and there are the mills." The community was officially known as Tyrahnena from 1866 until 1867 when the name was changed back to Lake Mills. Teyranena (or Tyranena) was claimed to be a Winnebago name for Rock Lake meaning 'lake water.' (Stennett, 91)

Lake Nebagamon [nuh BAG uh muhn]. Douglas. Village (1907). *Nebagamon* is from Ojibwa but the meaning is uncertain. Father Chrysostom Verwyst, a keen observer of Ojibwa language and culture in the last decades of the nineteenth century, claimed the origin is *nibegomowin*, which he glossed 'watching for game at night in a boat.' Joseph Nicollet, on one of his expeditions mapping the Upper Mississippi River Basin, noted in his journal for August 1837 the "Sleeping Bear River, also called Nibegomowin" (150). Based upon Nicollet's interpretation, Vogel (*Indian Names*, 141) suggests that Ojibwa *nibawin* 'sleep, sleeping' and *nabek* 'male bear' may have been blended into Nebagamon." This is an unsatisfying etymology but I can offer none better. The post office was established as Lake Nebagemain in May 1893, Otto Berg, postmaster.

Lake Owen. Bayfield. Probably named by Frank H. Drummond for John Owen, a founder of the Rust-Owen Lumber Company. Both Drummond and Owen were directors of the Drummond & Southwestern Railway Company, a logging railroad organized about 1890. See Drummond; see Owen.

Lakeport. Pepin. Previously known as Johnstown for John McCain, a raft pilot on the Mississippi River and the site owner, who laid out what he thought would become a significant shipping site on the shore of Lake Pepin in 1846. (Forrester, 285)

Lake Tomahawk. Oneida. Town (organized as Tomahawk Lake in 1914; changed to Lake Tomahawk in 1928) and ppl. Founded by the Milwaukee, Lake Shore & Western railroad in 1892. Named from Tomahawk Lake, itself reportedly so named because the outline of the lake resembled a tomahawk, the Native American striking weapon. (Stennett, 130)

Lake Waubesa [waw BEE suh]. Dane. Lake Waubesa was formerly known as Second Lake and as Swan Lake, from Ojibwa *wabisi* 'swan.' The name was proposed in 1854 by Lyman C. Draper, secretary of the Wisconsin Historical Society, reportedly from the fact that an unusually large swan had been shot near the lake. (Cassidy, *Dane County Place-Names*)

Lake Wissota [wi SOT uh]. Chippewa. Lake Wissota was created by the Minnesota-Wisconsin Power Company in 1915. The name, a blend of Wisconsin and Minnesota, was chosen by chief engineer Louis G. Arnold. (Vogel, *Indian Names*, 238)

Lakewood. Oconto. Town (organized as Wheeler in 1905; changed to Lakewood in 1959) and ppl. Founded by the Chicago & North Western railroad through its subsidiary, the Western Town Lot Company, in 1897. The name of the Lakewood station was transferred to the post office and subsequently to the community. The name was likely chosen for the positive associations of "lake" and "wood." (Stennett, 92)

Lamar [luh MAR]. Polk. Named for Lucius Quintus Cincinnatus Lamar (1825–93), a distinguished public servant and jurist of the last quarter of the nineteenth century. Lamar fought for the South in the Civil War, after which he represented Mississippi in the U.S. House of Representatives and Senate, was secretary of the interior, and was appointed to the U.S. Supreme Court by President Grover Cleveland in 1888. Lamar was a respected national political figure, and five U.S. counties, as well as several dozen communities and townships, are named in his honor. The post office was established in January 1899, Ludwig Andrews, postmaster. (McKenney, 5)

Lamartine [LAM er teen]. Fond du Lac. Town and ppl. The town was organized in 1847 as Seven Mile Creek. The name was changed the following year to honor Alphonse Marie Louis de Prat de Lamartine, the French politician and poet who was instrumental in founding the French Second Republic following the Revolution of 1848, which was prominent in news reports of the time. (Worthing)

Lamont [luh MAHNT]. Lafayette. Town (1889) and ppl. Named for Daniel S. Lamont, private secretary to President Grover Cleveland during Cleveland's first term and secretary of war during Cleveland's second term, serving 1893–97. The name was probably proposed by settlers from New York, Lamont's home state. The Lamont post office was established in June 1886 by postmaster Alfred Charles. (*Lafayette County Bicentennial Book*, 131)

Lampson. Washburn. Named by Wallace C. Winter, general superintendent of the Chicago, St. Paul, Minneapolis & Omaha railroad for Jonas T. and Frank L. Lampson, father and son, respectively, from Labette County, Kansas, who established a general store at the site about 1902. (Stennett, 180)

Lanark [LAN ahrk]. Portage. Town (1856). Named for Lanark, Ontario, Canada, and for Lanark, Scotland. Thomas Swan, a native of Lanark, Scotland, immigrated to Lanark, Ontario, as a ten-year-old. Arthur Minto was born near Lanark, Scotland, and, apparently coincidentally, immigrated to Lanark, Ontario, as well. Both Swan and Minto immigrated to Portage County in the early 1850s and proposed the name Lanark. The post office was established in September 1883, Thomas Riley Jr., postmaster. (*Commemorative Biographical Record of the Upper Wisconsin Counties*, 287, 396)

Lancaster [LAN kas ter]. Grant. City (1878). In August 1836, Glendower M. Price purchased the site of Lancaster on news that the Wisconsin Territorial Legislature was in the process of creating Grant County from Iowa County. Price laid out the community in spring 1837 with the proposed name Ridgeway. Price's friend Charles Wooster apparently suggested the name Lancaster, for his former home, Lancaster, Pennsylvania. Price himself was from Philadelphia. (Holford, 399)

Land O' Lakes. Vilas. Town (organized as State Line in 1907; changed to Land O' Lakes in 1948) and ppl. About 1878 Rudolph Otto established a sawmill west of present Land O' Lakes. In 1905 Otto's mill was bought by the Mason-Donaldson Lumber Company, which established the Donaldson post office in 1907. Much of the site burned in 1908 and was rebuilt along the railroad tracks as State Line, for its location on the Wisconsin-Michigan border. In 1926 George St. Claire, a resort operator and civic leader, suggested changing the name from Donaldson to Land O' Lakes to make the area more attractive to tourists. (Nehring, 19–20)

Landstad [LAN stad]. Shawano. Origin uncertain. The Landstad post office was established in June 1882 by Sven G. Morgan, who may have chosen the name to honor Magnus Brostrup Landstad (1802–80), a Norwegian minister, hymnist, and poet whose Landstad Hymnbook was popular in the nineteenth and early twentieth centuries. This is the only community so named in the United States.

Langes Corners [LANGZ]. Brown. Founded by Aaron, Henrietta, and Fred Lange in the early 1890s. The Langes post office was established in May 1900, Frank Sindzinski, postmaster. (Cassidy, *Brown County*)

Langlade [LANG layd]. The county and community are named for Charles Michel de Langlade (1729–1800), often called the Father of Wisconsin. Langlade, son of a French father and Ottawa mother, established a trading post at Green Bay in the mid-1740s. After participating in the French and Indian War and the Revolutionary War, he settled at Green Bay permanently and became a prominent and prosperous citizen. Langlade was created as New County in 1879 through the efforts of Squire A. Taylor, who had logging and lumber interests on the Wolf and Lily Rivers. In February 1880, the legislature approved changing the name from New County to Langlade County. The name change was probably suggested by Lyman C. Draper, secretary of the Wisconsin Historical Society. The post office was established in June 1873, Charles H. Lazelere, postmaster. (Dessureau, 12)

Lannon [LAN uhn]. Waukesha. Village (1930). Early settler William Lannon, from Louth, Ireland, laid out Lannon Springs about 1847. In 1890 Englishman Joseph Hadfield, who owned several limestone quarries around Lannon, platted the community of Hadfield, with a railroad spur connecting Hadfield with quarrying operations in Waukesha. The Lannon Springs post office, established in May 1854, was discontinued in 1862; when the office was reestablished, both Hadfield and Lannon Springs requested the name, along with Stone City, the residential complex near Hadfield's quarries. According to local historian Ruth Schmidt, the petition for the new post office carried the name Hadfield, which was overwritten with Stone City, which in turn was crossed out and replaced with Lannon. No one knows who made the changes, but the Lannon post office opened in August 1890, with Olavius Olsen, postmaster. (R. Schmidt, 6–7)

Laona [lay O nuh]. Forest. Town (1903) and ppl. Founded with construction of the Chicago & North Western railroad in 1899. The name Laona was apparently the result of a clerical error. The name on the plat was to have been Leona, for Leona Johnson, the daughter of local businessman Norman Johnson, but it was either misread or misheard and recorded as Laona. The post office was established in January 1900. See Forest. (Stennett, 92)

Lapham Junction [LAP uhm]. Jackson. Named for Increase Allen Lapham (1811–75), one of Wisconsin's early scientists. Lapham's weather observations, made from what is now known as Lapham Peak in Waukesha County, led to the creation of the National Weather Service by Congress in 1870. (McBride, 64)

La Pointe [luh POYNT]. Ashland. Town (1845) and ppl. An abbreviation of La Pointe de Chequamegon, a name given by early French explorers and traders to the needle of land composed of Chequamegon Point and Long Island, which projects into Chequamegon Bay south of Madeline Island. The name may antedate the Jesuit priest Claude Jean Allouez's establishment of the mission La Pointe du Saint Esprit 'the point of the holy spirit' in 1665. La Pointe apparently referred to the Chequamegon Bay area generally before it became restricted to the site on Madeline Island. Chequamegon is a French spelling of an Ojibwa word referring to a narrow strip of land projecting into a lake or bay, perhaps related to *jabonigan* 'a needle.' The post office was established in October 1843, Charles W. Borup, postmaster. (Vogel, *Indian Names*, 177–78)

La Prairie. Rock. Town (1849). French for 'the meadow.' The name was considered appropriate to the area and proposed by Samuel Porter Wheeler of a prominent Wheeler family. His father, Justus Wheeler, was the first town chair. (McLenegan, 13)

Lark. Brown. The first settler in Lark was August Wendorf in 1883. He was later joined by Frank C. Saenger, who operated a cheese factory and kept a general store. When he established the post office in January 1893, Saenger chose the name Lark, for the songbird. Intentional or accidental, the name is a play on words, since *Saenger* is German for 'singer.' (*Town of Morrison*, 31)

Larrabee. Waupaca. Town. Named for Charles Hathaway Larrabee, a justice on the Wisconsin Supreme Court in the 1850s. When the township was organized in 1860 Larrabee was a U.S. representative from Wisconsin. Larrabee in Manitowoc County is named for Charles Larrabee as well.

Larsen. Winnebago. Formerly known as Lee's Crossing for landowner Halvor Lee. The community grew around a flag stop on the Chicago & North Western railroad named for Philip Larsen, who kept a general store at the site from the late 1880s. The post office was established by Lars Nelson in December 1898. (Stennett, 92)

LaRue [luh ROO]. Sauk. Named for William G. LaRue, a mining engineer from Duluth, Minnesota, who, along with Henry Grotophorst and Benjamin Dean, organized the Sauk County Land and Mining Company to extract and process the local iron ore. LaRue was established about 1903 to house and supply the mining community. (Cole, *Standard History*, 412)

Lauderdale [LAWD er dayl]. Walworth. Named for James Lauderdale, a prominent local citizen and officeholder. Lauderdale, from Washington County, New York, served in the Wisconsin Assembly in 1853 and 1856. The post office was established in April 1881, Chester B. Williams, postmaster. (Beckwith, 831)

La Valle [luh VAL]. Sauk. Town (organized as Marston in 1851; changed to La Valle in 1861) and Village (1883). Presumably an adaptation of French *la vallée* 'the valley.' The name may have been chosen by Schuyler P. Barney, the first postmaster, when the office was established in 1856. (Stennett, 93)

Lawrence. Brown. Town (1847). Named for Boston financier Amos Lawrence, a founder and namesake of Lawrence University in Appleton. The community of Lawrence, named for the township, was platted in 1871 and is now part of Little Rapids. See Appleton. (Cassidy, *Brown County*)

Lawton. Pierce. Probably named for Lawton Peterson, who kept the store in which the first post office was established by postmaster Oscar Peterson in

1894. The relationship between the Petersons (if any) is unknown. (Johnson and Wilmot, 20)

Lead Mine. Lafayette. Formerly known as Democrat. Named for the lead mines in southwest Wisconsin. The post office was established in September 1883, William Buxton, postmaster.

Lebanon [LEB uh nuhn]. Dodge. Town (1846). Founded about 1843 by settlers from the province of Brandenburg, Germany, primarily Lutherans seeking relief from religious pressure by the Prussian state church. The colony was organized by William Woltmann, a Pomeranian pastor, who chose the name for the biblical Lebanon. (Whyte, 105)

Ledgeview. Brown. Town (1994). Organized as De Pere in 1839; the name was changed to Ledgeview in 1994. Named from the Niagara Escarpment, known in Wisconsin as "the ledge" or "the bluff," a limestone ridge (technically a cuesta) which extends some 250 miles through eastern Wisconsin, from Waukesha and Dodge Counties on the south through Fond du Lac and Brown Counties and along the eastern shore of Green Bay. In September 1874, Frederick Hjorth established the Ledgeville (or Ledgerville) post office, which gave its name to the short-lived community of Ledgeville and the Ledgeville school in Wrightstown township. See Niagara. (Cassidy, *Brown County*)

Leeman [LEE muhn]. Outagamie. Named for the Leeman family. Charles S. Leeman brought his wife and at least thirteen of their children from Abbot, Piscataquis County, Maine, sometime before 1850. Leeman's son Matthew established the Leeman post office in May 1881. ("Lehman-L Archives")

Lehigh [LEE heye]. Barron. Probably named by Soo railroad officials from the Lehigh Valley of Lackawanna County, Pennsylvania, where Lehigh is the name of a river, a county, a university, and several dozen other natural and artificial features. Lehigh is ultimately from a Delaware (Algonquian) word with the general meaning 'branched' or 'forked. The post office was established in December 1890.

Leland [LEE luhnd]. Sauk. Named for Cyrus Leland, who emigrated from Worcester County, Massachusetts, in the late 1830s. Leland, a lawyer and justice of the peace, served in the Wisconsin Legislature in 1849. The post office was established in April 1893, Henry Simon, postmaster. (Cole, *Baraboo*)

Lemington [LEM ing tuhn]. Sawyer. Probably named by settlers from Lemington, Essex County, Vermont, itself named for Lemington Spa, Warwick, England. The post office was established in May 1916, Silas J. Johnson, postmaster.

Lemonweir [LEM uhn wihr]. Juneau. Town (1849) and ppl. Named from the Lemonweir River. The origin of this intriguing name, occurring only in Wisconsin, is unknown. It has been claimed that Lemonweir is adapted from French *la mémoire* 'memory'; is from a Native American name meaning 'where the deer rut' or perhaps 'effluent'; is named in honor of Jim Lemonweir, descendant of a French Indian trader named Lenonair; and was named *lemo-wee* 'river of memory' by an Indian who saw the location in a dream, reminding him of where he had earlier lost a wampum bag. Of these, *la mémoire* is the most likely, *Lemonweir* being perhaps a popular etymology of *la mémoire* (which Americans would hear as [lah memwahr]). Alternatively, Lemonweir and perhaps also Lenawee, the name of several features in Bayfield County, may be popular etymologies from or adaptations of a yet to be discovered ancestral form. (Svob, 88)

Lena. Oconto. Town (1892) and Village (1921). Settled in the 1870s, largely by French Canadians and known as Maple Valley. The present name was proposed in 1879 with establishment of the post office by George R. Hall, postmaster at Oconto, in honor of his wife, Helena, known as Lena. (Rucker, *From the McCauslin*, 79)

Lennox [LEN iks]. Oneida. Named for Lenox, Massachusetts, itself named for Charles Lennox, seventeenth-century Duke of Richmond. See Jennings. (Stennett, 93)

Lenroot [LEN root]. Sawyer. Town (1909). Irvine Luther Lenroot (Swedish Lönnrot) (1869–1949) was a leading political figure of early twentieth-century Wisconsin. He served in the Wisconsin Assembly (1901–5), the U.S. House of Representatives (1909–18), and U.S. Senate (1918–27). (Landelius and Jarvi, 247)

Leon [LEE ahn]. Monroe. The Leon post office, the Town of Leon, and the community of Leon were named in the early 1850s for Nuevo León, Mexico, where U.S. and Mexican forces met in the Battle of Monterrey in September 1846. The local account is that D. Mortimer West, the first postmaster, suggested the name Miranda, after his wife, but the Mexican War was fresh in memory, and newspaper accounts of the encounter at Nuevo León were widespread. The Town of Leon in Waushara County is probably named from the same incident. (Richards, 522)

Leonards. Bayfield. Named for Frederick C. Leonard of Eau Claire, who had extensive logging and lumber interests in the vicinity. The post office was established in November 1899 by Carrie McCarthy. (Stennett, 181)

Leopolis [lee AHP uh luhs]. Shawano. Founded in 1872 by the site owner, Nathaniel M. Edwards, a Milwaukee civil engineer, originally from Haverhill, Massachusetts. Edwards's reasons for choosing the name are unknown. Perhaps a transfer from Leopolis, the Latin name of L'viv (Lwów), a city now in western Ukraine. This is the only Leopolis in the United States. (McDevitt, 147)

LeRoy. Dodge. Town (1846) and ppl. The source of the name is uncertain. LeRoy is probably a transfer from Genesee County, New York, likely proposed with establishment of the post office in 1848, perhaps by postmaster Obadiah Crane.

Leslie [LES lee]. Lafayette. The site was purchased about 1875 by Madison Y. Johnson, president of the Galena & Southern Wisconsin railroad. Named for Johnson's son, Leslie. Formerly known as Grandview and as Belmont. (Stennett, 94)

Lessor [LES er]. Shawano. Town (1870). Named for Thomas J. Lessor, from Vermont, who built the first house in the area in 1867. ("Thomas J. Lessor")

Levis [LEV is]. Clark. Town (1856). Named for Mahlon and William Levis, brothers from Bucks County, Pennsylvania, who established two mills in Jackson County and a third in the Levis area beginning in the 1840s. The Levis post office in Jackson County was established in May 1888, Hans O. Moen, postmaster. (Scholtz)

Lewis. Polk. Formerly known as Knappville, for Oscar Knapp, from New York State. Knapp owned several steamboats and oversaw other businesses from his base in Osceola. In 1900 he sold part of his land holdings to Charles E. Lewis, a Minneapolis grain dealer, who laid out the community of Seven Pines, now an area east of Lewis on Knapp Creek. The post office was established in January 1913, William H. Emrich, postmaster. (Christiansen, 44)

Lewiston. Columbia. Town (1852) and ppl. Named for Edward F. Lewis, who emigrated from New York State in 1849. Lewis served as Columbia County sheriff in the late 1850s. The post office was established in July 1858, Robert Ball, postmaster. (Butterfield, *History of Columbia County*, 605)

Leyden [LAYD n]. Rock. Possibly a transfer from Leyden, Massachusetts, or Leyden, New York, but more likely named directly by Dutch settlers for Leyden (Leiden) in the Netherlands. The post office was established in July 1850, James McMillan, postmaster. (Stennett, 91)

Liberty. There have been at least a dozen Wisconsin communities or townships called Liberty, most of which were named, in Stennett's words "from the sentiment of the American people" (94). The Town of Liberty, Manitowoc County, was organized in 1857 as Buchanan, for recently elected President James Buchanan. The name was changed to Liberty in 1861, largely because of dissatisfaction with Buchanan's position on slavery. Liberty in Vernon County was organized in 1858 largely through the efforts of Allen Rusk, brother of Jeremiah Rusk, the namesake of Rusk County and future governor of Wisconsin. Liberty Pole in Vernon County was named from the presumption that the first flagstaff or "liberty pole" in the county was raised at the site on Independence Day in 1848. Liberty Grove in Door County was originally settled by members of the Norwegian Moravian colony at Ephraim (q.v.), one of whom was Zacharias Morbek. According to Holand, Morbek "complained that liberty was dying out in Gibraltar [and] he got a portion of Gibraltar set off in 1859 as a separate town, [which] he called Liberty Grove" (367). (Falge, 313; *History of Vernon County*, 518, 621)

Lily. Langlade. Named from the Lily River, itself presumably named from the river flowers. The post office was established as New in October 1878 and changed to Lily in March 1890.

Lima [LEYE muh]. The town of Lima in Sheboygan County was named in 1849 at the suggestion of Hiram Humphrey, for Lima, Livingston County, New York, itself named for the city in Peru. Limas in Rock and Pepin Counties are likely transfer names as well, from Lima, New York, or Lima, Ohio. The name of Lima township in Grant County is apparently a play on words, named for the local lime kilns. (Buchen, 337)

Lime Ridge. Sauk. Village (1910). Named from the prominent limestone ridge west of the community. The name was chosen by Charles Cushman, the first postmaster, when the office was established in 1859. (Cole, *Baraboo*)

Lincoln. In addition to Lincoln County, named for Abraham Lincoln, there are more than a dozen Lincoln communities and towns in Wisconsin; most were named around the time of his election in 1860 or his assassination in 1865. The community of Lincoln in Kewaunee County was first known as Grandlez, named by Belgian settlers for Grand-Leez, Gembloux, Belgium. Also named for Abraham Lincoln is Old Abe, a bald eagle carried for much of the Civil War by Company C of the Eighth Wisconsin Volunteers. Old Abe was captured about 1860 and died in 1881 after a fire in the Wisconsin capitol. See Eagle Point.

Lind. Waupaca. Town (1852). Named by George W. Taggart, the first postmaster in 1850, for the Swedish opera star Jenny Lind. In the early 1850s Lind was in the midst of a spectacularly successful musical tour of the eastern United States. (Landelius and Jarvi, 247)

Linden. Iowa. Town (1849) and Village (1900). Formerly known as Pedler's [*sic*] Creek, named for Patrick O'Meara, "the Dodgeville peddler." O'Meara traveled throughout the lead region, selling pins, needles, and other such notions. The post office operated as Pedler's Creek from March 1843 until December 1845 when the name was changed to Linden at the suggestion of postmaster and shopkeeper John Wasley, who laid out the community in 1855. The reasons for Wasley's choice of the name are unknown. Linden is a popular place name, occurring in more than half the states, often named for the linden tree (basswood). (*History of Iowa County*, 812)

Lindina [lin DEYE nuh]. Juneau. Town (1854) and ppl. Named by Milton Maughs, the founder of Mauston (q.v.), for his wife, Melinda, whom he called Lindina. (*Juneau County*, 47)

Lindsey [LIN zee]. Wood. Platted in 1891 by Solomon L. Nason and George Hiles as a station on the Milwaukee, Dexterville & Northern railroad. Named for Freeman D. Lindsay [*sic*]. Originally from New York, Lindsay was a mill operator, served in the Wisconsin Assembly in 1877, and was one of the organizers of the Black River railroad. See Nasonville; see Hiles. (R. Rudolph)

Linn. Walworth. Named for Lewis F. Linn, U.S. senator from Missouri, 1833–43, and a half brother of Henry Dodge. Linn was a forceful advocate of western expansion and teamed with his fellow Missouri senator, Thomas Hart Benton, on a number of crucial national issues, notably statehood for Washington and Oregon. The town was organized in January 1844, three months after Linn's death. See Dodge; see Benton. (Beckworth, 367)

Lisbon [LIZ buhn]. Juneau. Town (organized in 1853 in Adams County). See New Lisbon.

Lisbon. Waukesha. Town (1838). The first permanent settler was Thomas Spencer Redford, who emigrated from western New York State to Milwaukee in 1836, walking most of the way. The name is probably a transfer from Lisbon, New York, or Lisbon, New Hampshire. James and Richard Weaver, father and son, both born in Sussex, England, were instrumental in the founding of Lisbon and Sussex, Wisconsin. James Weaver established the Lisbon post office in February 1846. See Sussex.

Little Black. Taylor. Town (1875) and ppl. Named from the Little Black River. The post office was established in November 1888 by August Frels. See Black River Falls.

Little Chicago. Marathon. Probably named for "big Chicago" on Lake Michigan in Illinois. Formerly known as Ziegler for George Ziegler, who kept the first general store in the area. Frank Gere established the Ziegler post office in October 1891. (Zamzow, 29)

Little Chute. Outagamie. Village (1899). Little Chute is a translation of *La Petite Chute* 'the little falls,' the name given by French traders and trappers to the smaller of two waterfalls on the Fox River. In 1835 the Dutch priest

Father Theodore J. Van den Broek established a mission that became the St. John of Nepomucene Catholic Church. In 1848 Van den Broek brought a group of settlers from the Netherlands who formed the nucleus of *Nepomuc*, the name under which the community was first platted. Nepomuc is a city near Pilsen in the Czech Republic, and St. John of Nepomuc is the patron saint of Bohemia. See Vandenbroek. (Truttschel, 107)

Little Eau Claire. Marathon. Named from the Little Eau Claire River. See Eau Claire.

Little Falls. Monroe. Town (1856). In 1851 William Printz and Abe Forsyth emigrated from Ohio and established a lathe mill on what became known as Printz Creek. The particular falls for which the town was named is unknown. (Koehler, *History of Cataract*, 5)

Little Falls. Polk. About 1865 George Gove became the first permanent settler in the area. The Little Falls post office was established in October 1874 by Edward Schumacher, who reportedly chose the name from a small waterfall on the Apple River. (Christiansen, 44)

Little Hope. Waupaca. The first land claim at the site was entered in November 1854 by James A. Lathrop, who dammed the Crystal River and established a sawmill and gristmill the following year. The source of the name is unknown. It was likely named for a larger community named Hope, of which there are more than two dozen in the United States. (*Our Heritage*, 196)

Little Kohler. Ozaukee. Named for Martin Koller [*sic*], who emigrated from Bavaria about 1847. Koller donated land for the church, called the Koller Kirche in his honor, and cemetery. When the post office was established in 1888, the spelling was changed to Kohler and "Little" was added, perhaps to distinguish this community from Kohler, a now-vanished settlement a mile to the southeast. (Eccles, 7)

Little Norway. Dane. The site of Little Norway was settled by Osten Olson Haugen, from Telemark, Norway, in the 1850s. A tourist attraction and musuem was established in the late 1920s as Nissedahle, at the inspiration of Isak Dahle, a Norwegian American businessman from Chicago who sought to reproduce a traditional Norwegian farm with authentic buildings and farming implements. Dahle took the name from *Nissedal* in Telemark, Norway, with the ending modified to incorporate his surname and claimed that the name meant 'valley of the elves.' In Scandinavian lore the nisser are household spirits or gnomes. Little Norway closed in 2012. (Cassidy, *Dane County Place-Names*)

Little Rapids. Brown. Named for the lesser rapids at this point compared to the greater rapids farther up the Fox River at Kaukauna. Little Kaukauna, as the community was formerly known, was settled in the early 1820s and renamed shortly after Prescott Boynton established the Little Rapids post office in September 1873. See Kaukauna. (Cassidy, *Brown County*)

Little Sturgeon. Door. Named from Little Sturgeon Bay, probably by Freeland B. Gardner, generally recognized as the founder of Little Sturgeon. Born in New York State, Gardner established a sawmill at the site in the mid-1850s. (Rohe, *Ghosts of the Forest*, 268)

Little Suamico. Oconto. Town (organized as Suamico in 1858; changed to Little Suamico in 1860). Named from the Little Suamico River. See Suamico.

Little Wolf. Waupaca. Town (organized in 1852 as Centerville; changed to Little Wolf in 1854). Named from the Little Wolf River. Also known as Meiklejohns Mills. Peter Meiklejohn, from Washington County, New York, was one of the first Waupaca County supervisors in 1851. (Wakefield, 181)

Livingston. Grant, Iowa. Village (1914). Previously known as Dublin, named by Irish settlers for Dublin, Ireland. The name was changed for site owner Hugh Livingston when the Chicago & Tomah railroad line was extended from Galena, Illinois, to Montfort, Wisconsin, in the late 1870s. Livingston came to the United States from Ireland in 1848 and joined in the California gold rush, where he made enough money to purchase a thousand acres in southwestern Wisconsin. The post office was established in February 1880, Thomas Watson, postmaster. (Olafson and Livingston, 2, 3)

Loddes Mill [LAHDZ]. Sauk. Named for Martin Loddes, born in Westfalen (Westfalia), Prussia. Loddes came to Sauk Prairie in 1850 where he established several gristmills. (*History of Sauk County*, 802)

Lodi [LO deye]. Columbia. Town (1849) and City (1941). The area was named about 1846 by first postmaster and site owner, Isaac H. Palmer. Palmer, from Chautauqua County, New York, was the first probate judge of Dane County and served in the Wisconsin Territorial Legislature. According to his daughter, Palmer was an amateur historian with a special interest in Napoleon's campaigns, and he chose the name for Lodi in northern Italy, where Napoleon defeated an Austrian army in 1796. (Martinson, 6)

Loganville. Sauk. Village (1917). Named for a Mr. Logan from New York State, the first permanent settler, who built a cabin near the site in the winter of 1854. Logan's given name has been variously reported; the 1880 *History of Sauk County* calls him Chauncey, Chancy, and Chancey. However he spelled his name, he was a justice of the peace, a successful sawmill operator, and the namesake of Loganville. (Derleth, 41)

Lohrville [LOR vil]. Waushara. Village (1910). Named from the Lohrville post office, established in October 1904 by Elsie Gautschi. The office was named for Charles Lohr, from Hesse-Darmstadt, Germany, owner of the Lohr Granite Company of Milwaukee, which purchased much of the stone quarried in the area. (Evans, 13)

Lomira [lo MEYE ruh]. Dodge. Town (organized as Juneau in February 1849; changed the following month to Lomira) and Village (1899). The origin of the name is unclear. A popular story is that the name was chosen by Samuel Schoonover in honor of his daughter Margaret Lomira. By another account, Schoonover's daughter was Elmira, not Lomira, and Lomira is an adaptation of Elmira. Interestingly, both Elmira Schoonover and Lomira Schoonover appear in census records of the mid-1800s. According to local historian Jane Kietzer (2), the name was created by Caleb Warren Marston, a leading citizen of Dodge County, who blended *Lo*, from the name of his sister, Lovina, with *mira*, from Elmira, his birthplace in New York State. The post office was established as Springfield in May 1849 and changed to Lomira in April 1850. This is the only Lomira in the United States.

London. Dane, Jefferson. Founded in 1881 by Archibald Armstrong, a grain dealer who emigrated from Ireland as a child in the 1850s. The source of the name is uncertain. Armstrong may have felt an affinity for London, England, or Derry (Londonderry), Ireland. Or perhaps officials of the Chicago & North Western railroad, which established a station shortly after Armstrong laid out the community, had their own reasons for choosing the name. The post office was established in April 1882, William Armstrong, postmaster. (Liebenow, 1–2)

Lone Rock. Juneau. Established by settlers from Denmark in the 1870s and named for the isolated rock outcropping northeast of Camp Douglas. (*Juneau County*, 50)

Lone Rock. Richland. Village (1886). Laid out next to the Milwaukee & Mississippi railroad station by Dr. James N. Casell in the fall of 1856. Named from Lone Rock, at the time a prominent sandstone landmark used as a navigational aid by boatmen and travelers. Quarrying has reduced the size of the formation to near invisibility. (Durbin, 177)

Lookout. Buffalo. According to Mary Ann Pattison, "The name goes back to the Indians who used the bluff nearby as a lookout post, and because Chauncey Cooke likened it to Lookout Mountain, which he had seen during the Civil War" (101). The post office was established in September 1882, Charles Britton, postmaster.

Lorain [luh RAYN]. Polk. Town (1872). Probably named for Lorain Ruggles, a highly valued Union spy during the Civil War. In the late 1860s Ruggles published several popular books recounting his espionage activities. The choice of the name may have been influenced by settlers from Lorain, Ohio. The post office was established in December 1875. (Christiansen, 14)

Loreta. Sauk. Loreta (also spelled Loreto and Loretta) took its name from the post office, established as Lorettoburgh in June 1875 by Lorenz Spitzlberger and named for Loretto Norris, wife of Edward Norris, the founder of Delton (q.v.). The Lorettoburgh office was discontinued in 1876 and reestablished as Loreto in 1900. (Cole, *Baraboo*)

Loretta [luh RET uh]. Sawyer. Named by Edward Hines, who founded the Hines Lumber Company of Chicago in 1892, for his wife and daughter, both named Loretta. See Hines.

Louis Corners. Manitowoc. Named for and by Louis C. Senglaub, county clerk, who established the post office in January 1878.

Louisburg. Grant. Founded in 1846 as Lewisburg and named for Lewis Curtis, an early settler in the late 1820s and site owner. The spelling was apparently changed when Louis Reifsteck established the post office in 1884. For a time, Louisburg seems to have shared with South Jamestown the nickname Puckerville, which, according to local lore, arose from a batch of moonshine whiskey so powerful it would "pucker a mule." (Butterfield, *History of Grant County*, 738; *Grant County History*, 262)

Lowell [LOL]. Dodge. Town (1846) and Village (1894). Clark Lawton and Henry Finney established a mill on Beaver Dam River in the mid-1840s. Several sources claim that Lawton chose the name for Lowell, Massachusetts, but more likely the source is his birthplace, Lowell, Oneida County, New York. (*History of Dodge County*, 570)

Lowville. Columbia. Town (1846) and ppl. Named for first settler Jacob Low, a New York merchant who relocated to Wisconsin in 1843. Low established the Lowville post office in 1846 and later served in the Wisconsin Legislature. (J. Jones, 427)

Loyal. Clark. Town (1865) and City (1948). Loyal is probably a patriotic name, chosen to show loyalty to the federal union at the close of the Civil War. By some accounts Oliver Hill, a Civil War veteran from Wisconsin, suggested the name. The Loyal post office was established in August 1869, John Graves, postmaster. (Curtiss-Wedge, *History of Clark County*, 623)

Loyd. Richland. Laid out in 1854 by site owners Robert B. Stewart and Ebenezer M. Sexton, the namesake of Sextonville (q.v.). The site was surveyed—and apparently named—by Joseph Irish, a Methodist minister, state senator, and official of Lawrence University in Appleton. The origin of the name is uncertain; perhaps it was named for an early settler or for Lloyd, New York, by the first postmaster, Jacob Fellows, when the office was established in 1855. Loyd may be an Americanized spelling of Welsh Lloyd. (Butterfield, *History of Crawford and Richland Counties*, 1287)

Lublin [LOOB lin]. Taylor. Village (1915). Named by Marvin Durski, a Chicago land agent, for his birthplace, Lublin, in eastern Poland. The post office was established by Peter B. Stadler in September 1907. (*History of Taylor County*)

Lucas [LOO kuhs]. Dunn. Lucas, both Town and post office, were organized in the 1860s and were named for early settler Samuel Lucas. Born in England, Lucas immigrated to the United States as a teenager in the early 1860s and to Dunn County about 1867 where he became a prominent landowner instrumental in organizing the Town of Wilson. (Dunn County Historical Society, 31)

Luck. Polk. Town (1869) and Village (1905). The origin of the name is unknown. Luck is a rare place name, occurring only in Wisconsin and North Carolina. According to a local legend, Luck was halfway between St. Croix Falls and Clam Falls and if travelers from either place could reach the other before nightfall they considered themselves to be "in Luck." The name may have been suggested by Daniel Smith, who was instrumental in organizing the township and who is reported to have said, "I propose to be in Luck the rest of my life." The post office was established in September 1869 by William Foster, who may have had his own reasons for naming the office Luck. (Christiansen, 9, 15, 45)

Luco [LOO ko]. Fond du Lac. Named in the 1840s from Luco Creek, itself reportedly named for boatbuilder Luke La Borde, known as Luco. La Borde founded the now vanished community of Delhi in Winnebago County in 1848. (Worthing)

Ludington [LUHD ing tuhn]. Eau Claire. Town (1876) and ppl. Named in honor of Harrison Ludington (1812–91), twice mayor of Milwaukee and the thirteenth governor of Wisconsin, serving 1876–78.

Lufkin [LUHF kin]. Eau Claire. Named for the Lufkin family. George Lufkin was a prominent local farmer, noted for the production of sugar beets in the early 1900s.

Lugerville [LOO ger vil]. Price. Named for Frank, John, and Lewis Luger, brothers from St. Paul, Minnesota, who established Lugerville as a residential community for employees of the Luger Lumber Company in the early 1900s. (Greene, 5–6)

Lund [LUHND]. Pepin, Pierce. Probably named for Lund, near Karlskoga, Värmland, Sweden; possibly named from Swedish *lund* 'grove' as descriptive of the area. The post office was established in May 1858, Jeremiah Newville, postmaster. (Landelius and Jarvi, 248)

Lunds [LUHNZ]. Shawano. Named for one or more Lund families. John Lund, a Norwegian farmer and businessman, operated a cheese factory at Lund's Corners from the late nineteenth century.

Luxemburg [LUHKS uhm berg]. Kewaunee. Town (1883) and Village (1908). Named from the Luxembourg post office (with current spelling) by settlers from the Grand Duchy of Luxembourg. The office was established in April 1880, Peter Hanbrick, postmaster. (Simonar, 4)

Lykens [LEYE kinz]. Polk. Named with establishment of the post office in May 1898 by postmaster Willard W. Seery for his birthplace, Lykens Township, Crawford County, Ohio, itself named for Lykens, Dauphin County, Pennsylvania, itself named for early settler Andrew Lykens ("Willard Wickham Seery")

Lymantown [LEYE muhn town]. Founded about 1900 as West Park Falls by brothers Edward and Roy Lyman, carpenters from Michigan. The community formally became Lymantown about 1910. (Goc, *100 Years on the Flambeau*, 23–24)

Lyndhurst. Shawano. Lyndhurst was apparently created by an officer of the Chicago, St. Paul, Minneapolis & Omaha railroad simply because it was euphonious. According to Stennett, the name "has no specific meaning" (97).

Lyndon. Sheboygan. Town (1849). Probably named for Lyndon, Caledonia County, Vermont, itself named for Josias Lyndon, an eighteenth-century governor of Rhode Island. (Buchen, 338)

Lynn. Clark. Town (1862) and ppl. Founded about 1856 by George Ure and Gottlieb Sternitzky. The origin of the name is uncertain. It may be derived from the local flora. As Scholtz points out, the U.S. government surveyor's notes on the area in the mid-nineteenth century mention large numbers of basswood trees, which were also called Linden or Lynden trees, often shortened to Lynn or Lyn.

Lynxville. Crawford. Village (1899). Formerly known as Haney's Point, for early settlers John and James Haney. The name Lynxville was apparently chosen by U.S. government surveyors in the mid-nineteenth century for the steamboat *Lynx*, which had brought them to the area. The site was surveyed about 1857 by the noteably named Pizarro Cook. (Butterfield, *History of Crawford and Richland Counties*, 720)

Lyons. Walworth. The town was organized in 1844 as Hudson, named for Hudson, New York, and renamed Lyons in 1865, taking the name of the

Lyons post office, itself named for a local Lyon family. Thomas Lyon, together with his sons, Willam, David, Thomas, and Isaac, arrived in the area from Chatham, New York, about 1837 and proceeded to establish a sawmill and later a gristmill. The post office was established by Thomas Lyon Jr. as Lyondale in 1843; this name was changed to Hudson the following year and to Lyons in January 1848. (Beckwith, 372)

Mackford. Green Lake. Town (1849). Named from Mack's Ford, the Grand River crossing named for justice of the peace Hiram "Mack" McDonald. The thriving community McDonald expected never materialized but the name remained. The post office was established in March 1878, Samuel Wadleigh, postmaster. (Reetz, 37)

Mackville. Outagamie. Probably named for and by Robert G. McGillan, who established the Mackville post office in December 1862.

Madge. Washburn. Town (1915) and ppl. Named from the Madge post office, established in May 1894, itself named for Madge Devereaux, daughter of James Devereaux, general superintendent of the Crescent Springs railroad in the 1880s. (Chappelle, *"Why of Names,"* 25)

Madison. Dane. Town (1846) and City (1856). The city of Madison was founded in 1836 by land speculator and politician James Duane Doty, who owned more than one thousand acres of land in the four lakes area. Doty successfully lobbied the legislature to choose his projected city as the capital of first the territory and subsequently the state of Wisconsin. Doty was an admirer of James Madison, fourth president of the United States, and named the city in his honor. See Doty.

Madsen. Manitowoc. Named for a prominent Madsen family. Andrew J. Madsen emigrated from Norway to the area in the late 1840s. (Falge, 2:468)

Magnolia. Rock. Town (1846) and ppl. The local account is that Joseph Prentice, an early settler from New York, planted several magnolia trees in the area in the early 1840s. The magnolias did not survive Wisconsin's harsh winters, but such was their novelty that the the community and township remember them with the name. (*History of Rock County*, 516)

Maiden Rock. Pierce. Town (organized as Pleasant Valley in 1857; changed to Maiden Rock in 1869) and Village (1887). Maiden Rock developed from a logging camp known as Harrisburg, established in 1855 by brothers Albert and Amos Harris. The Harrises were joined by miller John D. Trumbull, from Massachusetts, who formally laid out the community as Maiden Rock, named from the rock ledge overhanging the Mississippi River on the eastern edge of Lake Pepin, which was named from the Maiden Rock legend, one of the lovelorn Indian maiden tales that populate the American namescape from coast to coast. Details differ, but the legends have in common a beautiful Indian princess who is betrothed to a man she does not love and kept from the man she does. Rather than being forcibly married, she ascends a height and leaps to her death, and her broken body is recovered by her remorseful relatives. The legend of Maiden Rock is long standing and Wisconsin is well stocked with similar stories; for a selection, see D. Brown, "Indian Lover's Leaps." See Monona.

Maine. Marathon. The town was organized in 1866 and named for Uriah E. Maine, a county surveyor and sheriff in the early 1860s. The post office was established in January 1871 by John Kufahl. (Marchetti, 548)

Maine. Outagamie. Town (1868). Named in 1854 by Davis Stinson, George Speers, Paul Greely, and John Whitmore, for the state of Maine, their former home. (Balliet, 86)

Malone. Fond du Lac. Named for Thomas H. Malone, superintendent of the Sheboygan Division of the North Western railroad in the 1870s. The post office was established in June 1877, Anton Schmitz, postmaster. (Worthing)

Malvern. Oneida. Malvern might be a transfer name, brought to Wisconsin by settlers from Malvern, Pennsylvania, or Malvern, Ohio, itself named from Malvern, Pennsylvania. More likely, however, the name was given in honor of the Civil War battle of Malvern Hill, Virginia, where Union forces withstood a number of Confederate assaults in July 1862 and in which the Fifth Wisconsin Volunteers took part. The ultimate source of the name is the community of Malvern and the Malvern Hills of southwest England. The Malvern post office operated from November 1902 until February 1904.

Manawa [MAN uh wah]. Waupaca. City (1954). The origin and interpretation of Manawa is unknown. There is little to support the suggestions that Manawa was the name of a local Ojibwa leader and much less that it means 'I am out of tobacco,' both etymologies that have been seriously proposed. A possible source is Ojibwa *minewa* 'again, more.' Minewa Beach in Fond du Lac County may be a variant. (Vogel, *Indian Names*, 227)

Manchester. Green Lake. Town (organized as Albany in 1849; changed to Hardin in 1852; changed to Manchester in 1856). The community was laid out in 1856, probably by members of the Hoyt family and named for one of the Manchesters in New England or directly from Manchester, England. The post office was established in August 1856 by William A. Millard, from Ballston, New York. (Reetz, 33)

Manchester. Jackson. Town (1857). Named by Henry Quackenbush for Manchester, New York, or Manchester, New Hampshire, both of which were named for Manchester, England. (*Jackson County, a History*, 35)

Manitowish [MAN i tuh wish]. Iron. Named from the Manitowish River. The name is based upon *manito* 'spirit.' In his *Dictionary of the Otchipwe Language*, Bishop Frederic Baraga, who ministered to the Ojibwa in the mid-nineteenth century, defines *Manitowish* as 'small animal (a marten, a weasel, etc.).' The Manitowish post office was established in December 1890, George W. Ross, postmaster. See Manitowoc.

Manitowish Waters. Vilas. Town (organized as Spider Lake in 1927; changed to Manitowish Waters in 1939) and ppl. The community developed around a series of resorts established along the shores of several nearby lakes beginning in the early years of the twentieth century.

Manitowoc [MAN i tuh wahk]. County (1836), Town (organized as Conroe in 1838; changed to Manitowoc in 1839), and City (1870). Named from the Manitowoc River. Manitowoc is the plural of *manito*, a general Algonquian word meaning 'supernatural being, diety, spirit.' In early reports, the Manitowoc River was called the "river of spirits," the "river of good spirits," and, contradictorily, the "river of evil spirits." Manitowoc Rapids was founded by Jacob W. Conroe, from Middlebury, Vermont. Conroe established the Manitowoc Rapids post office in September 1836. The city of Manitowoc was founded shortly thereafter by William and Benjamin Jones, organizers of the Chicago-based Manitowoc Land Company. (Falge, 312, 345)

Mann. Marathon. Probably named for Curtis Mann, from Buffalo, New York, who operated a sawmill on the line of the Wisconsin Central railroad in the 1870s. The Mannville post office was established in February 1875 and discontinued in July 1892. (Marchetti, 137)

Maple Bluff. Dane. Village (1930). Named from Maple Bluff, a promontory extending into Lake Mendota, reportedly on which grew a remarkable grove of sugar maples. Earlier known as Sugar Grove and MacBride's Point, for Irish immigrant James MacBride, who settled in the area about 1850. The communities of Lakewood, Fuller's Woods, and MacBride's Point incorporated as the village of Maple Bluff about 1930. (McLean, 5, 22)

Marathon [MEHR uh thahn]. County. Marathon County was organized in 1850, largely through the efforts of Walter D. McIndoe, who represented Portage County in the Wisconsin Assembly in 1850 and Marathon County in 1854–55. He was U.S. representative from Wisconsin in the early 1860s. McIndoe probably chose the name from Marathon, the battlefield in Greece where an Athenian force defeated a Persian army in 490 BC. According to legend, a Greek messenger ran from Marathon to Athens bringing news of the victory.

Marathon City. Village. Named from the county, Marathon City was established by the Pittsburgh German Homestead Society in 1856. (Straub, 8, 9)

Marblehead. Fond du Lac. Named for the local quarries where limestone rather than marble is mined. The name may have been chosen by August and William Nast, who established the Nast Brothers Lime and Stone Quarry in the early 1870s. See Nasbro. (Worthing)

Marcellon [mahr SEL uhn]. Columbia. Town (1849) and ppl. Marcellon is probably an adaptation, intentional or accidental, of Massillon, brought to Wisconsin by settlers from Massillon in northeastern Ohio. According to James Jones's *History of Columbia County* (421), the town was to have been called Massillon but that name was erroneously recorded as Marrsellon, later revised to Marcellon. The post office was established in June 1847, Thomas D. Wallace, postmaster. This is the only Marcellon in the United States.

March Rapids. Marathon. In 1887, Thomas H. March, from Albion, New York, by way of southern Illinois, bought a sawmill on the Big Eau Pleine River around which a small settlement called Hope had developed. March laid out the community of March about the time he established the March post office in April 1892. (*Stratford Centennial Book*, 15)

Marcy. Waukesha. Origin uncertain. Likely a transfer by settlers from Marcy, Oneida County, New York, itself named for William Marcy, governor of New York in the 1830s. The Marcy post office operated from 1847 until July 1903.

Marengo [muh RENG go]. Ashland. Town (1907) and ppl. Named from the Marangouin (Marangoin) River, a tributary of the Bad River, itself named from *maringouin*, Mississippi Valley French for 'mosquito.' By popular etymology, Marangoin became Marengo, strongly influenced by Marengos in the eastern states, some of which were named for Marengo in northern Italy, where Napoleon defeated an Austrian army in 1800.

Maribel [MEHR uh bel]. Manitowoc. Village (1963). Named from the Maribel medicinal springs. The origin of the name is unknown. According to Stennett, "The name has no real significance, as it was manufactured for the springs" (98). There is no evidence to support a local account that the name was chosen by Father Francis X. Steinbrecher for the month of May with "bell" added for effect. The post office was established in August 1906, Joseph A. Kellner, postmaster.

Marietta [MEHR ee et uh]. Crawford. Town (1855). The name has been attributed to a young woman named Marietta who was tried and acquitted of theft in one of the first criminal cases prosecuted in the area. According to a local account, the defendant "so favorably impressed the officials . . . they named the township after her." More likely, however, Marietta was named for Marietta, Ohio, by the first postmaster, Oliver E. Wise, at the suggestion of his wife, Ada, who was born in southeast Ohio, near Marietta, itself named for Marie Antoinette, Queen of France in the late eighteenth century. (Butterfield, *History of Crawford and Richland Counties*, 626; Butteris)

Marinette [MEHR uh NET]. County (1879) and City (1887). Named for Marinette Chevalier, a French-Ojibwa métisse who settled in the area in 1822 with her second husband, trader William Farnsworth, with whom she took an active role in their joint business ventures. Her original given name is uncertain; it may have been Marie Antoinette, of which Marinette is a blend, or, as some have suggested, an existing diminutive associated with Marie Antoinette, the French queen executed around the time of Marinette's birth. John B. Jacobs Jr., Marinette's son by her first husband, established the post office in February 1853, which he named in honor of his mother. Jacobs was chair of the first township board of supervisors and platted what is now the central business district of Marinette in 1858. (Krog, 32)

Marion. Shawano, Waupaca. City (1898). First known as Perry's Mill, for the sawmill operated by Joseph W. Perry. About 1875 the site was bought by and platted for Ambrose McDonald and Daniel Ramsdell. The surveyor, Benjamin Franklin Dorr, chose the name, either for Francis Marion, the famous guerrilla fighter of the Revolution, or for Marion, Ohio, itself named for Francis Marion. (Adams, 7, 9)

Markesan [MAHR kuh san, MAHR kuh zan]. Green Lake. City (1959). Previously known as Granville, apparently a shortening of Grandville, a name derived from the Grand River. The community was laid out in 1849 by site owners John Chapel and Charles E. Russell. The local account is that Henry Wright, proprietor of the general store and the first postmaster in 1849, suggested the name from Marquesan, the adjectival form of Marquesas. The Marquesas Islands were in the news at the time because they had recently been annexed by France and became part of French Polynesia. The islands themselves were named for the Marquis of Cañete, the viceroy of Peru. (S. Smith)

Markton. Langlade. Previously known as Dobbston, named by Thomas M. Dobbs, who operated the first sawmill in the area from about 1874. After Thomas Dobbs left the area, the site was bought by George Roix and renamed for his son, Markton. The Dobbston post office operated from

June 1877 until July 1894 and was reestablished as Markton by Nettie Roix in July 1896. (Dessureau, 205)

Marlands [MAR lunz]. Vilas. In the 1930s Frank Mars, founder of the Mars Candy Company, makers of Mars Bars, Milky Way, and Snickers, built a summer resort on Fence Lake which he named for himself. (Meyers)

Marquette. Marquette County, organized in December 1836, and the Town (1843) and Village (1958) of Marquette in Green Lake County are named for Père Jacques Marquette (1637–75), a French Jesuit priest. He and Louis Jolliet were the first Europeans to explore the upper Fox, lower Wisconsin, and middle Mississippi River valleys on their historic 1673 expedition, which took them from Green Bay to the mouth of the Arkansas River.

Marshall. Dane. The village of Marshall has had at least four names. About 1837 brothers Augustus and Zenas Bird and Aaron Petrie organized a small settlement around their tavern on the Maunesha River. The tavern burned, giving rise to the site's first name, Bird's Ruins. In 1850, shopkeeper and site owner Asahel Hanchett laid out the community of Hanchettville. When the Chicago, Milwaukee & St. Paul railroad built through the area in the late 1850s, the station was called Howard City, reportedly for a Mr. Howard who was instrumental in attracting the railroad. In the early 1860s Hanchett sold his holdings to Samuel Marshall, a Madison banker and real estate broker, and since then the community has been known as Marshall. Asahel Hanchett established the post office as Hanchettville in 1848; the name was changed to Marshall in February 1862. (Trachte)

Marshall. Richland. Named for the Marshall family. Among the first settlers were Ohioans John and Simon Marshall, who came in the spring of 1852. A family member, Joseph Marshall, was a prominent figure in Richland County and a justice of the peace when the township was organized in 1854. (Butterfield, *History of Crawford and Richland Counties*, 1115)

Marshall. Rusk. Town (1902). Named for Marshall Sergeant, an early settler, Civil War veteran, first township chair, and second sheriff of Rusk (then Gates) County. (*Commemorative Biographical Record of the Upper Lake Region*, 209)

Marshfield. Fond du Lac. Town (1855). Much of the area now comprising the Town of Marshfield was organized as the Town of Kossuth (q.v.) in April 1852. That name was vacated less than a year later and the town was reorganized in 1855 as Marshfield. The origin of the name is unknown; Worthing suggests it is descriptive of the nearby wetlands.

Marshfield. Wood. Town (1875) and ppl. A tavern operated by brothers Louis and Frank Rivers from about 1868 provided the nucleus for the community of Marshfield, a name of uncertain origin. It may be a transfer; there are

Marshfields in Massachusetts, New York, New Hampshire, and Vermont, all states that contributed substantial numbers of settlers to early Wisconsin. It may be a railroad name. The Wisconsin Central, which built through the Marshfield area in the early 1870s, was particularly fond of naming stations for the New England homes of their officers, legal staffs, and bond holders. It may be from a personal name; Samuel Marsh was one of the site owners, and his nephew John J. Marsh laid out Marshfield. The fact that the Marsh family was from Massachusetts further obscures the source of the name. Robert Rudolph claims that Marshfield was named from the Wisconsin Central station, itself named for Marshfield, Massachusetts, by Gardner or Charles Colby, officials of the railroad. Several of these sources may have contributed to the name Marshfield. (Kleiman, 3; Stennett, 99)

Marshland. Buffalo. Perhaps named from a tract of marshy land that was drained and converted into a fertile field. The post office was established in January 1875, Asa Hedge, postmaster. (Stennett, 100)

Martell [mar TEL]. Pierce. Town (1854) and ppl. Laid out in the summer of 1856 as Rising Sun. Renamed for Joseph Martell, who, along with Xerxes Jock and several other French Canadians, settled in the area in the late 1840s. The post office was established in September 1858, Ole Rasmuson, postmaster. (Wiff, 2, 6, 25)

Martinsville. Dane. The first known settler was Joseph Knipschild, who emigrated from Westphalia, Germany, in 1846. Knipschild was instrumental in organizing the St. Martin's Catholic church in 1850, from which the community takes its name. The post office was established in August 1900, Leonard Vetter, postmaster. (Cassidy, *Dane County Place-Names*)

Martintown. Green. Named by and for Nathaniel Martin, who came to the area from Virginia about 1848 and established a dam and sawmill on the Pecatonica River. The community and post office were known as Martin until the Illinois Central railroad was built through in 1888. (Butterfield, *History of Green County*, 750)

Marxville. Dane. Named for site owner Johann Marx, who emigrated from Brandenburg, Germany, about 1857. The local story is that Marx provided a free barrel of beer at the naming caucus. The post office was established in April 1886, Jacob Back, postmaster. (Cassidy, *Dane County Place-Names*)

Marytown. Fond du Lac. Named from the Church of the Visitation of the Blessed Virgin Mary, organized by German Catholic settlers in the late 1840s. The post office was established in September 1854 by John Kraus. (Worthing)

Mason. Bayfield. Town (organized as New Mason in March 1924; changed to Mason in May 1924) and Village (1925). Named by site owner John A.

Humbird, probably for the Fraternal Order of Freemasons. Several of Humbird's associates were reported to be enthusiastic Masons. The post office was established in June 1883, Hiram A. Hunt, postmaster. See Humbird. (Stennett, 183)

Mather [MA ther]. Juneau. Named from the Mathers post office, established by John L. Mather, from Orange County, New York, in January 1876. (Richards, 385)

Matteson [MAT suhn]. Waupaca. Town (1856). Named for Roswell and Miranda Matteson, from New York State, the first settlers in the area, who arrived in the summer of 1855. The post office was established as Embarras, named from the Embarrass River, in March 1856, David Matteson, postmaster. (Ware, 62)

Mattoon [ma TOON]. Shawano. Village (1901). Named for the site owner, businessman George B. Mattoon. Born in Troy, New York, Mattoon established the Mattoon Manufacturing Company, specializing in household furniture, in Sheboygan in 1881. The post office was established in December 1895, Christian F. Ladwig, postmaster. (*Portrait and Biographical Record of Sheboygan County*, 315)

Mauston [MAWS tuhn]. Juneau. City (1883). Mauston is an adaptation of Maughs Town, platted in 1854 for site owner and gristmill operator Milton M. Maughs, known as General Maughs for his service with the Illinois militia during the Black Hawk War of 1832. The post office was established as Maughs Mills in September 1854, James M. Maughs, postmaster. (*Juneau County*, 10)

Maxville [MAKS vil]. Buffalo. Town and ppl. The township was organized in 1857 as Bear Creek and renamed later that year as Bloomington. The name was changed to Maxville in 1858 in honor of a Mr. Maxvell [*sic*], about whom little is known. Joseph Scafe, the first postmaster at Maxville in 1858, had a heavy Yorkshire accent, and the townsfolk, for their own entertainment, often asked him to spell Maxville. In the words of Curtiss-Wedge's 1919 *History of Buffalo and Pepin Counties*: "An amusing anecdote is still told by the old settlers in connection with this name. . . . [W]hen asked to spell the new name of the town [Scafe] would reply, 'It is spelled with a hem, a hai, a hex, a we, a hi, a double hell and a he'" (94).

May Corner. Marinette. Named for the Anton May family, early settlers from St. Lawrence County, New York, in 1855. (*Commemorative Biographical Record of the West Shore of Green Bay*, 586)

Mayfield. Washington. In 1852 site owners Andreas Reiderer and George Fleischmann laid out the community that Reiderer named Mayfield, a translation of the name of his birthplace, Maienfeld, Canton Graubünden,

Switzerland. The post office was established in July 1860, Henry Toedli, postmaster. (Quickert, 43)

Mayville. Clark. Town (1873). Named for Charles Sumner May, an early settler from Pennsylvania by way of Illinois, himself named for Charles Sumner, U.S. senator from Massachusetts in the 1850s and 1860s. See Sumner. (Scholtz)

Mayville. Dodge. City (1885). Founded by the May and Foster families in 1845. Chester May, from Oneida County, New York, and Alvin Foster located a significant deposit of iron ore near present Neda. They bought the site and later sold it to the Wisconsin Iron Company. Mayville, named for Chester May, was formally platted by Alvin Foster in 1847. (Martinson, 3, 9)

Mazomanie [may zuh MAY nee]. Dane. Town (organized as Farmersville in 1848; changed to Black Earth in 1851; changed to Mazomanie in 1859) and Village (1885). Mazomanie was settled largely through the efforts of the British Temperance Emigration Society of Liverpool, England, which by the 1850s had located several hundred colonists in the area. The traditional story is that Edward H. Brodhead, superintendent and chief operating engineer of the Milwaukee & Mississippi railroad, took the name from Manzemoneka, the Winnebago warrior who had killed Pierre Paquette, a well-known trader at Fort Winnebago, in 1836. Brodhead found the name, which he simplified to Manzomanie, quite appropriate since it meant 'iron walker,' which he chose to interpret prophetically as 'iron horse,' since the railroad was coming to the valley. There is, however, a more direct and more likely source of the name. Mazomanie was the name of at least two generations of leaders of the Sioux on the Minnesota River in the second quarter of the nineteenth century. The elder, whose name is recorded as *Mazo-manie* 'Iron That Walks,' signed a treaty at Prairie du Chien in 1830, and the younger (probably his son) was signatory to the 1858 treaty of Washington, where his mark is *Maz-zo-ma-nee* 'Walking Iron.' Hercules Dousman, a director of the Milwaukee & Mississippi railroad and a former fur trader in the Prairie du Chien area, may have suggested the name to Brodhead. The post office was established as Mazo Manie in January 1856, Gilbert T. Whitney, postmaster. (Cassidy, *Dane County Place-Names*; Vogel, *Indian Names*, 63)

McAllister. Marinette. Probably named for site owner Donald J. McAllister, who emigrated from New Brunswick, Canada, in the 1860s. McAllister was active in a number of logging operations and was president of the Brown-George Lumber Company in the 1890s. The post office was established in January 1895, Olof Lombard, postmaster. (*Commemorative Biographical Record of the West Shore of Green Bay*, 489)

McCartney. Grant. Named for Orris McCartney, originally from Washington County, New York. McCartney was a local official, a Grant County supervisor, and a member of the Wisconsin Territorial Legislature in the 1840s. The post office was established in February 1896, Daniel Dodge, postmaster.

McCord. Lincoln, Oneida. Probably named for Myron Hawley McCord (1840–1908), a state senator in the 1870s, U.S. representative from Wisconsin in the late 1880s, and governor of Arizona Territory in the late 1890s. The post office was established in August 1892, James C. Paul, postmaster.

McFarland. Dane. Village (1920). Named for William H. McFarland, who emigrated from London, England, in the early 1830s. He became construction superintendent of the Milwaukee & Mississippi railroad and donated land for the station in 1856. Modern McFarland includes the site of the City of the Second Lake (Lake Waubesa), a community proposed by James Duane Doty on the Yahara River that never developed beyond an 1836 plat. McFarland is the official form of the name, but MacFarland and Macfarland are also found. (Houghton, Licht, and Nielsen, 4, 14)

McKinley. Named for William McKinley (1843–1901), twenty-fifth president of the United States, in office 1897–1901. McKinley in Polk County was organized in November 1897, shortly after McKinley was elected president. McKinley in Taylor County was organized in May 1902, several months after McKinley was shot and killed by anarchist Leon Czolgosz in Buffalo, New York.

McMillan. Marathon. Town (1888) and ppl. Founded by Benjamin Franklin McMillan, from New York State. McMillan and his brother, Charles, operated a sawmill on the Plover River from the late 1860s. The former community of McMillan was located several miles north of Marshfield. The post office was established in August 1881, Samuel B. Powell, postmaster. (Stennett, 100)

McNaughton [mik NAWT n]. Oneida. Originally a railroad siding established to serve the primary sawmill of the Bradley and Kelly Lumber Company. Named for either James McNaughton, the Wisconsin Central railroad's superintendent of motive power in the 1890s, or Dougall W. McNaughton, the first postmaster in 1890, or both. (R. Martin, 82)

Mead. Clark. Town (1895). Named for William Henry Harrison Mead, township chair and member of the Clark County Board. Mead, from New York, was an agent for the Gates Land Company. See Rusk County. (Scholtz)

Mecan [mi KAN]. Marquette. Town (1856) and ppl. Named from the Mecan River. An adaptation of Ojibwa *mikana* 'road, pathway.' Mikana (q.v.) is a variant. (Vogel, *Indian Names*, 127)

Medary [muh DER ee]. La Crosse. Town (1853) and ppl. Named for Samuel Medary, a leading figure in the Democratic Party and an influential newsman. Medary was territorial governor of Minnesota and of Kansas, both in the 1850s. Medary, South Dakota, and Medaryville, Indiana, are also named in his honor. Previously known as Winona Junction. (Stennett, 101)

Medford. Taylor. Town (1874) and City (1889). Named with construction of the Wisconsin Central railroad by Boston financier Gardner Colby, or his son Charles, both presidents of the railroad, for the Medford area of Boston, Massachusetts, itself named for Medford, England. (Stennett, 164)

Medina [muh DEYE nuh]. Dane. Town (1848). Named in the late 1840s by Charles Lum, Sardine Muzzy, and others from Medina, Ohio. Muzzy married Lum's daughter, Elorsey Caroline, in Medina, Ohio in 1827. (Keyes, 363)

Medina. Outagamie. First known as Youngs Corner, for an early settler named Young (probably Samuel Young) who established a hotel at the site in the mid-1850s. Zehner (65) claims that the community was named by settlers from Medina, Ohio, but Medina, New York (for which Medina, Ohio, was probably named), is also a possible source. The name, in fact, may have been proposed by Josephus Wakefield, from Watertown, New York, who established the Medina post office in February 1852. The town of Medina existed from 1856 until 1858 when the name was changed to Dale. The dozen or so Medinas in the United States are ultimately named from Medina, Saudia Arabia, one of the holy cities of Islam.

Medina Junction. Winnebago. Originally a coaling dock and water tank established by the Wisconsin Central railroad about 1872. Named for its proximity to Medina in Outagamie County. (Stennett, 101)

Meehan. Portage. Named for Patrick and James Meehan, brothers who operated a sawmill on the Wisconsin River in the 1870s. James Meehan represented Portage County in the Wisconsin Assembly in 1878. The post office was established in March 1876, Leonard Niles Anson, postmaster. (Rosholt, *Our County, Our Story*, 329)

Meekers Grove. Lafayette. Named for Moses Meeker, who was instrumental in developing the lead industry of southwestern Wisconsin in the 1820s. Meeker established the post office in the summer of 1857. (Butterfield, *History of Lafayette County*, 562)

Meeme [MEE mee]. Manitowoc. Town (1849) and ppl. Previously known as the Irish Settlement. Meeme is an adaptation with phonetic spelling of Ojibwa *omimi* 'dove' or 'pigeon,' and was probably chosen because of the large numbers of wild pigeons in the area. Mimi Lake in Bayfield County is a variant, and Pigeon River, which empties into the Meeme River near Meeme, is a translation. The post office was established in February 1848, Henry B. Edson, postmaster. (Vogel, *Indian Names*, 151)

Meenon [MEE nuhn]. Burnett. Town (1899). From Ojibwa *minan* 'blueberries.' The word root, *min*, may also be the source of Minong (q.v.) in Washburn County. (Vogel, *Indian Names*, 160)

Meggers. Calumet, Manitowoc. Named for shopkeeper Andreas (Andrew) Meggers, who emigrated from Schleswig-Holstein, Germany, in the early 1850s. The post office was established in June 1886 by Andrew Meggers's son Henry. ("Andrew Meggers")

Mellen. Ashland. City (1907). Samuel O. Bennett, regarded as the first settler in Mellen, called his homestead Iron City, after the Gogebic-Penokee iron range. Early in 1888, after construction of the Penokee branch of the Wisconsin Central railroad, the nascent community took the name of the Mellen post office, established in January 1887 by Amos Markee. Although several accounts claim the community was named for Charles Sanger Mellen, general manager of the Union Pacific railroad, the namesake is most likely William Solon Mellen, general manager of the Wisconsin Central at the time of Mellen's naming. The confusion between the two men named Mellen stems largely from the fact that both were later associated with the Northern Pacific railroad. With Mellen as a growing junction point, the smaller settlement of Penokee, several miles south of Mellen, waned and ultimately disappeared. (*Journey into Mellen*, 28)

Melnik. Manitowoc. Named for Mělnik in the Czech Republic, twenty miles north of Prague. The name was probably proposed by Joseph Duchac, from Bohemia, who kept the first general store in the area and served as the first chair of the Town of Neva in 1883. The post office was established in March 1887, Frederick Shimonek, postmaster. (Dessereau, 218)

Melrose. Jackson. Several Douglas families from Scotland settled in the area around 1840. Robert Douglas established a ferry across the Black River that became the nucleus for a community known as the Douglas Settlement and also as Dumfries, for Dumfries in southern Scotland. The name was formalized as Melrose, with establishment of the post office by postmaster Mark Douglas in April 1855, for the town and ruined abbey in southeastern Scotland that provided the setting for Sir Walter Scott's novels *The Abbot* and *The Monastery*. (*Jackson County Reader*, 17)

174

Melvina [mel VEYE nuh]. Monroe. Village (1922). Founded in 1866. Named by site owner and first postmaster Charles Hunt, from Chautauqua County, New York, in honor of his wife, Amanda Melvina Hunt. (*Monroe County*, 41)

Menasha [muh NASH uh]. Winnebago. Town (1855) and City (1874). Founded in the late 1840s by Charles Doty, son of and secretary to Wisconsin territorial governor James Duane Doty, and Curtis Reed, brother of Harrison Reed, a founder of Neenah. Sarah Doty, wife of James Doty, is generally credited with proposing the name. From Menominee *menehseh* 'island,' perhaps referring to Doty Island, now shared by Menasha and Neenah. The post office was established in November 1849, James K. Lusk, postmaster. (Vogel, *Indian Names*, 178)

Menchalville [MEN chil vil]. Manitowoc. Named for one or more Menchal families. Vaclav Mencil [*sic*] emigrated from Mělnik, Bohemia, now in the Czech Republic, in 1854. Stephen Menchal established the post office, which he kept in his store, in March 1895. (Rucker, *History of Czech Settlements*, 6)

Menominee [muh NAH muh nee]. County. Also Menomonee Falls in Waukesha County and Menomonie [*sic*] in Dunn and Waukesha Counties. Menominee is derived from Ojibwa *manomin* 'wild rice.' *Manomini*, the 'wild rice people,' was the name given by the Ojibwa to the Menominee, for whom wild rice was a major food source. By 1670 the name Menominee referred to both the Menominee people and to at least one of the three Menominee or Menomonee rivers in Wisconsin. In 1961 the U.S. Congress ended all federal support for the Menominee, and in response the Wisconsin Legislature organized Menominee County from what until that time had been the Menominee reservation. Menomonie in Dunn County grew around a sawmill established in 1822 by James H. Lockwood and Joseph Rolette. The mill was bought in 1846 by John H. Knapp, later joined by Henry L. Stout as proprietors and namesakes of the Knapp, Stout & Co., one of the largest timber operations of nineteenth-century Wisconsin. Stout's son, James Huff Stout, also associated with the lumber company, was the founder in 1893 of the Stout Manual Training School in Menomonie, subsequently known as the Stout Institute, Stout State College, Stout State University, and now the University of Wisconsin–Stout. (Dunn County Historical Society, 36)

Mentor [MEN ter]. Clark. Town (1866). The name was suggested by George W. King for his former home in Lake County, Ohio, itself named for early settler Hiram Mentor. King was clerk of the county board and served in the Wisconsin Assembly in 1871. (Scholtz)

Mequon [MEK wahn]. Ozaukee. City (1957). Mequon is from a Native American language, but its source and derivation are uncertain. Several writers have suggested that Mequon, translated as 'white feather,' was the daughter of Chief Waubeka or that the namesake is "a locally famous Indian" named McKwon or Mekwan, meaning 'arrow.' Others suggest that a Native American name for Pigeon Creek was Mequon-sippi from *mequon* 'pigeon.' Increase Lapham, one of Wisconsin's first scientists, wrote the name as Mequanigo well into the 1840s, suggesting that Mequon may be a simple shortening of Mukwanigo (see Mukwonago). A major problem in determining the derivation of *mequon* is that the word root is general Algonquian and has taken on different meanings among Algonquian speakers of different regions. A variant is *Miquon* in Montgomery County, Pennsylvania, where the meaning is clearly 'feather' or 'quill.' Another variant is Maquon in Knox County, Illinois, derived from *A-ma-quon-sip-pi*, 'squash river' or 'mussel shell river.' Mussel shells were used as utensils and one translation of *A-ma-quon-sip-pi* was 'spoon river.' Surveyor Thomas Cram made what may be the first recording of the name about 1839 when he wrote "Micwon River" for the tributary of the Milwaukee River now called Cedar Creek. The name was formalized with establishment of the Mequon River post office in June 1840. (Eccles, 2; Stennett, 101; Vogel, *Indian Names*, 227)

Mercer. Iron. Town (1909) and ppl. Possibly named for a local lumberman named Mercer, but Stennett suggests that an organizer of the town named Mercer chose the name in honor of General Hugh Mercer (1725–77), who served with distinction in the French and Indian War and died at Princeton, New Jersey, during the American Revolution. At least seven U.S. counties are named in honor of Hugh Mercer. The post office was established in March 1895, Edward Staples, postmaster. (Stennett, 101)

Meridean [mehr uh DEEN]. Dunn. Origin unknown. By one local account the community is named for Mary Dean, the wife of trader and trapper Ira Dean, who drowned in the Chippewa River near Happy Island in the 1860s. By another, a young girl named Mary Dean was on a steamboat in the Chippewa River when she became violently ill and died. Her mother and the steamboat crew buried her at an unknown location on the river bank. Some accounts claim the ghost of little Mary Dean continues to haunt Happy Island. However, Meridean may be a simple mistranscription of Meridian, from the Meridian post office, established in 1874 and named for its location on or near the ninetieth meridian, which runs through Dunn County. (Curtiss-Wedge and Jones, 216–17)

Merrill [MEHR uhl]. Lincoln. Town (organized as Jenny in 1857; changed to Merrill in 1881) and City (1883). The area was first known as Bollier or

Beaulieux, for a French Canadian trader whose post was on the Wisconsin River in the early 1840s. About 1847 Andrew Warren Jr. established a sawmill, store, and hotel at the site and gave the falls and the nascent community their first formal name, Jenny Bull. The origin of Jenny is unknown. Local folklore claims that Jenny was the name given to a promiscuous Potawatomi woman by grateful rivermen, traders, and trappers. (And, indeed, Jenny has been often used as a generic for prostitute.) Jenny Bull, usually shortened to Jenny, was changed to Merrill in 1881 for Sherburn Sanborn Merrill, at the time general manager of the Chicago, Milwaukee & St. Paul railroad. Sherburn Merrill is also the namesake of Merrill Park, a Milwaukee community that grew around the large service complex established by the railroad in the early 1880s. The post office was established in February 1859 as Jenny and changed to Merrill in June 1881. See Bull. (Olsen, *Roots of the North*, 90)

Merrillan [MEHR uh luhn]. Jackson. Village (1881). Founded in 1870 with construction of the West Wisconsin railroad by site owners Leander and Benjamin Merrill. The name is clearly derived from Merrill, but details are unclear. By one account the source is "Merrill &," from the Merrill & Loomis general store. The post office was established as Merrillon in October 1870, James L. Loomis, postmaster; the spelling was changed to Merrillan in April 1894. (*Jackson County, a History*, 20)

Merrimac [MAIR uh mak]. Sauk. Town (1854) and Village (1899). Formerly known as Matt's Ferry, for Chester Mat(t)son, who operated a ferry across the Wisconsin River from the mid-1840s. The name was formalized as Merrimack, for Merrimack, New Hampshire, early in 1855. Merrimac is an Algonquian word meaning 'deep place' among Algonquian speakers in New England and 'catfish' in the Midwest. According to local historians Charlotte Olson and Michael Goc, the Wisconsin name was suggested by Emily Train; both she and her husband, lawyer James G. Train, were born in Merrimack County, New Hampshire. Walter P. Flanders of Milwaukee, generally considered the founder of Merrimac and also a native of Merrimack, New Hampshire, bought Mattson's ferry service in 1849, the year the post office was established by Chester Matson as Collamer, named for recently appointed U.S. postmaster general Jacob Collamer. The spelling has alternated between Merrimac and Merrimack. (Goc, *Many a Fine Harvest*, 177)

Merton. Waukesha. Town (organized as Warren in 1842; changed to Merton in 1848) and Village (1922). The post office petition of 1847 called for the name Warren, for a local Warren family. When this name was rejected, the application was resubmitted by William Odell with the name Merton, apparently suggested by Mary Shears, wife of miller Henry Shears, who would be the second postmaster, for one of the several Mertons in England. Mary Shears was born in Windermere, in the English Lake County. (Haight, 296)

Meteor. Sawyer. Town (1919) and ppl. Named from the local story that a meteor had once fallen in the vicinity. The post office was established in June 1906, Eugene F. Miller, postmaster. (Chappelle, *Around the Four Corners*, 204)

Metomen [muh TO muhn]. Fond du Lac. Town (1846). Named by Francis D. Bowman, the first settler of Alto, who said the name was Menominee for 'grain of corn.' Menominee *mita men* 'strawberry,' literally 'heart berry,' has also been suggested, as has Ojibwa *menomin*, the source of *Menominee* (q.v.). (McKenna, 262; Vogel, *Indian Names*, 164)

Metz [METS]. Waushara, Winnebago. Origin uncertain, but likely a transfer from the city of Metz in northeastern France, near the borders of France, Germany, and Luxembourg. The post office was established by Frederick T. Niemuth in March 1898 and was discontinued in May 1908.

Middle Inlet. Marinette. Town (1910) and ppl. Named from Middle Inlet, the stream lying between Lower Middle Inlet and Upper Middle Inlet, all of which flow into Lake Noquebay. The post office was established in December 1890, Edward W. Dropp, postmaster.

Middle Ridge. La Crosse. The community that grew around the Catholic mission of St. Peter from about 1870 was known as St. Peter's until the Middle Ridge post office was established in May 1878 by John Schomers. The office was named from its location at the approximate middle of the prominent ridge running through the area. (Hundt)

Middleton. Dane. Town (1848) and City (1963). Named from the Middleton post office, established in September 1846 and apparently named for Middleton (Middletown), Vermont, by postmaster Harry Barnes. The community was informally known as Peatville for the local peat deposits. Burgess Slaughter, active in the harvesting and sale of peat, established the Peatville post office in December 1856. After construction of the Milwaukee & Mississippi railroad in the early 1860s, the community was formally platted and the name of the post office was changed to Middleton Station. (Butterfield, *History of Dane County*, 899; Cassidy, *Dane County Place-Names*)

Midway. La Crosse. Founded as Halfway Creek, named from the stream, by James B. Canterbury, one of the incorporators of the Stevens Point, Wausau & Northern railroad. The name was changed to Midway Station with construction of the railroad. The post office was established in January 1872 by Hiram F. Smiley. (Stennett, 102)

Mifflin. Iowa. Town and ppl. Named for George Mifflin Dallas, vice president of the United States when the town was organized in 1849. The community was laid out by Joel Clayton, a local tavern keeper (and the namesake of Clayton, California). The post office was established in September 1848, Franklin Andrews, postmaster. See Dallas. (*History of Iowa County*, 820)

Mikana [MEYE kuh nuh, mi KAN uh]. Barron. From Ojibwa *mikana* 'road.' Circumstances of choosing the name are unknown. Mecan in Marquette County is a variant. The post ofice was established in June 1902, Thomas Losby Jr., postmaster. (Vogel, *Indian Names*, 127)

Milan [MEYE luhn]. Richland. Milan is a popular place name, occurring in more than a dozen states. Milan, Wisconsin, may have been named directly for the Italian city, but more likely the name was brought to Wisconsin from an eastern Milan, perhaps Milan, New York, or Milan, Ohio. The post office operated from August 1857 until April 1860.

Milladore [MIL uh dor]. Wood. Town (1882) and Village (1933). Previously known as Mill Creek. Apparently Milladore was chosen as the name of the post office in late 1875 by postmaster Orlow A. Everts. The source of the name is unknown. According to Robert Rudolph, "Supposedly the inspiration for the new name was either a fictitious place in a book the postmaster was reading . . . or the name of a sleeping car on the Wisconsin Central RR." This is the only Milladore in the United States.

Millard [MIL erd]. Walworth. Named for Millard Fillmore (1800–1874), thirteenth president of the United States, who assumed the office in 1850 upon the death of Zachary Taylor. The post office was established in February 1851 by Hiram Taylor.

Mill Center. Brown. Apparently named for the concentration of local lumber mills, reported to be a dozen or more in the late 1850s. The post office was established as Mill Centre, Sylvester Wright, postmaster, in July 1867. (Cassidy, *Brown County*)

Millhome [MIL hom]. Manitowoc. Named in the 1860s by Simon Hollensteiner of Germany, who established a sawmill in 1863, a general store in 1865, and the post office in 1872. Apparently, Hollensteiner created Millhome by combining *mill* and *home*. (Falge, 424)

Millston. Jackson. Town (1874) and ppl. Founded by Hugh Brooks Mills, from St. Lawrence County, New York, who first worked as a laborer in the pineries around Shawano. He later established his own sawmill and became a prosperous businessman and civic leader. Mills named the community for himself in the early 1870s and established the post office in February 1874. (*Biographical History of Clark and Jackson Counties*, 145)

Milltown. Polk. Town (1869) and ppl. About 1886 Jerome Patterson established a general store and post office, which he named for himself, about a mile from the present site of Milltown. When the railroad was built east of Patterson, many of the buildings were moved to trackside. The new community took the name of the township, itself probably named by Irish immigrant Patrick Lillis, who gave two reasons for his choice: that Milltown was in honor of Milltown, Ireland, his former home, and that the name is ironic because "there is not a stream large enough for a mill site in the entire township." The Patterson post office was changed to Milltown in March 1899. (Folsom and Edwards, 31)

Millville. Grant. Apparently named for the local mills. Elihu Warner and his sons built the first sawmill in 1840; William Kidd, the first gristmill in 1844; and Joseph Horsfall, the first woolen mill in 1850. The post office was established in May 1852, Charles C. Drake, postmaster. (Butterfield, *History of Grant County*, 869)

Milton. Rock. City (1969). Early settlers in the late 1830s included Joseph Goodrich and Stephen Butts, generally considered the founders of Milton. The original petition for a post office called for the name Grainfield, which was reconsidered and formally submitted as Prairie du Lac ('meadow of the lake'), which was apparently rejected because it was too similar to Prairie du Sac. The source of the present name Milton is uncertain. There are several dozen Miltons in the United States, including Massachusetts and Pennsylvania, home states of the founders. Some Miltons are transfers from England, others are contractions of Mill Town, others are for the seventeeth-century poet John Milton, and still others are for prominent Milton families. There is a local story that Butts called his Pennsylvania home Paradise Lost and his Wisconsin home Paradise Regained, suggesting that he chose the name for the author of poems so named, but this may be nothing more than a nice story. The post office was established in September 1839, Joseph Goodrich, postmaster. (*Bicentennial History of Milton*, 65)

Milwaukee [mil WAW kee]. County and City. The first known Europeans to settle in what is now Milwaukee were the French Canadian traders Baptiste Mirandeau and Jaques Vieau, who established a trading post in 1795. They were followed by "the fathers of Milwaukee," Solomon Juneau, who established Juneautown on the east bank of the Milwaukee River about 1825; George Walker, who laid out Walker's Point in 1835; and Byron Kilbourn, a surveyor from Green Bay, who founded Kilbourntown in 1839. The three communities merged as Milwaukee in the mid-1840s. The county, created by the Michigan Territorial Legislature in September 1834, and the city, incorporated in 1846, are named from the Milwaukee River, the name of which has been recorded variously, from Mahnawaukie through Meeleewaugee, Miloake, Milaucky, and Milwaucki to Milwaukee, which became official in 1844. Milwaukee is from a word common to Potawatomi, Ojibwa, Menominee, and other Algonquian languages, meaning 'good land.' Baraga derives the name from Ojibwa *mino* 'good' and *aki* 'earth, soil.' The post office was established in March 1835, Solomon Juneau, postmaster. Milwaukie in Clackamas County, Oregon, was named by settlers from Wisconsin in the late 1840s. See Theresa. (Vogel, *Indian Names*, 134–35)

Mindoro [min DOR o]. La Crosse. Probably named by Lloyd Lewis for the western Philippine island of Mindoro. Lewis established the post office in February 1852. This is the only Mindoro in the United States.

Mineral Point. Iowa. Town (1849) and City (1857). Named for the extensive deposits of lead ore, known as "mineral," which provided much of the economic base for southwest Wisconsin and northwest Illinois from the late 1820s. In its early days Mineral Point was known as Shake Rag Under the Hill, or simply Shake Rag. In Mineral Point, it was said, wives waved dishrags to let their miner husbands know that it was dinnertime. Shakerag Street which runs by Soldiers Memorial Park in Mineral Point perpetuates the name. The Mineral Point post office was established in March 1836 by William Henry. (G. Shepard, 56)

Minnesota Junction. Dodge. Named from the projected Wisconsin terminus of the Chicago, Milwaukee & St. Paul railroad. The post office was established in January 1861, Stephen R. S. Audres, postmaster. (Stennett, 103)

Minocqua [muh NAHK wuh]. Oneida. Town (1889) and ppl. Few Wisconsin names have inspired as much speculation as has Minocqua. Among the interpretations that have been proposed are 'noon day,' 'stop and drink,' 'a pleasant place to be,' 'fair maiden,' 'good woman,' 'bad woman,' 'place of blueberries,' and, of course, references to an Indian chief and his beautiful daughter. In spite of these creative suggestions, the source of the name and its meaning are straightforward but not nearly so romantic. Minocqua is from Ojibwa *minakwa* 'a clump of trees.' (Bright; Miazga, 17)

Minong [MEYE nahng]. Washburn. Town (1893) and Village (1915). Founded about 1888 by the first postmaster, Josiah Bond, on the line of the Chicago, St. Paul, Minneapolis & Omaha railroad, which was being extended to Superior. Minong is Ojibwa, possibly from *mino*, 'good,' plus *ong* 'place,' but more likely built upon *min*, which refers to blueberries or huckleberries. Minonk, Woodford County, Illinois, is a variant. (Vogel, *Indian Names*, 162)

Misha Mokwa [mish uh MO kwuh, mish uh MAH kwuh]. Buffalo. From Ojibwa *mishi* 'big' and *makwa* 'bear.' In his narrative poem *Hiawatha*, Longfellow calls Misha Mokwa "the Great Bear . . . the terror of the nations." Mudjekeewis kills Misha Mokwa with a blow to the forehead, breaking its skull "as ice is broken when one goes to fish in Winter." The post office was established in April 1871, James W. Kelly, postmaster. See Moquah. (Bright)

Mishicot [MISH i kaht]. Manitowoc. Town and Village (1950). Mishicot grew around a sawmill established by Alfred Smith about 1844. Probably named for Mishicot, a Potawatomi leader of the early nineteenth century, who was also known as Neatoshing. Several interpretations of *Mishicot* have been proposed, including 'turtle,' 'a swatch of cloth,' and 'hairy leg,' but the significance of the name—if any—is unknown. The town was organized as Mishicot in 1852; the name was changed by German settlers to Saxonburg in 1853 and back to Mishicot later that year. (Vogel, *Indian Names*, 48)

Mitchell. Sheboygan. Town. Organized in 1850 as Olio, named from the Olio post office, established by George H. Smith in September 1849. Buchen is probably correct when he notes that Olio is "an archaic word meaning a wide-mouthed earthen pot" and the name was suggested by the "kettles," the depressions in the local glacial drift. The name was changed to Mitchell (with English spelling) in 1851 at the request of Irish settlers to honor John Mitchel, the Irish nationalist and political journalist who was incarcerated in the British penal colony in Bermuda when the town was organized. (Buchen, 303)

Modena [mo DEEN uh]. Buffalo. Town (1861) and ppl. Probably named by early settler William Odell for Modena, Ulster County, New York, itself named for Modena in northern Italy. The post office was established in June 1862, Benjamin F. Babcock, postmaster. (Curtiss-Wedge, *History of Buffalo and Pepin Counties*, 96)

Moeville [MO vil]. Pierce. Named by and for Norwegian immigrant Ingvar S. Moe, who established the Moeville post office in January 1891.

Molitor [MAHL uh ter]. Taylor. Town (1886). Named for the Molitor family from Mensdorf, Luxembourg. William Molitor was one of the first settlers in 1878. (*Commemorative Biographical Record of the Upper Lake Region*, 255)

Monches [mahn CHES]. Waukesha. Founded in the 1840s by Irish settlers as O'Connellsville, named for Daniel O'Connell, the early nineteenth-century Irish political and social leader known as the Liberator. The name was changed with establishment of the post office in February 1848. Named for Monches, a local Native American of Ojibwa-Potawatomi ancestry. According to Whelan (44–45), the name change from O'Connellsville to

Monches was largely political, promoted by English settlers intent upon ridding the area of a reminder of Ireland.

Mondovi [mahn DO vee]. Buffalo. Town (1881) and City (1889). Formerly known as Farrington for first settler Harvey Farrington and his brothers, Harlow and Lorenzo, from Naples, New York, who laid claim to the site in the Pancake Valley in the summer of 1855. The name Mondovi was chosen about 1857 by Elihu B. Gifford, reportedly the only person in the vicinity who subscribed to a newspaper. Gifford claimed he came across the name in an account of Napoleon's victory over the Sardinians at Mondovi, Italy, in 1796. Twenty years after the naming of Mondovi, Wisconsin, Gifford and a group of settlers moved to the Pacific Northwest and founded Mondovi, Washington, twenty miles west of Spokane. These are the only Mondovis in the United States. (Rockwell, 99)

Monico [MAHN uh ko]. Oneida. Town (1900) and ppl. Probably named by surveyor Benjamin Franklin Dorr for the Mediterranean Principality of Monaco, but the reasons for his choosing the name are unknown. This is the only Monico (so spelled) in the United States. (Doucette et al., 105)

Monona [muh NO nuh]. Dane. City (1969). Named from Lake Monona, the third in the chain of four lakes that originates with Lake Kegonsa to the southeast and progresses through Lakes Waubesa and Monona to Lake Mendota. The lakes were known to the Winnebago as *Taychopera* 'the four lakes.' Lake Monona and and Lake Mendota were given their present names about 1849 by Frank Hudson, a surveyor who platted one of the first additions to Madison. Hudson claimed that he had happened upon the name Monona while reading accounts of local Indian legends. The source of the name is uncertain. In 1945 Frederic Cassidy gave the first full account of the naming of the four lakes and concluded that Monona was a transfer from Monona in Clayton County, Iowa, which, according to legend, was named for an Indian maiden, who, believing her lover had been killed by her own people and refusing to be wed to someone she does not love, throws herself from a precipice into the Mississippi River. This story has all the hallmarks of popular lore and differs only in detail from dozens of other stories of distraught Indian maidens leaping to their deaths that are regular features of American mythology. Writing several decades after Cassidy, historian Virgil Vogel suggested that the name may have made its way into the legends encountered by Hudson from a melodrama first performed about 1820. In *Oolaita, or the Indian Heroine* the American playwright Lewis Deffebach reworked the Indian maiden suicide for love motif. In Deffebach's drama, the elderly Monona (a man in this telling) seeks to marry the younger Oolaita, the Sioux chief's daughter, who loves the youthful, virtuous Tallula. In order to avoid a loveless marriage,

Oolaita throws herself (from a high precipice, of course) into Lake Pepin. Vogel's proposal has a great deal to recommend it, especially when we consider that the names of several other characters in Deffebach's drama (Tallula first among them) became place names in the Midwest at approximately the same time. See Maiden Rock. (Cassidy, "Naming of the Four Lakes"; Vogel, *Indian Names*, 94)

Monroe. County. Organized in March 1854. Named for James Monroe (1758–1831), fifth president of the United States, in office 1817–25. The name was probably suggested by William F. Terhune, at the time a member of the Wisconsin Assembly living in Viroqua. Terhune was a native of New York State, which also has a county named for James Monroe. Terhune proposed the names of Victory (q.v.) and Vernon County (q.v.) as well.

Monroe. Green. Town and City (1882). Present Monroe grew from two distinct plats, each named New Mexico. The first was established by Jacob Andrick in 1836 or 1837, the other a short time later by Joseph Payne. After a great deal of confusion and contention as to which was the "true" community and thus would have the honor of serving as the county seat, Daniel Harcourt, a Methodist minister and county commissioner, proposed the communities unite as Monroe, for James Monroe, fifth president of the United States. The post office was established as New Mexico in March 1837 and changed to Monroe in December 1839. (Butterfield, *History of Green County*, 923)

Montana. Buffalo. Town (1867) and ppl. Named for the Territory of Montana, organized in 1864. The post office was established in July 1873, Fred Zeller, postmaster.

Montello [mahn TEL o]. Marquette. Town (1851) and City (1938). Montello was founded about 1849 as Seraglio (Seralyo), a name apparently suggested by Jason Daniels for a site he had passed by during his service in the Mexican War. At about the same time, several Dart(t) families, one of which became the namesake of Dartford (now Green Lake), emigrated from New England. Joseph R. Dart suggested the name Montello, which he said he had found in a novel. The post office was established in September 1850, Justus N. Dartt, postmaster. (Stennett, 17, 26)

Monterey [mahn tuh RAY]. Waukesha. Named in the summer of 1847 by the first postmaster, Alexander W. Hackley, in recognition of the capture of Monterrey by U.S. forces during the Mexican War in 1846. (*History of Waukesha County*, 773)

Montfort. Grant. Village (1893). Previously known as Wingville, named from Wingville township. The community was platted as Montfort for the site owners, Benjamin Eastman and Francis Dunn, in the spring of 1848. The source of the name is uncertain. The local account is that the name refers to a makeshift blockhouse erected during the Black Hawk War of 1832, suggesting that Montfort means 'hill of the fort.' The post office was established in May 1849, Jacob Benner, postmaster. (Holford, 723)

Monticello [mahn tuh SEL o]. Green. Village (1891). Founded by Alexander Foster Stedman, who established the Monticello post office in 1846. Most of the several dozen Monticellos in the United States are named directly or indirectly from Thomas Jefferson's Virginia estate. Monticello, Wisconsin, is most likely a transfer from a Monticello farther east, perhaps from Monticello in Steadman's home state of Ohio. (Bingham, 190)

Montpelier [mahnt PEEL yer]. Kewaunee. Town (1856). The name was suggested by Thomas Paddleford, the first permanent settler, for his former home, Montpelier, Vermont, itself named for Montpelier, France. The post office was established in August 1862, Henry Christman, postmaster. (*Kewaunee, Wisconsin*)

Montreal [MAHN tree AHL]. Iron. City (1924). The city was named from the Montreal Mining Company, which mined copper and iron ore in the area from the middle of the nineteenth century. The company took its name from the Montreal River, which forms part of the boundary between Wisconsin and Michigan's Upper Peninsula before emptying into Lake Superior northwest of Ironwood. The name is ultimately from Montreal, Quebec, 'royal mountain,' so named by the French colonial leader Jacques Cartier about 1535. The post office was established in January 1901, Donald E. McDonnell, postmaster.

Montrose [mahn TROZ]. Dane. Town (1847). Named for Montrose, Susquehanna County, Pennsylvania, itself named from French *mont* 'hill,' combined with rose, for Robert H. Rose, an early settler and landowner. The name may have been proposed by Peter W. Matts, who also founded Paoli (q.v.), which he named for Paoli, Pennsylvania. An early nickname for the community was Jimtown, for blacksmith Jim Wilson. The post office was established in July 1878, Samuel Sherman, postmaster. (Cassidy, *Dane County Place-Names*)

Moon. Marathon. Named from the Moon post office, established in December 1891 by Zimri Moon, whose ancestors founded Moonville, Indiana, in the 1830s.

Moquah [MO kwah]. Bayfield. From Ojibwa *makwa* 'bear.' The post office was established in April 1903, Wilmer E. Wesche, postmaster. Mukwa (q.v.) is a variant.

Morgan. Oconto. Town (1902) and ppl. Named from the Morgan post office, established by Levi Cleveland in September 1881. According to local historian Donald Schroeder, the namesake is a Mr. Morgan who was instrumental is securing the post office. This would most likely be railroad agent Herbert Morgan Jr, originally from New York State. ("Town of Morgan")

Morgan. Shawano. Named for Ole E. Morgan, who established a sawmill at the site about 1910. (Michael)

Morris. Shawano. Town (1881). Probably named for Maurice Deleglise, who emigrated from Switzerland about 1848. "Morris" is an informal pronunciation of "Maurice." Deleglise's connections to the area are unclear. See Antigo. (Pukall)

Morrison. Brown. Town (1853) and ppl. Named for the first known settlers, Alphonse and Harriet Morrison. Alphonse Morrison was a Methodist circuit rider and a schoolmaster in De Pere before moving to the area in February 1851. The community of Morrison dates to the fall of 1855 when Philip Falck, from Hesse-Darmstadt, Germany, opened a general store in his home. Falck established the post office in 1859. (*Town of Morrison*, 1, 6, 15)

Morrisonville. Dane. The Morrison family emigrated from Dundee, Scotland, to Milwaukee in 1842 and to Dane County in the summer of 1843, where they were among the first settlers in what became Windsor Township. James Morrison established the Morrisonville post office in May 1871 and laid out the community around the Sugar River Valley railroad station about 1873. (Cassidy, *Dane County Place-Names*)

Morse. Ashland. Town (1890) and ppl. Founded about 1882 and known locally as Jacobs, named for William H. Jacobs, a partner in the Bad River Lumbering and Improvement Company. Formally named about 1890 for August W. Morse, general manager of the local works of the Penokee Lumber Company. (*History of the Glidden Four-Town Area*, 32)

Morton Corner. Pierce. Named for one or more Morton families. William Morton, Harway Morton, and their families are enumerated in the 1880 census and listed as farmers in the Town of Martell.

Moscow [MAHS ko]. Iowa. Town (1860) and ppl. In 1847 Chaunc(e)y Smith, from Bradford County, Pennsylvania, built a cabin and gristmill near Moscow, which he laid out in 1850. The direct source of the name is uncertain. There have been some fifty communities in the United States named Moscow and the name may have been transferred from a Moscow in an eastern state. However, Thompson, Lauper, and Disrud (7, 10), suggest that Moscow may be a shortening by popular etymology of Muscoutin, the name of a tribe of Native Americans who reportedly had a village in the area at the time of the Black Hawk War in 1832.

Mosel [MOZ uhl]. Sheboygan. Town (1853) and ppl. The name was suggested by Julius Wolff for the Mosel (Moselle) River, which forms part of the boundary between Germany and Luxembourg. Wolff was born in Germany and was one of the organizers of the town of Rhine (q.v.). The post office was established in March 1869, Andrew Festerling, postmaster. (Buchen, 338)

Mosinee [MO zuh NEE]. Marathon. Town (1856) and City (1931). In 1839 John Moore established a sawmill on the Wisconsin River at a site known as Little Bull Falls. Joseph Dessert purchased Moore's mill and the community was known as Dessert's Mill until 1857 when the Little Bull Falls post office was moved from the east to the west side of the river. According to local accounts, several leading citizens, including postmaster Truman Keeler, felt that Little Bull Falls was "vulgar" and particularly embarrassing for ladies who had to use the name as part of their return address. A more genteel name was needed and Joseph Dessert proposed Mosinee for a local Ojibwa leader whose name appears as Mosinee and Mon-so-ne in early documents. The likely meaning is 'moose tail,' clearly much more refined than "Little Bull." See Bull. (*Mosinee Centennial*)

Mosling [MOZ ling]. Oconto. Previously known as Linwood for the local linn (basswood) trees. Formally named in 1897 for John P. Mosling, a local merchant and the first postmaster. (Stennett, 105)

Moundville. Marquette. Town (1851). Presumably named from the effigy mounds built by Native Americans and common in the area when European settlers first arrived. The post office was established in April 1851, R. B. Brown, postmaster.

Mountain. Oconto. Town and ppl. Platted by the Western Town Lot Company for the Chicago & North Western railroad in 1896. Named from the Mountain post office, established in 1889 by Andrew C. Frost, the namesake of Frostville (q.v.). According to Stennett, Mountain "was named from its location in a deep valley between very high and precipitous hills. It got this name in the early state days, when the stages had to climb these hills, or, as the drivers called them—'mountains'" (105).

Mount Calvary. Fond du Lac. Village (1962). Mount Calvary grew around and takes its name from the Mount Calvary Catholic church established by the order of St. Francis in the 1850s. The complex eventually included the Capuchin monastery, the convent of Notre Dame, and St. Lawrence seminary. The area is known as the Holyland for the number of communities that developed around churches, including St. Peter, St. Cloud, St. Anna, Mount Calvary, and Marytown. (McKenna, 255–56)

Mount Hope. Grant. Town (1865) and Village (1919). Mount Hope grew around the Brunson Institute, a school named for the Reverend Alfred

Brunson, established on land donated by William Whitesides and Thomas Taylor in the mid-1850s. There are several dozen Mount Hopes in the eastern states, and one of these may have been the inspiration for Mount Hope, Wisconsin. Alternatively, the name may have been chosen simply for its positive associations. The Hermitage post office was transferred to Mount Hope in June 1855. (Holford, 657)

Mount Horeb [HOR uhb]. Dane. Village (1899). Named from the Mount Horeb post office, established in the home of postmaster George Wright in 1861 and named for the bibical Mount Horeb. Wright was a Methodist Episcopal minister who was elected township treasurer and later served in the state legislature. The area was known for a flagpole called the Liberty Pole or *Staangji* 'the pole' by Norwegian settlers. (Sebenthall, 9)

Mount Ida. Grant. Town (1877) and ppl. Named from the Mount Ida post office, established in April 1857 by Samuel L. Borah. The name was reportedly suggested by Marie Baxter for its location as one of the highest points in the area. Ida was a popular woman's name at the time and may have been chosen to honor a local Ida. (*Grant County History*, 298)

Mount Morris. Waushara. Town and ppl. Named from Mount Morris, the 1,137-foot elevation in Mount Morris County Park. As Reetz tells it, the summit was known simply as "the mountain" until Gunnar Gunderson and Solomon Morris each sought to have it named for himself (118). To decide who should have the honor, they had a foot race to the top. Apparently Morris won. The post office was established in July 1854 by Andrew J. Tanner.

Mount Sterling. Crawford. Village (1936). Mount Sterling, both the summit and the community, are named for William T. Sterling, an early settler who came to the lead region from Kentucky in the 1840s. Sterling served as clerk to the Wisconsin Territorial Legislature and as state assemblyman in 1848 and 1850 and established the post office in February 1851. (Butterfield, *History of Crawford and Richland Counties*, 734)

Mount Tabor [TAY ber]. Vernon. More than a dozen states have a Mount Tabor; most of these are named from the isolated summit in northern Israel, mentioned several times in the Bible. Wisconsin may be one of these, but a more likely source is John C. Tabor, who established the post office in 1856.

Mount Vernon. Dane. Named by Virginians Joel and George Britts for George Washington's Virginia estate. Joel Britts purchased the site in the late 1840s; in 1852, George Britts laid out the community and began operating a sawmill on Mount Vernon Creek. (Cassidy, *Dane County Place-Names*)

Mount Zion. Crawford. Founded about 1866 and named from the Mount Zion Methodist church. (Butteris)

188

Mukwa [MUHK wah]. Waupaca. Town (1852). A shortening of Mukwonago (q.v.). From Ojibwa *makwa* 'bear'; related to Mukwonago (q.v.). Moquah in Bayfield County is a variant.

Mukwonago [muhk WAHN uh go]. Waukesha. Town and Village (1905). From Potawatomi 'bear's lair.' It is unclear if the name referred to the presence of actual bears, if it was a totemic or a clan name, or if it was the name of an individual. The Wisconsin Territorial Legislature established the township in January 1838 as Mequanego; the present spelling became official about 1844. (*History of Waukesha County*, 756; Vogel, *Indian Names*, 140)

Murat [MYOO rat]. Ozaukee. Apparently founded and named by Dr. Conrad E. Nystrum of Medford. Nystrum chose the name in honor of his relatives, especially his uncle, John A. Murat of Stevens Point. Nystrum gave the lake on which the community is located his middle name, Esadore. ("Conrad E. Nystrum Obituary")

Murry. Rusk. Town (1913) and ppl. Named for one of several Murray families who emigrated from New Brunswick, Canada. By 1880 Jim Murray had operated a sawmill on the Little Weirgor River for several years. The spelling was formalized as Murry with establishment of the post office about 1902. (*Rusk County History*, 28)

Muscoda [MUHS kuh day]. Grant. Town (1851) and Village (1894). Formerly known as Savannah and as English Prairie. The community grew around a smelting furnace used to process lead ore built about 1836 by William S. Hamilton, son of Founding Father Alexander Hamilton and a prominent figure in early southwest Wisconsin. *Muscoda* is a general Algonquian word (e.g., Ojibwa *mashkode*), meaning 'prairie' or 'meadow.' Mascoutah, Illinois, Muscatine, Iowa, and Muskoda, Minnesota, are variants. In Longfellow's poem *Hiawatha*, Nokomis, Hiawatha's grandmother, fell from the full moon "on the Muskoday, the meadow/ On the prairie full of blossoms." The Savannah post office was established in May 1836 and discontinued in November 1837; the English Prairie post office was established in May 1838 and discontinued in May 1842; the Muscoda post office was established in July 1842. (Holford, 693)

Muskeg [MUHS keg]. Bayfield. Muskeg, common to Potawatomi, Menominee and other Algonquian languages, refers to a marsh or bog, e.g., Ojibwa *mashkig* 'swampy ground.' Place names derived from Muskeg are found throughout the Great Lakes region. Muskego, Wisconsin, and Muskegon, Michigan, are variants. (Bright)

Muskego [muhs KEE go]. Waukesha. Muskego was originally established in 1839 near the Waukesha-Racine county line by settlers from Telemark, Norway, led by John Luraas. The city of Muskego, incorporated in 1964, and the former Town of Muskego, organized in 1838, took their names from Big and Little Muskego Lakes. Anson H. Taylor established the Muskego Centre post office in July 1848; he later represented the district in the Wisconsin Legislature. (Bright; Damaske, *Along the Right-of-Way to East Troy*, 11)

Myra [MEYE ruh]. Washington. Founded in 1858 by Jacob Young, the first postmaster, and Chauncey Gray. The local account is that Young's wife, Emma, chose the name from the Book of Acts, which mentions the village of Myra in Lycia. (*Town of Trenton & Village of Newburg*, 9)

Nabob [NAY bahb]. Washington. The origin of the name is uncertain, but a possible source is *nabob*, meaning 'soup' in Ojibwa (*napop* in Menominee). The Nabob post office was established in February 1899 by Peter Hacker, and the name may have been chosen for its pleasant sounds rather than for its meaning. This is the only community called Nabob in the United States, although there are several natural features so named in the western states.

Namekagon, Namakagon [NAM uh kah guhn]. Bayfield. Town (1913) and ppl. The town and community take their names from the Namekagon River, itself named from Ojibwa 'place of sturgeons,' based upon *name* 'sturgeon.' In Longfellow's narrative poem *Hiawatha* the sturgeon is called "Mishe-Nahma, King of Fishes." The Namakagon post office was established in Burnett County in November 1866. It lasted less than one year but was reestablished in Washburn County in November 1888. This is the only Namekagon in the United States. (Vogel, *Indian Names*, 155)

Namur [nah MOR]. Door. Named by settlers from Namur, the city and province in Wallonia, southern Belgium. The post office was established in June 1872, Clement Geniesse, postmaster. (Hale, 122)

Naples. Buffalo. Town (1857). John LeGore, from New York State, was one of the first permanent settlers, arriving in 1845. His wife, Pauline Farrington LeGore, a member of the Farrington family that settled Mondovi, proposed the name for her birthplace, Naples, Ontario County, New York, itself named for Naples, Italy. (Pattison, 15)

Nasbro [NAZ bro]. Dodge. Probably a shortening and blending of Nast Brothers, from the Nast Brothers Lime and Stone Company, founded by August and William Nast. The brothers operated several lime kilns and stone quarries from the 1870s. The post office was established in July 1913 by tavern keeper Hugh Isadore. (McKenna, 105)

Nasewaupee [naz uh WAH pee]. Door. Town (1859). Named from the post office established in 1858 by Nelson W. Fuller, who, with his brother,

Elijah, had emigrated from New York State a short time before. The post office was probably named for a Menominee leader whose village was on Little Sturgeon Bay and whose name was recorded as Nasewaupee, Nasawaupee, and Naseqaupee. (Holand, 439)

Nashotah [nuh SHOT uh]. Waukesha. Village (1957). From Ojibwa *nijode* 'twin.' Neshota was apparently a Native American name for the site of Two Rivers, where West Twin River merged with East Twin River before flowing into Lake Michigan. The Neshota River, Shoto in Manitowoc County, Wisconsin, and Nijode Lakes, Michigan, are variants. (Vogel, *Indian Names*, 136)

Nashville. Forest. Town (1909) and ppl. Named for Garrett V. Nash, who established the Nashville post office in October 1902.

Nasonville [NAY suhn vil]. Wood. Named for Solomon Nason, who, with his brother William, arrived in the area from Maine in 1854. Solomon Nason established a sawmill, opened a general store, established the Nasonville post office in February 1859, was instrumental in the formation of Lincoln township, and was elected without opposition to the Wisconsin Assembly in 1877. (Jones and McVean, *History of Wood County*, 276)

Naugart [NAW gahrt]. Marathon. Named by settlers from Naugard, the city then in Pomeranian Germany. The post office was established in October 1866, August Schmidt, postmaster. (Zamzow, 38)

Navarino [nav uh REE no]. Shawano. Town (organized as Mayville in May 1874; changed to Navarino in December 1874) and ppl. The origin of the name is uncertain. The town and community may have been named for Navarino Bay (Pylos), Greece, a seaport where a major battle in the war for Greek independence from the Ottoman Empire was fought in 1827, or been transferred from Navarino, New York, the only other present Navarino in the United States, perhaps by the first postmaster, Truman Hilliker, in 1874. For another Navarino in Wisconsin, see Green Bay.

Necedah [nuh SEE duh]. Juneau. Town (1853) and Village (1870). Necedah grew around a sawmill established about 1848 by Thomas Weston. The community was platted in the mid-1850s by Weston or his partners in the Necedah Lumber Company. Named from Necedah Lake, from Ho-Chunk (Winnebago) *ne ce day-ra*, literally 'water yellow lake' plus a noun indicator. The lake apparently took its color from an accumulation of pine needles. (Vogel, *Indian Names*, 131)

Neda [NEE duh]. Dodge. Neda was first known as Sterling's Mill, for Theodore Sterling, who operated a sawmill on what is now Neda Creek in the late 1840s. The community became Iron Ridge with establishment of the Iron Ridge mine and post office in 1849. Neda was in use by about

1910. The origin of the name is uncertain. Neda may be the name of the wife or daughter of an early settler or may be transferred from an existing Neda mine. (Frederick, "A Study of the 'Iron Ridge' Mine," 2)

Neenah [NEE nuh]. Winnebago. Town (1847) and City (1873). Winnebago Rapids was established in the 1830s to teach industrial and farming skills to Native Americans, in Goc's words, "to 'civilize' the Menominee people" (*Land Rich Enough*, 21). Neenah, which includes Winnebago Rapids, was founded about 1843 by site owners Harrison Reed, editor of the *Milwaukee Sentinel* newspaper, and Wisconsin territorial governor James Duane Doty. Neenah is from Ho-Chunk (Winnebago) for 'water.' The local tradition is that Doty pointed to the Fox River and asked his Ho-Chunk guide, "What is the name of this?" The guide replied, "*Nina*" ('water'). The post office was established in March 1844, Harrison Reed, postmaster. (Vogel, *Indian Names*, 174)

Neillsville [NEELZ vil]. Clark. City (1882). In the summer of 1845, James and Henry O'Neill moved their lumber milling operations from Black River Falls to the site of present Neillsville. The community was formally platted for James O'Neill in 1855. O'Neill, originally from New York, became a Clark County judge and served in the Wisconsin Legislature from 1865. (Curtiss-Wedge, *History of Clark County*, 162)

Nekimi [nuh KEE mee]. Winnebago. Town (organized in 1847 as Brighton; changed to Nekimi in 1850). Nekimi is from Ojibwa or Menominee, the name of either a local berry or for the bush on which the berry grows. Recorded forms include *Ne-kim-me-nah* and *Neekimeneen*. In the 1820s ethnologist Henry R. Schoolcraft described the berry as "black and taste-less, a little larger than the whortleberry." The post office was established in July 1849 as Nekama, David Chamberlain, postmaster. (Vogel, *Indian Names*, 163)

Nekoosa [nuh KOO suh]. Wood. City (1926). Formerly known as Whitney's Rapids for early settler Daniel Whitney, who erected a sawmill on the Wisconsin River in the early 1830s. Whitney's milling interests were eventually taken over by the Nekoosa Lumber Company, which reorganized as the Nekoosa Paper Company and platted the community in 1893. The name is built on Ho-Chunk (Winnebago) *ni* 'water' and has been interpreted as 'rapid waters,' 'large water,' and 'swift running water.' This is the only Nekoosa in the United States. (Buehler, 8)

Nelma. Forest. Named for Nelma Brooks, daughter of Arberry and Sylvania Adeline Brooks and granddaughter of Alvin Spencer, the founder of Alvin, Wisconsin (q.v.). ("Memories of Forest Co.," 182)

Nelson. Buffalo. Town (1857) and Village (1978). First known as Nelson's Landing, named for James Nelson, an Englishman who established a refueling station for Mississippi riverboats in the mid-1840s. The post office was established by Ernest A. Walker in October 1860. (Rockwell and Rzepiejewski, 504)

Nelsonville. Portage. Village (1913). Named for Englishman Jerome Nelson, who established a sawmill on the Tomorrow River in the mid-1850s. Nelson served with distinction in the Civil War and represented Portage County in the Wisconsin Assembly in 1887. The post office was established in April 1871, Edmund Creed, postmaster. (*Commemorative Biographical Record of the Upper Wisconsin Counties*, 46)

Nenno [NEN o]. Washington. Named for Nicholas "Nick" Nenno, who emigrated from Prussia about 1833. Nenno operated a brewery and kept a hotel and general store. The community was named for Nenno when the post office was established by George Smith in June 1857. ("History of the Nenno Family")

Neopit [nee O pit]. Menominee. Named for Neopit 'four in a den,' a son of Oshkosh, who was elected Menominee leader in the mid-1870s and became a judge of the Menominee tribal court in the early 1880s. The Menominee nation named their largest community in honor of Neopit shortly after his death in 1913. (Vogel, *Indian Names*, 40)

Neosho [nee O sho]. Dodge. Village (1902). In 1847, shortly after he arrived from New York State, Lucas Van Orden established the post office and laid out the community. *Neosho* is from a Siouan language, probably Ho-Chunk (Winnebago), with the general meaning 'principle river' or 'primary water.' The details of the naming are unknown. As a place name, Neosho is also found in Kansas and Missouri. (Bright)

Nepeuskun [nuh POOS kuhn]. Winnebago. Town (1849). Named from the post office, established in September 1849. Nepeuskun is an adaptation of *nepiaskon* 'cattails,' the Menominee name of Rush Lake (q.v.). (Bright)

Neptune. Richland. Dr. Joseph Sippy established the Neptune post office and platted the community of Neptune about 1855. The reasons for Sippy's choosing the name are unknown. (Butterfield, *History of Crawford and Richland Counties*, 1080)

Nerike. Pierce. Named by settlers from Nerike (modern Närke), the landskap (traditional province) in Svealand, south central Sweden. This is the only Nerike in the United States. (Landelius and Jarvi, 249)

Neshkoro [nesh KOR o]. Marquette. Town (1852) and Village (1906). Formerly called Dakinsville for early settlers Ebenezer and Helen Dakin; informally known as Whiskey Corners for the local stills. The name became Neshkoro with establishment of the post office by Horace W. Barnes in 1850. The origin of the name is uncertain and has generated a number of local stories, most of which are products of inventive minds, e.g., that Neshkoro is from *Nash* and *Kora*, early settlers, or from a Native American language meaning 'clear water' by one account or the incompatible 'twisted rock' by another. A more plausible proposal is reported by Reetz and credited to Charles Robinson, editor of the *Green Bay Advocate* newspaper. Robinson noticed that the post office application was submitted by hotelkeepers Alvah and Matilda Nash and called for the name Nashboro, which may have been misread and recorded as Neshkoro. A further possibility is that the name derives from Ho-Chunk (Winnebago) *nee-skoo* 'salt river.' (Reetz, 77, 79; Vogel, *Indian Names*, 136)

Neuern [NYOO ern, NER uhn]. Kewaunee. Neuern is the German name of Nýrsko, a community in the Pilsen region of the Czech Republic. Neuern, Wisconsin, was probably named with establishment of the post office in June 1895 by Anton Grassel, who emigrated from Austria in the 1880s. This is the only Neuern in the United States.

Neva [NEE vuh]. Langlade. Town (1883) and ppl. Reportedly named for "Chief Neva," supposedly a local Ojibwa leader. Perhaps from a general Algonquian word of unknown origin and derivation. Neva (likely a different person) was the brother of Niwot, leader of the Arapaho in Colorado in the 1860s. The post office was established as Melnick in November 1881 by Joseph Duchac, from Bohemia. That office closed in 1886 and was re-established as Neva in June 1892 by postmaster James Gillis. See Melnik. (Dessureau, 214)

Nevels Corners [NEV uhlz]. Richland. Named for the Nevel family. George W. Nevel, from Pennsylvania, had established a farm in the area by the late 1850s. (Scott)

Nevins. Clark. Named from the Nevins post office, established in November 1879, Thomas J. LaFlesh, postmaster. The office was named for Sylvester L. Nevins, a La Crosse lumberman who represented the district in the state senate in the mid-1870s. Nevins was the brother-in-law of Cadwallader C. Washburn, eleventh governor of Wisconsin and the namesake of Washburn County. ("Good Old Days")

Newald [NOO awld]. Forest. Platted in 1905 by the Western Town Lot Company for the Chicago & North Western railroad; named for Leopold J. Newald, the first banker in Gillett. Also known as Ross for early settler Charles Ross. (Lang; Stennett, 106)

New Amsterdam. La Crosse. In February 1853, some one hundred colonists under the leadership of Oepke H. Bonnema left Harlingen in the Netherlands, bound for New Orleans. After several months of unbelievable hardship they arrived in Wisconsin, where Bonnema laid out New Amsterdam. Bonnema was the first postmaster in 1858 and the namesake of Oepke Street. For a time the community was known as Frisia or Friesland for the province in the Netherlands. (Lucas)

New Auburn. Chippewa. See Auburn.

New Berlin [noo BER luhn]. Waukesha. City (1959). Settled in the late 1830s; named by Sidney Evans, for his former home, New Berlin, Chenango County, New York. The origin of the New York name is uncertain. but most likely it is a transfer from Berlin in eastern New York State, or Berlin, Connecticut. The post office was established in May 1837 by Waterman Field. See Berlin. (*History of Waukesha County*, 768)

Newbold. Oneida. Town (1898) and ppl. Named for Frederick Newbold, president of the Newbold Land and Lumber Company and nephew of Frederick W. Rhinelander, president of the Milwaukee, Lake Shore & Western railroad, for whom Rhinelander, Wisconsin, was named. (Stennett, 106)

Newburg. Washington. Village (1973). Founded in 1847 by Barton Salisbury, the namesake of Barton (q.v.). In the mid-1840s, Salisbury dammed the Milwaukee River and built a sawmill, a gristmill, and an ashery. (Quickert, 44)

New Denmark. Brown. Town (1855). Founded by Danish settlers, largely from Langeland in southeastern Denmark, in the late 1840s. The community was formerly known as Cooperstown for the Cooperstown post office, established in April 1848 by Allen A. Cooper. See Denmark. (J. Rudolph, 25)

New Diggings. Lafayette. Town (1849) and ppl. In 1824 a group of lead miners from Galena, Illinois (the "Old Diggings"), established Natchez a mile or so from the present "New Diggings." The name became New Diggings about 1844 with establishment of the post office by Henry Potwine. A number of mining sites in the lead region of southwest Wisconsin and northwest Illinois took the name Diggings or Digs (e.g., Irish Digs, Hardscrabble Digs). Of these, New Diggings is one of the few names that have survived. (*Lafayette County Bicentennial Book*, 140)

New Fane [FAYN]. Fond du Lac. New Fane takes its name from the post office established in April 1852 by Thomas Willcox and named for Newfane [*sic*], Niagara County, New York, itself named for Newfane, Vermont, itself named in the 1750s for John Fane, the Earl of Westmoreland. New Fane includes the former community of Eblesville, founded about 1855 by Andrew Eble, from Baden, Germany. (Worthing)

New Franken [FRANG kuhn]. Brown. New Franken is derived from German *Unterfranken* (Lower Franconia), an administrative region of Bavaria and the former home of a number of early settlers. A dozen families arrived in the area in the summer of 1845, followed by others later that year. The community was known as the Bavarian Settlement, the Dutch Settlement, and New Franconia until about 1852 when the New Franken post office was established by John M. Burkard. (D. Martin, 319)

New Glarus [GLEHR uhs]. Green. Town (1849) and Village (1901). In 1845, facing an increasingly dire economic situation, leading citizens of the canton of Glarus in eastern Switzerland formed an immigration society and sent Nicholas Duerst and Fridolin Streiff to locate and purchase a site suitable for colonization. Just over one hundred Swiss settlers arrived later that year at New Glarus, named in honor of their former home. The name is ultimately from Latin *clarus* 'clear,' referring to a largely treeless area. (M. Taylor, 20)

New Haven. Dunn. Town (1866). The origin of the name is uncertain. The first New Haven in the United States was established in the mid-seventeenth century in Connecticut. From there the name spread to more than forty locations. New Haven, Wisconsin, is likely a transfer from New England, the name perhaps suggested by John Holly Knapp, a founder of Menomonie (q.v. at Menominee) with a Connecticut background. See Knapp.

New Holstein [HOL steen, HOL steyen]. Calumet. Town (1849) and City (1889). The origins of New Holstein go back to the mid-1840s when George A. White, the founder of Calumetville (q.v.) met Ferdinand Ostenfeld, who had recently returned from Schleswig-Holstein in northern Germany. Together, Ostenfeld and White organized a group of some seventy colonists, who embarked from Hamburg in early April 1848. Ostenfeld is credited with naming the community. As Wulff so aptly puts it, "This name would remind [the settlers] of the area from which they had come, and might suggest to others . . . that this was a good place to settle" (7). The post office was established in May 1850, Rudolph Puchner, postmaster.

New Hope. Portage. Town (1856) and ppl. The origin of the name is unknown. By one account, at a contentious meeting in which agreement on a name could not be reached, someone called out, "We must have new hope," which inspired the name. The present community grew around a store kept by Peer Benson from the mid-1870s in an area then known as Benson Corners. Because of its positive and promising associations. New

Hope is a popular place name; there are well over one hundred communities and townships so named in some thirty states. (Seefelt, 3, 4)

New Lisbon [LIZ buhn]. Juneau. City (1889). New Lisbon was laid out by Amasa Wilson in 1855. Perhaps named for its location in Lisbon township, although local accounts claim that New Lisbon is a transfer from the town of Lisbon in Waukesha County, or from Lisbon, Columbiana County, Ohio, or both. County clerk Larmon Saxton, reported to be from Lisbon, Ohio, with relatives in the Waukesha area, is usually given credit for choosing the name. The post office was established in August 1854 as Mill Haven, then in Adams County; changed to New Lisbon in March 1868. (*Juneau County*, 40)

New London. Outagamie, Waupaca. City (1877). First known as Johnson's Trading Post for the small general store at the confluence of the Wolf and Embarrass Rivers opened about 1850 by William Johnson. Methodist minister Reeder Smith, a founder of Lawrence University in Appleton and the site owner, chose the name for New London, Connecticut, his father's birthplace. The post office was established in February 1854, William McMillin, postmaster. See Appleton. (Truttschel, 103)

New Lyme [LEYEM]. Monroe. Town (1872). Perhaps a transfer from New Lyme, Ashtabula County, Ohio, but more likely a transfer from one of the several Lymes in New England, perhaps Lyme, New Hampshire, or Lyme, New York. The name is ultimately from Lyme, England.

New Munster [MUHN ster]. Kenosha. Named in the 1840s by settlers from Münster, Germany. New Munster reportedly was known for a time as "whiskey hill" because of the large number of drinking establishments per capita. ("Kenosha County, WI Placenames")

New Paris. Sheboygan. About 1867 Joseph Schwartz established what he called Central Mills. Several years later he sold at least one of the mills to Vallier Wattier, who laid out part of the site as Paris, presumably named for Paris, France, Wattier's birthplace. (Ziller, 332)

Newport. Columbia. Town (1852). Newport was founded about 1852 on the west bank of the Wisconsin River. In 1857 Byron Kilbourn had the tracks of his La Crosse & Milwaukee railroad laid several miles north, creating Kilbourn City (now Wisconsin Dells) and leading to the disappearance of Newport, which is remembered only in the name of the township. The name was apparently proposed by Thomas Laffan for his birthplace, Newport (Ballyveaghan), County Mayo, in western Ireland. Laffan immigrated to Canada in 1841 and to Wisconsin in 1850. He was a hops farmer and held several local offices. (*Memorial and Biographical Record . . . of Columbia, Sauk, and Adams Counties*, 530)

New Prospect. Fond du Lac. Previously known as Jersey, named by early settlers from New Jersey. The name was formalized in 1861 when the New Prospect post office was established by Benjamin Romaine, himself from Bergen County, New Jersey. (Worthing)

New Richmond. St. Croix. City (1885). Formerly known as Cold Springs. In the early 1850s Benjamin Foster established a sawmill on the Willow River. About 1850 Henry Russell laid out the community of Fremont, named for western explorer John C. Fremont, and the Hudson development firm of Gridley and Day laid out Gridley. In 1858 Richmond Day surveyed the combined site, which was named Richmond in his honor. "New" was added when the post office was established in September 1858, presumably to avoid confusion with another Richmond in Wisconsin. (*New Richmond Centennial*, 9, 21)

Newry [NYOO ree]. Vernon. Newry may have been named directly from Newry in County Down, Ireland, but more likely was transferred from Newry in an eastern state, perhaps Newry, Pennsylvania, or Newry, Maine, themselves named for Newry, Ireland. The Newry post office was established in January 1868, Peter Bredel, postmaster.

Newton. Manitowoc. Town (1850) and ppl. Named for John Newton, a sergeant in the Revolutionary War, active in the Carolinas. Newton and William Jasper, his companion in arms, would be minor figures in American history were it not for *The Life of General Francis Marion*, by Mason L. Weems, a highly romanticized and largely fictitious tale of how Newton and Jasper—alone of course—subdued a squad of British regulars and rescued a group of American volunteers who were being marched to Savannah to be hanged. The book, first published in 1809, went through many editions and made Francis Marion, Sergeant Jasper, and Sergeant Newton American heroes and assured that their names would be spread over much of the Midwest. (Stennett, 107)

Newton. Vernon. Laid out in 1856 by Orin Calkins, first chair of the Town of Bergen. The namesake is probably one of several local Newton families, perhaps that of blacksmith Andrew Newton. (*History of Vernon County*, 557)

Newtonburg. Manitowoc. Named for its location in the Town of Newton. The post office was established by Henry Meyer in March 1855.

Niagara [neye AG ruh]. Marinette. Town (1910) and City (1992). Named from the Niagara post office, established in May 1897 by John Stoveken, from Herkimer County, New York. The office was named either for Niagara Falls, New York, or for the Niagara Escarpment, the long, low flat-faced ridge known in Wisconsin as "the ledge" or "the bluff," which runs from western New York State through the Great Lakes, follows the western shore of Lake Michigan through the Door peninsula, and ends near the Wisconsin-Illinois border. See Ledgeview.

Nichols. Outagamie. Village (1967). Named for the Nichols family. Nelson Nichols emigrated from Jefferson County and had become an established farmer by the 1860s. (Ryan, 1106)

Nix Corner. Eau Claire. Named for Andrew Nix, a German Catholic born in Dusseldorf who emigrated in 1871 to escape religious persecution. Nix, a smith and shopkeeper, established the Nix post office in October 1888. (*Osseo Area Bicentennial Book*)

Nobleton. Washburn. Named for Nathan B. Noble, a Rice Lake banker and president of the Rice Lake Manufacturing Company, which produced "hair dusters, clothes racks, fire kindlers and other novelties." The post office was established in October 1889, Even M. Kirkely, postmaster. (Forrester, 346)

Nokomis [nuh KOM uhs]. Oneida. Town (1948). From Ojibwa *nokomis* 'my grandmother.' In Longfellow's epic poem *Hiawatha*, Nokomis, "daughter of the moon," is Hiawatha's grandmother.

Nora. Dane. Named from the Nora post office, established in April 1869. Andrew A. Prescott, the first postmaster, sought a Norwegian name for the office and created Nora, a name intended to suggest Norway. After all, this was, in Cassidy's words, "a very Norwegian settlement." Also known as Nora Corners. (Cassidy, *Dane County Place-Names*)

Norma. Chippewa. According to Stennett (185), the community was named for Vincenzo Bellini's popular opera *Norma*, first performed in 1831.

Norman. Kewaunee. The area around Norman was settled in the mid-1850s largely by Bohemians, who named the community Klatovy, for the city now in the eastern Czech Republic. The name was formalized as Norman with establishment of the post office in November 1874. Joseph Bohman, an early settler, may have proposed the name, perhaps for a family member. (Dopke and Slikkers, 27)

Norrie [NOR ee]. Marathon. Town (1886) and ppl. Named for Gordon Norrie of New York City, treasurer of the Milwaukee, Lake Shore & Western railroad in the 1880s and 1890s. (Stennett, 108)

Norske [NORSK]. Waupaca. Norske is a general term for all things related to Norway or the Norwegian people. Details of the naming are unknown. The post office was established in January 1900, Andreas Merde, postmaster.

North Andover. Grant. North Andover grew around a gristmill and store opened on Rattlesnake Creek by Douglas Oliver about 1850. The name is apparently a transfer from North Andover, Massachusetts. The local story is that Oliver purchased machinery for his mill that was shipped from North Andover, Massachusetts, and this informal name became formalized when the post office was established in June 1867. (Holford, 719)

North Bend. Jackson. Town (1907) and ppl. Named from the north bend of Black River at the mouth of Mill Creek. The post office was established in May 1856, Thomas Douglas, postmaster. (*Jackson County, a History*, 38)

North Cape. Racine. Likely named by Norwegian settlers for the North Cape (Nordkapp) on the island of Magerøya in extreme northern Norway. The post office was established in August 1858 by Knud Adland.

North Clayton. Crawford. Named from its location in the northeast corner of Clayton township. The post office was established in May 1870, John H. Winn, postmaster. (Butteris)

Northeim [NOR theyem]. Manitowoc. Named from Northeim (Nordheim) in central Germany. The area was formerly known as Mann's Landing, named for the dock established in the early 1860s by Samuel Mann. The name of the Mann's Landing post office was changed to Northeim in January 1870.

North Freedom. Sauk. Village (1893). Originally known as Hackett's Corners for several Hackett families who had emigrated from Hackettstown, New Jersey. The railroad station was established about 1874 as Bloom, named for site owner George W. Bloom. When iron ore production increased in the 1880s, the area became known as Bessemer, in honor of Henry Bessemer, inventor of the first practical process for converting pig iron into steel. About 1890 the community formally took the name of the North Freedom post office, established in February 1872 and named for its location in the northern part of Freedom township. (Cole, *Baraboo*)

Northland. Waupaca. Apparently named for its location in the northern part of Waupaca County by Ole A. Buslett, who emigrated from Oppland, Norway, in 1868. Buslett established the post office in 1890, edited several Norwegian-language newspapers in the 1890s, and served in the Wisconsin Assembly in 1909.

Northline. St Croix. The post office was established as Hudson Junction or as North Wisconsin Junction in 1878, named for the junction of two lines of the Chicago, St. Paul, Minneapolis & Omaha railroad. The community was formally named Northline about 1906, apparently from the Northline school. (Ericson)

North Prairie. Waukesha. Village (1919). Named from North Prairie, itself probably named by Robert Sugden, from Yorkshire, England, one of the first Europeans to explore the area and a representative in the Wisconsin

Assembly in the early 1850s. The name was formalized in 1852 when the Milwaukee & Mississippi railroad established North Prairie Station. In the 1910s there was an unsuccessful attempt to change the name to Morey for Robert Gideon Morey, who operated a milk condensery from 1917 (later purchased by the Pet Milk Company). (Kabitzke, 13)

North Red Wing. Pierce. North Red Wing, named for its location one mile north of Red Wing, Minnesota, is one of the few Wisconsin communities located west of the main channel of the Mississippi River. Red Wing is an English translation of French *l'aile rouge*, itself a translation of the name of several Siouan leaders of the early nineteenth century. In 1821 the ethnologist Henry Rowe Schoolcraft wrote, "At twelve o'clock we arrived at the Sioux village of Talangamane, or the Red wing, which is handsomely situated on the west banks of the river, six miles above Lake Pepin."

Norwalk [NOR wawk]. Monroe. Village (1894). Founded in the early 1870s by site owners Christian Hettman and Selium McGary. Named by McGary for his former home, Norwalk, Huron County, Ohio, itself named for Norwalk, Connecticut. Norwalk is from an eastern Algonquian word, probably meaning 'point of land.' (Richards, 409)

Norway. Racine. Town (1847). The first group of Norwegian settlers, which arrived in the spring of 1840, was led by John Luraas, from Tinn, Norway, and included Johannes Johannesen, from Drammen, Norway. The post office was established in May 1847, Even H. Heg, postmaster. See Muskego. (Palmer and Pederson, 11)

Norway Grove. Dane. Named for or by Norwegain settlers, many of whom arrived in the late 1840s. The post office was established in March 1872, Helge Tollefson, postmaster. (Cassidy, *Dane County Place-Names*)

Nutterville. Marathon. Founded about 1878 by site owner James W. Nutter. The Nutterville post office operated from December 1889 until July 1901.

Nye [NEYE]. Polk. Named for the Nye brothers, who grew up on a farm near River Falls. Edgar Wilson "Bill" Nye (1850–96) was a distinguished American journalist and humorist, ranking with Mark Twain and Artemus Ward. The quip "Wagner's music is better than it sounds" is attributed to Nye. Bill Nye's brother Frank Mellen Nye (1852–1935) was a lawyer and a U.S. representative from Minnesota in the 1900s. The post office was established in August 1892, Frank A. Brandt, postmaster. (Ericson)

Oak Center. Fond du Lac. Named by Perry H. Smith, an officer of the Chicago & North Western railroad, reportedly for the presence of a prominent grove of oak trees. The post office was established in June 1857 as Oak Centre. (Stennett, 109)

Oakdale. Monroe. Town (organized in 1857 as Leroy; changed to Oakdale in 1862) and Village (1988). The post office was established as Le Roy Station in March 1864, William Y. Baker, postmaster. (Richards, 528)

Oakfield. Fond du Lac. Town (organized in 1846 as Lime for the local limestone quarries; changed to Oakfield in 1847) and Village (1903). Reportedly named by early settler Jacob Brewster, perhaps for Oakfield, Genesee County, New York. The post office was established in May 1850, William Isaac Ripley, postmaster. (Stennett, 109)

Oak Grove. Dodge. Oak Grove welcomed its first permanent settler in the early 1840s when a Major Pratt built a combination residence and tavern. The area was first known as Fairfield for Fairfield, Connecticut, the birthplace of prominent settler James Ferris Clason. For unknown reasons, the name was changed to Oak Grove about 1844. The 1880 *History of Dodge County* suggests the name is ironic and was chosen "from the fact that there was no oak grove in the neighborhood" (552). Oak Grove is a popular place name; there are more than 150 communities in the United States so named.

Oak Hall. Dane. The community was named from a combination hotel and meeting hall established in the 1850s. The structure, reportedly built of oak logs, thus the name, became a popular rest stop on the road from Milwaukee to Mineral Point because its location allowed teamsters to bypass Nine Springs Hill in Fitchburg, known locally and to travelers as Break Neck Hill. Also known as Fitchburg Corners. See Fitchburg. (*Fitchburg Bicentennial*, 45)

Oak Hill. Jefferson. Founded as Pleasant Valley by Abiathar Waldo, a merchant from Bennington, Vermont. Renamed from the Oak Hill post office, established in 1847 by Miles Holmes. The community was known informally as Punk, a shortening of Pumpkin (Punkin) Hollow. (Gnacinski and Longley, 92)

Oasis [o AY suhs]. Waushara. Town (organized as Norwich in 1851; changed to Oasis in 1852). Named from the Oasis post office, established in April 1851 by farmer and businessman Walter W. Beach, originally from Chittenden, Vermont. The reasons for Beach's choice of the name are unknown. (*History of Northern Wisconsin*, 1117)

Oconomowoc [o KAHN uh muh wahk]. Waukesha. Town (1844) and City (1875). Oconomowoc was platted in 1848 for site owner John S. Rockwell, a director of the Milwaukee & Watertown railroad and a community benefactor. In 1887 Peter Vieau, brother of Amable Vieau, who established the first trading post in the area in the 1820s, claimed that Oconomowoc was a shortening of *o ko nee me wing*, meaning "a fall, and gathering of beautiful waters in the lakes." Several additional interpretations of Oconomowoc have been proposed, including 'meeting of the waters,' 'river of lakes,' even 'bones.' The actual source is more prosaic. About 1890 Chrysostom Verwyst, a Catholic priest who lived and worked among the Ojibwa for thirty years, recorded Ojibwa *okonimawag* 'beaver dam.' The post office was established in March 1847 as Oconomowock. (*History of Waukesha County*, 378; Vogel, *Indian Names*, 142)

Oconto [o KAHN to]. County. Oconto Falls. City. Named from the Oconto River. The origin and meaning of Oconto have been debated for decades. In the early 1900s Henry Legler proposed an unspecified Menominee word for 'black bass' as the source, because several early nineteenth-century maps apparently label the Oconto River the Black Bass River. An Ojibwa origin has also been suggested, based on the entry *akando* in Baraga's Ojibwa dictionary, which he glosses 'I watch; I lurk; I lie in ambush.' Rather, Oconto is from Menominee *Okaqtow*, perhaps derived from *okaw*, referring to the northern pike or pickerel. Swanton's *The Indian Tribes of North America* defines *Oka'to Wini'niwuk* as 'Pike Place people,' a subdivision of the Menominee living at the mouth of the Oconto River. The only other Oconto in the United States is in Custer County, Nebraska, undoubtedly a transfer from Wisconsin. (Vogel, *Indian Names*, 154)

Odanah [o DAY nuh]. Ashland. In 1841 Leonard Hemenway Wheeler, a Congregational clergyman from Massachusetts, began ministering to the Ojibwa at La Pointe in the early 1840s. In 1845 he founded an agricultural settlement that he named Odanah, from Ojibwa *odena* 'village.' Wheeler established the Odanah post office in October 1855. (*Dictionary of Wisconsin Biography*)

Ogdensburg. Waupaca. Village (1912). Founded by Caleb S. Ogden in 1854. Ogden, from Delaware County, New York, was a county judge and founder of the *Waupaca County Republican* newspaper. (*History of Northern Wisconsin*, 1006)

Ogema [O guh mah, O guh muh]. Price. Town (1882) and ppl. In the mid-1870s the area was known as Dedham from the Wisconsin Central railroad station, named for Dedham, Massachusetts. By about 1877 the community had assumed the name Ogema, either from the Ojibwa generic *ogima* 'chief' or from a particular Ojibwa leader. A redundantly named "Chief Ogemageshic" is reported in early records. (Forrester, 363)

Oil City. Monroe. Platted in 1870 and named in response to the speculations (rumors, as it turned out) that oil was to be found in the area. There was considerable commotion and anticipation over the development and presumed prosperity of an "oil city." (*Monroe County*, 134)

Ojibwa [o JIB way]. Sawyer. Town (1919) and ppl. Ojibwa was founded on the Chippewa River in 1917 as the showcase settlement of Benjamin Faast's Wisconsin Colonization Company. The editors of the *Wisconsin Magazine of History* were consulted on the important matter of choosing an appropriate name for what was being promoted as a modern, planned community. The editors offered Carver, for Jonathan Carver, who explored the area in the 1760s; Corbin, for Jean Baptiste Corbin, an early fur trader; and Sha-da-wish, for a local Ojibwa leader. Other names considered at the time were Wiscoapolis, Kitchitwa, and Nawakwa. Company officials rejected these proposals in favor of Ojibwa, which they claimed was "a historical name that should be preserved." See Chippewa County. (Janik, 46)

Okauchee [o KAW chee]. Waukesha. Okauchee developed around a sawmill established by Orson Reed at an outlet of Okauchee Lake about 1840. Reed's mill provided lumber for the plank road from Milwaukee to Watertown. Okauchee is from a Native American language but its source and derivation are uncertain. Several origins have been suggested, including *okatci* 'something small' and *okidji* 'pipestem.' Vogel proposes Ojibwa *okitchi* 'to the right side,' which he claims refers to the location of Okauchee Lake in reference to Lac La Belle to one looking north. The post office was established in October 1850, Albert McConnell, postmaster. (Vogel, *Indian Names*, 132)

Okee [o KEE]. Columbia. From Algonquian *aki* or *aukee* (as in Milwaukee), meaning 'land,' 'country.' Platted in 1858 for mill owner Seth Bailey. The name was likely chosen by Bailey's business partner, Miller Blachley (Blakeley). The Okee post office operated from April 1858 until May 1908. (J. Jones, 384)

Oliver. Douglas. Village (1917). Named from the Oliver Iron Mining Company, established in the early 1890s by Henry W. Oliver. Born in Ireland, Oliver was an American industrialist who spent much of his life in Pittsburgh, Pennsylvania, where his company became one of the largest manufacturers of bar iron in the United States. Oliver was instrumental in developing the resources of the Mesabi Iron Range in Minnesota. The post office was established in September 1914, William J. Blaha, postmaster. (Cole, *Baraboo*)

Olivet [ah luh VET]. Pierce. Named from the Olivet post office, established in July 1870 by Benjamin H. Preston. Olivet may have been a transfer from one of the several dozen Olivets (or Mount Olivets) in the eastern states, but most likely the office was named directly for the biblical Mount of Olives, called Olivet in the Book of Acts.

Oma [O muh]. Iron. Town (1911). Finnish for 'own,' as in 'our own.' By a local account, at a meeting to choose a name, a Finnish settler called out

"*Oma Kaupunki*" (our town), which was enthusiastically endorsed. A Finnish proverb, *oma tupa, oma lupa* (one's own house, one's own freedom) has become associated with the Town of Oma. (Techtmann, 136)

Omro [AHM ro]. Winnebago. Town (organized as Butte des Morts in 1849; changed to Bloomingdale in 1849 and to Omro in 1852) and City (1944). The community was laid out about 1849 by Joel Taylor, Elisha Dean, and Nelson Beckwith on a site known as Smalley's Landing. By one account, local businessmen drew letters from a hat until a pronounceable word was formed; by another, Omro is a blend of the last two letters of Bloom, from Bloomingdale township, and the last two letters of Kero, reportedly the name of an early trading post. Omro, however, is probably a phonetic spelling of Amereau, for Charles Amereau, an early blacksmith and trader who apparently had established a post near the site by the early 1840s. The post office was established in August 1850, William P. McAllister, postmaster. (M. Smith, 33)

Onalaska [ahn uh LAS kuh]. La Crosse. Town (1854) and City (1887). Thomas G. Rowe, who founded Onalaska about 1851, took the name from Thomas Campbell's 1799 poem *The Pleasures of Hope*, which includes the line "The wolf's long howl from Oonalaska's shore." Oonalaska is one of the eastern Aleutian Islands (now spelled Unalaska) from Aleut *nawan-alaxsxa* 'the mainland along there.' Another of Campbell's poems, *Gertrude of Wyoming*, popularized Wyoming (q.v.) as a place name. The name Onalaska appears in several states, thanks to William A. Carlisle, owner of the Carlisle Lumber Company of Onalaska, Wisconsin. Carlisle established lumber camps in Arkansas, Texas, and Washington, and named each one Onalaska. (Bright; Vogel, *Indian Names*, 96)

Oneida [o NEYE duh]. County (1885). Town in Outagamie (1903), and ppl. in Brown County. Named for the Oneida, one of the six nations of the Iroquois of New York State. About 1820 the Protestant missionary, visionary, and eccentric Eleazar Williams proposed to relocate to Wisconsin the Oneida, Brotherton, and other Christian Indians of New England, who were rapidly losing their traditional homelands. Although many Oneida opposed the move, Williams prevailed and some 150 people were settled east of Green Bay in the early 1820s. *Oneida* is traditionally taken to mean 'people of the standing stone,' from a large stone at one of the Oneida villages in New York. (Vogel, *Indian Names*, 24)

Ono [O no]. Pierce. As with most unfamiliar and nontransparent names, Ono has generated its share of popular etymologies. Johnson and Wilmot report that one of their informants declared "a group of settlers got together to decide on a name for the settlement. When the first suggestion was heard, one of the group jumped up and cried 'oh, no' and from this they decided on the name" (24). Ono, however, was named by Civil War veteran Morris Holt. In Holt's own words, "In 1868 I got up a petition to the post ofice department asking for a post office to be established. . . . I had two names in view, but had not decided which to take; one day, as I was reading in my Bible, I saw the word Ono; that decided me at once." The Ono described in the Old Testament as "the valley of artisans" is now known as Kiryat-Ono, east of Tel Aviv, Israel. The Ono, Wisconsin, post office was established in June 1870, John K. Hunter, postmaster. The community is one of four so named in the United States; the others are in California, Kentucky, and Pennsylvania. (*Pierce County's Heritage*, 5:14)

Ontario [ahn TEHR ee o]. Vernon. Village (1890). Ontario was laid out in 1857 by Giles White, the first settler of Whitestown (q.v.), who had established a sawmill at the site several years earlier. The name was suggested by Oscar H. Millard for his birthplace, Ontario County, New York, itself named for Lake Ontario. (*History of Vernon County*, 748)

Oostburg [OOST berg]. Sheboygan. Village (1909). Named from the Oostburg post office, which postmaster Peter Daane established in his general store in December 1869. Daane choose the name for his birthplace in Zeeland, Netherlands. Daane may have been related to Pieter Zonne, who led Dutch settlers to Cedar Grove (q.v.) in the 1840s. (Buchen, 262)

Oregon. Dane. Town (1847) and Village (1883). Settlement began in the early 1840s when Charles P. Mosely built a tavern and hotel on the Madison–Janesville road. The town was named for the Oregon country of the Pacific Northwest, probably at the suggestion of Rosel Babbit. The community was platted as Oregon in 1847 but continued to be called Rome Corners, an earlier name, until 1864 when the Beloit & Madison railroad established Oregon station. (*Souvenir of Oregon Centennial*, 13, 39)

Orfordville. Rock. Village (1900). Platted in 1855 as Orford. The name was apparently suggested by surveyor Joseph T. Dodge for Orford, New Hampshire, his former home, itself named in the eighteenth century for Robert Walpole, the Earl of Orford and Britain's first prime minister. The post office was established in May 1857, George Helmbolt, postmaster. (*History of Rock County*, 665)

Orienta [or ee EN tuh]. Bayfield. Town (1903). The community, known simply as "mouth of Iron River," was formally named in September 1892 with establishment of the Orienta post office. The name was suggested by Patrick Hynes or by postmaster John Haney, partners in the Iron River Boom and Improvement Company. The source of the name is uncertain. Orienta soil, a fine, sandy loam, has become associated with the area, but it is unclear if naming of the soil preceded naming of the post office or the other way around. Orienta is also a place name in Florida, New York, and Oklahoma.

Orihula [or uh HOO luh]. Winnebago. Formerly known as Merton's Landing for Andrew Merton, a farmer and local official who emigrated from Germany in the mid-1840s. The origin of the name is uncertain but most likely is a transfer with modification from Orihuela, a city in Valencia, Spain. The name was probably suggested by Merton when the Town of Orihula was organized in 1855. The name of the town but not the community was changed to Wolf River in 1861. The post office was established in September 1865, George Theby, postmaster. (Lawson, 352; Munroe, p.c.)

Orion [OR ee uhn]. Richland. Town (organized as Richmond in 1848; changed to Orion in 1860) and ppl. The community was founded as Richmond in the 1840s by Thomas Mathews and his father-in-law, John R. Smith, who operated a ferry across the Wisconsin River to Muscoda. With establishment of the post office in 1851, the name was changed to Orion at the suggestion of local judge Alvin (or Alban) B. Slaughter, whether for the constellation Orion the Hunter or in honor of a friend or associate. Orion, pronunced [OR ee uhn], was a fairly common male name at the time. (Butterfield, *History of Crawford and Richland Counties*, 1133–34)

Ormsby. Langlade. Named for William Ormsby of Milwaukee, who, with several others, formed the Northern Woodland Company and erected a sawmill about 1902, the year the post office was established. (Dessereau, 226)

Osborn [AHZ born]. Outagamie. Town (1858). Organized largely through the efforts of James Simpson, generally regarded as "the Father of Osborn," who purchased land in the area about 1850. The name is apparently an popular etymology of Ausbourne, for William and John Ausbourne, early immigrants from Ireland who settled near Seymour about 1857. (Balliet, 83)

Osceola [ah see O luh]. Fond du Lac. Town (1850). Polk. Town (organized in 1852 as Leroy; changed to Osceola in 1853) and Village (1886). Named for Osceola (also known as Billy Powell), the Seminole leader whose bravery and perseverance in the face of U.S. military opposition in the Second Seminole War of the late 1830s made him a national folk hero. Osceola became a popular place name and now appears in more than twenty states. Osceola in Polk County was founded as Osceola Mills in 1848 by William Kent and his brothers, Thomas and John, from New Brunswick, Canada. The name was changed from Leroy in the 1850s and was proposed by either William Kent, who owned the site, or by James Livingston. Osceola is from Muskogee *asi*, a ceremonial drink made from the yaupon holly, and *yahola*, 'the shouter' or 'the exhorter.' (Gordon and Grant, 23)

Oshkosh [AHSH KAHSH]. Winnebago. Town (organized in 1839 as Winnebago; changed to Oshkosh in 1852) and City (1853). From 1827 until his death in 1858, Oshkosh (the name means 'claw' or 'hoof') was regarded by the U.S. government as leader and speaker for the Menominee people. The city of Oshkosh was formally named in 1840, apparently at the suggestion of trader Robert Grignon. Other names considered at the time were Athens, Fairview, and Osceola. Written *Ois-cose, Osk-Osh,* and *Oskosh,* the [s] of the initial syllable had assimilated to the [sh] of the second syllable by the time the post office was established as Osh Kosh in 1840. Oshkosh, Minnesota, and Oshcosh, North Dakota, are also named directly for Oshkosh the person. Oshkosh in Garden County, Nebraska, was named by settlers from Oshkosh, Wisconsin. (Freda and Miller, 21; Vogel, *Indian Names,* 38)

Osseo [AHS ee o]. Trempealeau. City (1941). The origin of *Osseo* has prompted a number of guesses and speculations, from Spanish *oso* 'bear' to an "Indian" word (variously reported to be Ojibwa, Potawatomi, or "other") meaning 'river' or 'stone.' The editors of the 1917 *History of Trempealeau County* record a delightful popular etymology: "A fanciful explanation given by some of the early settlers is that an Indian, seeing the improvement made by the white men, exclaimed, Oh! See! Oh! thus giving the name Osseo" (271–72). In truth, the source of the name and its meaning, if indeed there is one, are unknown. The community was possibly named from the poem *Hiawatha,* where Longfellow calls Osseo "the son of the Evening Star." Longfellow most likely got the name from the nineteenth-century ethnologist and Indian agent Henry Rowe Schoolcraft, but Schoolcraft was notorious for taking bits and pieces from actual words and confecting them into pseudo-Indian names. Schoolcraft's fertile mind may have created Osseo from parts of Algonquian words he had encountered in his studies and in his interviews with Native Americans along the Great Lakes. A Schoolcraft origin is supported by the fact that the name occurs only in the lake states of Wisconsin, Michigan and Minnesota. The post office was established as Sumner in February 1858 and changed to Osseo in July 1867. (Curtiss-Wedge and Pierce, 271–72; Stennett, 186)

Ostrander [O strand er]. Waupaca. Named for James W. Ostrander, who at age seventeen emigrated from Onondaga County, New York, to Waupaca where he purchased a furniture factory in what became known as Ostrander Mills. Much of the factory's machinery was moved to Wausau and by 1910 the community had largely vanished, leaving behind only the name. (Cooney, 11; *"Ghost" Towns of Waupaca County*)

Otis. Lincoln. Probably named for Otis H. Waldo, president of the Milwaukee & Northern railroad in the 1870s. See Waldo.

Otsego [aht SEE go]. Columbia. Town (1849) and ppl. Named by settlers from Otsego County, New York, itself likely named from an Onondaga word meaning 'misty place.' The post office was established in November 1847, Cyrus Root, postmaster.

Ottawa [AHT uh wuh]. Waukesha. Town (1843) and ppl. The first settler was Talbot C. Dousman, the founder of Dousman (q.v.). Hans Crocker, a Milwaukee lawyer and real estate promoter, proposed the name Ottawa about 1840. The Ottawa are an Algonquian people, many of whom lived in the Ashland area of Lake Superior in the late seventeenth century. The name is customarily taken to mean 'traders.' (*History of Waukesha County*, 775)

Ottman Corners. Pierce. Named for brothers Nelson, Christopher, and James Ottman, originally from Schoharie County, New York, who came to the area about 1859. The Ottman post office was established in March 1886 with the name-worthy Ingebright Bundlie as postmaster. ("Nelson Ottman")

Oulu [OO loo]. Bayfield. Town (1904) and ppl. Named from the Oulu post office, established in September 1903 by Andrew Lauri, who chose the name for his birthplace, Oulu, a province and city in central Finland on the Gulf of Bothnia. This is the only Oulu in the United States. (*Historical Sketches of the Town of Oulu*, 20)

Outagamie [OWT uh gay me]. County (1851). The French Jesuit missionary Claude-Jean Allouez recorded the name about 1666. Outagamie is from *otakamik*, 'people of the other shore, people on the other side,' the Ojibwa name for the Meskwaki (Fox). The particular "shore" or "side" referred to is uncertain. (Bright)

Owen [O uhn]. Clark. City (1925). Owen was founded by and named for the John S. Owen Lumber Company, which began operations in the area about 1893. The company was an Owen family affair: John S. Owen was president and treasurer; his brother Edward A. Owen was second vice president; his son Aloney R. Owen was first vice president; and his son John Owen Jr. was secretary. (*City of Owen*, 4)

Oxbo (Oxbow). Sawyer. Named from the sharp, oxbowlike bend on the Flambeau River south of the community.

Oxford. Marquette. Town (1852) and Village (1912). By one local account the name is a popular etymology of Axford, from William Axford, an influential early settler. Equally likely, William Axford may have transferred the name from Oxford, Warren County, New Jersey, where he had lived before coming to Wisconsin. The similarity of Axford and Oxford may have made the choice of the name inevitable. The post office was established as Crooked Lake in 1851 and changed to Oxford in 1854. (Reetz, 86)

Ozaukee [o ZAW kee]. County. Organized in 1853 from Milwaukee County. From Ojibwa *osaki*, literally 'people of the outlet,' referring to the Sauk (Sac) people. See Sauk.

Pacific. Columbia. Town (organized in 1849 as Winnebago Portage; after several name changes, changed to Pacific in 1854). Named by Nathan H. Wood, the first town chair and the first postmaster in 1854. Wood's reasons for choosing the name are unknown, but there was a great deal of interest in California and the Pacific coast at the time, generated in part by the gold rush of 1848 and California statehood in 1850. (*Commemorative Biographical Record of the Fox River Valley Counties*, 83)

Packwaukee [pak WAW kee]. Marquette. Town (1851) and ppl. Named from the Packwaukee post office, established in July 1850 by William Euen Jr. The origin of the name is uncertain. Perhaps from Ojibwa *bagwaki* 'forest opening,' built upon *bagwa* 'thin, shallow' plus *aki* 'land,' with (*w*)*aki* becoming "waukee" through analogy to Milwaukee, Pewaukee, Zilwaukee, and other such. Allusions to a Native American leader named Packwaukee appear from time to time, but his existence is difficult to confirm. (Vogel, *Indian Names*, 132)

Paddock Lake. Kenosha. Village (1960). Named for one or more Paddock families. William D. Paddock brought his family to the area from New York State in the summer of 1838. (*Commemorative Biographical Record of Racine and Kenosha Counties*, 422)

Padus [PAY duhs]. Forest. Laid out by the Chicago & North Western railroad in 1904; named from the Padus post office, established in April 1901. According to local folklore, Owen Smith, a civil engineer who assisted in surveying the railroad line, claimed "the name came from a former mill owner's dog. [I was] sitting on the porch when the owner came out . . . with the dog following him. Chas. Rietz ask [*sic*] him what he called the dog. He said he reckoned his name was Padus as that was what he answered to. Chas. Rietz said . . . call this town Padus, it will never be anything but a dog town anyway" (Lang, n.p.). More likely, when the Indiana Lumber Company established the post office, a Mr. Muir proposed the name for the Padus River in Italy, Padus being the Latin name of the Po River. This is the only Padus in the United States. ("Miscellaneous Laona Area News Items")

Palmer. St. Croix. Named for landowner William Palmer, who emigrated from England to New York State in the early 1840s and to Wisconsin in the 1860s. The post office was established in December 1893, William McConnell, postmaster. (Ericson)

Palmyra [pal MEYE ruh]. Jefferson. Town (1846) and Village (1866). Founded by David J. Powers, who emigrated with his family from Athens, Vermont, in 1837. Powers, along with his brother, Samuel, were hoteliers in White-water and established a sawmill and gristmill on the Scuppernong River in the early 1840s. In 1843 John Fish platted the community, which David Powers named for the biblical Palmyra, the ancient city in Syria. Powers later served in the Wisconsin Assembly and Fish was the first postmaster in 1844. (Lehner, 13–15)

Paoli [pay O leye, pay O lee]. Dane. Laid out in 1849 by tavernkeeper and county sheriff Peter W. Matts, who chose the name for Paoli, his former home in Chester County, Pennsylvania, itself named for Pasquale Paoli, leader of an eighteenth-century Corsican revolt against Genoa. (Cassidy, *Dane County Place-Names*)

Pardeeville. Columbia. Village (1894). Founded in the summer of 1850 and named for site owner John S. Pardee, a Milwaukee merchant and diplomat. In 1854 President Franklin Pierce appointed Pardee consul to San Juan del Sur, Nicaragua, the Pacific terminus of the sea route to California. (Butter-field, *History of Columbia County*, 871)

Parfreyville [PAR free vil]. Waupaca. Founded by Englishman Robert Parfrey, who operated a gristmill on what is now Parfrey's Glen Creek from the early 1850s. Parfreyville flourished for a time but began to decline when the railroad was built through Waupaca in the early 1870s. (Ware, 398)

Paris. Grant. Town (1849). About 1830 Martial (or Martil) Detantabaratz, reportedly a former dragoon in the French army, laid out a settlement named for Paris, France, on the Platte River, a short distance above its confluence with the Little Platte. The Town of Paris retains the name of the community that vanished shortly after Detantabaratz's death in 1842. (Holford, 763)

Paris. Kenosha. Town (1842) and ppl. Named about 1836 by early settler Seth Butler Myrick for his former home, Paris, Oneida County, New York, itself named for eighteenth-century community benefactor Isaac Paris. (Taylor and Holme, 12)

Park Falls. Price. City (1912). Named for the waterfall on the Flambeau River formerly known as Muskellunge Falls. By the late 1870s, following construction of the Wisconsin Central railroad, the area was known as Flambeau Crossing or North Fork. In 1885 Henry Sherry of Neenah purchased the site from Ezra Cornell, the namesake of Cornell (q.v.), and established a sawmill that provided the nucleus for the future city of Park Falls. The name became official in 1889 when the North Fork post office was changed to Park Falls. While the source of "Falls" is obvious, the origin of "Park" is unclear. Historian Michael Goc writes, "Park Falls . . . takes its name from the park-like stand of mature pine that once surrounded the Falls" (*100 Years on the Flambeau*, 8), while Behling cites the early report of an official of the Wisconsin Department of Education that claims that the namesake is Gilbert L. Park, a judge of the seventh judicial circuit of which Price County was a part (21).

Park Ridge. Portage. Village (1938). The original documents of incorporation called for the name Plover Hills but this was overwritten with Park Ridge. Who made the change and why are unknown. (Rosholt, *Our County, Our Story*, 349)

Parnell [pahr NEL]. Sheboygan. Named by Thomas Heraty, born in County Mayo, Ireland, in honor of Charles Stewart Parnell (1846–91), Irish nationalist and leader of the Irish home rule movement. Parnell was widely known in the United States in 1888 when the Parnell post office was established. (Buchen, 339)

Parrish. Langlade. Town (1889) and ppl. Founded about 1887 by the Prairie River Lumber Company as Mitchell, named for William H. Mitchell, a Chicago businessman and treasurer of the lumber company. Renamed several years later for the company president, James C. Parrish of New York. (Rohe, *Ghosts of the Forest*, 243)

Patch Grove. Grant. Town (1848) and Village (1921). Named for early settler Henry Patch, who built a cabin west of the present community in 1836. The site was laid out in the 1840s by Enos P. Finn, a founder of Wyalusing. The Patch Grove post office was established in 1838 with Henry Patch, postmaster; the name was changed to Ursine (Latin for 'bearlike') in 1851 and changed back to Patch Grove in 1852. (Holford, 614)

Patzau [PAT zoo]. Douglas. Patzau is the German form of Pacov [PAHT sof], a community in the Czech Republic. The post office was established in November 1913, George W. Holmes, postmaster.

Paukotuk [POW kuh tuhk]. Winnebago. Likely named for a Sauk leader of the early nineteenth century. The 1825 Treaty of Prairie du Chien lists as one of the signatories Pau-ko-tuk, glossed as 'the open sky.'

Pearson. Langlade. Named from the Pearson post office, established by postmaster (Joseph) Pearson Hughes in June 1893. (Hermolin, p.c.)

Peck. Langlade. Town (1891). Named for George W. Peck (1840–1916), the seventeenth governor of Wisconsin (1891–95). Peck, who founded newspapers in Ripon and La Crosse, was also a writer of note, best known for the "Peck's Bad Boy" series of books, which were immensely popular in the late nineteenth and early twentieth centuries. (Dessureau, 226)

Peebles [PEE buhls]. Fond du Lac. Named for site owner Ezra Peebles. According to local lore, when the Sheboygan & Fond du Lac railroad established a station in the 1870s, railroad officials asked Peebles how much he would pay to have the station named after him. He replied, "Not a damn cent—but if you want to name it after me, you can." And they did. The post office was established in June 1877, Robert Conklin, postmaster. (Worthing)

Peeksville. Ashland. Town (1915) and ppl. Little is known about the Mr. Peek who gave his name to the town and community of Peeksville beyond the fact that he opened a hardware store at the site in the late 1880s and may have been employed by the Wisconsin Central railroad. The post office was established in July 1887 by Callie J. Wagley. (*History of the Glidden Four-Town Area*, 37)

Pelican. Oneida. Town (1883) and Pelican Lake, ppl. Probably a translation of Ojibwa *zhede* 'pelican.' The Pelican Lake post office was established in August 1882, Stephen B. Roberts, postmaster. See Chetek.

Pelishek Corners [PEL uh shek]. Brown, Manitowoc. Largely a Bohemian settlement, named for one or more Pelishek families (several spellings), which were established in the area by 1870. (Cassidy, *Brown County*)

Pella [PEL uh]. Shawano. Town (1860) and ppl. Pella was platted in 1887 for site owner William Smith and named from the township, which was most likely named by settlers from Pella, Marion County, Iowa, itself named in the mid-1840s by the Reverend Hendrik Scholte for Pella in ancient Palestine, a place of refuge for early Christians. (McDevitt, 212)

Pell Lake. Walworth. Named from Pell Lake, itself named for site owner Ira A. Pell. Originally from Vermont, Pell brought his family to the area in the mid-1840s. Local lore claims that Pell drowned in the lake that bears his name. (Beckwith, 230)

Pembine [PEM beyen]. Marinette. Town (1913) and ppl. The name is probably derived from Ojibwa *anepeminan* 'summer berry.' Apparently surveyors for the federal government in the 1840s recorded the name of the Pemebonwon River as *Pemene-Bon-Won*, which was shortened to *Pemene*, now the name of the falls on the Menominee River between Wisconsin and Michigan, and modified to *Pembine*. A variant, Pembina, occurs in Minnesota, Missouri, and North Dakota. The post office was established in June 1887, David A. Crusoe, postmaster. (Bright; *Marinette County Centennial*, 5)

Pence [PENS]. Iron. Town and ppl. Pence was platted in 1890 by the Milwaukee, Lake Shore & Western railroad and named for John W. Pence, vice president of the Amazon Iron Mining Company and a partner in the mining firm of Pence and Snyder of Minneapolis. The town was organized in 1900 as Montreal, changed to Clement for township chair Clement Bertagnoli in 1923, and to Pence in 1924. (Stennett, 112)

Pennington. Price. Named for Edmund Pennington, who worked his way from brakeman to president of the Minneapolis, St. Paul & Sault Ste. Marie railroad in the early twentieth century. He was also director of the First National Bank of Minneapolis. See Starks. ("Edmund Pennington Obit")

Pensaukee [pen SAW kee]. Oconto. Town (1856) and ppl. Named from the Pensaukee River, itself probably named from Ojibwa *pindsagi* 'inside the mouth of a river.' The name was probably chosen by Freeland B. Gardner, for whom Gardner Township in Door County is named. Gardner established a sawmill at the site in 1850. (Vogel, *Indian Names*, 133)

Pepin [PEP uhn]. County (1858), Town (organized as North Pepin in 1856), and Village (1860). Named from Lake Pepin, a widening of the Mississippi River between Pepin County, Wisconsin, and Goodhue and Wabasha Counties, Minnesota. The lake is most likely named for one or more Pepin families from Trois Rivières, Quebec. Several Pepins appear in the early records, including a patriarch Guillaume dit Tranchemontagne and his descendants Pierre and Jean. One or both of the latter likely accompanied Daniel Greysolon, the Sieur du Lhut, from Montreal to what is now Duluth, Minnesota, in 1679. Exactly when the lake was first called Pepin is unknown, but the name was in use as early as 1700, making it one of the oldest recorded place names in Wisconsin. The name was well established by the mid-1760s when Jonathan Carver wrote in his journal, "Arrived at Lake Pepin calld by some Lake St. Anthony." (Kellogg, 227; *Pepin County History*)

Peplin. Marathon. Founded by John, Stephen, and Tony Warzella, who established a sawmill, store, and blacksmith shop about 1910. The source of the name is uncertain. Peplin may be a direct transfer from Peplin in northern Poland or a modification of Pelplin, south of Gdansk.

Perkinstown. Taylor. Named for Albert J. Perkins, businessman and mayor of Medford in the early 1880s. The post office was established in April 1891, Emma Rees, postmaster.

Perry. Dane. Town (1849). Named for Commodore Oliver Hazard Perry, U.S. Navy hero who distinguished himself in the War of 1812 during the battle of Lake Erie and in 1815 in the Second Barbary War in the Mediterranean. The post office was established in July 1857, Anaun Sanderson, postmaster. (Butterfield, *History of Dane County*, 929)

Pershing [PER shing, PER zhing]. Taylor. Town. Named for John J. Pershing (1860–1948). At the time of township formation in July 1919, Pershing was commander of American forces in Europe at the end of World War I.

Peshtigo [PESH tuh go]. Marinette. Town (1858) and City (1903). The city and town of Peshtigo are named from the Peshtigo River. Beyond this rather obvious fact, very little is known about the origin of the name or the circumstances surrounding the naming. It is generally assumed that *pestigo* is Menominee, although this is not certain. Several meanings have been proposed, as varied as 'wild goose river,' 'rapids,' and 'snapping turtle.' While many names have a history and a meaning, the etymology of *Peshtigo* may be that it simply referred to a band of Native Americans who lived along the river that bears their name. (Vogel, *Indian Names*, 41)

Petersburg. Crawford. Founded by and named for Peter Haskins, from New York State, who established a blacksmith shop and gristmill about 1855. (Butterfield, *History of Crawford and Richland Counties*, 1074)

Pewaukee [pee WAW kee]. Waukesha. Town (1840) and Village (1876). Settled about 1837, when Asa Clark erected a sawmill, hotel, and church. Pewaukee is built upon *aki* or *(w)aukee*, meaning 'land' or 'location' in several Algonquian languages. The significance of the initial syllable is unclear. Sources in Ojibwa *nibiwaki* 'swampy place' and Menominee *pee-wau-nau-kee* 'place of flint' have been proposed, and meanings such as 'clean land,' 'dusty place,' 'snail lake,' and 'shell lake' have been suggested. (Vogel, *Indian Names*, 180)

Peyton. Douglas. Named for Hamilton M. Peyton, born in Geneva, New York. Peyton immigrated to Wisconsin in the mid-1850s and established a bank in Superior in 1858. He later formed the Peyton, Kimball & Barber lumber consortium. ("Hamilton M. Peyton")

Phelps. Vilas. Town and ppl. Phelps grew around a collection of resorts and fishing camps built in the 1880s, one of which was established on North Twin Lake by Seth Conover, for whom the Town of Conover is named. The township was organized in 1905 as Hackley, named from the Hackley post office, established in November 1902 and named for Charles H. Hackley, a partner in the Hackley Phelps Bonnell Company, which established a sawmill on North Twin Lake about 1900. Hackley was renamed for another of the partners, William Phelps, upon his death in 1912. (*Historical/Architectural Resources Survey*, 21)

Phillips. Price. City (1891). Platted in September 1876 and named for Elijah B. Phillips, general manager of the Wisconsin Central railroad. With Charles Colby he formed the Phillips and Colby Construction Company in the early 1870s to build the railroad through to Lake Superior. See Colby. (*Phillips, Wisconsin*, 11)

Phipps. Sawyer. Founded about 1881; named for William H. Phipps, mayor of Hudson in the 1880s, state senator in the 1890s, and land commissioner for the Chicago, St. Paul, Minneapolis & Omaha railroad. (Stennett, 186)

Phlox [FLAHKS]. Langlade. Apparently named for the North American phlox, which grew wild in the area, but naming details are unknown. The post office was established in December 1880 by John Jansen, from Gelderland, Netherlands.

Piacenza. Winnebago. Piacenza grew around a collection of summer cottages built by Walter L. Miller about 1889. Miller or his associates probably chose the name for the city and province of Piacenza in northern Italy. This is the only Piacenza in the United States, although the Latin form of the name, Placentia, is a community in Orange County, California, and the name of several lakes and other hydrographic features in a number of states. (Munroe, p.c.)

Pickerel. Langlade. Formerly known as Twin Lakes, the community was named either directly for the fish genus, which includes northern pike and muskelunge, or is a translation of Menominee *okaw*, referring to the pickerel. The name was apparently changed in 1904 when the post office was established. See Oconto. (Hermolin, p.c.)

Pickett. Winnebago. Named for site owner Armine Pickett, who served in the Wisconsin Assembly in the early 1860s. The post office was established as Weelaunee in May 1850, changed to Pickett's Station with construction of the railroad in the 1870s, and to Pickett in 1883. (Lawson, 339)

Piehl [PEEL]. Oneida. Town (1908). Named for Frederick H. Piehl, chief operating officer of the Gagen Land and Cedar Company and a prominent local business and civic leader in the early twentieth century. ("Fred Piehl")

Pierce. County. In 1853 the Wisconsin Legislature organized two new counties; each was named for a president of the United States: Pierce, for Franklin Pierce of New Hampshire, fourteenth president of the United States, in office 1853–57, and Polk, for James K. Polk, who was president when Wisconsin became a state in 1848.

Pierce. Kewaunee. Town (1859). The local story is that the township was named for James Pierce, who took part in the Canadian insurgency of 1837, was banished from Canada, fled to Kewaunee County, and became a local folk hero. (*Kewaunee, Wisconsin*)

Pierceville. Dane. Named for the Pierce family, early settlers who arrived in the area about 1840. The post office was established in February 1849 with William A. Pierce, one of the original settlers, as postmaster. (Cassidy, *Dane County Place-Names*)

Pigeon. Trempealeau. Town (1875). Also Pigeon Falls. Village (1956). Named from the Pigeon Falls post office, established in April 1873 by Hans Johnson and named for the rapids on Pigeon Creek. The stream took its name from the flocks of wild pigeons or from Ojibwa *omini* 'pigeon, dove.' Meeme (q.v.) is a variant. Pigeon Falls was platted in 1894 and named from the township by community founder and benefactor Peder Ekern, who emigrated from Norway about 1868. (Curtiss-Wedge and Pierce, 225, 270)

Pike River. Bayfield. Named for Elisha Pike from Toledo, Ohio, generally acknowledged as the first permanent settler in Bayfield County. Pike established a sawmill on what became known as Pike's Creek about 1855. Robinson D. Pike, Elisha's son, founded the Pike Lumber Company in the late 1860s. (Stennett, 186)

Pikeville. Kenosha. Pikeville is derived from Pike Creek, an early name for the area around Kenosha. The name of the stream was a translation of Ojibwa *kinoji* 'pike.' See Kenosha.

Pilsen [PIL suhn]. Both the community of Pilsen in Kewaunee County and the township in Bayfield County (1909) were named for Pilsen (Plzeň) in western Bohemia in the Czech Republic. The Pilsen post office was established in April 1881, Andrew Mahlek, postmaster. (Rucker, *History of Czech Settlements*, 6)

Pine Grove. Brown. According to a local account the community was named for a stand of pine trees saved from cutting and dedicated as a park by the site owner, Anton Nachtweg. The Pine Grove post office was established, discontinued, and reestablished several times between December 1862 and December 1907, when it closed permanently. (Cassidy, *Brown County*)

Pine Knob. Crawford. Butteris writes: "[The] name derived from the landmark in this community. It is a huge, rocky mound with native white pines and other trees growing up along the sides and on the top. Years ago, it had a clump of tall pine trees on top, which could be seen for miles around emerging over the horizon of the more or less wooded area" (n.p.).

Pine River. Waushara. Founded about 1849 by Ensign Noble and Benjamin Franklin Frisbie. Frisbie and his wife, Perthenia, emigrated from Vermont and established a tavern and hotel in 1850. The name was reportedly inspired by a particularly large pine tree near the establishment. (Reetz, 119)

Pipe. Fond du Lac. A shortening of "peace pipe," itself from French *calumet*, literally 'little reed,' referring to the peace pipe of ceremonial importance to a number of Native American groups. Calumetville (q.v.) is just north of Pipe.

Pipersville. Jefferson. Named in 1840 for and by the first postmaster, Benjamin Piper, who emigrated from New York State about 1836.

Pittsfield. Brown. The Town of Pittsfield was organized in 1852 and named by Isaac Knapp, one of the township organizers, for his former home, Pittsfield, Berkshire County, Massachusetts. The Pittsfield post office was established in June 1892 in Brown County, August Goethe, postmaster. (Cassidy, *Brown County*)

Pittsville. Wood. City (1887). Named for one or more Pitts families. In 1856 Oliver W. Pitts left Bedford County, Pennsylvania, with his memorably named bride, Freelove Chase, and established a sawmill on the banks of the Yellow River where he was joined by his father, Luke Noble Pitts, and other members of the Pitts family. Pitts' Mill was formally platted as Pittsville by George Hiles and Lawrence Ward in 1883. (Jones and McVean, *History of Wood County*, 221)

Plain. Sauk. Village (1912). Adam and Solomon Cramer, their mother, and Adam's son, John, arrived from Ohio at the site of present Plain in 1851. The area became known as Cramer's Corners and informally as Logtown. The community was likely named by Catholic Austrian and Bavarian settlers for the Shrine of Our Lady of Maria Plain in Salzburg, Austria, a pilgrimage site since the seventeenth century. The post office was established in July 1860, Bela V. Bunnell, postmaster. (Cole, *Baraboo*; Goc, *Many a Fine Harvest*, 165)

Plainfield. Waushara. Town (1854) and Village (1882). Previously known as Norwich, a transfer from New England. The name was formalized with establishment of the post office in October 1854 by Elijah C. Waterman, the first postmaster and site owner, for his former home, Plainfield, Vermont. (Reetz, 121)

Platteville [PLAT vil]. Grant. Town (1849) and City (1876). In the 1820s the area was known as the Platte River Diggings for the local lead mines. John B. Rountree, James B. Campbell, and several others became the first permanent settlers and mine owners in 1827. The following year Rountree opened a general store, and the site subsequently became known as Lebanon. In 1828 or 1829 Rountree applied for a post office to be called Platteville, in Rountree's words, "named at my Suggestion, because of its Location in the vicinity of the Platte River" (Mining & Rollo Jamison Museum). The source of the name of Platte River is unknown. Stennett has proposed that the river was named in the late eighteenth century by French explorers, from *plat* 'flat, dull, shallow,' referring to the relative width and little depth of much of the stream. The more famous Platte River in Nebraska was called *Rivière Plate* 'flat river' by French explorers, a translation of the Oto or Omaha name of the river. However, there is no reason to believe that the Platte River of Nebraska influenced the naming of the Platte River of Wisconsin. (Stennett, 114)

Pleasant Springs. Dane. Town (1848). According to Butterfield's 1880 *History of Dane County*, "Pleasant Springs receives its name from a large spring . . . and numerous smaller ones" (911). Cassidy (*Place Names of Dane County*) calls the name "subjectively descriptive."

Plover [PLOV er]. Portage. Town (1849) and Village (1971) and Town in Marathon (1890). Named from the Plover River, which, in Rosholt's words, takes its name "from the Semipalmated Ring Plover, a shore-bird with long pointed wings and short tail similar to the Kildeer" (*Our County, Our Story*, 360). By the late 1830s the developing community was known as the Plover Portage, named for the strip of land over which canoes were carried between the Wisconsin and Wolf Rivers. The name became Plover by 1850, was changed to Clayton in 1857, and later to Algernon, perhaps for Algernon B. Crosby, a local official. More name changes were to come: Stanton in 1858, for either Edwin Stanton, who became Lincoln's secretary of war, or Elizabeth Cady Stanton, the women's rights activist, and finally Plover in 1864. The post office was established in January 1845 as Plover Portage; changed to Plover in January 1850. (Riley)

Plum City. Pierce. Village (1909). About 1857 land speculator Frank Moser laid out the community, which he named for its location on Plum Creek, itself probably named for the local wild plums. Moser added City to the name in hopes that the community would become a center of commerce and a major economic force in west central Wisconsin. Moser established the post office in January 1866. (McBride, 219)

Plum Lake. Vilas. Town. Organized in 1911 at the urging of Herbert M. Warner, a lumberman and resort owner who was one of the first settlers on Plum Lake in 1899. (Jones and McVean, *History of Lincoln, Oneida, and Vilas Counties*, 356)

Plummer Point. Winnebago. Named for site owner Levi Plummer.

Plymouth. Juneau. Town (1854). Among the early settlers were the Fowler brothers from Vermont: John, David, Rueben, and George. Named for a Plymouth in New England, likely Plymouth, Vermont, or Plymouth, Massachusetts. (*Juneau County*, 50)

Plymouth. Sheboygan. Town (organized as Plymouth in 1849; changed to Quitquire or Quitquioc in 1851; changed back to Plymouth in 1852) and City (1877). Plymouth grew around an early tavern and hotel known as the Cold Spring House, operated by Thomas J. Davidson from the mid-1840s. Davidson established the Plymouth post office in September 1846 and laid out the community of Plymouth about 1848, which he reportedly named for Plymouth, Connecticut, where his early sweetheart was buried. About 1851, east of Plymouth, Martin Flint platted a community he called Quitquioc, a name of unknown origin, although several possible sources have been proposed. Buchen suggests a derivation from *Ta-quit-qui-oc*, meaning 'crooked creek,' perhaps a Native American name for the Mullet River. However, John Warren Hunt, in his 1853 *Wisconsin Gazetteer* writes: "The real derivation of the word is from the Menominee, Quitlztlqueouowouwoc, which signifies a sulphur or mineral spring" (183). Plymouth is the official name of the town and city, but as Hildebrand notes, "Quitquioc lives on in the name of the high school yearbook and the golf course at Elkhart Lake." (Buchen, 243; Hildebrand, 89–91)

Pokegama [po KEG uh muh]. Douglas. Named for its location near the Little Pokegama River. Pokegama is a popular name for geographic features in northern Wisconsin and eastern Minnesota, but this is the only community so named in the United States. There are at least five lakes named Pokegama in Wisconsin, in Barron, Burnett, Sawyer, Vilas, and Washburn Counties. Pokegama is an adaptation of Ojibwa *bakegama* 'where a lake is divided by a projecting point.' (Vogel, *Indian Names*, 133)

Poland. Brown. Probably named for the country of Poland. The post office was established in August 1891, John Conrad, postmaster. (Cassidy, *Brown County*)

Polar. Langlade. Town (1881) and ppl. Formerly known as Mueller's Lake for early settler Moritz Mueller. The Polar post office was established in February 1882, named for Hi(ram) B. Polar (Poler), an early fur trader described by Dessureau as an "English prospector, Indian trader and Stopping Place proprietor of the Wolf River country" (231).

Polk [POK, POLK]. The Town of Polk in Washington County, organized in 1846, and Polk County, created from St. Croix in 1853, were named in honor of James K. Polk (1795–1849), eleventh president of the United States, serving 1845–49. Polk was president when Wisconsin became a state in 1848. Polk's vice president was George Mifflin Dallas, the namesake of both Dallas and Mifflin (q.v.).

Polley [PAH lee]. Taylor. Named from the Polley post office, established in April 1907 by James Polley, who emigrated from New Brunswick, Canada, about 1870.

Polonia [puh LON ee uh]. Portage. The area was known as Poland Corners for settlers from Poland until 1867, when the post office was established as Ellis, named for Albert Gallatin Ellis, multiterm mayor of Stevens Point in the 1860s. Polonia, a Latinized form of Poland, was founded east of Ellis about 1874 by Father Joseph Dabrowski, born in Zoltance, Poland, as a site for the Sacred Heart Catholic Church. The only other Polonia in the United States is in Minnesota. (Rosholt, *Our County, Our Story*, 139)

Poniatowski [pah nuh TOW skee]. Marathon. The local account is that a group of Polish settlers suggested the community be named for Frederick Rietbrock, but he proposed instead that it be named for their illustrious countryman, Józef Antoni Poniatowski (1763–1813), who served militarily with the Austrian Empire, the Polish-Lithuanian Commonwealth, and Napoleon's Grande Armée. The post office was established in June 1881, Joseph Chesak, postmaster. This is the only Poniatowski in the United States. See Rietbrock. (Nowicki and Kolpack, 21)

Popple River. Forest. Town (organized as Newald in 1914; changed to Popple River in 1926) and ppl. Named from the Popple River. Popple is an alteration of "poplar," referring to aspen or poplar trees. As a place name, Popple is found primarily in New England and in Michigan, Wisconsin, and Minnesota.

Porcupine. Pepin. Named from Porcupine Creek. The 1985 *Pepin County History* records two local stories regarding the origin of the name, either or both of which may have some basis in fact. By one, "When surveyors came down from Eau Claire to help [Miles Durand] Prindle plot the City of Durand, they had driven around the county. They saw a porcupine in the area of the little town, so when talking about this section, they would say, 'Remember, where we saw the porcupine.'" By the second, "[Levi] Place, a great hunter, went hunting and shot a very large porcupine. He nailed it to a tree and thence called the creek and settlement by that name" (20). The post office was established in October 1877, James Shaw, postmaster.

Portage [PORT ij]. County (1936). City (1854) in Columbia County. French for 'carrying place,' referring specifically to the mile-and-a-half strip of land where canoes were carried between the Fox and Wisconsin Rivers. Portage is probably a translation of a Native American name, often reported to be Winnebago *wau-wau-o-nah* 'carry on one's shoulder,' now reduced to Wauona, the name of today's walking trail between the rivers. ("Portage Canal Society, History")

Port Andrew. Richland. Named for and by the first permanent settler, "Captain" Thomas Andrew, a riverboat pilot, who, with his brother-in-law, Englishman John Coumbe, operated a ferry across the Wisconsin River from the early 1850s. (Durbin, 197)

Port Arthur. Rusk. Founded about 1905 and named for Port Authur, Manchuria (now known as Lushun, at the tip of the Liaodong peninsula, China), itself named about 1860 for British naval officer William Arthur. The seige of Port Arthur in February 1904 signaled the start of the Russo-Japanese War and was widely reported in American newspapers. (*Rusk County History*, 27)

Port Edwards. Wood. Town (1874) and Village (1902). About 1840 John Edwards and his business partner, Henry Clinton, assumed ownership of a sawmill at a site on the Wisconsin River known as Frenchtown, named for an early settlement of French Canadians. The post office was established as French Town in February 1859 and changed to Port Edwards in honor of John Edwards in January 1864. (Jones and McVean, *History of Wood County*, 245)

Porter. Rock. Town (1847). Named for a locally prominent Porter family, likely related to Dr. John Porter, U.S. Senator Daniel Webster's personal friend and physician in the early nineteenth century. (*History of Rock County*, 522)

Porterfield. Marinette. Town (1887) and ppl. Named for John Porterfield, a Marinette grocer and hotelier. The post office was established in December 1885, Robert McWilliams, postmaster. (*History of Northern Wisconsin*, 592)

Porters. Rock. Named for Philo Porter, site owner and township treasurer. The Racine, Janesville & Mississippi railroad established Porter's Station in 1856. (McLenegan, 24)

Portland. Dodge. Town (1846) and ppl. Monroe. Town (1856) and ppl. Portland in Dodge County was laid out as Campbell's Settlement by Canadian Alexander Campbell about 1847. The name was changed in January 1853 when the post office was established as Portland, named for Portland, Maine, the home state of Jedediah Kimball, who represented the district in the Wisconsin Assembly in 1849, and his brother, Hannibal. Portland in Monroe County was also named for Portland, Maine. ("Village of Portland")

Port Washington. Ozaukee. Town (organized in 1846 in Washington County) and City (1882). In late 1835 surveyor George Ostrander platted the north shore of Sauk Creek as Wisconsin City for site owners Wooster Harrison and James Doty, the future governor of Wisconsin Territory. The popular name was Sauk Washington or Washington City until about 1844, when the name was formalized as Port Washington at the suggestion of George C. Daniels, a tavern owner and county commissioner. (Stennett, 115)

Port Wing. Bayfield. Town (1901) and ppl. Founded by Theodore N. Okerstrom, who emigrated from Sweden to St. Paul, Minnesota, in 1867. Okerstrom became a successful lumberman and laid out Port Wing in 1892. The namesake is Colonel Isaac H. Wing, a Civil War veteran and a Bayfield lawyer. ("Port Wing, Wisconsin")

Poskin [PAHS kin]. Barron. Founded about 1887 as Cosgrove by Peter Cosgrove, the first permanent settler. The name was changed by October 1889, recognizing Mary Poskin, the Native American wife of Andrew Tainter, who oversaw the local Knapp, Stout lumber camp and for whom the Town of Tainter in Dunn County is named. (Curtiss-Wedge and Jones, 1036)

Post Lake. Langlade. The community was named from Upper or Lower Post Lake. One or both of the lakes was first known as Trading Post Lake, where an Indian trading post was located. The post office was established in May 1884, Henry J. Seamon, postmaster. (Hermolin, p.c.)

Postville. Green. In 1858 Gilbert Post built the fourth house in Postville, in part of which he kept a general store. (Bingham, 232)

Potosi [puh TO see]. Grant. Town (1849) and Village (1887). The area, originally known as Snake Hollow, was settled soon after significant deposits of lead ore were discovered in the late 1820s. Potosi, from the native Bolivian language Aymara, was the name of a famous silver mine during Spanish rule and became associated with fabulous wealth. The name was transferred from Bolivia to San Luis Potosí in Mexico and to Potosi, Missouri. Missouri miners in turn brought the name to southwestern Wisconsin. In 1839, Lafayette, Van Buren, and several other small communities consolidated as Potosi. (Holford, 515)

Potter. Calumet. Village (1980). Earlier known as Muskratville and as Rantoul Centre. Formally named for Orin R. Potter, who built a sawmill on the Manitowoc River in 1859 and operated a lumberyard from about 1860. ("Village of Potter")

Pound. Marinette. Town (organized as Coleman in 1893; changed to Pound in 1903) and Village (1914). Named from the Pound post office, established in March 1883. Both the village of Coleman (1903) and the town of Pound honor Thaddeus Coleman Pound (1833–1914), Wisconsin state representative in the 1860s, lieutenant governor in the early 1870s, and U.S. representative in the late 1870s and early 1880s. Thaddeus Pound was the grandfather of poet Ezra Pound. (*Marinette County Centennial*, 5)

Powell. Iron. Named for John Wesley Powell (1834–1902), geologist and explorer, best known for the 1869 Powell Geographic Expedition to the Southwest, which included the first known passage through the Grand Canyon. The post office was established in April 1908, William Sherman, postmaster. (Stennett, 115)

Powers Lake. Kenosha. Named for James B. Powers, the Town of Wheatland's first constable in the 1840s. The Lagoon post office, established in August 1896, was changed to Powers Lake in October 1900.

Poygan [POY guhn]. Winnebago. Town (1852). Named from Lake Poygan, itself named from Menominee *pawahekan* 'where wild rice is harvested,' referring to Lake Poygan's extensive beds of wild rice, a major food source for the Menominee. The post office was established in July 1852 as Powaickum and changed to Poygan in April 1859. (Bright; Vogel, *Indian Names*, 110)

Poynette [poy NET]. Columbia. Village (1892). Laid out about 1837 by James Duane Doty, a land speculator and politician who later became the second governor of Wisconsin Territory. Doty named the community Pauquette, for Pierre Pauquette, a French Winnebago interpreter and agent for John Jacob Astor's American Fur Company in Prairie du Chien. In 1850 John Thomas filed an application for the Pauquette post office, but the petition was misread and approved as Poynette. The community was formally platted the following year, taking the name of the Poynette post office. (J. Jones, 300)

Poy Sippy [poy SIP ee]. Waushara. Town (1854) and ppl. Poy Sippy is a shortening of Poygansippi, probably a Native American name for the Pine River, perhaps so named because it flows into Lake Poygan. *Poy* is from the same source as Poygan (q.v.) and *sippi* is general Algonquian for 'river.' The name may have been chosen by site owner and first postmaster George Hawley, who established a sawmill on Pine River in the 1850s. (Reetz, 124; Vogel, *Indian Names*, 111)

Praag [PRAHG]. Buffalo. Named for the city of Prague now in the Czech Republic by site owner William Mattausch (Mattauch), who emigrated from Bohemia in the late 1850s and laid out the community on his farm about 1876. The post office was established in June 1898 as Praag, Reinhard Mattausch, postmaster. ("Descendants of Unknown Mattausch")

Prairie du Chien [PREHR ee duh SHEEN]. Crawford. Town (1849) and City (1872). Jonathan Carver, who explored the area in the 1760s, gave the first known account of the name, writing that the plain was "called by the French, la Prairies les Chiens, which signifies the Dog Plains" (31). On several occasions Carver mentions that local Native Americans frequently used dogs in their hunts, suggesting that the prairie was named for canines. However, Carver also writes "La Prairie le Chien," where "dog" is singular, which led the eminent Wisconsin historians Louise Clark Kellogg and Reuben Gold Thwaites to claim that the "dog" in question was a leader of a Fox band whose village was nearby. Quite possibly, the word translated by the French as "chien" referred to both the animals and to one or more Native Americans named "dog." (Kellogg, 69; Vogel, *Indian Names*, 193)

Prairie du Sac [PREHR ee duh SAK]. Sauk. Town (1849) and Village (1885). French for 'Sauk meadow,' 'meadow of the Sauks.' Sac was the customary French spelling of Sauk. The prairie was named by French explorers and traders, probably in the early eighteenth century. The first permanent European settler was David B. Crocker, who laid claim to much of the area and established a general store about 1839, the year the post office was established by Cyrus Leland. See Sauk. (Goc, *Many a Fine Harvest*, 179)

Prairie Farm. Barron. Town (1874) and Village (1901). Founded in the late 1840s by the Knapp, Stout Lumber Company as the new headquarters of its logging and milling operations. The local story is that William Wilson, one of the original owners of Knapp, Stout, chose the name as appropriate for an enterprise that was created to provide crops for both company employees and their draft animals. The first farm was established in 1856. (Gordon and Curtiss-Wedge, 1126–27)

Pratt Junction. Oneida. Probably named for George W. Pratt, lumberman and owner of the Wolf and Wisconsin Rivers railroad in the 1880s.

Pray. Jackson. Formerly known as Tremont, named from the Tremont post office, established in December 1874 by Artemis Emery and likely named for the Tremont section of the Bronx, New York. The name was changed to Hatfield in 1875. In the late 1870s, Herman Pray Jr., from New York State by way of Michigan, built a sawmill and became master of the Hatfield post office, which he renamed for himself in 1878. (*Biographical History of Clark and Jackson Counties*, 178)

Preble [PRE buhl]. Brown. Town (1859) and ppl. Probably named for Commodore Edward Preble (1761–1807), a distinguished officer credited with bringing organization and discipline to the early U.S. Navy. Preble served brilliantly in the Tripolitan War against the Barbary pirates in the early 1800s. The post office was established in November 1861, Edward Rothe, postmaster.

Prentice. Price. Town (1886) and Village (1899). The namesake is often claimed to be Jackson L. Prentice, a mid-nineteenth-century surveyor based at Stevens Point. More likely, however, the name was chosen for and probably by Alexander Prentice, the first postmaster and one of the owners of the Jump River Lumber Company, which founded the community in 1882. (Forrester, 364)

Prescott. Pierce. City (1857). Named for Philander Prescott, originally from Phelps, New York, a translator and interpreter in negotiations between the federal government and the Sioux. In 1827 Prescott and other officials from Fort Snelling, Minnesota, formed a land company that founded Elizabeth at the mouth of the St. Croix River, named for Elizabeth Schaser, generally believed to be the first non-Native American child born in the area. The site was purchased, formally platted, and renamed for Prescott about 1852 by Orrin T. Maxon, the first postmaster. The town was organized as Elizabeth in 1849 and changed to Prescott in 1851. (Cotter, 2–3)

Presque Isle [presk EYEL]. Vilas. Town (1907) and ppl. Formerly known as Fosterville for John J. Foster, who established a sawmill and planing mill at the site in 1905, and, from about 1910, as Winegar for William S. Winegar, a prominent lumberman. The present name did not become official until 1955. *Presque Isle* 'almost an island,' was probably first used by early French explorers to refer to a peninsula having the appearance of an island but connected to the mainland by a narrow land bridge. (*Historical/Architectural Resources Survey*, 22)

Preston. Adams. Town (1855). Named by John Thomas Marsden, who established the Preston post office in March 1855. Marsden was born in one of the several Prestons in England, most likely Preston, Lancashire. ("John Thomas Marsden")

Preston. Grant. Named for the first postmaster, Matthew Preston, born in Yorkshire, England. Preston established the office in the summer of 1880.

Preston. Trempealeau. Town (1855). Named for the Preston family of New England, ancestors and relatives of Susan H. Reynolds, who, with her husband, Edmond, was one of the earliest settlers, arriving in the 1850s. (Curtiss-Wedge and Pierce, 271)

Price. Price County (1879), the Town of Price in Langlade County (1883), and the community of Price in Jackson County are named for William T. Price (1824–86). Born in Pennsylvania, Price came to Black River Falls in 1846 and became a successful lumberman and lawyer. He served in both the Wisconsin Assembly and Senate and represented the district in the U.S. House of Representatives from 1883 until his death in 1886. Price County was to have been called Flambeau County but the name was changed while the bill was in committee; William Price was president of the state senate at the time. (*History of Northern Wisconsin*, 765)

Primrose. Dane. Town (1849) and ppl. Named from the Primrose post office. According to a local account, when the office was established in the home of Robert Spears in April 1847, the choice of a name "was left to the ladies," and Mrs. Spears suggested Primrose from a song she had heard her father sing, which began "On Primrose Hill there lived a lass." This did not sit well with Mrs. Miriam Chandler, who opined that Primrose was "too sweet" and that Hillsburgh would be a better name. Mrs. Chandler's objection notwithstanding, Primrose was adopted enthusiastically by those assembled. (Keyes, 383)

Princeton. Green Lake. Town (organized as Pleasant Valley in 1849; changed to Princeton in 1852) and City (1920). Previously known as Treats Landing for the first permanent settler, Royal C. Treat. The name was chosen either by Royal Treat or by his brother, Henry, most likely for Princeton, Bureau County, Illinois, itself probably named for Princeton, New Jersey. (Reetz, 43)

Pukwana Beach [pook WAH nuh]. Fond du Lac. From Ojibwa *bakwene* 'to be smoky.' The name may have been taken from Longfellow's *Hiawatha*, where Gitche Manito smokes the calumet to summon the tribes to council. Longfellow calls the rising smoke "the Pukwana of the Peace Pipe." A Pukwana post office operated in Monroe County for several years in the late 1850s. The only other Pukwana in the United States is in Brule County, South Dakota. (Vogel, *Indian Names*, 91)

Pulaski [puh LAS kee]. Brown, Oconto, Shawano. Village. (1910). Named for Kazimierz (Casimir) Pulaski, the Polish national who served in the Revolutionary War with George Washington at Valley Forge, commanded the Continental cavalry, and died a hero's death during a charge into the British lines at Savannah, Georgia, in 1779. Pulaski is one of several communities that John J. Hof(f) organized in the nineteenth century. In 1875 the Agrarian Company of Milwaukee employed Hoff to organize settlements and sell lots in the area northwest of Green Bay. Of Norwegian ancestry himself, Hoff first tried to promote Norwegian immigration to the area. When this effort failed, he appealed to the Poles of Milwaukee and then to those of Poland. Hoff established at least five settlements: Pulaski, Sobieski, Kosciuszko, Hofa Park, and Maple Grove. He proved a generous benefactor to the communities he founded, donating land for public purposes and money to social and civic organizations. The post office was established in April 1891, Valentine Peplinski, postmaster. (Larsen and Caylor, 5)

Pulaski. Iowa. Town. Nobleman Vincent Dziewanowski fled Poland after taking part in the failed revolution of 1830, and by 1836 he had found his way to the Wisconsin lead region. The town of Pulaski was organized in 1849 and named for Kazimierz (Casimir) Pulaski, either at Dziewanowski's suggestion or in recognition of his Polish heritage because he had become a successful businessman and a respected member of the community. Dziewanowski is thought to be the first Polish immigrant to settle permanently in Wisconsin. Pulaski is a popular place name; some fifty U.S. communities or townships are named in Casimir Pulaski's honor. (Mikoś, 11)

Pulcifer [PUHL suh fer]. Shawano. Named for Daniel Haight Pulcifer, newspaper publisher, politician, and civic leader. A native of Vermont, Pulcifer was editor of the *Plover Times*, served in the Wisconsin Assembly in 1867 and 1879, and was the first mayor of Shawano. (*Commemorative Biographical Record of the Upper Wisconsin Counties*, 29)

Purdy. Vernon. Named for county judge William S. Purdy, who represented the district in the state senate in 1863.

Quarry. Manitowoc. Named from the local lime and stone quarrys. The post office was established in May 1900, John Mallman, postmaster.

Quincy [KWIN see]. Adams. Town (1852). Prompted by its location in Adams County, the town was named for John Quincy Adams (1767–1848), sixth president of the United States (1825–29). The community of Quincy disappeared when Castle Rock Lake was created in the late 1940s by the Wisconsin River Power Company. The Quincy post office operated from March 1854 until June 1915.

Quinney [KWIN ee]. Calumet. Named for Austin E. and John W. Quinney, Mohican brothers who led a contingent of Stockbridge settlers from New York first to Indiana and then to Wisconsin in the 1820s. The name itself is probably an English popular etymology of Mohican *quinecan* 'dish.' The post office was established in January 1867, Matthias Johnson, postmaster. See Stockbridge. (Vogel, *Indian Names*, 56–57)

Racine [ruh SEEN]. County and City (1848). The city was founded about 1834 by Gilbert Knapp, a Great Lakes ship captain from Massachusetts. The site became known as Port Gilbert, in honor of Knapp, but this name never caught on and gave way to Racine when the name of the Root River post office was changed in April 1836. *Racine*, French for 'root,' is a translation of a Native American name for the Root River, first recorded by the Franciscan missionary Jean François Buisson de St. Cosme in 1698 as *Kipikaoui*. The name is probably from Potawatomi *chepekataw sebe* 'root river' (which by popular etymology became Chippecotton), translated into French as Rivière Racine and subsequently into English as Root River. The yearbook of Washington Park High School in Racine is still called *Kipikawi*. (Vogel, *Indian Names*, 193)

Radisson [RAD uh suhn]. Sawyer. Town (1905) and Village (1953). Named at the suggestion of Edwin E. Woodman, secretary of the Chicago, St. Paul, Minneapolis & Omaha railroad in honor of Pierre-Esprit Radisson, a French adventurer and trader, who, along with his brother-in-law, Médard Chouart, the Sieur des Groseilliers, explored the southern shore of Lake Superior in 1659. Radisson was one of the founders of the Hudson's Bay Company, and his narratives of the natural landscape and Native American life were widely read. Radisson is the namesake of communities in Quebec and Saskatchewan and also of the Radisson hotel chain. See Woodman. (Stennett, 187)

Radspur. Bayfield. The origin of this intriguing name is unknown. Perhaps from German *Radspur* 'wheelroad, wheeltrack.' This is the only Radspur in the United States.

Randall. Burnett. Perhaps named for Alexander Randall, the namesake of Randall in Kenosha County (q.v.), but more likely the namesake is James J. Randall, an early settler from New Hampshire, who, along with his wife, Fannie, appears for the first time in the 1880 census. The post office was established in February 1885, Sven Johan Bengston, postmaster. ("Burnett County Communities")

Randall. Kenosha. Town (1860). Named for Alexander Randall (1819–72), the sixth governor of Wisconsin, serving 1858–62. Randall was later minister to the Vatican and U.S. postmaster general. Randall is also the namesake of Camp Randall Stadium on the University of Wisconsin campus in Madison. The stadium was built on the site of Camp Randall, a training facility for Union troops from Wisconsin during the Civil War. It is unclear if Randall in Burnett County was also named for the governor.

Randolph. Town (1849) in Columbia County; Village (1870) in Columbia and Dodge Counties. Probably named by site owner John Converse for his birthplace, Randolph, Vermont, itself named for colonial statesman Edmund Randolph. Converse was postmaster when the office was changed from Polk Prairie to Randolph in December 1849. The community was platted as Converseville when the Milwaukee & La Crosse railroad station was established about 1857. (*History of Dodge County*, 555)

Random Lake. Sheboygan. Village (1907). Founded about 1870 by the Milwaukee & Northern railroad as Greenleaf, named for Emery B. Greenleaf, general manager of the railroad and the namesake of Greenleaf in Brown County (q.v.). Renamed about 1872 for Random Lake. The origin of the name is uncertain. A possible source is the surveying term "random line," a trial line run in such a way as to avoid obstacles between survey stations. The area was surveyed for the federal government in the mid-1830s. (Buchen, 270)

Range. Polk. Rangeline. Marathon. Range and Rangeline are artifacts of the federal government's survey of Wisconsin that began in the early 1830s and partitioned the territory into townships and ranges. Each range was a distance of six miles east or west from one of the principle meridians. The building that housed the Range post office in Polk County sat on the line dividing ranges 15W and 16W, in other words, the fifteenth and sixteenth ranges west of the fourth principle meridian. (Ericson)

Rankin [RANG kin]. Kewaunee. Named in honor of Joseph Rankin (1833–86), from Passaic, New Jersey. Rankin served in the Wisconsin Assembly and Senate and represented the district in the U.S. Congress from 1883 until his death in 1886. The post office was established in May 1886, Fred H. Plinke, postmaster.

Rantoul [ran TOOL]. Calumet. Town (1855). Named for Robert Rantoul Jr., U.S. representative and senator from Massachusetts in the 1850s. Rantoul was a forceful proponent of railroad expansion in the Midwest and was a major stockholder in the Illinois Central railroad. Rantoul in Champaign

County, Illinois, is also named in his honor. The post office was established in January 1859, Timothy Mulcahy, postmaster.

Rantz [RANTS]. Oneida. According to Jennifer Rantz, the community was named for her grandfather Anthony, a Minocqua architect. Rantz was also agent for the Wisconsin Valley division of the Chicago, Milwaukee & St. Paul railroad, and when he noted that two stations had similar names, the railroad renamed one in his honor about 1900. ("Re: Rantz")

Raymond [RAY muhn(d)]. Racine. Town (1846) and ppl. Named for Elisha Raymond and his son, Alvin, who were among the first settlers in the mid-1830s. The first town meeting was in Elisha Raymond's cabin and he served as the first postmaster, beginning in March 1846. (F. Stone, 122)

Readfield [RED feeld]. Waupaca. Named for Charles Readfield or Redfield, who held several local and county offices, including that of Waupaca County register of deeds in the 1850s. The post office was established in May 1855, John Littlefield, postmaster. ("Outagamie County")

Readstown [REEDZ town]. Vernon. Village (1898). Daniel Read, from Tioga, New York, built the first gristmill and the first permanent house in the area in the late 1840s. He laid out and named the community in 1855. (*History of Vernon County*, 605)

Red Banks. Brown. Named from the banks of red clay that lie along the eastern shore of Green Bay, northeast of the community.

Red Cedar. Dunn. Town (1860) and ppl. Named from the Red Cedar River, a translation of Ojibwa *miskwawakokang* 'where there are red cedars.' Joseph Nicollet, during his expedition mapping the Upper Mississippi basin in the 1830s, recorded the "Mishwagokag, or Red Cedar River, which falls into the Chipppeway river" (Vogel, *Indian Names*, 160).

Red Cliff. Bayfield. Possibly a partial translation of Ojibwa *passabika* 'steep cliff,' but more likely Red Cliff is descriptive of one or more natural formations in the area. The post office was established in April 1896, George D. Ellis, postmaster.

Redgranite. Waushara. Village (1904). The area was known for its stone quarries by 1889 when William Bannerman's Berlin Granite Company began operations. Owners of the Wisconsin Granite Company formalized the name about 1904 to agree with that of the post office, established in 1897. Redgranite reflects both the main industry of the community and the color of the polished stone. (Evans, 2)

Reedsburg. Sauk. Town (1850) and City (1887). In the mid-1840s deposits of iron and copper ore were uncovered near present Reedsburg and several mines were opened, attracting the interest of David C. Reed, then living near Big Foot Prairie. Reed purchased several hundred acres near the mines and in the late 1840s established a sawmill that formed the nucleus of Reedsburg (originally Reedsburgh). (*Souvenir Program and Centennial History*, 5, 6)

Reedsville. Manitowoc. Village (1892). Founded by George Reed and Jacob Lueps about 1854 and named for Reed, a Manitowoc lawyer and railroad promoter. Reed was an incorporator of the Chicago, Milwaukee & Green Bay railroad in 1851. The choice of the name may have been influenced by Horatio Gates Howard Reed, chief engineer and later superintendent of the Milwaukee, Lake Shore & Western railroad. Formerly known as Mud Creek. (Stennett, 117; Zarnoth, 2)

Reeseville [REES vil]. Dodge. Village (1899). Named for early settler Samuel Reese, who built the first grain elevator in the area about 1844. The community was laid out by Reese's son, Adam, the first postmaster in 1857 and the first station agent for the Chicago, Milwaukee & St. Paul railroad in 1858. (Hubbell, 251)

Reid [REED]. Marathon. Town (1917). Named for Alexander H. Reid, judge of Wisconsin's sixteenth circuit in the early twentieth century. (Marchetti, 602)

Reifs Mills [REEFS]. Manitowoc. Named for the Reif family. Peter Reif emigrated from Cobelantz, Germany, in the late 1840s and established a sawmill and gristmill about 1850. ("Rudolph Reif")

Reighmoor [RAY mor]. Winnebago. Reighmoor is a community of lakefront homes on Lake Butte des Morts. Named for Stephen Reigh, an official of the Globe Realty Company, which founded the community in the 1920s. (Munroe, p.c.)

Remington. Wood. Town (1868). Named for Henry W. Remington, from Lorain, Ohio, who established a general store about 1859. Remington became an officer of the Wisconsin Valley railroad, served on the Wood County board, and represented the district in the Wisconsin Assembly in 1865. (Hiles and Hiles, 10, 69)

Requa [REK wuh]. Jackson. First known as Hanson, for a local landowner, and in the 1880s as Garfield for President James A. Garfield. Renamed by Norwegian settlers, either from an area in Norway known as Reque [*sic*] or from one or another Norwegian family who had taken Reque as their surname. (Stennett, 187)

Reseburg [REES berg]. Clark. Town (1893) and ppl. Named for William R. Reseburg, who emigrated from Prussia in 1856. Reseburg served in several local offices, including chair of Withee Township in the early 1880s. The post office was established in July 1894, Herman Holzhausen, postmaster. (Scholtz)

Retreat. Vernon. Apparently named for the path of Black Hawk's retreat to the Mississippi River, where the final battle of the Black Hawk War took place at Bad Axe during the first days of August 1832. The post office was established in February 1855, William P. Clark, postmaster. (Vogel, *Indian Names*, 185)

Rewey [ROO ee]. Iowa. Village (1902). Founded in the summer of 1880 and named for the site owner, Jefferson W. Rewey, from Tioga County, New York. He represented the district in the Wisconsin Assembly in 1868 and again in 1881. (Stennett, 117)

Rhine [REYEN]. Sheboygan. Town (1851) and ppl. One of the organizers of Rhine was Julius Wolff, a Sheboygan County sheriff and local official, who emigrated from Brandenburg, Germany, in the late 1840s. Wolff chose the name of Mosel (q.v.). Rhine was named for the Rhineland region of Germany. The Rhine post office was established in March 1863. (Buchen, 339)

Rhinelander [REYEN lander]. Oneida. City (1894). Formerly known as Pelican Rapids for the cascades in the Pelican River. The community grew around a trading post, sawmill, and tavern established by Canadian John Curran about 1859. In the mid-1870s the site was purchased by Edward D. Brown of Stevens Point and his sons Anderson, Webster, and Edward, who developed the local lumber industry. The Milwaukee, Lake Shore & Western railroad extended a line to the site in the early 1880s, and in appreciation the Browns renamed the community for Frederick W. Rhinelander Jr., president of the railroad and a prominent social and financial figure of New York City. Rhinelander is known as Hodag City for the legendary horned creature created by humorist Eugene Shepard in the 1890s. (Olsen, *Rhinelander Story*, 10–11)

Rib Falls, Rib Lake, Rib Mountain. Marathon, Taylor. The Town (1885) and Village (1902) of Rib Lake in Taylor County are named from Rib Lake, the source of Big Rib River, for which the towns of Rib Falls (1876) and Rib Mountain (organized as Flieth in 1905; changed to Rib Mountain in 1930) and the community of Rib Falls in Marathon County are named. "Rib" is a translation of an Ojibwa word based upon *opikwan* 'back' (anatomical). It is unclear if *opikwan* meant 'rib' as well as 'back' or if the meaning of 'back' was extended to 'rib' in the process of translation. (Bright)

Rice Lake. Barron. Town (1874) and City (1887). Platted in 1870 by the Knapp, Stout Lumber Company, which owned some hundred thousand acres of local timber land. From Ojibwa *manomin* 'wild rice,' which was translated by early French traders as *folle avoine*, 'wild oats,' in turn translated into English 'wild rice.' *Manomin* is also the source of the name

Menominee (q.v.). The post office was established in July 1872, Martin W. Heller, postmaster. (Stennett, 189)

Richardson. Polk. Named from the Richardson post office, established in 1881, itself probably named for the first postmaster, Eugene Richardson. See Turtle Lake; see Joel. (Stennett, 189)

Richfield. Washington. Town (1846). Founded and likely named by Philip Laubenheimer, who emigrated from Hesse, Germany, in 1842. Laubenheimer kept a tavern and general store and later erected a grain elevator on the line of the La Crosse & Milwaukee railroad. The post office was established in June 1854, Bertram Schwarz, postmaster. (Quickert, 45)

Richford. Waushara. The town was organized as Adario in 1853 and perhaps named for Adario, Ohio, the only other Adario in the United States, or for Adario, a Wyandot leader brought to popular attention by several mid-nineteenth-century dramas. Nathaniel Woodruff proposed the name change in 1855 for Richford, Franklin County, Vermont, his former home. The post office was established as Adario in June 1851 and changed to Richford in July 1859. (Reetz, 131)

Richland. County. Organized in 1842. There are more than two hundred Richlands in the United States, making this one of the more popular place names. I can only speculate on the origin of the name in Wisconsin. It may be a transfer from an eastern state; it may be—as some local boosters claim—that Richland is indicative of the nature of the soil; it may be hopefully optimistic of abundant crops and livestock; or it may have been chosen simply to attract settlers through the positive images that the name Richland evokes.

Richland Center. Richland. City (1887). Founded by Ira Hazeltine, originally from Vermont, in the summer of 1851. Named for its location near the center of Richland County. The post office was established in April 1854, Leroy D. Gage, postmaster. (Scott)

Richmond. The name originated in England, where it first meant 'rich' or 'splendid' hill; from there it was transferred to New England, and now it occurs in some forty states. There have been at least four Richmond townships in Wisconsin. In Shawano County the town, organized in 1856, and the community were named for Abial Richmond, from Ohio, a land speculator who platted the first section of what is now the city of Shawano in 1856. In Walworth County, the Town of Richmond, organized in 1841, was named by early settlers Thomas and Perry James for Richmond, Rhode Island, their former home. The post office was established in July 1844, Perkins S. Childs, postmaster. Other Richmond townships are in St. Croix and Richland Counties. (Beckwith, 384; Michael)

Ridgeville. Monroe. Town (1855). Formerly called the Dividing Ridge, named for a ridge that reportedly separates the watershed of Sparta and Cole's Valley from that of Indian Creek. Named from the Ridgeville post office, established in June 1854 by Benjamin Welch (Welsch). (*Monroe County*, 88)

Ridgeway. Iowa. Town (1849) and Village (1902). Earlier known as Patesville for Jacob Pate, who built one of the first smelting furnaces in the area in the late 1820s. Renamed, probably in 1839, with establishment of the post office, apparently for a prominent dividing ridge running west through the county from near Blue Mounds. (G. Shepard, 69)

Rietbrock [REET brahk]. Marathon. Town (1879). Named for Fred Rietbrock, the founder of Athens (q.v.). Rietbrock was a quintessential nineteenth-century businessman. A Milwaukee lawyer, he was involved in city politics and had interests in the Rietbrock Land and Lumber Company, the Abbotsford & Northwestern railroad, and the First National Bank of Wausau. The outreach efforts of Rietbrock's Helendale Farms (named for his wife, Helen) significantly increased the quantity and improved the quality of livestock in Wisconsin. (Sjostrom, 95)

Riley. Dane. Founded in 1881 as Sugar River Station, a stop on the Chicago & North Western railroad, by Riley brothers Robert and William, who emigrated from New York about 1850. The site became known as Riley's Station and as Riley with establishment of the post office in May 1882. (Cassidy, *Dane County Place-Names*)

Ring. Winnebago. The origin of the name is unknown, but a possible source is Ring (An Rinn) in southern Ireland, an area that contributed significantly to the settling of Wisconsin in the 1860s. The post office was established in May 1870, James H. Walker, postmaster.

Ringle [RING guhl]. Marathon. Town (1901) and ppl. Named for John R. Ringle of Wausau, landowner and president of the Ringle Brick Company. Ringle was elected to both the Wisconsin Assembly and Senate and was mayor of Wausau in 1884. The post office was established in August 1891 by Ruth Abbott. (Marchetti, 577)

Rio [REYE o]. Columbia. Village (1887). Founded in 1864 by Nathan B. Dunlap, from Weathersfield, Ohio, and named from the Rio post office, established in the spring of 1852. The source of the name is unknown. According to a local tradition, Delos Bundy requested the post office be named Ohio for the home state of a number of early settlers, but the petition was approved with the name Rio, perhaps from a misreading or illegibility of Ohio. Other proposals are that the name is from Rio de Janiero, Brazil, or from the Rio Grande River, a familiar name in the recent Mexican War.

Rio, however, is most likely a transfer from Rio Grande, Gallia County, Ohio, itself named for the Rio Grande River. Both the Ohio and Wisconsin names are pronounced [REYE o]. (*Columbia County*, 54)

Rio Creek. Kewaunee. Named from Rio Creek. The stream was probably named—either seriously or facetiously—by a Kewaunee volunteer returning from Texas, where several Wisconsin regiments were part of a force that patrolled the Rio Grande valley following the Civil War during the Second Mexican Empire. The post office was established in June 1888, August Kirchmann, postmaster.

Riplinger [RIP ling er]. Clark. Named for the Riplinger family. Frank Riplinger emigrated from Trier, Germany, in the 1850s. He was a Civil War veteran, and in the late 1870s he and his sons, Fred and Ben, established a general store in the area then known as Osborne. Fred Riplinger was the first postmaster in 1916. (Curtiss-Wedge, *History of Clark County*, 664)

Ripon [RIP uhn]. Fond du Lac. Town (organized as Ceresco in 1845; changed to Ripon in 1856) and City (1858). The community of Ripon was founded in 1849 by David Mapes, John S. Horner, and several others. Horner, secretary of Wisconsin Territory in the 1830s, proposed the name for Ripon, North Yorkshire, England, his ancestral home. In the early 1850s Mapes and Horner established Brockway (now Ripon) College. Present Ripon includes the utopian socialist commune of Ceresco, which was founded in 1844 by the Wisconsin Phalanx, followers of the socialist ideas of Charles Fourier, and dissolved by 1850. (Pedrick, 30)

Rising Sun. Crawford. Named by Truman H. Wilder, who established the post office in March 1856. According to a local account, two solid weeks of rain accompanied Wilder's arrival in the area. When the rain finally stopped, he was thankful for "the rising sun." (Butterfield, *History of Crawford and Richland Counties*, 739)

River Falls. Pierce. Town (organized as Greenwood in 1854; changed to River Falls in 1858) and City (1875). In the spring of 1854 Nathaniel and Oliver Powell, originally from Madrid, New York, laid out a community they called Kinnickinnic, named from the Kinnickinnic River. The following year Charles Hutchinson established a post office he called River Falls. In 1856 George Pratt founded Greenwood Falls, named from the township, south of Kinnickinnic. The names were often confused. As Schoenick notes, "The post office of River Falls [was] located in the Village of Kinnickinnic in the township of Greenwood [and] the inhabitants . . . [used] any of the three names they desired" (3). In 1858 the Pierce County Board of Supervisors formalized the name as River Falls and changed the name of Greenwood township to River Falls. See Kinnickinnic.

Roberts. St. Croix. Village (1945). Formerly known as Warren or Warren Center for its location in the town of Warren. The community grew around the Roberts station on the West Wisconsin railroad, established in 1873 and named for John Bannister Gibson Roberts, chief engineer and superintendent of the railroad. (Stennett, 189)

Rochester. Racine. Town (1838) and Village (1912). In late 1836 William H. Waterman, future mayor of Racine, made the first land claim in present Rochester. About 1839 the community was laid out by Philo Belden, who later served in the Wisconsin Assembly and Senate and was a Racine County judge in the 1890s. Joshua Hathaway, who surveyed Racine County's townships in 1836–37, claims that he had chosen the name Waukeeshah for the settlement that he and several others were planning to establish, but Belden's Rochester prevailed, most likely named by settlers from Rochester, New York. (Ela, 8)

Rock. County (1836) and Town (1838). The name of Rock County has occasioned its share of popular etymologies, such as "named for its rocky soil," "named from Rock Prairie," "named from the 'big rock' on the north side of the river in Janesville," all suggesting that the name was created by and first used by Europeans, which is not the case. Rather, the county is named from the Rock River, known to the Miami and Illinois as *assini-sippi*, literally 'rock river,' probably named for the two-mile-long, thousand-acre block of limestone in the Mississippi River between the cities of Rock Island–Moline, Illinois, and Davenport-Bettendorf, Iowa. *Assini-sippi*, translated by French explorers, appears on maps of the early eighteenth century as Rivière de la Roche 'river of the rock,' in turn translated into English as Rock River. In the mid-1780s Thomas Jefferson proposed the name Assenisipia for one of the new states to be created from the Northwest Territory, to consist of much of present southern Wisconsin and northern Illinois. (*History of Rock County*, 357; Stennett, 29; Vogel, *Indian Names*, 175)

Rockbridge. Richland. Town (1850) and ppl. Founded by Ira S. Hazeltine in the summer of 1851. Hazeltine, from Vermont, held several local offices and represented the district in the Wisconsin Assembly in 1867. The name was presumably taken from a nearby natural bridge. (Butterfield, *History of Crawford and Richland Counties*, 1183)

Rockdale. Dane. Village (1914). Founded in 1836 as Clinton, for Clinton, New York. Replatted in 1885 as Rockdale. The source of the name is uncertain. It may be a transfer from one of several Rockdales farther east. (Cassidy, *Dane County Place-Names*)

236

Rock Elm. Pierce. Town (1865) and ppl. Named for rock elm (*Ulmus Thomasii*), the species of elm used in the construction of furniture. The post office was established in December 1863, Eli Heerman, postmaster. (Johnson and Wilmot, 27)

Rockland. Brown. Town (1856). Presumably named from the prominent limestone ridge that runs through the township. (J. Rudolph, 25)

Rockland. Manitowoc. Town (1856). According to Falge, Rockland "derives its name from the numerous outcroppings of coral limestone of the Kettle Range" (315).

Rockmont. Douglas. Apparently named from a nearby rocky summit. Formerly called Amnicon (q.v.). (Stennett, 190)

Rock Springs. Sauk. Village (1894). In 1845 Stephen Van Rensselaer Ableman, a carpenter who was elected colonel in the New York state militia, immigrated to Wisconsin, where he founded Excelsior. Ableman was also founder and president of the Baraboo Air Line railroad, which established Ableman Station about 1870. The names of the community and post office were changed to Rock Springs in 1875. Particulars of the naming are unknown. See Excelsior. ("Preserving the Past for the Future")

Rockton. Vernon. Laid out about 1873 by Van S. Bennett, reported to be the largest landowner in Vernon County. Bennett served in both the state assembly and senate in the 1870s and 1880s. Jesse Harness, who established the post office in June 1869, likely chose the name "to be in harmony with the rough and rocky surface of the country near the village," according to the 1884 *History of Vernon County* (751).

Rodell. Eau Claire. Perhaps named for a local Rodell family, or an employee of the Chicago & North Western railroad. By a local account Rodell is an early twentieth-century modification of Rosedale, the original name of the Chicago & North Western station, itself apparently named from the Rosedale school. Whatever the source of the name, this is the only Rodell in the United States. ("Area History of Rodell, Wisconsin")

Rogersville. Fond du Lac. Named for the Rogers family. Elisha and Emerson Rogers, following other members of their family, settled the area about 1848. The post office was established in July 1894, Edward P. Seaman, postmaster. (Worthing)

Rome. Adams. Town (1857). Named by William W. Burhite, Joseph Smith, and other settlers from Rome, Oneida County, New York, itself named for Rome, Italy. (Goc, *From Past to Present*, 35)

Rome. Jefferson. Named for Rome, New York, by Ambrose Seely, the site owner, in the fall of 1848. Seely, his brothers Davis and Dempster, and his sister Betty, settled in the area earlier that year. (Gnacinski and Longley, 95, 168)

Roosevelt. The towns in Burnett (1903) and Taylor (1905) Counties and the community in Oneida County, founded in 1907, were named for Theodore Roosevelt (1858–1919), twenty-sixth president of the United States, in office 1901–9.

Rose. Waushara. Town (1855). Perhaps named by settlers from Rose, Wayne County, New York. The post office was established as Rose Centre in January 1877, Jeremiah C. Pierce, postmaster.

Rosecrans [ROZ kranz]. Manitowoc. Probably named in honor of William Starke Rosecrans, who gained fame as a Union general in the Civil War. Rosecrans was instrumental in Union victories at Iuka and Corinth, Mississippi, in 1862. The post office was established in May 1863, John Bruss, postmaster.

Rosendale [ROZ uhn dayl]. Fond du Lac. Town (1846) and Village (1915). Origin unknown. As a place name Rosendale occurs in five states, including New York, which contributed a number of early settlers to this part of Wisconsin. Stennett speculates that Rosendale is a combination of German *rosen* 'roses' and English *dale* 'valley' (120). Butterfield's *History of Fond du Lac County* claims the name was "most appropriate" for the area "because it was such a perfect dale of roses" (767).

Rosholt [RAHSH uhlt]. Portage. Village (1907). Named from the Rosholt post office, established in March 1893, itself named for John Gilbert Rosholt, a sawmill owner who would be instrumental in attracting the Chicago & North Western railroad a decade later. One of the names proposed for the office was apparently Russellville because, as Malcolm Rosholt tells it, "the name Rosholt at that time was consistently slurred to 'Russell' by the non-Norwegian speaking people of the community" (Rosholt, *Town 25 North*, 174).

Rosiere [ro ZIHR]. Door, Kewaunee. Probably named by settlers from Rosières, Belgium, southeast of Brussels. Rosier is French for 'rosebush.' The post office was established in October 1871, Charles Rubens, postmaster.

Rostok [RO stahk]. Kewaunee. Probably named by German settlers for Rostok, a city in Mecklenburg-Vorpommer on the Baltic Sea. The post office was established in July 1899, Joseph W. Skala, postmaster.

Rothschild [RAHTH cheyeld]. Marathon. Village (1917). Founded about 1910 by the Marathon Paper Mills Company, which later became part of the Weyerhaeuser lumber conglomerate. The particular Rothschild for whom the community is named is uncertain. A local story claims that the community was named for the famous European Rothschild investment banking firm, but, as Durbin (60) points out, for more than half a century before the founding of the village, a landmark obstruction in the Wisconsin River was known to rivermen as Rothschilds Rock(s), probably the immediate source of the name.

Rowleys Bay [ROL eez]. Door. Founded by Samuel Ashbel Rogers, who established a sawmill and trading post about 1874. Named for Peter Rowley, a native of New York State who migrated to Kaukauna in 1834, after stops in Pennsylvania and Ohio. In the late 1830s Rowley moved to the site that now bears his name. A lifelong adventurer, he served in the War of 1812, moved frequently along the Door peninsula (even though he was supporting a family of seven), and at age sixty-six enlisted as a drummer in the Union army during the Civil War. (Thomas, 125–27)

Roxbury. Dane. Town (1849) and ppl. Named at the suggestion of James Steele for his former home, Roxbury, Delaware County, New York. The amanuensis of the evening recorded the name as Rocksbury, a spelling that persisted for several years. The post office was established in March 1852, John F. Cutting, postmaster. (Cassidy, *Dane County Place-Names*)

Royalton. Waupaca. Town (1853) and ppl. Reportedly named for Ellis N. Royalton, who established the first general store in the area in 1853. Perhaps a transfer from New York or Vermont. The post office was established as North Royalton in December 1854, Bradford Phillips, postmaster. (*History of Northern Wisconsin*, 1100).

Rozellville [ro ZEL vil]. Marathon. Named from the Rozellville post office, established in October 1877 by Michael Rozell, from Fishkill, Dutchess County, New York. (*Stratford Centennial Book*, 16)

Rube. Manitowoc. Named for Reuben D. Smart, a Manitowoc County sheriff who served in the Wisconsin Assembly in 1875. The post office was established in September 1884, Joseph Thalhammer, postmaster. (Falge, 314)

Rubicon [ROO buh kahn]. Dodge. Town (1846) and ppl. The first settlement in the area was known as Upton, probably named by settlers from Upton, Worcester County, Massachusetts. The Upton post office operated from 1848 until 1852, when the name was changed to Rubicon. The ultimate source of the name is the Rubicon River in Italy, which Julius Caesar famously crossed in 49 BC, precipitating a Roman civil war, but the immediate source of the Wisconsin name is unknown. William Garrett, a teacher reported to be well versed in European history, has been given credit for proposing the name, as has Thomas Cram, an engineer and an important figure in the mapping of the Great Lakes region in the 1830s and 1840s. (*Remembering the Past! Rubicon Township Sesquicentennial*, 36)

Ruby. Chippewa. Town (1906) and ppl. Named for Ruby Hawn, daughter of Ed(d) L. Hawn, an officer of the Ruby Lumber Company, which established a sawmill at the site in 1901. Hawn also served as the first postmaster in Ruby, beginning in 1903. See Arnold. (Nagel and Deuel, 6, 8)

Rugby Junction. Polk. Origin uncertain. Likely named by officials of the Wisconsin Central railroad when the tracks were extended to join those of the Chicago, Milwaukee and St. Paul about 1886. The namesake may be Rugby in Warwickshire, England, an important railroad junction in the latter half of the nineteenth century.

Rudolph. Wood. Town (1856) and Village (1960). The local story is that a meeting to choose a name was held at the home of Horace Hecox. While the meeting was in progress, one-year-old Frederick Rudolph Hecox provided both amusement and a name for the township. (R. Rudolph)

Rural. Waupaca. The area around present Rural was known as Nepawan, reported to be a Native American name for the falls in the Crystal River. The post office was established as Nepawan in July 1852 with Lyman Dayton as postmaster and changed to Rural in March 1855. The reasons for the choice of the name are unknown. See Dayton (Waupaca County). (*Our Heritage*, 200)

Rush Lake. Winnebago. Also Rushford. Town (1847). Named from Rush Lake, a translation of Menominee *nepiaskon* 'reeds, bulrushes.' See Nepeuskun. (Vogel, *Indian Names*, 167)

Rusk. County. Town (1901). When he learned that a new county was to be organized, James L. Gates, a Milwaukee land speculator who owned several hundred thousand acres in the area, offered to donate $10,000 for construction of government buildings if the county were named for him. The Wisconsin Legislature obliged and created Gates County in 1901. Gates failed to honor his pledge, however, and in June 1905 the legislature changed the name to Rusk in honor of Jeremiah McLain Rusk (1830–93), a Civil War hero, member of the U.S. House of Representatives (1871–77), governor of Wisconsin (1882–89), and secretary of agriculture under President Benjamin Harrison (1889–93). The Town of Rusk (1889) in Burnett County is also named for Jeremiah Rusk. (*Rusk County History*, 5)

Rusk. Dunn. Founded about 1870 as Baldwin by the West Wisconsin railroad, named for railroad president Daniel A. Baldwin. The name was changed to Wilson in January 1872 for William Wilson, who donated ten acres of land for a community center, and in February 1873 changed to Rusk, for Jeremiah M. Rusk, the namesake of Rusk County, at the time a U.S. representative from Wisconsin. See Baldwin. (Stennett, 190)

Russell. Sheboygan. Town (1853). Named for John Russell, a shoemaker from New York State and a pioneer settler in 1848. The post office was established in February 1855, John L. Sexton, postmaster. (Buchen, 339)

Russell. Trempealeau. Named for a local Russell family, probably that of William Russell, who emigrated from Clackmannan, Scotland, and kept a general store from the mid-1870s. The post office was established in September 1882, William Hunter, postmaster. (Gamroth, 11)

Rutland. Dane. Town (1846) and ppl. Laid out about 1846 and named by Sereno W. Graves and Jonathan Lawrence for Rutland, Vermont, itself named for Rutland, Massachusetts, in turn named for Rutland, the former county in central England. (Butterfield, *History of Dane County*, 388)

Sabin [SAY buhn]. Richland. Named for one or more Sabin families. Oliver Corwin Sabin, David Sabin, and Dr. Eli Sabin are mentioned in early histories and appear on census rolls of the 1860s and 1870s. The post office was established in June 1886, Robert Marshall, postmaster. (Kepler and Bower, 2)

St. Anna [AN uh]. Calumet, Sheboygan. Named from St. Anna's parish church, established in 1848 by a congregation of German Catholics from New Holstein and named for St. Anne, Jesus's grandmother. The post office was established in April 1867, Michael Bolz, postmaster. (Minaghan and Vanderhoef, 14)

St. Anthony. Washington. Probably named from the St. Anthony of Padua Catholic Church. (Reinders and Melberg, 26)

St. Cloud. Fond du Lac. Village (1909). Founded in 1868 for the Sheboygan & Fond du Lac railroad by site owner Henry Moersch. According to local historians, Moersch's brother suggested the name St. Claude, apparently for St. Claude, France, but when the timetable was printed the station carried the name of the more familiar St. Cloud. The printer may have taken St. Claude as a misspelling of St. Cloud, perhaps influenced by St. Cloud, Minnesota, itself named from St. Cloud, France. ("Saint Cloud History")

St. Croix [KROY]. County (1840). Named from the St. Croix River. The source of the name is uncertain; it may have been chosen for unknown reasons by Daniel Greysolon, the Sieur du Lhut (for whom Duluth, Minnesota, is named) who explored the area around western Lake Superior in the 1670s. In the early 1680s the Recollect priest Louis Hennepin called the river Rivière Tombeau 'river of the tomb,' and in 1689 Nicholas Perrot, a French explorer and trader, in claiming much of northern Wisconsin for France, recorded "Rivière de Sainte-Croix." Several sources for St. Croix, French for 'Holy Cross,' have been proposed: that the name was taken from a rock formation that resembled a cross in the river near St. Croix Falls; that French missionaries saw a cross in the river where it entered the Mississippi; and, in one of the more hopeful suggestions, that early missionaries were struck by the fact that (to them, at least) the dark, umber waters of the St. Croix River formed a cross as they blended with the more lucent waters of the Mississippi. A further proposal, advanced about 1699 by the fur trader and explorer Pierre-Charles Le Sueur, is that the name commemorates a French trader named St. Croix, whose vessel was wrecked at the river's mouth. To these proposals I add the possibility that the name may have been transferred from an existing St. Croix. Fort St. Croix was established by the French at the headwaters of the St. Croix River in the early 1680s and may have given its name to the river rather than the other way around. Several military installations named St. Croix were established by the French in North America, including Fort Ste. Croix, Quebec, constructed as early as 1535 by Jacques Cartier. See Dunn's *The St. Croix* (26–29) for an informative, detailed discussion of the naming of St. Croix.

St. Croix Falls. Polk. Town and City (1958). Named for the falls on the St. Croix River, possibly a translation of Ojibwa *kakabikang* 'where there is a waterfall.' First settled by Franklin Steele, a partner in the St. Croix Lumber Company, which established a sawmill at the site about 1838. The name may have been chosen by Caleb Cushing, a major figure in the economic development of the St. Croix valley. The post office was established in July 1840 as the Falls of St. Croix, William Holcombe, postmaster. See Cushing. (Nyberg)

St. Francis. Milwaukee. City (1951). This south Milwaukee suburb has its origins in the Convent of the Sisters of St. Francis of Assisi, established in the summer of 1849 by lay Franciscans from Ettenbeuren, Bavaria, at the request of John Martin Henni, the first bishop of Milwaukee. The name was reinforced in 1856 when Father Henni dedicated the Seminary of St. Francis de Sales, which sits next to the convent, in honor of St. Francis de Sales, Bishop of Geneva, canonized in 1665. (Stennett, 121)

St. Germain [jer MAYN]. Vilas. Town (organized as Farmington in 1907; changed to St. Germain in 1930) and ppl. Named from Big and Little St. Germain Lakes, themselves named for Jean François St. Germain, a French Canadian soldier who left the service in the late seventeenth century, married an Ojibwa woman, and established a line of traders and interpreters. (Vogel, *Indian Names*, 85)

242

St. John. Calumet. The community grew around the St. John Catholic Church, founded by German settlers in the early 1860s. The post office was established in June 1872, Matthias Brown, postmaster.

St. Joseph. La Crosse. A shortening of St. Joseph's Ridge. When Catholic settlers arrived in the 1840s, they named the ridges in the area after saints. This particular ridge was probably named for Joseph, the husband of Mary. (St. Mary's Ridge is nearby.) The post office was established in June 1875, John Hammes, postmaster. (Petersen, p.c.)

St. Joseph. St. Croix. Town. Organized in 1858, apparently as Bochea, named for Peter Bouchea, reportedly the first permanent settler in St. Croix County. While still in committee, the name was changed to St. Joseph, apparently at the insistence of Joseph Bowron, who operated a sawmill on the Willow River from the early 1850s. Bowron may have suggested the name at least partially for himself. (Ericson)

St. Kilian. Fond du Lac, Washington. Named from the St. Kilian Catholic church, built in 1848. The church was dedicated to St. Kilian, the Irish missionary martyred in Bavaria in 689. The post office was established in December 1874, Ferdinand Heisler, postmaster. (*Winding through the Town of Wayne*, 108)

St. Lawrence. Washington. The site was purchased by John Martin Henni, bishop of Milwaukee, presumably on which to build the St. Lawrence seminary, which was established at Mt. Calvary instead. The post office operated from May 1867 until December 1911. (Reinders and Melberg, 16)

St. Marie. Green Lake. Town. According to Colonel John Shaw, originally from Johnstown, New York, and one of the earliest permanent setters in 1845, St. Marie is a shortening of an earlier French name. About 1855 Shaw wrote, "On the opposite bank of Fox River, is a large spring, called by the early French, La Cote St. Marie" (231). In Mississippi valley French, côte referred to a hill or a river bank.

St. Martins. Milwaukee. Formerly known as Franklin Village, named from Franklin Township. The community was probably named for St. Martin, the fourth-century Bishop of Tours, by Father Martin Kundig, a Swiss priest who came to the area in the early 1840s and established Holy Assumption parish in the spring of 1847. (Damaske, *Along the Right-of-Way to East Troy*, 5)

St. Mary's. Monroe. Named from St. Mary's Catholic church, founded by German settlers in the late 1850s. The post office was established in November 1860, Caspar Schmitz, postmaster. (Richards, 510)

St. Nazianz [NAY zee uhnz]. Manitowoc. Village (1956). In 1854, to escape an often hostile political and religious environment, a group of German

Catholics under the leadership of Father Ambrose Oschwald immigrated to Manitowoc County and established the utopian colony of St. Nazianz, named from Nazianzus in Asia Minor and its fourth-century bishop St. Gregory Nanzianzen. When Oschwald died in 1873, the commune collapsed and several members sued for private title to lands formerly held in common. Some of the property was given to the Society of the Divine Savior, which established a religious education center at the site. This is the only Nazianz in the United States. (*St. Nazianz*, 3–4)

St. Peter. Fond du Lac. Named from the St. Peter church, founded by German Catholic settlers about 1866 in an area known as the Holyland. The post office was established in August 1893, Joseph Differ, postmaster. See Mount Calvary.

St. Rose. Grant. Named from the St. Rose Catholic church, founded as St. Rose Church of the Prairie by Father Samuel Mazzuchelli in 1851. The church was probably named for St. Rose of Lima, early seventeenth-century patron saint of Latin America and the Philippines. The post office was established in May 1856, William Miller, postmaster. (Butterfield, *History of Grant County*, 832)

Salem [SAYL uhm]. Kenosha. Town (1838) and ppl. Formerly known as Brooklyn. The name was proposed by John Cogswell for Salem, Massachusetts, his former home, about 1838. The town and community of Salem in Pierce County are likely transfers from a Salem farther east. (Stennett, 122)

Salmo [SAL mo]. Bayfield. Probably a shortening of *salmo salar*, the scientific name of the Atlantic salmon. According to Stennett (190), the name was suggested by the fish commissioner of Minnesota for the Landlocked salmon, a subspecies of the Atlantic salmon. This is the only Salmo in the United States.

Salona [suh LON uh]. Door. Naming details are uncertain, but Salona was likely named directly for a Salona in Greece, one of which in central Greece figured prominently in the Greek War of Independence from the Ottoman Empire in the 1820s and 1830s. Wisconsin has had at least two Salona post offices; one operated in Racine County from March 1840 until May 1842, the other in Door County from August 1881 until January 1904.

Sampson. Chippewa. Town. Named for Rear Admiral William T. Sampson, a hero of the Spanish-American War, who distinguished himself during the naval battle of Santiago de Cuba in early July 1898. The town was named four months later. (Susedik, 2–3)

Sanborn. Ashland. Town (1899) and ppl. Probably named in honor of Albert W. Sanborn. Originally from Vermont, Sanborn settled in Ashland by 1888 and represented the county in the state senate in the early 1900s.

Sandusky [san DUHS kee]. Sauk. Named in the early 1850s by Joshua Holmes and several others for their former home, Sandusky, Ohio, itself named from a Wyandot word for clear, pure water. The post office was established in September 1855, William Dano, postmaster. (Derleth, 41)

Saratoga [sehr uh TO guh]. Wood. Town (1857). Named from the Saratoga post office, established in October 1855 by John Ensign. Probably named for an eastern Saratoga, perhaps Saratoga, New York, site of the well-known mineral springs. Saratoga is a popular place name, occurring in nearly half the states. (R. Rudolph)

Sarona [suh RO nuh]. Washburn. Town (1904) and ppl. Founded about 1898 as a utopian community by a Mennonite religious colony from southwestern Minnesota organized as the Sarona Christian Social Association. Sarona, claimed to mean 'beautiful pastures' or 'valley of flowers,' is adapted from Saron, mentioned once in the New Testament. The name was probably proposed by Abraham Hiebert, the first commune president. By 1890 the colony had dissolved and the communal property was divided among the remaining members. This is the only Sarona in the United States. ("Along the Galician Grapevine")

Sauk. County. The Sac, or Sauk, are a Native American people of the Central Algonquian language group, along with the closely related Fox and Kickapoo. The Sac were formerly resident in Wisconsin, Illinois, and Michigan. The name is an English modification of Saki in French, from Ojibwa *osaki* 'people of the outlet,' itself an adaptation of *asakiwaki*, the Sac's name for themselves. Ozaukee is a variant. The "outlet" probably refers to the Saginaw River in Michigan, generally considered the ancestral home of the Sac. Sauk City was founded about 1840 as Haraszthy by Hungarian immigrant "Count" Agoston Haraszthy, whom Durbin calls "a colorful, restless, enthusiastic dreamer" (156). He kept the first general store in the area, oversaw a brick kiln, and operated a ferry across the Wisconsin River. He failed in a number of ventures, including several attempts to develop local wineries; he was later instrumental in developing the vineyards of Sonoma, California. The post office was established in November 1839 as Prairie du Sac, Cyrus Leland, postmaster; the name changed to Sauk City in December 1852. See Prairie du Sac. (Bright)

Saukville. Ozaukee. Town (1848) and Village (1915). Founded about 1846 by William Payne (Paine), who emigrated from England in the mid-1820s. Payne kept a store and tavern and operated a sawmill near Sheboygan. Named for the Sauk people. See Sauk. (Buchen, 80)

Saunders. Douglas. Named for Edward N. Saunders, a coal and railroad magnate of St. Paul, Minnesota. Saunders was an officer of the Northwestern

Fuel Company and the Northwestern Coal Railway Company from the late 1870s.

Sauntry [SAWN tree]. Douglas. Named for William Sauntry of Stillwater, Minnesota. Sauntry directed the Ann River Logging Company of Minnesota, which cut much of the pine on the St. Croix River in the 1890s. (Stennett, 191)

Sawyer. County (1883). Named for Philetus Sawyer of Oshkosh (1816–1900), a prominent and prosperous lumberman. Emigrating from Vermont to Wisconsin in the late 1840s, Sawyer was elected to the Wisconsin Assembly in 1857 and again in 1861. He served in the U.S. House of Representatives (1865–75) and was a U.S. senator from Wisconsin (1881–93).

Saxeville [SAKS vil]. Waushara. Town (organized in 1851 as Ontario; changed to Saxeville in 1855) and ppl. Named from the Saxeville post office, established by postmaster Edward Saxe in March 1852. Saxe opened a general store and hotel about 1850. He raised a company of volunteers during the Civil War and was killed at the Battle of Shiloh in Tennessee in 1862. (Reetz, 135)

Saxon. Iron. Town (1892) and ppl. Previously known as Dogwood. The name may have been proposed by settlers from Saxony, Germany, but Techtmann (142) suggests that the name is a popular etymology from the phrase "sacks on," used to say that mail sacks had been loaded onto a train. The post office was established in May 1889, Horton J. Stone, postmaster.

Saylesville [SAYLZ vil]. Dodge. Probably named for William Sayles, from Massachusetts. In 1850 Sayles owned some two thousand acres in the area.

Saylesville. Waukesha. Named about 1888 for a local Sayles family, perhaps that of William Sayles, the probable namesake of Saylesville in Dodge County, or that of Stephen Sayles, who, with his sons, Donison, Whitman, and Mortimer, left Bellingham, Massachusetts, in 1837 and, after an arduous trip of nearly two months, arrived in the area, where they established several sawmills and gristmills. The post office was established in April 1894, Harry McMillan, postmaster. (*Historic Genesee Township*)

Sayner [SAY ner]. Vilas. Founded by and named for Orrin W. Sayner, who built the first resort, the Sayner Lodge, in 1892. Sayner was the first postmaster in 1898. (Hintz and Hintz, 32)

Scandinavia. Waupaca. Town (1853) and Village (1894). An early name was Eidanger, for the community in Telemark, Norway. Eidanger was shortened to Danger and pronounced much like English *danger*. To avoid the obvious associations with *danger*, the name was changed to Scandinavia sometime before 1856 when the Scandinavia post office was established by Ole Reine. (Dunlavy, 13)

Schleswig [SHLES wig]. Manitowoc. Town. Organized in 1855 as Able, named for an early settler. The name was changed in 1856 for Schleswig in northern Germany at the request of Henry F. Belitz, the founder of Kiel (q.v.) and the first town chair. The post office was established in October 1860, August Krieger, postmaster. (Falge, 241)

Schneyville. Green. See Shueyville.

Schoepke [SHEP kee]. Oneida. Town (1897). Named for August F. Schoepke, who emigrated from Prussia in the mid-1850s. Schoepke, a miller, storekeeper, hotelier, and first station agent for the Milwaukee, Lake Shore & Western railroad, was instrumental in the formation of the township. (Doucette et al., 12)

Schofield [SKO feeld]. Marathon. City (1951). In the early 1850s Dr. William Scholfield, a physician and surgeon from Mineral Point, bought a sawmill on the Eau Claire River and laid out the community of Eau Claire, now Schofield. Scholfield was the first mayor of Stevens Point in 1859, and by the 1870s the spelling of his name had become Schofield. The post office was established as Sherman in January 1865, changed to Schofield Mills in 1874, and to Schofield in 1881. (Rhyner)

Schultz. Green. Probably named from the Schultz post office, established in October 1889 by postmaster Fred W. Schultz.

Scott. The towns Scott in Crawford (1855) and Sheboygan (1849) Counties were named for Winfield Scott (1786–1866), an immensely popular nineteenth-century American military commander.

Scott. Brown. Town. Organized in November 1859 with the proposed name of Liberty, which did not meet with general approval. John P. Arndt, chair of the Brown County board, suggested Pochequette, a faux-French variant of *pucihkit*, a Menominee name for Green Bay, which proved even less acceptable. It is not entirely clear why Scott was ultimately selected. According to a local story, Robert Gibson, originally from Scotland, proposed the name for the Scottish poet and novelist Sir Walter Scott. It seems more likely, however, considering when the town was named, that the namesake is General Winfield Scott, a hero of the War of 1812 and the Mexican War and a popular—though unsuccessful—Whig candidate for president in the election of 1852. (Cassidy, *Brown County*)

Scott. Burnett. Town (1909). According to a local account, a Mr. Scott won the naming rights from a coin toss and named the town after himself. More likely the name was chosen by George L. Miller, an attorney whose practice was at Prairie du Chien, in honor of General Winfield Scott, an American hero whose military career extended from the War of 1812 through the Civil War. Scott was one of the most well-known and popular

Americans following the Mexican War, and dozens of communities and townships are named Scott or Winfield in his honor. (Ericson)

Scott. Columbia. Named for Winfield Scott. At the time of township formation in 1849 Scott was a national hero for his leadership during the Mexican War. The name was suggested by Henry Ammiras Darrow, who emigrated from Ohio to Wisconsin in 1839. (*Memorial and Biographical Record . . . of Columbia, Sauk, and Adams Counties*, 499)

Scott. Lincoln. Town (1881). Named for Thomas B. Scott, born in Scotland. In 1848 Scott immigrated to Wisconsin, became a successful lumberman, served several terms in the Wisconsin senate in the 1870s, and was the first mayor of Merrill in 1881. (Jones and McVean, *History of Lincoln, Oneida and Vilas Counties*, 720)

Scott. Monroe. Town (1880). Named for Andrew Scott, thought to be the first permanent settler. Scott built a cabin near the site in 1850. (Richards, 538)

Sechlerville [SEK ler vil]. Jackson. Named for Jacob R. Sechler, who emigrated from Pennsylvania in the mid-1850s. The community grew around a general store kept by Sechler and James Mason. The Sechlerville Seminary, a private school, was housed in a room above the store. (*Jackson County, a History*, 19)

Sedgwick [SEJ wik]. Ashland. Named for Edward V. Sedgwick, an official of the Duluth, South Shore & Atlantic railroad in the 1880s and 1890s.

Seeley. Sawyer. Named for Theodore B. Seeley, chief dispatcher for the Chicago, St. Paul, Minneapolis & Omaha railroad in the 1880s. (Marple, 100)

Seif [SEYEF]. Clark. Town (1900). Named for Frederick J. Seif, who was instrumental in organizing the township, served as the first town chair, and was mayor of Neillsville in the 1910s. (Scholtz)

Seminary Springs. Dane. Named for the several springs that are the sources of Door Creek. The land for a seminary was authorized by Congress in 1838. The present community takes its name from the Seminary Springs Farm, so named about 1910. (Cassidy, *Dane County Place-Names*)

Seneca [SEN uh kuh]. Most if not all of the half dozen Senecas in Wisconsin are transfers from one of the Senecas in New York, themselves named for the Seneca, an Iroquoian people of upper New York State. Seneca in Crawford County, Wisconsin, was surveyed in 1857 by Pizarro Cook for site owner and first postmaster Samuel P. Langdon. The name was suggested by Nicholas Morgan, from Seneca County, New York. Seneca in Wood County was organized as Hemlock, named from Hemlock Creek, in 1857; the name was changed to Seneca in 1861. (Butterfield, *History of Crawford and Richland Counties*, 718; R. Rudolph)

Sevastopol [suh VAS tuh pol]. Door. Town. Organized in November 1859 as Laurieville, named for Robert Laurie and the Laurie family, which contributed significantly to the development of the stone industry in Door County. Three months later the name was changed at the suggestion of Peter Joseph Simon to Sebastopol (misspelled as Sevastopol), for the Russian port on the Black Sea, which was prominent in the news of 1854–55 when it was besieged for nearly a year by Allied forces during the Crimean War. (Holand, 323)

Seven Mile Creek. Juneau. Town (1853). Named from Seven Mile Creek, thought to be approximately seven miles upstream from the mouth of the Lemonweir River.

Sextonville. Richland. Named for Ebenezer M. Sexton, one of the founders of Loyd (q.v.). Originally from New York State, Sexton was a lawyer and businessman and also the first postmaster in 1849. (Butterfield, *History of Crawford and Richland Counties*, 1071)

Seymour. The towns of Seymour in Lafayette (1868) and Outagamie Counties (1867) (and probably in Eau Claire County as well) were named for Horatio Seymour, multiterm governor of New York in the 1850s and 1860s, a well-known politician, and a candidate for president of the United States on the Democratic ticket in 1868. He also owned significant tracts of land in Wisconsin. (Butterfield, *History of Crawford and Richland Counties*, 1071; Butterfield, *History of Lafayette County*, 606)

Shamrock. Jackson. Known as Kelly's Corner for Charles and Margaret Kelly until 1881, when the Shamrock post office was established by David Mann. The name was apparently suggested by William Hunter, who had recently returned from a visit to Ireland. (*Jackson County, a History*, 35)

Shanagolden [shan uh GOL duhn]. Ashland. Town (1907) and ppl. Shanagolden grew around a sawmill established about 1901 on the Chippewa River by the Nash Lumber Company, founded by Thomas Nash, his sons Guy and Jim, and William Vilas, for whom Vilas County is named. The community was known as Nashville until 1902 when the post office was established as Shanagolden, named by Thomas Nash for Shanagolden, County Limerick, Ireland, ancestral home of the Nash family. Shanagolden is from Gaelic *Sean Ghualainn* 'old shoulder,' probably named for a prominent hill or ridge. This is the only Shanagolden in the United States. (Engel and Bunde, 26)

Shantytown. Marathon. The name is most likely a leftover from and a reminder of nineteenth-century lumber operations in northern Wisconsin where a shanty was a building in a lumber camp, a shanty-boy cleaned sleeping quarters and stables, and a shanty-nasty was a logger who stayed behind after all the timber had been cut. The Shantytown post office operated from November 1888 through July 1909.

Sharon [SHAIR uhn]. Walworth. Town (1843) and Village (1892). Named by Josiah Topping for Sharon, Schoharie County, New York, itself named for Sharon, Connecticut. Sharon in Portage County may also be a transfer or may have been named directly from the biblical "Rose of Sharon." Sharon is a popular place name, occurring in more than thirty states. (Beckwith, 7)

Shawano [SHAW no]. County (1853) and City (1874). The first permanent settler in Shawano was Charles D. Wescott, namesake of the Town of Wescott (q.v.). From the early 1840s Wescott operated a sawmill for the Farnsworth and Moore Lumber Company at what was then known as Falls of the Wolf River. Shawano County was organized as Shawanaw; the spelling was officially changed to Shawano in 1864. The county is named for one of two Menominee leaders. The elder Shawano was appointed "Grand Chief of the Menominees" by the British governor of Canada in 1778; his name was recorded by French scribes as Chawanon, from Menominee *osawanow* 'southerner,' respelled phonetically as Shawano. The name of the younger Shawano appears as Shaw-wan-noh and Shaw-wan-on in treaties signed as late as 1848. (Moede, 6, 11; Vogel, *Indian Names*, 41)

Shawtown. Eau Claire. Named for Daniel Shaw, who emigrated from Maine and established a sawmill at the outlet of Half Moon Lake in 1856. Although the name Shawtown still appears on many maps, the community was annexed to Eau Claire in the early 1930s and is now better known as Mount Washington, presumably named for the town of Washington. The Shaw post office operated from April 1896 through September 1903. (Forrester, 216)

Sheboygan [shuh BOY guhn]. County (1836), Town (organized as Morgan in 1838; changed to Sheboygan in 1839), and City (1853). Also Sheboygan Falls. Town (1849) and City (1913). About 1820, William Farnsworth, husband of Marinette Chevelier, the namesake of Marinette (q.v.), established a trading post on the Sheboygan River. Farnsworth later purchased much of what is now downtown Sheboygan, which was formally platted in the winter of 1835–36 by William Payne and Oliver Crocker. Early recordings of the name dating from the late 1680s include Chabonigan, Ship-wi-wai-gan, Shab y a gun, and Chab-way-way-gun, which were often folk-etymologized as Chipwagon or Shipwagon. The post office was established as Shebowagan in April 1836; the spelling was changed to Sheboygan later that year. The name is from the Sheboygan River, several sources of which have been proposed. In 1844 Increase Lapham, one of Wisconsin's first scientists, wrote, "The original Indian name of this river . . . meaning is, 'the river that comes out of the ground'" (102). Surveyor Joshua Hathaway repeated this claim, adding that the name was from Ojibwa with the general meaning 'great noise' or 'rushing underground water.' More recently, the Native American name scholar Virgil Vogel suggested that Sheboygan is a blend with shortening of Ojibwa *kitchi* 'great' and *opwagan* 'pipe' or 'pipe stem.' A more likely source, however, is Menominee *sapiwehekaneh*, glossed in Leonard Bloomfield's Menominee Lexicon 'at hearing distance in the woods; at Sheboygan.' Cheboygan, Michigan, is a variant. (Buchen, 331–33; Kellogg, 229; Vogel, *Indian Names*, 111)

Shelby. La Crosse. Town (1867) and ppl. Named from the post office, established in April 1863. Jacob Beckel, the first postmaster, chose the name for his former home, Shelby, Richland County, Ohio, itself named for Isaac Shelby, a distinguished Revolutionary War officer and the first governor of Kentucky. (Butterfield, *History of La Crosse County*, 859)

Sheldon. Rusk. Village (1917). Formerly known as Fern. The community was formally organized in 1906 when the Wisconsin Central railroad was built through the area. The station was named for Edward W. Sheldon of New York, a director of the railroad. The post office was established in December 1906, Edward D. Lacy, postmaster. (*Rusk County History*, 29)

Shell Lake. Washburn. City (1961). Named from Shell Lake. Probably a translation from a Native American language, perhaps Ojibwa, based upon *esag* 'clams.' See Clam Falls.

Shennington. Monroe. Founded and named in the early 1890s by Fred H. Shennington, who established the first store in the area and was a community benefactor, donating land for both the German and Danish Lutheran churches. (*Monroe County*, 180)

Shepley. Shawano. Probably named for Ether L. Shepley of St. Paul, Minnesota, vice president of the Northwestern Coal Railway Company in the first decades of the twentieth century. The post office was established in April 1907, August Pukall, postmaster.

Sheppard [SHEP erd]. Jackson. Named for Andrew Sheppard, from Canada by way of Galena, Illinois. Beginning in the 1840s, Sheppard established more than a dozen sawmills and several gristmills on Black River. (*History of Northern Wisconsin*, 413)

Sheridan. Both the Town of Sheridan (1867) in Dunn County and the community in Waupaca County are named for Philip Sheridan, Union general in the Civil War whose popularity was at a peak in the late 1860s. The post office was established in January 1865.

Sherman. Clark. Town (1873). Named for William Tecumseh Sherman, well-known general in the Union army. (Scholtz)

Sherman. Iron. Town. Organized in 1907 as Emerson, named for David W. Emerson, who formed the Emerson Land Company about 1905 and served as the first town chair. Renamed in 1918 for William Sherman, the second town chair. (Techtmann, 142)

Sherman. Sheboygan. Town. Organized in 1850 as Abbott, named for Reuben Abbott, the first town chair. The name was changed to Sherman in March 1865. According to Buchen, "During the Civil War . . . the Abbotts were southern sympathizers. . . . Angered at their attitude, the people not only forced them to leave the town, but they had the name of the town changed to Sherman" (340–41). The namesake is William Tecumseh Sherman, the famous Union general.

Sherry. Wood. Town (1885) and ppl. Named for businessman Henry Sherry. About 1880 Sherry and a business partner founded the firm of Briggs and Sherry and established a sawmill on Mill Creek. Apparently Sherry Junction in Langlade County is also named for Henry Sherry, who kept the first general store in the area in the early 1890s. (Dessureau, 237; R. Rudolph)

Sherwood. Clark. Town and ppl. Sherwood was organized in January 1874 as Perkins, named for landowner Daniel Perkins. The name was changed to Sherwood Forest in 1876 and shortened to Sherwood in 1900. According to Kay Scholtz, Elizabeth LaFlesh suggested the name, "as the area resembled her homeland in England and her literary interest." McBride (12), however claims that former Wisconsin governor Cadwallader Washburn, the namesake of Washburn County, proposed the name. Washburn had business interests in the area at the time.

Shields [SHEEL(D)Z]. Dodge. Town (1848). Named for James Shields (1806–79), a general during the Mexican War and a U.S. senator who represented three states (1849–79): Illinois, Minnesota, and Missouri. The Town of Shields in Marquette County, organized in 1852, is probably named for him as well. (Hubbell, 253)

Shiocton [sheye AHK tuhn]. Outagamie. Village (1903). Shiocton was founded by Woodford Dominicus Jordan, a surveyor turned merchant and lumberman from Casco, Maine, who in 1850 purchased a site on the Wolf River that became known as Jordanville or Jordans Landing. Jordan platted the site in 1857 as Shiocton, named from the post office established in October 1855 by Matthew G. Bradt and from the Shioc River. A persistent story claims the river was named for Shioc or Shiocton, a Menominee war leader whose main village was nearby. But a Menominee by that name does not appear in the available historical records. Most likely Shioc is a shortening of Menominee *manomehsayak*, based upon *manomeh* 'wild rice.' Shioc was laid out north of Shiocton, and for several years the communities contended for the title of leading village in the Town of Bovina. Shioc fell out of contention when the dam burst and washed away the mills. (Bright; Truttschel, 111)

Shirley. Brown. Named from the Shirley post office, established in July 1895, William C. Falck, postmaster. According to a local account, several citizens were discussing a name for the post office in Falck's general store when one of them happened to notice the brand name Shirley on the suspenders that another was wearing and said this would be a good name for the office. (Cassidy, *Brown County*)

Shopiere [sho PEER]. Rock. Formerly known as Waterloo. The name was formalized as Shopiere about 1848 by a committee consisting of James Buckley, a local doctor; Louis P. Harvey, the first postmaster (and later governor of Wisconsin); and John Hopkins, the site owner. Buckley is usually credited with suggesting the name. In 1985 Frederic Cassidy, the eminent Wisconsin names scholar, called Shopiere "an unresolved onomastic puzzle." Now, nearly thirty years later, that puzzle remains unsolved. Cassidy is surely correct when he characterizes Shopiere as "a pseudo-French phrase [which] has been 'phonetically' respelled in an English-like way." That "pseudo-French phrase" is often—but without support—taken to be *chaux* 'lime' and *pierre* 'stone,' literally 'limestone,' the name being suggested by the local limestone deposits. Another possibility, however, is that *Shopiere* is an English spelling of *chaud pierre*, literally 'hot stones,' perhaps referring to the process of converting limestone into quicklime or slaked lime. (Cassidy, "From Indian to French to English," 55)

Shorewood Hills. Dane. Village (1927). In 1912 developer John C. McKenna and the University Bay Land Company platted College Hills west of the University of Wisconsin, intended to appeal to university employees. A decade later the Shorewood subdivision was established on Lake Mendota. The communities merged and incorporated as Shorewood Hills in 1927. (Cassidy, *Dane County Place-Names*)

Shortville. Clark. Founded by the Short brothers: James, Andrew, John, Stephen, and George, who settled in the area about 1870. Three of the Shorts had been granted land by the government as payment for their services during the Civil War. Andrew Short was the first postmaster in February 1880. (Curtiss-Wedge, *History of Clark County*, 665)

Shoto [SHO to]. Manitowoc. Founded by the Neshoto Lumber Company in the late 1830s. *Shoto* is a shortening of Neshoto, from Ojibwa *nijode* 'twin.'

The Shoto post office operated from June 1894 until September 1904. See Nashotah.

Shueyville. Green. DeLorme's *Wisconsin Atlas and Gazetteer* shows Schneyville about one half mile east of Clarno on county road P. The name, however, is a typographical error for Shueyville, named for John W. Shuey, who operated a sawmill at the site from about 1846. Shuey was a township official who established the Shuey's Mills post office in June 1854. The pronunciation is regularly [SHOO ee vil]. I am indebted to historian Matt Figi for much of this information.

Shullsburg [SHUHLZ berg]. Lafayette. Town (1843) and City (1889). Named for Jesse Shull, from Pennsylvania. After serving in the War of 1812, Shull became an agent for John Jacob Astor's American Fur Company, trading fur pelts in the Galena-Dubuque area. In the 1820s Shull uncovered substantial lead deposits and became a miner and smelter in the area of present Shullsburg. The post office was established in March 1846, Andrew W. Harrison, postmaster. (*Sesquicentennial History of Shullsburg*, 17–19)

Sigel [SEE guhl]. The towns of Sigel in Chippewa and Wood Counties were named in honor of Franz Sigel, a German military officer who had taken part in the 1848 German Revolution. Sigel immigrated to the United States in 1852, and when the townships were organized in 1863 he was a brigadier general in the Union army. Sigel was a popular and dashing Civil War hero, and a number of places were named for him, including Sigel, Pennsylvania, and Sigel Township, Minnesota. (R. Rudolph)

Silica. Fond du Lac. The post office was established as Summit Station in April 1873 and changed to Silica in April 1898. According to Stennett, Silica (quartz sand) "is supposed to describe the soil around the place" (124).

Silver Creek. Sheboygan. Reportedly named for Silver Creek, Chautauqua County, New York. Naming details are unknown. The post office was established in May 1872, John F. Moehrl, postmaster. (Buchen, 341)

Silver Lake. Kenosha. Founded by John Bullen in 1836. Bullen built a bridge across the Fox River and operated the first tavern in the vicinity, the Ackanuckochowoc House, which he claimed meant 'great bend.' Silver Lake is reportedly a translation of a Native American name for the lake. (Lacher, 140)

Sinsinawa [sin SIN uh wah, sin suh NAH wuh]. Grant. Named from the Sinsinawa River. Although such meanings as 'home of the young eagle,' and 'rattlesnake' have been proposed, the name is Algonquian having to do with 'stone' or 'stony' and probably means 'stony in the middle,' likely referring to a characteristic of the Sinsinawa River. Spellings have varied: Sin-sin-ah-wah, Sinsinaway, Sinsiniwaw, Sinsinnewa, Sissinaway, among others. The post office was established in December 1839 as Sinsinawa Mound. (Vogel, *Indian Names*, 181)

Sioux [SOO]. The Town of Sioux Creek (1929) in Barron County and the community of Sioux in Bayfield County take their names from Sioux Creek and Sioux River, respectively. Sioux is a shortening of French *Nadouessioux*, a noun apparently related to an Algonquian verb having to do with speaking a different language. The Ho-Chunk (Winnebago) people are related to the Santee or Eastern Dakota Sioux who were once resident in large parts of western Wisconsin.

Siren. Burnett. Town (1913) and Village (1948). Settled largely by Swedish colonists in the 1880s. The application for a post office, prepared in 1895 by Charles Segerstrom, called for the name *Syren*, Swedish for 'lilac.' Apparently there were few Swedes in the Post Office Department at the time and officials changed Syren to the more familiar Siren. (Landelius and Jarvi, 251)

Sister Bay. Door. Village (1912). Named about 1870, apparently by Increase Claflin, an early settler and explorer, from Big Sister Bay and Little Sister Bay, themselves reportedly so named because they resembled one another — like sisters. (Thomas, 93)

Skanawan [SKAY nuh wahn]. Lincoln. Town (1910). Named from Skanawan Creek. Skanawan is an adaptation of Ojibwa *oshkinawe* 'young man.' Skinaway, the name of a lake in Barron County, is a variant. (Vogel, *Indian Names*, 46)

Slab City. Shawano. Probably named after slabs, the first cut of logs consisting largely of bark and of little value as building material. Byron Fullerton established a sawmill in the area about 1890. Cheap houses made of slabs were referred to as slab shanties. See Shantytown.

Slades Corners. Kenosha. Named for Thomas Slade, from Genesee County, New York, who settled in the area about 1840. The post office was established in December 1878, Paul E. Sauer, postmaster. ("Kenosha County, WI Placenames")

Slinger [SLING er]. Washington. Village (1869). A shortening of Schleisingerville, the original name of the community founded by Baruch Schleisinger Weil, from Strasbourg, Alsace, France, who purchased land in the area in the mid-1840s. Weil served in several local offices and represented the district in the state senate in 1853. The name was formally changed to Slinger in 1921. Other names considered at the time included Tyrone and Cream City. (*History of Washington and Ozaukee Counties*, 393)

Slovan [SLO vuhn]. Kewaunee. *Slovan* 'slav' may have been named for Czech or Slovak settlers generally, for a particular settler or family so named, or from an institution with Slovan as part of its name. The *Slovan Amerikansky*

'American Slav' newspaper began publication in Racine in 1860. The Slovan post office was established in July 1878, Joseph Ouradnik, postmaster. This is one of two Slovans in the United States; the other is west of Pittsburgh, Pennsylvania.

Smelser [SMEL zer]. Grant. Town (1849). Named for Jonas Markee Smelser, from Bourbon County, Kentucky, in the early 1830s. Smelser held several local offices, including town chair. See Georgetown. (Holford, 738)

Snells. Winnebago. Named for Amos J. Snell, a wealthy Chicago businessman from Little Falls, New York, who had extensive lumber and farming operations in the area in the 1860s. Snell was considered by some to be a flint-hearted financier, and he was murdered in Chicago in 1888. The post office was established as Snell's Station in May 1876, David Reed, postmaster. ("SooLine History")

Sniderville. Brown, Outagamie. Named for and by John Snider, from Cayuga County, New York. Snider established the post office in December 1859. ("Snider-L Archives")

Sobieski [so BIS kee]. Oconto. Named for John III Sobieski (Jan Sobieski), military leader and king of Poland in the last quarter of the seventeenth century. Sobieski is one of several Wisconsin communities established to attract Polish colonists in the late nineteenth century by John. J. Hof (Hoff). The post office was established in January 1894 as Sobieska, the feminine form of Sobieski. See Pulaski.

Soldiers Grove. Crawford. Village (1888). Soldiers Grove, formally established in 1866, grew around a dam and sawmill built about 1855 by Joseph Brightman. The name appears to have been given in respect of a contingent of soldiers who camped nearby. According to local historian William Ward, "The best explanation of 'Soldiers Grove' is that soldiers in pursuit of Indians, in the Black Hawk War, camped in a pine grove on the bank of the Kickapoo about where the village is located" (43). Another possibility is that the name commemorates the encampment of several regiments of Union soldiers on their way south during the Civil War.

Solon Springs [SOL uhn]. Douglas. Town (1907) and Village (1920). Founded in 1883 as White Birch, a translation of Ojibwa *wigwassikang* 'place of birch trees.' In 1896 the name was changed for Thomas Solon, who founded the Solon Springs Bottling Company to market medicinal water from the local springs. Solon subsequently invented and patented a vending machine that delivered the water (and other beverages) automatically. (*Commemorative Biographical Record of the Upper Lake Region*, 102)

Somerset. St. Croix. Town (1856) and Village (1915). Samuel and Hudson Harriman, from Orland, Maine, established a sawmill and gristmill on the

Apple River about 1850. Samuel Harriman was the area's first storekeeper in 1856 and platted the community, which he named for Somerset, Maine, or Somerset, England, reportedly his ancestral home. The post office was established in May 1856. (Lamm and Janke, 3)

Somo [SO mo]. Lincoln. Town. Organized in June 1905, largely through the efforts of Henry H. Stolle, longtime chair of the town board. Named from the Somo River. Somo is probably a shortened form of an Algonquian word, but the derivation and meaning are unknown. The only other Somo in the United States is in Mason County, Kentucky. The post office was established in November 1892, John C. Clarke, postmaster. See Tripoli. ("Tripoli")

Soperton [SO per tuhn]. Forest. Named from the Soper Lumber Company, established in Chicago in 1859 by James and Albert Soper, from Rome, New York. The community was founded about 1905 by James Jr. and Alex Soper. (Stennett, 121)

South Fork. Rusk. Town (1916) and ppl. Named from the South Fork of the Flambeau River. The community was formerly known as Czestochowa, named by Polish settlers for the city of Częstochowa in southern Poland.

South Wayne. Lafayette. See Wayne.

Sparta. Monroe. Town (1854) and City (1883). Laid out by the Pet(t)it brothers, George and William. According to Koehler, the Petits' mother chose the name because of her belief that "the pioneers who came to the area were just as brave and suffered hardships with as much fortitude as the ancient Spartans" (*Sparta*, 14). Sparta is a popular place name, occurring in about half of the continental states. The post office was established in January 1852, William F. Pettit, postmaster.

Spaulding [SPAWL ding]. Jackson. Named for miller and businessman Dudley J. Spaulding, originally from Johnstown, New York. The site was settled by his father, Jacob, in the late 1830s. The post office was established in July 1878, Joseph Winter, postmaster. (*Jackson County, a History*, 27)

Spencer. Marathon. Town (1876) and Village (1902). Probably named by Gardner Colby for Spencer, Massachusetts, with construction of the Wisconsin Central railroad. The Waltham post office (also named for a community in Massachusetts) was changed to Spencer in July 1874. See Colby. (Jantsch, 3)

Spider Lake. Sawyer. Town (1920). Named from Spider Lake, one of five lakes making up the Spider Chain, collectively so called, according to local accounts, because they resemble the shape of a giant spider. ("Spider Chain of Lakes Association")

Spirit. Price. Town and ppl. Spirit Falls. Lincoln. Named from the Spirit River, itself likely a translation of Ojibwa or Potawatomi *manito* 'spirit.' The township was organized in 1879 as Brannan, probably named for Brannan, Sweden, by Knute Ostergren, who, as agent for the Wisconsin Central railroad, was responsible for settling a large number of Scandinavians in the area in the 1870s. The name was changed to Spirit in 1921. ("Rib Lake Historical Society Newspaper Notes")

Spokeville [SPOK vil]. Clark. Probably named from the sawmill operated by Joseph C. Marsh, who established the post office in February 1885. Marsh's mill specialized in splitting shingles and manufacturing spokes for wagon wheels. This is the only Spokeville in the United States. (*Biographical History of Clark and Jackson Counties*, 141)

Spooner [SPOO ner]. Washburn. Town (1889) and City (1909). In 1879 the North Wisconsin Railway was built north of present Spooner. Shortly thereafter, the railroad moved its operations south where it joined the Chicago & North Western at what became known as Chicago Junction. The station was named by Edwin W. Winter, general superintendent for the Chicago & North Western, for John Coit Spooner (1843–1919), at the time a railroad attorney from Hudson. Spooner served in the Wisconsin Assembly and represented Wisconsin in the U.S. Senate (1885–91, 1897–1907). He was a popular politician and advisor to presidents Harrison, McKinley, and Theodore Roosevelt. (Stennett, 192)

Sprague. Juneau. Likely named for John F. Sprague and his son, Gleason, owners and publishers of the *Mauston Star* newspaper from the 1870s. The post office was established in February 1907, Michael A. Anthony, postmaster. (*History of Northern Wisconsin*, 377, 726)

Spread Eagle. Florence. Named from the Spread Eagle Chain of Lakes, themselves named by Artimus Curtis, who surveyed the area for the U.S. government in 1857. Stennett suggests that the lakes were so named because of their "fancied resemblance to an eagle with its wings widely spread." ("Florence, Wisconsin")

Spring Brook. Washburn. Town (organized as Veazie in 1880, named for William H. Veazie, a Minnesota lumberman; changed to Spring Brook in 1904). Named from a small stream that runs through the community, Spring Brook grew around a rest stop and logging camp established by Canadian Joseph Trepania (Trepanier) in the early 1880s on the line of the North Wisconsin railroad. The post office was established as Namekagon (q.v.) in November 1888 and changed to Spring Brook in November 1901. (*Commemorative Biographical Record of the Upper Lake Region*, 88)

Spring Green. Sauk. Town (1850) and Village (1869). Spring Green is a name that attracts popular etymologies. The most often repeated is that early settler Mary Williams chose the name because "to the north of her house, in the hollows facing the south, the green came so much earlier in the spring than in the surrounding country" (Cole, *Standard History*, 497).

Spring Prairie. Town (1838) and ppl. Walworth. Apparently named at the suggestion of Abigail Heminway (variously spelled) for the natural springs, whose waters formed Spring Brook. (Beckwith, 889)

Stangelville [STANG guhl vil]. Kewaunee. Named for one or more Stangel families. Jiri (George) Stangel and his family emigrated from Bohemia, now in the Czech Republic, in the early 1850s. ("George Stangel")

Stanley. Chippewa. City (1898). Lemuel Castle Stanley emigrated from Canandaigua, Ontario County, New York, in the late 1840s. In 1881, after building the Chippewa Falls & Western railroad, he platted the community of Stanley. The authors of *Stanley, Our Town*, describe Lemuel Stanley as "schoolmaster, farmer, merchant, banker, judge, mayor of Chippewa Falls—lumberman with a far flung interest, railroad builder, man of ability, vision and judgement," concluding "such was the man who happened to give his name to a community he never lived in" (6). The town of Stanley in Barron County is also named for Lemuel Castle Stanley.

Stanton. St. Croix. Town (1870) and ppl. Named for Edwin McMasters Stanton (1814–69), a politician and civil servant best known as Abraham Lincoln's secretary of war. The community was founded about 1880 as Ormes, likely named for an official or associate of the Chicago, St. Paul, Minneapolis & Omaha railroad. The name was changed to Stanton, for the township, about 1900. Edwin Stanton is also the namesake of townships in St. Croix and Dunn Counties, both also organized in 1870, shortly after his death. The Stanton post office operated from November 1880 until September 1913. (Stennett, 193)

Star Lake. Vilas. The local tradition is that Star Lake was named for the Starr brothers, Bob and Harry. Bob Starr was a surveyor and may have been working in the area in the 1880s when the site was bought by the Land and Log Company of Milwaukee. The name evolved from Starr Lake through Starlake to the current Star Lake. The post office was established in August 1895, Allen E. Williams, postmaster. (Rohe, *Ghosts of the Forest*, 297)

Stark. Vernon. Town (1858). Named for Ethan Allen Stark, born in Lyme, New Hampshire, and named for the Revolutionary War hero. Stark was active in local affairs, serving several terms as a Viroqua trustee.

Starks. Oneida. First known as Pennington for Edmund Pennington, president of the Minneapolis, St. Paul & Sault Ste. Marie railroad. The name was changed to Hobson in the early 1900s to honor Richmond Hobson, a hero of the Spanish-American War, and changed again by Leonard Starks, who bought the site and renamed it for himself about 1912. The post office was established as Hobson in June 1913 and changed to Starks six months later. See Pennington. (Doucette et al., 139)

Star Prairie. St. Croix. Town (1856) and Village (1900). Formerly known as Jewelltown for Trueworthy Jewell, the first chair of the Town of Stanton, who emigrated from Massachusetts in 1854. The local story is that a small party was traveling to Jewelltown from the New Richmond area and either Jewell's daughter, Emma, or her husband, Edmund Otis, looked at the sky and remarked, "How beautiful the stars are tonight over the priarie." Thus the name Star Prairie. The post office was established in April 1857, William E. Densmore, postmaster. (Silver)

State Line. Kenosha. Named for its location just north of the Wisconsin-Illinois border.

Stebbinsville [STEB uhnz vil]. Rock. Named for Harrison Stebbins, a teacher from Vermont. Stebbins represented the district in the state assembly in 1853 and established the Stebbinsville post office in 1875. (*Portrait and Biographical Album of Rock County, Wisconsin,* 715)

Stella. Oneida. Town (1921). Named from the Stella post office, established in January 1889, Edwin R. Armstrong, postmaster. The origin of the name is uncertain. According to Stennett, the namesake is Esther Johnson, whom the Irish satirist Jonathan Swift met when she was a child. Their unusual relationship continued for many years, and in his writings Swift referred to her only as Stella. (121)

Stephenson. Marinette. Town (organized as Crivitz in 1897; changed to Stephenson in 1905). Named for Isaac Stephenson (1829–1918), politician and community benefactor. Stephenson represented the district in the U.S. House of Representatives (1883–89) and the U.S. Senate (1907–15). The public library in Marinette was funded by Stephenson and named in his honor.

Stephensville [STEE vuhns vil]. Outagamie. Earlier known as Bruce's Mill for site owner William Bruce and later as Ellington Center, named from the Town of Ellington (q.v.). The mill property was later purchased by John Stephens, who platted the community in 1856 and named it for himself. (Balliet, 76–77)

Sterling. Polk. The town was organized in 1855 as Moscow, perhaps named for a Moscow in New England, and changed the following year to Sterling.

The source of the name is unknown. Sterling may have been brought to Wisconsin from New England; an early spelling of Stirling suggests a transfer from Stirling, New York, or Stirling, New Jersey. The original Sterling (Stirling) is in Scotland, and it has been suggested that James T. Cragin, who established the Stirling post office in September 1858, chose the name for his Scottish roots. (Ericson)

Sterling. Vernon. Town (1857). Named for Harvey Sterling, originally from Hagerstown, Maryland, who brought his family to the area in the summer of 1846. Harvey is probably the father of William T. Sterling, for whom Mount Sterling (q.v.) is named. (*History of Vernon County*, 644)

Stetsonville [STET suhn vil]. Taylor. Village (1949). Known informally as "63," presumably the mileage from a construction site where the Wisconsin Central tracks were laid in 1872. Later named for Isiah F. Stetson, who established the first sawmill in the area in 1875. (Latton, 191)

Stettin [ste TEEN]. Marathon. Town (1860). Named by German settlers for Stettin, in Prussia at the time and now part of Poland. The historical community of Stettin was founded three miles north of Marathon City on today's Stettin Drive. The post office was established in September 1864, Anton Maier, postmaster.

Steuben [STOO buhn]. Crawford. Village (1900). Previously known as Farris Landing for John T. Farris, who operated a ferry across the Kickapoo River from the 1850s. The circumstances surrounding the naming are unknown, but Steuben is likely a transfer from one of the several Steubens in New York State. The ultimate namesake is Friedrich Wilhelm Baron von Steuben, the Prussian officer who organized and trained the continental army during the American Revolution. The post office was established in April 1882, Henry C. C. Kast, postmaster. (Butteris)

Stevens Point. Portage. City (1858). The namesake of Stevens Point is probably George Stevens, the former postmaster and highway commissioner of Almond, Allegany County, New York. Stevens worked his way from St. Louis through Illinois to the Portage County area with a load of building and trading supplies in the late 1830s. The "point" or peninsula on the Wisconsin River where goods were transferred from land to river transportation was apparently known as Stevens Point by the mid-1840s, when Mathias Mitchell opened a hotel and travelers' rest called Raftsman's Home, which provided the nucleus for the present city. The name was in common use by 1849 when the Stevens Point post office was established. A less likely candidate has been proposed by William Stennett, historian and counsel for the Chicago & North Western railroad, who states without qualification that the namesake is the Reverend Jedediah D. Stevens, a

Presbyterian minister with missions at Mackinac, La Pointe, and elsewhere beginning in the late 1820s. (Durbin, 75; Stennett, 29)

Stevenstown. La Crosse. Named for Chase A. Stevens, a La Crosse lawyer and a director of the La Crosse & Milwaukee railroad. Stevens represented the district in the Wisconsin Assembly in 1855. The post office was established in July 1856, Ira Kilmer, postmaster. (Butterfield, *History of La Crosse County*, 414)

Stiles [STEYELZ]. Oconto. Town (organized as Howard in 1854; changed to Stiles in 1856) and ppl. The community was founded by logging entrepreneur Anson Eldred and named for his son and business partner, Howard Stiles Eldred, who was appointed first master of the Eldred post office in February 1882. The name was changed to Stiles several months later. About 1882 the tracks of the St. Paul Eastern Trunk railroad met those of the Chicago, Milwaukee & St. Paul north of Stiles, at what is now Stiles Junction, originally known as Leightown for early settler John Leigh. (Rucker, *From the McCauslin*, 68)

Stinnett [sti NET]. Washington. Town (1904). Named for W. W. Stinnett, who was appointed trainmaster and division superintendent of the Waverly branch of the Minnesota & Northwestern railroad in 1887, the year the post office was established by Edward A. O'Brien. (Stennett, 193)

Stitzer [STIT zer]. Grant. Named about 1878 by site owner William W. Ford for the Stoetzer family, especially local farmer Bernhard Stoetzer. German *Stoetzer* had been Americanized to *Stitzer* by the time the post office was established by Henry Fisher in March 1879. (Holford, 749)

Stockbridge. Calumet. Town (1844) and Village (1908). In the late seventeenth century, a group of Native Americans of Mohican descent were driven by repeated wars with Mohawks and European settlers from their ancestral home in the Hudson Valley of New York State to Stockbridge, Massachusetts, which provided the name by which they are now known. After the Revolutionary War many were relocated to western New York State and, in the 1820s and 1830s, to Wisconsin where they joined with the Lenape to form the Stockbridge-Munsee community. The Brothertons were relocated to Wisconsin at about the same time. See Brothertown. (Vogel, *Indian Names*, 26)

Stockholm. Pepin. Town (1858) and Village (1903). Stockholm is claimed to be the earliest successful Swedish settlement in Wisconsin, founded by Erik Peterson, from Karlskoga, Värmland, Sweden, in 1854. Peterson, with his brothers, Peter and Andrew, sailed from Sweden in 1849, destined for the California gold fields. Apparently, Erik Peterson left the others when they reached Chicago. After working in the pineries of the St. Croix valley,

Peterson returned to Sweden and brought back several families, which became the nucleus of Stockholm. The community was formally surveyed in the late spring of 1856 for the site owners, Erik Peterson, Jacob Peterson, and John Anderson. Swedenberg was suggested as the name of the community but "Stockholm on Lake Pepin" had greater support. Stockholm is one of about a dozen communities in the United States so named. (*Pepin County History*, 41)

Stockton. Portage. Town (1855) and ppl. In the early 1850s Nelson Blodgett built a hotel and tavern that he called the Stockton House, perhaps named for Stockton, Ohio, Blodgett's home state. He established the Stockton post office in 1858. (Rosholt, *Our County, Our Story*, 397)

Stoddard [STAHD erd]. Vernon. Village (1911). Named from the Stoddard post office, established in January 1863. Probably named by the first postmaster, William O. Bokee (Bochee), for Thomas Benton Stoddard, a lawyer from New York who was the first mayor of La Crosse in 1856 and a Wisconsin assemblyman in 1862. The community was founded by Henry H. White in 1886 with construction of the Chicago, Burlington & Quincy railroad. (De Cicco, 3)

Story. Dane. Known as Storytown from the late 1840s until the Story post office was established by Omer S. Shepard in January 1890. Shepard was the son of Hannah Story, daughter of Moses Story, who brought his family from Batavia, New York, to Wisconsin about 1847. (Cassidy, *Dane County Place-Names*)

Stoughton [STOT uhn]. Dane. City (1882). Named for and by Luke Stoughton, from Weathersfield, Vermont. Stoughton opened a general store and built a gristmill on the Yahara River in 1847. The post office was established in October 1848, Forest Henry, postmaster. (Butterfield, *History of Dane County*, 842)

Stratford. Marathon. Village (1910). Founded in 1891 with construction of the Milwaukee, Lake Shore & Western railroad by William Duncan Connor and named for his birthplace, Stratford, Ontario, Canada, itself named for Stratford, England. Connor was the twentieth lieutenant governor of Wisconsin (1907–9) and the son of Robert Connor, one of the founders of Auburndale (q.v.). (*Stratford Centennial Book*, 23)

Strawbridge. Lafayette. Named for landowner John Strawbridge, who is entered in the 1860 census as a teamster, born in Ireland. (McLernon, p.c.)

Strickland. Rusk. Town (1897) and ppl. Probably named from the Strickland post office, established in July 1895 in Chippewa County by postmaster Percy W. Strickland. The office was discontinued in July 1900 and reestablished in Rusk County in October 1903.

Strum [STRUHM]. Trempealeau. Village (1948). Named from the Strum post office, established in February 1885 by Ole Kittleson. The name was suggested by U.S. Representative William T. Price—for whom Price County is named—in honor of his friend Louis Strum, the Eau Claire County register of deeds. Apparently Strum was not pleased with this "honor" to the point of remarking, "It wasn't much of a place to have named for one." The name of the post office was changed in December 1887 to Tilden, for statesman and presidential candidate Samuel J. Tilden, who had died several months before, and changed back to Strum (apparently without Louis Strum's consent) toward the end of 1889. (Curtiss-Wedge and Pierce, 273)

Stubbs. Rusk. Town (1902). Named for Jabez C. Stubbs, a leading businessman of Weyerhaeuser and the first town chair. (*Commemorative Biographical Record of the Upper Lake Region*, 364)

Sturgeon Bay [STER juhn]. Door. Town and City (1883). Among the first permanent settlers in Sturgeon Bay were brothers Robert, Sam, and Oliver Perry Graham, who established a sawmill and related lumber industries about 1850. Oliver Perry Graham is generally considered the founder of Sturgeon Bay, and Robert Graham was the first postmaster in 1855. Sturgeon Bay is a translation of French *Baie des Eturgeons* 'bay of sturgeons.' The name was in use as early as the 1670s when the French Jesuit priest Claude-Jean Allouez recorded *La Portage des Eturgeons* 'the portage of the sturgeons,' where canoes were carried across the land barrier between Green Bay and Lake Michigan. The township was established as Otumba (likely a variant of Ottumwa, the name of an Algonquian village) in March 1857 and changed to Sturgeon Bay in February 1860. Also known as Tehema [*sic*], probably a transfer from Tehama County, California. (Holand, 304; Thomas, 22)

Sturtevant [STERD uh vuhnt]. Racine. Village (1907). Founded as Parkersville in 1854 by site owner Stillman Parker and renamed Western Union Junction after the railroad was built through Racine County in the mid-1850s. The community was renamed Corliss about 1901 when the Brown Corliss Engine Company of Milwaukee established a facility for manufacturing steam engines. Corliss Avenue in north Sturtevant perpetuates the name. The company went bankrupt in 1907 and the plant was taken over in 1923 by the B. F. Sturtevant Company of Boston, maker of industrial fans and air conditioners, which provided the source for the current name. (Redmann, 7, 8)

Suamico [SWAH muh ko]. Brown. Town (originally organized 1848) and Village (2003). Oconto. Town (organized as Suamico about 1850; changed to Little Suamico in 1860) and ppl. Named from the Suamico River. Suamico is probably derived from Ojibwa *osaw-amikwan-ong* 'at the place of the yellow beaver's tail,' based upon general Algonquian *amik* 'beaver.' Just below the mouth of the Suamico River is a sandbar known as Long Tail Point, which, along with Little Tail Point, were apparently seen metaphorically by some Native Americans as beavers' tails projecting into Green Bay. Early spellings of the name include Oussouamigong and Oussouamigoung. The post office was established in July 1857, John Bruce, postmaster. The name is unique to Wisconsin. (Cassidy, *Brown County*)

Sugar Bush. Brown. A translation of *La Sucrerie*, literally 'sugar refinery,' the name early Belgian settlers gave to the area, referring to the local sugar maple trees and the collection and processing of maple syrup. (Cassidy, *Brown County*)

Sugar Bush. Outagamie. Reportedly named by Michael Ruckdashel for a particularly striking sugar maple that grew nearby. The post office was established in February 1858, Robert Hutchison, postmaster. (Stennett, 128)

Sugar Camp. Oneida. Town (1898) and ppl. Early settlers around Rhinelander traded for maple syrup with the Ojibwa, who had been tapping the maple trees for centuries in an area that became known as the "sugar camp." Frederick R. Tripp, a hotel proprietor from Minocqua and the first township chair, established the Maple Grove Resort on Tripp Lake in 1891. When the name of the lake was changed to Sugar Camp Lake, Tripp renamed his vacation retreat the Sugar Camp Resort. The community of Sugar Camp was known as Robbins into the 1930s. (Kortenhof, 29, 67)

Sugar Creek. Walworth. Town (organized as Elkhorn in 1838; changed to Sugar Creek in 1846). Probably a translation of *sisbakwat sepee* 'sugar river,' a Potawatomi name for Sugar Creek. (Vogel, *Indian Names*, 107)

Sugar Island. Dodge. A translation of Ojibwa *sisibakwatokan* 'place where sugar is made.'

Sullivan. Jefferson. Town (1845) and Village (1915). Sullivan is named for John Sullivan (1740–95), an officer in the Continental Army and president (governor) of New Hampshire in the late 1780s. Sullivan was not only well known but commended in New England for his near-genocidal campaigns against the Iroquois in western New York State as punishment for their siding with the British during the Revolutionary War. The name John Sullivan has given rise to the baseless claim that the namesake is John L. Sullivan, the famous boxer of the 1880s. (Gnacinski and Longley)

Summit. There are several dozen locations in Wisconsin called Summit. Most were named because they are, or at least were thought to be, the highest points in the vicinity. Summit in Waukesha County was named for Summit Prairie, taken to be the highest point between the Fox and Rock river valleys. (*History of Waukesha County*, 784)

Sumner [SUHM ner]. Wisconsin's three Sumner townships—in Barron (1874), Jefferson (1858), and Trempealeau (1856) Counties—were named in honor of Charles Sumner (1811–74), U.S. senator from Massachusetts in the 1850s and 1860s. A determined opponent of slavery and a leading abolitionist, in May 1856 Sumner was beaten nearly to death on the floor of the Senate by Preston Brooks of South Carolina, prompting a number of sympathetic namings and renamings in his honor, especially in strong antislavery states such as Wisconsin.

Sumpter [SUHM(P) ter]. Sauk. Town. Organized as Kingston in 1849, named by early settlers Henry Teel and Charles Kern for Kingston, Luzerne County, Pennsylvania. The name was changed in November 1861 to show solidarity with the federal Union after the Confederate attack on Fort Sumter, South Carolina, in April of that year. Sumpter, with excrescent *p*, is a phonetic spelling of the informal pronunciation of Sumter. (Goc, *Many a Fine Harvest*, 185)

Sun Prairie. Dane. Town (1846) and City (1958). Named from Sun Prairie, itself named in June 1837 by New York architect August(us) A. Bird, commissioned by President Martin Van Buren to oversee construction of the Wisconsin capitol at Madison. Bird and some forty artisans had traveled for nine days from Milwaukee through persistent fog and rain, but when they came onto the prairie, in Bird's own words, "the sun suddenly appeared through a rift in the clouds and dispelled the gloom of the previous days, sending a thrill of joy to our hearts. . . . The prairie . . . was then and there . . . appropriately named 'Sun Prairie.'" The community was founded two years later by August Bird's brother Charles. (Cassidy, *Dane County Place-Names*)

Superior. Douglas. Town (1855) and City (1858). Also Superior Village (1949). Named from Lake Superior, known to the Ojibwa as *Kitchigami*, 'great water' or 'great lake,' called *Gitiche Gumee*, 'the shining Big-Sea-Water' in Longfellow's *Hiawatha*. French explorers in the middle years of the seventeenth century called the lake *Superieur*, 'upper lake' (as opposed to the lower lakes, particularly Lake Michigan). The city of Superior was founded in 1854 by a consortium organized as the Proprietors of Superior, among whom were several notable political figures of the day, including senators Stephen A. Douglas of Illinois, Jessie D. Bright of Indiana, and Robert M. T. Hunter of Virginia and congressmen William A. Richardson of Illinois and John C. Breckenridge of Kentucky. (Armour, 9)

266

Suring [SER ing, SOOR ing]. Oconto. Village (1914). Named for Julius "Joe" Suring, a storekeeper from Hayes and the first permanent settler in the area. Suring built a sawmill on an island in the Oconto River in 1881. The community became known as Mudville and, according to local historian Bruce Paulson, letters addressed simply to Mudville, Oconto County, were regularly delivered. Suring became the formal name of the village with establishment of the Chicago & North Western railroad station about 1896. Formerly known as Three Rivers.

Sussex. Waukesha. Village (1924). Probably named by Richard Weaver, who was born in Sussex, a former county in southern England. Weaver immigrated to Wisconsin in 1837 and represented the district in the Wisconsin Assembly and Senate in the late 1870s. The post office was established in January 1851, Richard Cooling, postmaster. Sussex includes the community of Templeton, founded on the line of the Wisconsin Central railroad in the mid-1880s and named for businessman and postmaster James Templeton. (*History of Waukesha County*, 983)

Swiss. Burnett. Town (1909). Named from the Swiss post office, established in September 1899. The local story is that Charles H. Chipman, the first postmaster, petitioned for a post office to be named Big Island. When that name was rejected, Chipman resubmitted the petition with the name Swiss, from his herd of Brown Swiss cattle, acclaimed by Edward Peet to be "the finest herd of blooded cattle in the county" (Riis and Koenen, 38).

Sylvan [SIL vuhn]. Richland. Town (1855). Sylvan and its derivative Sylvania (both from Latin *silva* 'forest') are popular place names because of their favorable associations; one or the other occurs in about half the states. The Wisconsin names may be transfers from eastern states.

Sylvester. Green. Town (1849). Named for Amos and Charles Sylvester, from Onondaga County, New York, who established a sawmill on the Sugar River in the late 1830s. The post office was established in May 1851, Charles F. Thompson, postmaster. (Butterfield, *History of Green County*, 1098)

Symco. Waupaca. Earlier known as Union Bridge and as Unionville for its location in Union township. The origin of the name is unknown. By a local account, when the post office was relocated from Unionville in 1865, the postmaster chose the name for a local Indian figure. Perhaps a modification of Suamico (q.v.). This is the only Symco in the United States. (Dunlavy, 14)

Tabor [TAY ber]. Racine. Named by Bohemian settlers for Tábor, a city in the western Czech Republic, itself perhaps named from Mount Tabor, west of the Sea of Galilee and mentioned in the Bible. The post office was established in July 1872, John Elias, postmaster. A second Tabor post office operated in Portage County from 1905 through 1911. The Mount Tabor post office was established in Vernon County in 1856, probably named for Mount Tabor and for the first postmaster, John C. Tabor.

Taegesville [TAG eez vil]. Marathon. Formerly known as Maine, named for its location in the town of Maine (q.v.). Renamed in the summer of 1891 when the Maine post office was changed to Taegesville by postmaster William Taege.

Taft. Taylor. Town. Named for William Howard Taft (1857–1930). When the town was organized in March 1909, Taft was the newly inaugurated twenty-seventh president of the United States.

Tainter. Dunn. Town (1869). Named for Andrew Tainter, a wealthy lumberman who held a one-fourth interest in the Knapp, Stout Lumber Company from the early 1850s. When his daughter Mabel died in 1886 at age nineteen, Tainter commissioned the Mabel Tainter Memorial Building, later called the Mabel Tainter Memorial Theater and now the Mabel Tainter Center for the Arts, in downtown Menomonie. The post office was established in December 1880, David D. Darling, postmaster. ("Mabel Tainter Memorial Theater")

Tamarack. Trempealeau. Named from Tamarack Creek, itself named for the stands of Tamarack trees, a species of larch. The post office was established in May 1871, Foster T. Gunem, postmaster.

Tarrant [TER uhnt]. Pepin. Named for George Tarrant, who emigrated as a teenager from Woolhampton, Berkshire, England, to Janesville in 1850. In 1863 Tarrant moved to Durand where he became a successful merchant and a founder of the Bank of Durand. He later served as mayor of Durand and in the Wisconsin Legislature in the early 1880s. The post office was established in February 1893, John K. Crawford, postmaster. (Forrester, 472)

Taus [TOWZ]. Manitowoc. Named for Taus, the German form of Czech Domažlice, a community and municipality in Bohemia in the western Czech Republic. This is the only Taus in the United States. The post office was established in June 1886, Joseph Zahorik, postmaster.

Tavera [tuh VEER uh]. Richland. Little is known about the origin of Tavera. The area was first known as Ellsworth Mills for the mills operated by Joseph S. Ellsworth in the mid-1850s and formally named from the Tavera post office, established in August 1893. Perhaps named for a local family, as Tavera is a (primarily Spanish, but also French) family name. Perhaps it is a transfer; Tavera is a community on the island of Corsica in the Mediterranean Sea. This is the only Tavera in the United States. (Scott)

Taycheedah [tuh CHEE duh]. Fond du Lac. Town (1847) and ppl. Founded about 1839 and named by James Duane Doty from Winnebago *teechira* 'camp by the lake,' reportedly the name of a Ho-Chunk village at the foot of Lake Winnebago. See Doty. (Bright; Stennett, 130)

Taylor. County. Named for William R. Taylor (1820–1909), governor of Wisconsin when the county was organized in 1875. Taylor came to Wisconsin from Ohio in 1848, served in the assembly and senate in the 1850s, and was Wisconsin's twelfth governor (1874–76). Taylor was known as the "farmer governor" for his work with the Grange and with state agricultural organizations. The choice of the name may have been influenced by David Taylor (1818–91), a prominent lawyer and circuit court judge in the 1870s and a Wisconsin Supreme Court justice (1878–91).

Taylor. Jackson. Founded as Taylor Station by the Green Bay & Western railroad in 1873. Named for Moses Taylor, New York financier, railroad investor, and president of the National City Bank of New York from the 1850s. (*Jackson County, a History*, 21)

Taylors Corners. Dane. Named for William R. Taylor, governor of Wisconsin and namesake of Taylor County (q.v.), who lived in the area in the 1840s. Also known as Kilian's Corners for the Kilian brothers, who purchased part of Taylor's property in the 1900s. See Taylor County. (Cassidy, *Dane County Place-Names*)

Tell. Buffalo. Named from the Tell post office, established in March 1893 by John Bernet, who probably chose the name for the legendary Swiss archer William Tell. Bernet emigrated from Bern, Switzerland, in 1856. Formerly known as Altdorf (Altorf), traditionally the location of the William Tell stories. (Pattison, 105)

Tennyson [TEN uh suhn]. Grant. Village (1940). Formerly known as Dutch Hollow. When the community was formally named in 1912, several "more appropriate" names were proposed, including St. Andrews, for the local Catholic church, Pluemerville, and Mullerville, for local Pluemer and Muller families. The source of the name is uncertain but the namesake is most likely Alfred, Lord Tennyson, the poet laureate of Britain in the last half of the nineteenth century. (*Grant County History*, 187)

Tess Corners. Waukesha. Named for Jakob Christian Joachim (Jacob) Tess, who emigrated from Prussia in the mid-1850s. Tess was a community benefactor, donating land for civil and religious purposes. (Vanden Heuvel, p.c.)

Texas. Marathon. Town (1858). Named for the state of Texas, in the news at the time for the recent end of the Mexican War.

Theresa [THRES uh, Thuh RES uh]. Dodge. Town (1848) and Village (1898). Theresa was established in the early 1830s as a fur trading post by Solomon

Juneau, one of the founders of Milwaukee. The community was formally organized in the late 1840s and named by Juneau in honor of his mother, Therese La Tulipe, his daughter Theresa, or both. See Juneau. (Barker and Tennies, 67)

Thiensville [THEENS vil]. Ozaukee. Village (1910). Thiensville grew around a gristmill established about 1842 by German immigrant Joachim Heinrich (John Henry) Thien. [THEEN] is an Americanized pronunciation of [TEEN]. (Eccles, 2)

Thiry Daems [THIR ee DAYMZ]. Kewaunee. Named for Constant Jean Baptiste Thiry, a Kewaunee County official born in Belgium, and Father Edward Daems, a Belgian Catholic priest. Thiry and Daems were instrumental in attracting Belgian settlers to the Door-Kewaunee area in the mid-nineteenth century. The post office was established in March 1874 as Darbellay, probably named for local official Joseph Darbellay, and changed to Thiry Daems in January 1875. ("Constant Jean Baptiste Thiry, Sr.")

Thompsonville. Racine. Named for Thomas F. Thompson, a grain merchant born in Voss, Norway, who immigrated to Wisconsin in 1844. The post office was established in February 1850, Emerson Lombard, postmaster. (Weber, 17)

Thornapple. Rusk. Town (1902) and ppl. Named from the Thornapple River, itself named for the abundance of thorn apples, fruits of the hawthorn tree. The only other Thornapple in the United States is in Barry County, Michigan, named from a different Thornapple River.

Thornton. Shawano. The source of the name is unknown. Perhaps a transfer from Grafton County, New Hampshire, or Chautauqua County, New York; perhaps in honor of Matthew Thornton, one of three delegates from New Hampshire who signed the Declaration of Independence.

Thorp. Clark. Town (1876) and City (1948). Named for Joseph G. Thorp, who emigrated from Otsego County, New York, in 1857. Thorp was founder and president of the Eau Claire Lumber Company from 1866 and a state senator in the late 1860s and early 1870s. (Scholtz)

Three Lakes. Oneida. Town and ppl. The town was organized in 1885 as Gagen, named for Daniel Gagen, the founder of Gagen (q.v.). It was renamed in 1909 for the Three Lakes post office, established in December 1885 and named for Maple Lake, Townline Lake, and Rangeline Lake. The names of Townline Lake and Rangeline Lake are artifacts of the nineteenth-century surveys that divided Wisconsin into townships and ranges. See Range. (Doucette et al., 12)

Tibbets. Walworth. Formerly known as Kendalls Corner, named for inn-keeper George Washington Kendall. Named for Samuel H. Tibbets

(Tibbits), from Windham County, Vermont, who opened a roadside tavern about 1842. The post office was established in August 1888, William H. Snyder, postmaster. (Beckwith, 421)

Tichigan [TISH uh guhn]. Racine. Probably a variant of Michigan, itself from Ojibwa *kitchi gami* 'great lake.' The post office was established in May 1893 as Tischigan, Amund T. Fjeld, postmaster. This is the only Tichigan in the United States. See Superior. (Bright)

Tiffany. Dunn. Town (1873). Named from Tiffany Creek, itself named for Pettis Tiffany. Little is known of this early settler, who built a cabin on the stream that bears his name in the early 1840s. The Tiffany Creek post office was established by Annie E. Hays in May 1873. (Ford and Dougherty, 7)

Tiffany. Rock. Apparently named for George Tiffany, from Avon, New York. In the 1840s Tiffany was a clerk and general assistant to Solomon Juneau in Milwaukee. His responsibilities included overseeing operations of the mail and stagecoach lines to and from Milwaukee. The post office was established in March 1857, Peter Smith, postmaster. (Wheeler, 57)

Tigerton. Shawano. Village (1896). Tigerton grew around the Newbold and Livingston sawmill, which began operations in the late 1870s. The village is named from the Tiger River, but the ultimate source of the name is unknown. According to Stennett, Tiger is an adaptation of a French name for the river that "cannot now be ascertained" (130). The post office was established in January 1880. This is the only Tigerton in the United States.

Tilden. Chippewa. Town (1883) and ppl. Named for Samuel J. Tilden, governor of New York and Democratic candidate for president in the disputed election of 1876. Tilden received a majority of the popular vote but after consideration and reconsideration of electoral ballots a congressional committee declared the winner to be the Republican, Rutherford B. Hayes. The post office was established in August 1900, William Schwartz, postmaster.

Tilleda [TIL uh duh]. Shawano. Perhaps named directly for Tilleda in Saxony-Anhalt, Germany, possibly by postmaster William Dumke, who emigrated from Prussia in the early 1860s; perhaps named for an early settler or family member named Tilleda. Tilleda is a rare female name but appears occasionally in early records. This is the only Tilleda in the United States.

Tioga [teye O guh]. Clark. The name was probably proposed by Nathaniel C. Foster for his birthplace, Tioga County, New York, itself named from a Mohawk word meaning 'junction' or 'fork.' See Foster. (Blang, 15)

Tipler. Florence. Town (1920) and ppl. Named for Arthur J. Tipler, a mill superintendent from Soperton, who partnered with William Grossman, a Green Bay accountant and lumber salesman, to form the Tipler-Grossman

Lumber Company in 1916. The name of the community became Tipler with establishment of the railroad station about 1918. (*Heritage of Iron & Timber*, 73)

Tisch Mills [TISH]. Manitowoc. Named for Johann Christian "Carl" Tisch, who emigrated from Eutin, Germany, established a sawmill and gristmill on the Mishicot River in the early 1860s, became a Kewaunee County judge in 1870, and served in the Wisconsin Assembly in 1877. (Falge, 330)

Tobin [TO buhn]. Kenosha. Named for early settler Patrick Tobin. Tobin emigrated from Ireland and by 1860 was an established farmer and land-owner. Also known as Tobin Road.

Token Creek [TO kuhn]. Dane. The name invites popular etymologies, and several have become local lore. By one, early settlers found a Winnebago totem in the area and from "totem" came "token." By another, Native Americans left "tokens" or offerings of tobacco to the spirits of Token Creek. Rather, Token is a popular etymology of Tokaunee, the leader of a small band of Ho-Chunk who had a village in the area in the 1830s. The Windsor post office was changed to Token Creek in February 1869 and to Token in June 1883. (Cassidy, *Dane County Place-Names*)

Tomah [TO muh]. Monroe. The Town (1856) and City (1883) are named for Thomas Carron, a Menominee leader in the Green Bay area in the late eighteenth and early nineteenth centuries. There is a local tradition (un-founded) that Tomah called a conference on Council Creek to encourage cooperation between Menominees and Winnebagos. Tomah is an English phonetic spelling of French Thomas. The post office was established in July 1855, Cady Hollister, postmaster. (Vogel, *Indian Names*, 43)

Tomahawk. The Town (1897) and City (1891) in Lincoln County are named from the Tomahawk River (also known as the Little Wisconsin River). The community was founded by William Bradley, who organized the Tomahawk Land and Boom Company as a subsidiary of the Chicago, Minneapolis & St. Paul railroad in 1886. The Town (1914) and community of Lake Tomahawk in Oneida County are named from Lake Tomahawk. The word Tomahawk originated in a Virginia Algonquian language and was brought to Wisconsin (and to most other states) by early settlers and explorers. Local accounts claim that Tomahawk Lake was so named because its shape was reminiscent of the head of the Native American war club. (Jones and McVean, *History of Lincoln, Oneida and Vilas Counties*, 68)

Tonet [to NET]. Kewaunee. Named from the Tonet post office. The office is named for a Belgian settler whose name appears on the 1870 census as Pierre Jonet and on the 1880 census as Peter Jonet. Apparently when the post office was established in 1887 the petition called for the name Jonet but it was misread as Tonet. This is the only Tonet in the United States. (*Commemorative Biographical Record of the Counties of Brown, Kewaunee and Door*, 708)

Tony. Rusk. Village (1911). Formerly known as Deer Tail, named from Deer Tail Creek. Renamed for village founder and first postmaster Anton Frank Hein, known as "Tony," with establishment of the post office in 1897. Hein was manager of a lumber company established by his father in the mid-1880s. (*Rusk County History*, 32)

Torun [TOR uhn]. Portage. The name was probably chosen by Julian Fierek for his birthplace, Torun (Toruń), on the Vistula River in north central Poland. Fierek established the Torun post office in January 1899. This is the only Torun in the United States.

Towerville. Crawford. Named for one or more Tower families from Underhill, Vermont. Joseph Tower and John Woodburn were among the early settlers in Utica township, arriving in the fall of 1853. John H. Tower was Towerville's first postmaster in 1857. (Butterfield, *History of Crawford and Richland Counties*, 731)

Townsend. Oconto. Town (1916) and ppl. Named for Charles Townsend, land agent for the Chicago & North Western railroad. According to Owen Smith, who assisted in surveying the area for the railroad right-of-way, "Townsend wanted the name put down as Reitzville after Charles Reitz. Reitz told me to put down the name of Townsend . . . which I did. [I]t became Townsend post office before Townsend knew what it was all about." The post office was established in July 1903, John P. Schmitt, postmaster. (Lang)

Trade Lake. Burnett. Town (1874) and ppl. Both Trade Lake and Trade River were sites of commerce between Europeans and Native Americans, and likely between groups of Native Americans before the arrival of Europeans. In the 1830s Joseph Nicollet recorded the river name *Attanwa Sibi* 'trade river,' from Ojibwa *atawe* 'to trade' (142) . The post office was established as Donersville, named by the first postmaster, Samuel Doner, in January 1870. The name was changed to Trade River in October 1870. (Vogel, *Indian Names*, 108)

Trego [TREE go]. Washburn. Town (organized as Mills in 1904; changed to Trego in 1906) and ppl. The community was formerly known as Veazie for early lumberman and land speculator George Veazie. Edwin E. Woodman, secretary of the Chicago, St. Paul, Minneapolis & Omaha railroad, claimed to have created Trego from Latin *tres* 'three' and *go* 'roads,' because trains arrived at the site from three directions. (Stennett, 194)

Tremble. Brown. Named for site owner Martin B. Tremble, a sawmill owner from Essex County, New York, who donated land for the right-of-way of the Milwaukee & Northern railroad in the late 1870s. (Cassidy, *Brown County*)

Trempealeau [TREM puh lo]. County (1854), Town (organized as Montoville in 1852; changed to Trempealeau in 1856), and Village (1867). Trempealeau is an adaptation of French *la montagne qui trempe à l'eau* 'the mountain that stands in the water,' itself a translation of Ho-Chunk *hay-nee-ah-chah* 'soaking mountain,' one of the Native American names for the rock island that rises some four hundred feet from the Mississippi River at Lake Pepin. The community of Trempealeau, first known as Reedstown, grew around a tavern established by fur trader James Reed in the late 1830s. Reedstown was platted as Montoville by Benjamin F. Heuston, Ira Hammond, and James Reed in 1852. Later that year the site was resurveyed and platted as Trempealeau. (Curtiss-Wedge and Pierce, 224, 230, 270)

Trenton. Towns in Dodge (1846), Pierce (1857), and Washington (1848) Counties. Trenton is a popular place name, occurring in some twenty states, most of which were named for the original Trenton in New Jersey, itself named in the early eighteenth century for and by the founder, William Trent. Trentons in Wisconsin may have been transfers by settlers from New Jersey, but just as likely may be for another Trenton, perhaps Trenton, Ohio. Trenton in Pierce County was laid out about 1855 by surveyors Wilson Thing and James Akers as Mount Pleasant at a site on the Mississippi River known as Thing's Landing. The post office was established as Pleasant View in the spring of 1856; the name of the office and the community was changed to Trenton later that year. (Ericson)

Trevor [TREV er]. Kenosha. Founded by the Wisconsin Central railroad and named for John B. Trevor, a New York financier who invested heavily in Wisconsin railroads in the 1880s. The post office was established in April 1887.

Trimbelle [TRIM buhl]. Pierce. Town (1855) and ppl. Named from the Trimbelle River. The origin of the name is unknown. Easton's speculation that the stream was named for a pretty girl, a "trim belle" (559), is classic popular etymology. Ericson is likely closer to the mark when he claims that the name was one of three given to streams in the area by government surveyors, probably about 1840. The community was laid out, apparently as Trim Belle, by Aaron and Joseph Cornelison in 1853. Although there are several Trimbles, this is the only Trimbelle in the United States.

Tripoli [TRI puh leye]. Lincoln, Oneida. Founded by Henry Herbert Stolle, from Oldenburg, Germany, who built a sawmill and opened a general store in the early 1900s. Several sources of the name have been proposed, mostly fanciful. By one, a railroad worker, for unknown reasons, wrote the name on a sign and planted it along the right-of-way; residents saw the sign and thought this would be a good name for their community. By another, Tripoli (which means 'three cities' in Greek) was seen as appropriate because the community was located near the intersection of Oneida, Lincoln, and Price Counties. Tripoli, ultimately from the North African city, may be a transfer; there are a dozen or so U.S. communities so named and one of these may have been the source of Tripoli, Wisconsin. Tripoli, New York, is an especially attractive possibility. (Arndt, 12)

Tripp. Bayfield. Town (1911). Named for Winfield E. Tripp, who emigrated from York County, Maine, in 1890. Tripp was postmaster at Iron River, judge of the municipal court, Bayfield County surveyor, and first chair of the Town of Tripp. (*Souvenir in Print and Pictures of the Fifty Year History of the Town of Tripp*, 5)

Trippville. Vernon. Founded by Dier N. Tripp, site owner and merchant from Nassau, New York. Tripp came to Vernon County in the summer of 1851, subsequently establishing a sawmill, a store, and a post office of which he was the first postmaster in 1871. (*History of Vernon County*, 569)

Troy. St. Croix. Town. Organized as Kinnickinnic in 1851; name changed to Troy in 1857. Possibly named by settlers from Troy, Ohio, but more likely for Troy, New York, itself named for the ancient city of Troy in Anatolia.

Troy. Sauk. Town (1857). According to Sarah Jane Keifer, who settled in Sauk County in 1846, "In regard to the name of Troy: When they were going to set off another town Henry Keifer [Sara Jane's husband] proposed to call it either Bloomfield or Troy, in honor of so many of the settlers coming from Bloomfield and Troy townships in Ohio" (Cole, *A Standard History of Sauk County*, 559). Keifer herself was born in Troy township, Richland County, Ohio.

Troy. Walworth. Town (1838) and ppl. When Walworth County was organized in 1838, a large northeastern section was known as Troy, named for Troy, New York. When that area was divided, the eastern part retained the name Troy and the western part became West Troy. A rather complicated series of actions followed. The Wisconsin Territorial Legislature renamed West Troy Meacham's Prairie, in honor of early settler Jesse Meacham. Displeased, for some reason, Meacham traveled to Madison and implored the legislature to change the name from Meacham's Prairie to Troy. The legislature did so, at the same time changing the name of the existing Troy to East Troy, which was formally platted as such by site owners Austin McCracken and Jacob Burgit in 1847. To encourage growth of the community, McCracken and Burgit offered free lots to anyone who would build a house at the site. The Troy post office was established in April 1837, Jesse Meacham, postmaster. (Damaske, *Along the Right-of-Way to East Troy*, 46–47)

Truax [TROO aks]. Eau Claire. Named from Truax Prairie, itself named for the Truax family. Peter and Cordelia Truax emigrated from New York State to Walworth County in 1854. Peter Truax became a successful lumberman, active in civic affairs. He was instrumental in building the first opera house in Eau Claire in the 1860s. (Bailey, 889)

True. Rusk. Town (1902). Named for Herbert W. True, a Glen Flora shopkeeper, lumberman, and community benefactor. True established the Hawkins post office in October 1888.

Truesdell. Kenosha. Named for Gideon Truesdell, originally from New York. Truesdell made a fortune in lumber and other business enterprises in the Kenosha and Chicago areas and represented the district in the Wisconsin Assembly in 1867. The post office was established in December 1876, Joel N. Woodworth, postmaster. ("Biography of Gideon Truesdell")

Truman. Lafayette. Probably named for Neff B. Truman, a landowner from New York State. The post office was established in July 1886, Frederick Fink, postmaster.

Tunnel City. Monroe. Named for the tunnel on the Chicago, Milwaukee & St. Paul railroad, opened in the late 1850s. (Hayward, 88)

Turtle. Rock. Town (1846). Named from Turtle Creek, which may have been named for the presence of turtles, from a turtle-shaped effigy mound, or for a turtle clan of Native Americans. At the time of the Black Hawk War in 1832, a large encampment of Ho-Chunk (Winnebago) was reported near the confluence of Turtle Creek and the Rock River. A short-lived community called Turtleville was founded several miles north of Beloit by John and Abel Lewis about 1838. (McLenegan, 13, 42)

Turtle Lake. Barron. Town (1879) and Village (1898). About 1870, Stephen F. Richardson built a sawmill near present Turtle Lake, which he called Skowhagen, a variant spelling of Skowhegan, his former home in Maine. With establishment of the post office in December 1879, the emerging community was formally named Turtle Lake from Upper Turtle Lake and Lower Turtle Lake. The naming of the lakes is uncertain. "Turtle" may be a translation of a Native American name, or a name given for unknown reasons by government surveyors. ("Barron County Communities")

Tuscobia [tuhs KO bee uh]. Barron. Tuscobia is a pseudo-Indian name confected from perceived Native American elements, perhaps influenced by Tuscola, Michigan, or Tuscola, Illinois. The Michigan name was coined by the nineteenth-century ethnologist Henry Rowe Schoolcraft, who created a number of artificial "Indian" names based loosely upon actual native materials. On one occasion Schoolcraft claimed that Tuscola meant 'warrior prairie' and on another that it meant 'level land.' The post office was established in September 1902, Mike J. Wagner, postmaster. This is the only Tuscobia in the United States.

Tustin [TUHS tuhn]. Waushara. Named for Thomas H. Tustin, a hardware merchant and one of the site owners. Formerly known as Fountain City for the artesian well dug by Charles Freer about 1855. (Velte, 32–33)

Twin Bluffs. Richland. With construction of the railroad in 1876, George Reed suggested the name for two bluffs, which, in Scott's words, "seemed to be standing guard over the little village." Also known as Bug Town, again in Scott's words, "because it was a little town without a school, a church, or a cemetery."

Twin Lakes. Kenosha. Village (1937). Named for its location at the northern tip of Lake Mary and Elizabeth Lake.

Two Creeks. Manitowoc. Town and ppl. The town was organized in 1859 as Rowley, named for early settler Peter Rowley, the namesake of Rowleys Bay (q.v.). The name was changed to Two Creeks in November 1861, presumably for two nearby streams that emptied into Lake Michigan. About 1860 Milwaukeean Guido Pfister and a business partner bought some fifteen hundred acres of shoreline and established a tannery, the Pfister and Vogel Leather Company, which became the nucleus of the community. (Wojta, 14–15, 17)

Two Rivers. Manitowoc. Town (1840s) and City (1878). Named from the streams now known as East Twin River and West Twin River. Hezekiah Huntington Smith, who arrived in the area from Connecticut in 1845, is generally regarded as the founder of Two Rivers. A classic entrepreneur and civic leader, Smith operated a sawmill, established a tub and pail factory, and was chair of the town board in the early 1860s. Two Rivers is a translation of Ojibwa *nijode* 'twin.' See Nashotah. (Gagnon, 27)

Tyran [teye RAN]. Florence. Origin uncertain. Tyran, a (rare) personal name, may have been the name of an early settler; but more likely Tyran is an adaptation of Teyranena (or Tyranena), possibly meaning 'lake water,' claimed to be a Winnebago name for one or more local lakes. This is the only Tyran in the United States. See Lake Mills.

Ubet [YOO BET]. Polk. Named from the Ubet post office, established in 1897 by David A. McCourt. The origin of the name is unknown but, as one reader pointed out, given the large number of Norwegians and Swedes in the area, the name may be related to what has become the catch phrase associated with Scandinavians, "You betcha!" There have been several Ubets in the United States, mostly names of mining operations in western states. This is the only current Ubet in the United States, but there is a You Bet in Nevada County, California. (Christiansen, 51)

Ulao [yoo LAY o, YOO lee o]. Ozaukee. Founded by James T. Gifford, the founder of Elgin, Illinois, who built a refueling station for steamships on Lake Michigan about 1840. The community was platted as Port Ulao by Daniel Wells and John Howe in 1853, taking the name of the Ulao post office established by Howe in the summer of 1850. Several explanations of the name have been proposed, one of the more ingenious being that the whistles of the engines of the North Western railroad screamed "YOU LAY O" as they approached the station. But Krier (38) is surely correct when she notes that Ulao is a Mexican War name, an alteration of Ulloa, likely chosen by a veteran named Weber, who had participated in the Battle of Vera Cruz in March 1847, when American troops under the command of Winfield Scott besieged and overran the castle of San Juan d'Ulloa, itself named for Francisco de Ulloa, who had navigated the western coast of Mexico as part of the Cortés expedition of 1539.

Underhill. Oconto. Town (1893) and ppl. Founded in the mid-1880s as a company town for employees of the William M. Underhill Lumber Company. Underhill, from Walcott, New York, purchased the site and established a sawmill on the Oconto River about 1883. ("Underhill, Wisconsin")

Union. There are more than a dozen communties or towns in Wisconsin named Union; most were named in honor of the federal union of states or to show solidarity with the Union during the Civil War. Union in Burnett County was named for the Union forces at the suggestion of David Fox, a captain of Pennsylvania volunteers in the Civil War. Fox laid out Veteran on the west side of Yellow Lake at the end of the war. The community was short-lived but the Veteran post office operated for twenty years, from 1897 until 1917. Union Church, where Racine, Waukesha, and Milwaukee Counties join, was so named in the 1850s when several religious denominations united to build one church open to all.

Unity. Clark. Town (1873) and Village (1903). In the early 1870s James Spaulding erected a sawmill that provided the nucleus for what would become the village of Unity. Early accounts are unclear, but apparently the station on the Wisconsin Central railroad was established as Brighton, named for one of the Brightons in New England, and the community initially took that name. Problems arose when the application for a Brighton post office was rejected. By a local account, early settler Amy Creed suggested the name Maple Grove. When this name, too, was rejected by the

Post Office Department, she then proposed Unity, reportedly because the community was "unified." The Unity post office was established in February 1873, John Sterling, postmaster. (*Unity, Wisconsin: Centennial*, 3)

Unity. Trempealeau. Town (1877). Dennis Lawler and Phineas B. Williams were early settlers about 1860. The local account is that both Lawler and Williams felt entitled to choose the name. When they drew straws for the honor, Williams drew the long straw and proposed the name Unity for his former home in Waldo County, Maine. (Curtiss-Wedge and Pierce, 271)

Upham [UHP uhm]. Langlade. Town (1894). Named for Wisconsin governor-elect William H. Upham (1841–1924). Born in Massachusetts, Upham came to Wisconsin in 1853, served in the Civil War, and became a successful lumberman. He was the eighteenth governor of Wisconsin, serving 1895–97. (Dessureau, 252)

Urne [ER nee]. Buffalo. Named for Ole J. Urne (or Urnes), who emigrated from Sogn, Norway, in 1865. The post office was established as Urne's Corners in March 1873. (Pattison, 105)

Utica [YOOT uh kuh]. There are at least four Uticas in Wisconsin: communities in Dane and Waukesha Counties and towns in Crawford and Winnebago Counties. All are transfers from Utica, Oneida County, New York, itself named for Utica, the ancient city in Tunisia.

Utley [UHT lee]. Green Lake. Utley is noted for the local deposits of black granite, which was mined and crushed for paving material. The community was named for Charles P. Utley, assistant superintendent of the Chicago, Milwaukee & St. Paul railroad, which built a spur to the quarries in the early 1880s. The post office was established in July 1883, James Densmoor, postmaster. (Reetz, 50)

Valders [VAL derz]. Manitowoc. Village (1919). Named for Valders, Norway, home of a number of early settlers, including Ole Evensen, who arrived in 1848. According to local accounts, when the Wisconsin Central railroad was extended westward from Manitowoc in the mid-1890s, the line was to run through Clarks Mills; however, when landowners refused to sell, a new route was plotted several miles south. With construction of the station, an official of the railroad reportedly asked for the local name and when none was offered, he asked the name of the church; the response was "the Valders church." The post office was established in September 1897, Otto G. Berge, postmaster. ("Village of Valders")

Valley Junction. Monroe. Apparently named for the Wisconsin Valley Line railroad built between Babcock and Tomah about 1872. (*Monroe County*, 161–62)

Valmy [VAL mee]. Door. Perhaps named for Valmy, France, site of a decisive conflict in 1792 in which the French army defeated Austrian-Prussian forces that were advancing toward Paris to end the French Revolution. The post office was established in July 1899 by Ella Simon. The only other Valmy in the United States is in Humboldt County, Nevada, founded in 1910 by the Southern Pacific railroad.

Valton [VAWLT uhn]. Sauk. The origin of this unique Wisconsin name is unknown. Historian Henry Cole (*Baraboo and Other Place Names in Sauk County*) suggests that Valton is "probably" a contraction of Vale Town or Valley Town. In his "History of Valton," however, Gilbert Mortimer writes: "Richard Mann, a preacher and landowner in Woodland, obtained the services of a surveyor who laid out the town of Valton in 1856. He requested that it be named after his home town of Valton, Ohio." I have been unable to verify the existence, present or past, of a Valton, Ohio. Valton is a rare given name and family name that may have originated as a Germanic pronunciation of the more well-known Walton. An early appearance of the name in English was in Vincenzo Bellini's 1835 opera, *I Puritani*, where Bellini apparently altered the name Walton, found in his source, to Valton. I am indebted to Linda Levenhagen for much of this information.

Van Buren. Grant. Laid out in the spring of 1839 by site owners Joseph Woolley, Thomas Palliser, and Joseph Petty. Named from the post office, established in September 1837 by Peter Coyle, itself named for Martin Van Buren, recently inaugurated as the eighth president of the United States. Little remains of Van Buren beyond a cemetery at the southwest corner of Potosi. (Holford, 519)

Van Buskirk. Iron. Named for Van Buskirk brothers George and Charles, who built a sawmill on the east branch of the Montreal River south of Hurley in the late 1880s. Charles was a prominent figure and civic benefactor of Lodi. The settlement did not endure. In Techtmann's words, "Today all that remains of Van Buskirk is a place name and the memories of the lumbermen and farmers who worked hard to make a living and a community here" (116).

Vandenbroek [VAN duhn bruhk]. Outagamie. Town (1902). Named for Father Theodore Van den Broek, who established a mission at Little Chute to minister to the Menominee in 1836. See Little Chute. (Balliet, 88)

Van Dyne [VAN DEYEN]. Fond du Lac. Named for Daniel R. Vandyne of Fond du Lac, the site owner. Born Daniel Van Duyne in New Jersey, Vandyne immigrated to Wisconsin in 1849 and purchased the property where the North Western railroad station was established and named for him about 1858. (*Van Dyne Centennial*, 4, 8)

Vaudreuil [vaw DRIL, vaw DREL]. Jackson. Founded by Edward J. Vaudreuil, formerly known as Edward J. Vodra, founder, president, and general manager of the E. J. Vodra Canning Company. Vaudreuil held several patents related to canning and vegetable processing. About 1907 he purchased some five thousand acres east of Black River Falls on which to locate farms, transportation, and homes to provide materials and support services for an independent, self-sustaining canning operation. The post office was established in August 1910, James Piper, postmaster. (*Jackson County, a History*, 41)

Veedum [VEE duhm]. Wood. Probably named by early settlers for Vedum (Kinne-Vedum), Västergötland, Sweden. By a local popular etymology, the name arose when a visitor asked two men who had recently arrived from Sweden what the name of the place was and received the reply *Vi dum* 'We don't understand.' The post office was established in January 1901, Hans Poulsen, postmaster. (Landelius and Jarvi, 252)

Veefkind [VEEF kind]. Clark. Henry Born Veefkind emigrated from Leyden in the Netherlands in 1876. He kept a general store and was instrumental in attracting the Wisconsin Central railroad, which named the station in his honor. The post office was established in June 1892, Edward Schultz, postmaster. (Curtiss-Wedge, *History of Clark County*, 2:533)

Vermont. Dane. Town (1855) and ppl. Named by settlers from the state of Vermont. The post office was established in May 1867, August B. Erbe, postmaster.

Vernon. County. Vernon County was organized as Bad Ax(e) County in 1851 and named from the Bad Axe River or the Town of Bad Axe, which had been organized several years before. Bad Axe is a translation of *la mauvaise hache*, as the river was known—for reasons unknown—to French voyageurs of the late eighteenth century. Because of the negative connotations of Bad Axe, in the early 1860s the name was changed to Vernon, probably at the suggestion of William F. Terhune, a local lawyer and state representative who also proposed the names of Victory (q.v.) and Monroe County (q.v.). The reasons for Terhune's choice are unclear but may have been influenced by Vernon in Terhune's native state of New York and by Mount Vernon, Virginia, the estate of George Washington. (*History of Vernon County*, 129)

Vernon. Waukesha. Town (1839). John Dodge, Prucius Putnam, and brothers Curtis and Orien Haseltine are the earliest known permanent settlers, all arriving from Vermont in 1836. The most likely source of the name is Vernon in Windham County, Vermont. The post office was established in March 1840, Asa A. Flint, postmaster. (*History of Waukesha County*, 791)

Verona [vuh RO nuh]. Dane. Town (1847) and City (1977). George, William, and Joseph Vroman established the Badger Mill about 1844 and named the community that grew around the mill for their former home, Verona, Oneida County, New York, itself named for Verona, Italy. The Verona post office was established in February 1847, Joseph Flick, postmaster. (Cassidy, *Dane County Place-Names*)

Vesper. Wood. Village (1948). Named from the Vesper post office, established by lumberman James W. Cameron in September 1878. The source of the name is uncertain: perhaps from Vesper, the Latin name for Venus, the evening star; for the finches called Vesper sparrows, noted for their evening song; for the sound like vesper bells of the wind blowing through the pine forests; or perhaps, less romantically, for Vesper, Onondaga County, New York, itself named for the evening star. See Hansen. (R. Rudolph; Stennett, 134)

Victory. Vernon. Founded in 1852 by William F. Terhune, Henry W. McAuley, Ira Stevens, and Hiram Rice. Named by Terhune, a pioneer lawyer from New York, in recognition of the defeat of the Sauk, which ended the Black Hawk War of 1832 at the Bad Axe River north of Victory. Terhune also suggested the names of Vernon County and Monroe County. (*History of Vernon County*, 734)

Vienna [veye EN uh]. Dane. Town (1849). Named by settlers from Vienna, Oneida County, New York, itself apparently named directly from the city in Austria. (Cassidy, *Dane County Place-Names*)

Vignes [VIG nuhs]. Door. Vignes(s), originally the name of a farm in Ryfylke, Norway, northeast of Stavenger, became a Norwegian family name and was subsequently transferred by Norwegian settlers to Wisconsin. The first postmaster was Mathias Nygard in 1891.

Viking. Pierce. Probably named in celebration of his Norse heritage by Hans Olson, who established the Viking post office in February 1892. (Ericson)

Vilas [VEYE luhs]. Vilas County, organized from Oneida in April 1893, and the Town of Vilas in Langlade County (1886) are named for William Freeman Vilas (1840–1908), one of Wisconsin's leading political figures in the second half of the nineteenth century. Vilas was born in Vermont, moved with his family to Wisconsin at the age of eleven, graduated from the University of Wisconsin at eighteen, made a fortune in northern Wisconsin lumber, rose to the rank of lieutenant colonel during the Civil War, and was U.S. postmaster general (1885–88), secretary of the interior

(1888–89), and senator (1891–97). In his will Vilas left several million dollars to the University of Wisconsin, where he had been a law professor and a regent. Vilas, in Baca County, Colorado, is also named for William Vilas.

Vilas. Dane. Named from the Vilas post office. When the Cottage Grove post office was moved to its present location in 1882, the Vilas post office was established at the original site of Cottage Grove. Named for William F. Vilas, for whom Vilas County is named. (Cassidy, *Dane County Place-Names*)

Viola [veye O luh]. Richland, Vernon. Village (1899). Laid out in the summer of 1855 by brothers Cyrus, Hartwell, and Jerry Turner. Apparently named in honor of Viola Buck, the Turner boys' teacher in Wyoming County, New York. A local story claims the namesake is Viola Mach (or Mack), reportedly the first settler's child to be born in the area, but she was likely named for the community rather than the other way around. (Scott)

Viroqua [vuh RO kwuh]. Vernon. Town (organized as Farwell in 1853; changed to Viroqua in 1854) and City (1885). The first permanent settlers at the site of Viroqua were Moses Decker and his sons Solomon and Reasoner from Mercer County, Illinois, in 1846. Decker was joined the following year by his wife, Elizabeth, and another nine children. In 1850 Decker laid out the community as Deckerville; he changed the name to Farwell in 1853 for Leonard J. Farwell, the sitting governor of Wisconsin. The name was further changed to Viroqua in May 1854, this time from the Viroqua post office, which had been established in November 1852. The choice, by either Decker or Luther Nichols, the first postmaster, probably recognizes a popular novel of the day, *Viroqua; or, The Flower of the Ottawas, a Tale of the West*, by Emma Carra, published in 1848. (The actual author is unknown since Emma Carra was a collective pseudonym used by a number of writers.) The novel, based loosely on historical events, tells of the romance between an English officer and Viroqua, the beautiful daughter of an Ottawa chief, set at the time of Pontiac's siege of Detroit in the early 1760s. This is the only Viroqua in the United States. (*Viroqua Centennial*; Vogel, *Indian Names*, 96)

Wabeno [wuh BEE no]. Forest. Town (organized as Cavour in 1897; changed to Wabeno in 1901) and ppl. Platted by the Western Town Lot Company for the Chicago & North Western railroad in 1897. Wabeno, literally 'man of the dawn,' is from Central Algonquian and refers to a brotherhood or class of conjurers, healers, and prophets. Wabenos were the "medicine men" or "sorcerers" of their tribes. Lumberman Charles Reitz probably chose the name, either directly from Ojibwa *wabanow*, or from *Hiawatha*, where Longfellow calls Wabeno "the magician." See Cavour. (Vogel, *Indian Names*, 92)

Wagner. Marinette. Town (1914) and ppl. Named for Joseph Wagner, who emigrated from Bohemia about 1860. Wagner was the first township representative to the county board. ("Marinette County, Wisconsin")

Waino [WAY no]. Douglas. Waino is an Americanized form of Wäinö, an older spelling of Väinö, a Finnish male name. The particular Väinö for whom the community was named is unknown. The post office was established in December 1900, Matti Harju, postmaster.

Waldo. Sheboygan. Village (1922). Founded about 1845 by Dr. Joseph Mallory as Joppa; later known as Onion River. In 1871 Norman Harmon bought the site intending to establish a community called Lora; however, the Milwaukee & Northern railroad named its station Lyndon and later Waldo, for Otis H. Waldo, a Milwaukee lawyer and president of the railroad. The post office was established as Onion River in September 1850 and changed to Waldo in February 1877. The community of Otis, north of Merrill in Lincoln County, is probably named for Otis H. Waldo as well. (Buchen, 264)

Waldwick. Iowa. Town (1849) and ppl. Waldwick was settled beginning in the 1830s. The origin of the name is uncertain. Waldwick is likely a transfer from Waldwick, Bergen County, New Jersey, the only other Waldwick in the United States. The post office was originally established in June 1850.

Wales. Waukesha. Village (1922). Named for their former home by Welsh settlers, the first of whom was John Hughes in 1840. The Chicago & North Western railroad established Wales Station in 1882. (Stennett, 134)

Walhain [WAWL ayn]. Kewaunee. Probably named for Walhain in central Belgium. The post office was established in September 1868, Michael Arndt, postmaster.

Walsh. Marinette. After the great Peshtigo fire of 1871, the remaining families of the Walsh area founded Rawnsville, named for Jacob Rawn, and established the Rawnsville post office, which operated for less than one year before being discontinued early in 1882. In the 1900s the Wisconsin & Michigan railroad changed the name of its station to Walsh, after John R. Walsh, president of the Chicago National Bank and a major stockholder in the railroad. The Walsh post office was established in July 1902 with Frank N. Bernardy, postmaster. (Grawey, 9)

Walworth. County (1838), Town (1839), and Village (1901). Walworth County was named at the suggestion of Samuel F. Phoenix, the founder of Delavan (q.v.), in honor of Reuben H. Walworth (1788–1867), at the time chancellor of New York, the highest ranking judicial office of that state. Phoenix and

Walworth shared a number of social and political views; both were active in the American Temperance Union and both worked for the abolition of slavery. The community of Walworth in Wayne County, New York, is also named for Reuben Walworth. George Walworth, perhaps a relative of Reuben, was an early settler from New York State who served in the Wisconsin Territorial Legislature in the 1840s. (Beckwith, 53; *Commemorative Biographical Record of the Counties of Rock, Green*, 419)

Wanderoos [WAHN duh rooz]. Polk. Formerly known as Dwight, the name was changed in 1917 for the primary employer in the area, the Wanderoos cheese factory, established in the early 1910s by Iver K. Wanderoos (occasionally written Wandersee). The Dwight post office operated from June 1901 until June 1904; the Wanderoos office was established in January 1917. (Christiansen, 40)

Warner. Clark. Town (1874). Named for Mark B. Warner, who emigrated from Genesee County, New York, to Black River Falls about 1855. Warner, a local farmer and businessman, served as township chair and supervisor. (Scholtz)

Warren. St. Croix. Town (1859). Probably named by early settler George Longworth for his former home, Warren Township, Lake County, Illinois, itself named for Warren, Herkimer County, New York, itself named for Revolutionary War general Joseph Warren. The post office was established in August 1862, Beach Sanford, postmaster. (Easton, 963)

Warrens. Monroe. Founded about 1868 with extension of the West Wisconsin railroad as Warren's Mills for the sawmills operated by George Warren and James Gamble. Gamble established the post office in April 1871. (Stennett, 196)

Warrentown. Pierce. In 1818 Lyman Warren emigrated from Massachusetts to the Lake Superior area and several years later to the Chippewa River valley where he became a successful trader and government subagent, working with the Ojibwa. Warren laid out Warrentown several miles upriver from Maiden Rock in the early 1850s. ("Truman Abraham Warren")

Wascott [WAHS kaht]. Douglas. Town (1910) and ppl. Wascott is a semi-acronym derived from the name of W. A. Scott, general manager of the Chicago, St. Paul, Minneapolis & Omaha railroad. The actual namesake, however, is uncertain because both Walter A. Scott and William A. Scott were general managers of the railroad in the 1890s. The post office was established in October 1902, Herbert G. Wilkes, postmaster. (Stennett, 196)

Washburn. County (1883). Town (1884) and City (1904) in Bayfield County. Named for Cadwallader Colden Washburn (1818–82), businessman, politician, and soldier. Born in Maine, Washburn established a legal practice at

Mineral Point in 1842. He represented Wisconsin in the U.S. Congress both before and after the Civil War. During the war he was colonel of the Second Wisconsin Volunteer Cavalry and brigadier general of volunteers. Washburn was the eleventh governor of Wisconsin (1872–74). In the late 1870s Washburn and his associates founded the corporation now known as General Mills. A number of schools and civic venues are named in his honor, including the Washburn Observatory at the University of Wisconsin–Madison. The town of Washburn in Clark County was named while Washburn was sitting governor.

Washington. Washington County, organized in 1836, and the half dozen Washington townships in Wisconsin are named for George Washington, first president of the United States.

Washington. Door. Town (1850) and ppl. Named from Washington Harbor, itself named for the *George Washington*, the flagship of a small flotilla bringing supplies to Green Bay to construct Fort Howard in 1816. The Washington Harbor post office was established in June 1854, Milton E. Lyman, postmaster. (Holand, 70–71)

Waterford. Racine. Town (1852) and Village (1906). Named for Waterford, Saratoga County, New York, probably by Levi Barnes and his son-in-law, Samuel Chapman, early settlers in the late 1830s. Waterford was platted about 1839 by Moses Vilas, who also surveyed the site of Racine in the late 1840s. (Butterfield, *History of Racine and Kenosha Counties*, 482; Damaske, *Along the Right-of-Way to Burlington*, 27)

Waterloo. Jefferson. Town (1847) and City (1962). Bradford Hill brought his family to the area in 1842 and they became Waterloo's first permanent settlers. The name commemorates the victory of the Duke of Wellington over Napoleon's forces at Waterloo, Belgium, which ended Napoleon's campaign and military career. The circumstances leading to the naming of Waterloo are unknown. Waterloo is a popular place name, occurring in some thirty states. By January 1847, when the Waterloo post office was established by Charles Topping, there were a dozen Waterloos in the eastern states and any one of these may have been brought to Wisconsin by early settlers.

Watertown. Jefferson. Town (1838) and City (1853). First known as Johnson's Rapids for founder Timothy Johnson, a carpenter from Connecticut, and the falls on the Rock River. The name was formalized in 1839 as Watertown, proposed by settlers from Watertown, Jefferson County, New York. According to local lore, a Native American name for the area was *Ka-Ka-Ree* 'big bend,' where the Rock River loops north of Watertown before continuing its southwestern journey into Illinois and the Mississippi River. (*History of Jefferson County*, 401)

Waterville. Waukesha. The source of the name is unknown. Since the mid-1840s, the community has been in decline. According to the 1880 *History of Waukesha County*, "Waterville, in 1845, was quite a little burg, and had its store, postoffice, public house, shops and comcomitants; but a change has come over the scene, and what was, is no more" (787). The Waterville post office was established in March 1846, Edmund Mellor, postmaster.

Waubeek [waw BEEK]. Pepin. Town (1858). Waubeek is probably a shortening of Ojibwa *Biwabik* 'metal, iron.' The town may have been named from Longfellow's *Hiawatha*, in which Mudjekeewis, Hiawatha's extra-worldly father, brags that nothing can harm him except the black rock, "the fatal Wawbeek." The now-vanished community of Waubeek, near the present Pepin-Dunn county line, grew around a sawmill operated by Cadwallader C. Washburn, governor of Wisconsin in the 1870s and the namesake of Washburn County (q.v.). (*Pepin County History*, 52)

Waubeka [WAW bi kuh]. Ozaukee. Possibly named for Waubeka (Waubika), reportedly a Potawatomi leader of the mid-nineteenth century whose village was on the Milwaukee River near present Waubeka. Possibly an adaptation of Potawatomi *wapikin* 'clay' or a variant of Waubeek (q.v.). (Vogel, *Indian Names*, 49)

Waucousta [wah KOOS tuh]. Fond du Lac. First settled by James Farr (Farrer), Peter Radliff, and Washington Noble in 1845. The name may have been inspired by the popular 1832 novel *Wacousta; or, The Prophecy*, by John Richardson, an officer in the British army. In the novel Wacousta is the fictional name of Reginald Morton, a renegade soldier who advised Pontiac during the 1763 uprising. The variant Waucosta occurs in Michigan and Iowa. The post office was established in August 1857, Anson S. Stowe, postmaster. (Vogel, *Indian Names*, 97)

Waukau [WAW kaw]. Winnebago. Founded by Luther Morton Parsons, who left the Fourierite settlement at Ceresco and established a sawmill at the site about 1847. Waukau has been claimed to mean 'zigzag,' 'a white bird flies along,' 'the spawn of a frog,' 'habitually,' and 'sweet flag.' Rather, Waukau is from Menominee, derived from either *wakoh* 'fox' or *wahkow* 'female sturgeon.' The community may have been named from Waukau Creek or from a Menominee village but more likely, Parsons or one of his associates chose the name from a family named Waukau. According to Waukau historian Ruth Westover, several Menominee had taken Waukau as their family name, at least for official purposes, before they moved to the Wolf River reservation in the 1850s (8–9, 16). The post office was established in July 1848, William H. Elliott, postmaster.

Waukechon [WAW kuh shahn]. Shawano. Town (1856). Named for a leader of the Embarrass River band of Menominee whose name appears on treaties of the 1850s as Waw-kee-che-un. The meaning is uncertain but has to do with 'bent' or 'crooked,' perhaps 'crooked nose.' The post office was established in June 1870, Parlan Semple, postmaster. (Vogel, *Indian Names*, 44)

Waukesha [WAW kuh shah]. County (1846), Town (1847), and City (1895). The name was proposed by Joseph Bond of Mukwonago, who represented the district in the territorial legislature when the county was organized. Apparently the name on the original bill was Wauk-shaw, which was changed "for euphony" to Waukesha while in committee. It is unclear if Waukesha was taken to be a native name for the Fox River or if it was chosen for one of several local Native Americans known as Wauk-tsha or Waukt-shaw. Joshua Hathaway, who surveyed much of Wisconsin for the federal government in the 1830s, claims to have been the first to transcribe the name, which he "obtained . . . from some Indian boys, . . . understanding it to be Pottawattamie for 'Fox,' which is a favorite name with the natives for all crooked rivers, whose course, in this respect, resembles the eccentric trail of that animal" (118). Hathaway also recorded the pronunciation as "Wau-*kee*-shah." From this reference Waukesha has been taken to be derived from Potawatomi *wekshi* or Ojibwa *wagosh* 'fox.' To these possible sources I would add Ojibwa *wakeshka* 'it is shining.' The post office was established as Prairie Village in April 1837, changed to Prairieville in July 1842, and changed to Waukesha in April 1847. (Bright; Damaske, *Along the Right-of-way to Waukesha*, 1)

Waumandee [WAW muhn dee]. Buffalo. Town (1853) and ppl. Named from Waumandee Creek. Waumandee is of Siouan origin, derived from *wamdi* 'big eagle' or 'war eagle,' and the immediate source of the name may be one of several nineteenth-century Sioux leaders. One, *Wa-man-de-tun-ka* 'big war eagle,' was known to English speakers in the 1820s as Black Dog; the name of another appears on an 1858 treaty as *Wa-min-dee-ton-kee*, glossed as 'large war eagle.' According to a local account, the name was proposed by Marvin Pierce, who was instrumental in the organization of Buffalo County and served as the first Buffalo County judge. The person who actually named Waumandee Creek, however, is more likely Thomas A. Holmes, who established Holmes Landing, the first permanent settlement in Buffalo County, now known as Fountain City (q.v.). Holmes was a fur trader with the Sioux and fluent in several Siouan languages. The post office was established in July 1858 and the community was formally platted in 1871. (Vogel, *Indian Names*, 53)

Waunakee [waw nuh KEE]. Dane. Village (1893). Laid off late in 1870 by site owners Louis Baker, George Fish, and Solomon Mardin (Martin) when the Chicago & North Western railroad line was extended from Madison.

The proprietors asked Simeon Mills, a pioneer settler of Madison and reportedly acquainted with several Native American languages, to suggest possible names for the community. One of Mills's proposals was Waunakee. Although the popularly accepted meanings are 'pleasant land' or 'pleasant earth,' the name is most likely from Ojibwa *wanaki* 'I inhabit a place in peace.' The area was formerly known as Leicester for the Leicester (often spelled phonetically as Lester) post office, named in 1852 by postmaster William Crow, for his former home in Leicestershire, England. The post office name was changed to Waunakee in October 1871. Waunakee signage claims that this is "the only Waunakee in the world." While I cannot speak for the world, I can say with confidence that this is the only Waunakee in the United States. (Cassidy, *Dane County Place-Names*)

Waupaca [waw PA kuh]. County (1851), Town (1851), and City (1878). Named from the Waupaca River, itself apparently named for a local Potawatomi figure known as Sam Waupaca, possibly the same individual whose name appears on the 1829 treaty of Prairie du Chien as *Way-pay-kay*. Several interpretations of the name have been proposed, including 'tomorrow,' 'pale water,' and 'looking ahead.' More likely, Waupaca is an Americanization of Potawatomi *wapeckow* 'is white-haired,' perhaps referring to Sam Waupaca. The post office was established in July 1850, Erastus C. Session, postmaster. (Vogel, *Indian Names*, 50)

Waupun [wuh PAHN]. Fond du Lac. Town (1842) and City (1878). Seymour Wil(l)cox, the first permanent settler in 1839, intended to call the site Madrid, after his birthplace in St. Lawrence County, New York. However, James Duane Doty, at the time Wisconsin Territory's representative in the U.S. Congress, changed the name on the post office application to Waubun, which was misread and approved as Waupun. From Potawatomi *wapan* 'it is day' or Ojibwa *waban* 'it is daylight,' meaning 'dawn' or 'early light of day.' In 1858 Juliette Kinzie published *Wau-Bun; or, The Early Day in the Northwest* in which she recounted her experiences in Chicago and at Fort Winnebago, where her husband, John, was Indian agent in the 1830s. In Longfellow's *Hiawatha*, Wabun is both the morning star and the east wind. Waubun, Minnesota, and Waubonsee, Illinois, are from the same source. The post office was established in May 1840, Seymour Willcox, postmaster. (*History of Dodge County*, 493–94)

Wausau [WAH saw]. Marathon. Town (1856) and City (1872). George Stevens, for whom Stevens Point is probably named, is generally credited with founding Wausau. Stevens established several sawmills in the area beginning in the late 1830s. Previously known as Big Bull Falls, the name Wausau was proposed by Walter D. McIndoe, who was instrumental in the organization of Marathon County. Wausau is from Ojibwa *wassa* 'distant, far,' perhaps, as Vogel suggests, for the long view from Rib Mountain (*Indian Names*, 138). The post office was established in May 1850, Charles Shuter, postmaster.

Wausaukee [wa SAH kee]. Marinette. Town (1887) and Village (1924). A variant of Wausau (q.v.). Named from the Wausaukee River. From Ojibwa *wassa* 'distant' and *aki* 'land.' The post office was established in January 1885 as Big Wausaukee, John S. Monroe, postmaster. (Bright)

Waushara [waw SHEHR uh]. County (1851). From Ho-Chunk (Winnebago) *waushara* 'fox.' Possibly named directly for the Winnebago leader whose name appears on the 1832 Fort Winnebago annuity list as *Wau-shay-ray-kay-kaw* 'the fox,' whose main village was on Fox Lake in present Dodge County. (Vogel, *Indian Names*, 64)

Wautoma [waw TO muh]. Waushara. Town (1851) and City (1901). Wautoma is a coined name, probably combining *Wau* from Wausau, Waushara, and others with *toma*, claimed to mean 'good earth' or 'good life,' but perhaps taken from an individual named Thomas. Earlier known as Shumway, for John P. Shumway, who established the post office in January 1850. See Tomah. (Stennett, 32, 136)

Wauwatosa [waw wuh TO suh]. Milwaukee. City (1897). First known as Hart's Mill for the sawmill established on the Menomonee River by Charles and Thomas Hart about 1837. The name was formalized as Wauwatosa about 1842 at the suggestion of Daniel Proudfit, who claimed that he had come across the name in a book on Indian treaties. Indeed the 1837 Treaty of Washington between the United States and the allied Sauk and Fox tribes has Wau-wau-to-sa as a signatory, but his name is mistranslated as 'great walker.' The correct source is Ojibwa *wawatessi* 'firefly.' In *Hiawatha* Longfellow depicts "the firefly Wah-way-taysee / flitting through the dusk of evening." (*City of Wauwatosa*, 3; Vogel, *Indian Names*, 158)

Wauzeka [waw ZEE kuh]. Crawford. Town (1857) and Village (1890). Founded about 1856 with construction of the Chicago, Milwaukee & St. Paul railroad. The name may have been chosen by site owner Hercules L. Dousman, one of the leading businessmen of the area, reported to be Wisconsin's first millionaire. Wauzeka is from Ho-Chunk (Winnebago) 'pine tree,' perhaps named from a particular Winnebago leader or local figure. (Butterfield, *History of Crawford and Richland Counties*, 750)

Waverly. Pierce. Waverly was popularized by the Waverley novels of Sir Walter Scott, beginning with *Waverley* in 1814, named for the protagonist, Edward Waverley. Waverly (with Americanized spelling) occurs in more than thirty states, and the Wisconsin name may be a transfer, perhaps from

New England or Ohio. The post office was established as Rock Elm in 1863 and changed to Waverly in 1878.

Waxdale. Racine. Named from the Johnson Wax Company, which was established as a flooring company in Racine in 1886. The name is a combination of *wax* and the rural-inspired *dale*.

Wayne. Lafayette. Town (1847). Named for Anthony Wayne (1745–96), a hero of the Revolutionary War and postwar campaigns against the Indians in Ohio. A number of places in the Midwest, including Wayne in Washington County, are named for "Mad Anthony" Wayne, so called in recognition of his personal courage and boldness on the battlefield. South Wayne, named for its location in Wayne township, was laid out by John P. Dickson (Dixon) in the late summer of 1858. (Butterfield, *History of Lafayette County*, 598)

Webb Lake. Burnett. Town (organized as Harrison in 1909; changed to Webb Lake in 1910) and ppl. A local account claims the name was decided by a coin toss won by a Mr. Harrison, but more likely the town was named for William Henry Harrison, famous Indian fighter, ninth president of the United States, and namesake of Harrison in Grant County. The Webb for whom Webb Lake was named is unknown. The post office was established as McDowell in March 1901; the name was changed to Weblake [*sic*] in August 1902. (Derrick, 58)

Webster. Burnett. Village (1916). Formerly known as Clam River. Renamed about 1896, perhaps for the New England statesman and orator Daniel Webster, who had substantial land holdings in northern Wisconsin in the 1830s and 1840s. However, according to the Village of Webster website, when Maggie Carroll and her husband petitioned for the establishment of a post office in 1896, they attached a note reading "the father of the American Dictionary is good enough for us." This would make the namesake Noah Webster, whose *American Dictionary of the English Language* was first published in 1822. ("Webster, Wisconsin")

Webster. Vernon. Town (1855). Probably named for Daniel Webster, Massachusetts senator, statesman, and orator, who had invested heavily in Wisconsin real estate in the 1840s. (*History of Vernon County*, 721)

Weedens. Sheboygan. Named for George W. Weeden, a county judge and chair of the Sheboygan County Board of Supervisors in the early 1870s. (Stennett, 137)

Wellington. Monroe. Town (1856). Named for Wellington Davis, an early settler from New York. The name was proposed by Benjamin Welch, the postmaster at Ridgeville, and landowners Thomas Young and Henry Pennewell. (*Monroe County*, 2)

Wells. Calumet, Manitowoc. Named for Owen A. Wells, a Fond du Lac lawyer who represented the district in the U.S. Congress in the 1890s. The post office was established in June 1894, Claus Menke, postmaster. (Falge, 316)

Wells. Monroe. Town (1871). The name was to have been Charleston, but while still in committee Wells was substituted, apparently at the suggestion of Milton Montgomery, for James Wells, a prominent early settler and the first township chair. Ironically, it seems that Wells had signed the petition to have the township named Charleston. (*Monroe County*, 130)

Wentworth. Douglas. Likely named from the Johnson-Wentworth Lumber Company. In the early 1890s lumber entrepreneur Samuel S. Johnson of Cloquet, Minnesota, organized the timber and milling company along with brothers Justin and George Wentworth, from Knox County, Maine. ("Justin K. Wentworth")

Wequiock [WEE kwee ahk]. Brown. The community was named from Wequiock Bay, an inlet on the eastern shore of Green Bay. Circumstances are unknown, but the name is likely based upon Ojibwa *wikweia* 'there is a bay.' The post office was established in June 1856, John B. A. Masse, postmaster. (Cassidy, *Brown County*)

Werley. Grant. Earlier known as Climbing Rock. The community was established with construction of the Chicago, St. Paul, Minneapolis & Omaha railroad in 1878. Named for Gottlieb Wehrle, with phonetic spelling. Wehrle emigrated from Baden, Germany, in 1822 and was elected to the Wisconsin Assembly in 1873 on the Reform ticket. (Holford, 711)

Wescott [WES kaht]. Shawano. Town (1901). Named for Charles D. Wescott, the founder of Shawano (q.v.), who established a sawmill on the Wolf River in the early 1840s. The post office was established in February 1887, August Kregal, postmaster. (McDevitt, 44)

West Allis. Milwaukee. City (1906). Formerly known as Honey Creek. In 1880 the Chicago & North Western railroad established the North Greenfield station, named for its location in Greenfield Township. That name lasted until the Reliance Iron Works of the Edward P. Allis Company outgrew its Milwaukee location. Allis joined with the Fraser and Chalmers company and, as Allis-Chalmers, manufacturers of heavy equipment and farm machinery, moved to what is now West Allis in 1902, at which time the name was formally changed from North Greenfield. (Muchka, 8–9)

West Bend. Washington. Town (1846) and City (1885). Dr. Erastus Bradley Wolcott, Wisconsin surgeon general and founder of the Wisconsin Medical Society in 1841, is generally recognized as the father of West Bend for the gristmill and sawmill he erected in the mid-1840s. The name, however, was most likely chosen by Byron Kilbourn, one of the founders of Milwaukee. One name under discussion was *Pikatomaea*, a blend of Native American and European elements. Kilbourn proposed a simpler name, one descriptive of the bend in the Milwaukee River at this point. (Williams, 3–5)

Westboro. Taylor. Town (1875) and ppl. Named about 1874 by the Wisconsin Central railroad for Westboro, Massachusetts, a Boston suburb. The post office was established in February 1875, Edwin A. Williams, postmaster. (*History of Taylor County*, 19)

Westby. Vernon. City (1920). Named for Ole T. Westby, who emigrated from Toten, Oppland, Norway, in the late 1840s and established a general store in 1867. The Chicago, Milwaukee & St. Paul railroad station and the post office were named for him in 1879. (*History of Vernon County*, 484)

West Denmark. Polk. Named from the West Denmark post office, established in the summer of 1877 by Martin C. Pederson. The office was apparently so named by Danish settlers because the site was indeed "west" of Denmark. (Ericson)

Westfield. Marquette. Town (1852) and ppl. Named from the Westfield post office, established in 1851 and named for Westfield, Chautauqua County, New York, by Robert Cochrane, the first postmaster. The community of Westfield was formally platted for Cochrane in 1856 by surveyor Pickens Boynton. (*Centennial Memories*, 151)

Westfield. Sauk. Town (1854). Named for the community of Westfield, now Loganville (q.v.). (Cole, *Baraboo*)

Westford [WEST ferd]. Richland. Town (1856). Named by Asa and Levi Lincoln, who kept the first general store in the area from the late 1850s. The Lincolns proposed the name for their former home, Westford, Otsego County, New York, itself named for Westford, Vermont. (Scott)

West Lima [LEYE muh]. Richland. The post office was established in 1856 as Hoosier, for the large number of settlers from Indiana, and renamed in 1860 for Lima, Ohio, at the suggestion of postmaster Jesse Harness and shopkeeper Joseph DeHart. (Butterfield, *History of Crawford and Richland Counties*, 983)

Weston. Clark. Town (1856). Named for Samuel F. Weston, who arrived from Somerset County, Maine, in the early 1850s. Weston oversaw several extensive logging operations in Clark County and became one of the largest landowners in Wisconsin. (Scholtz)

Weston. Dunn. Town (1865) and ppl. Named from the Weston post office, established in June 1874 by postmaster Andrew Harrison. The office was probably named for Daniel Weston, one of the first members of the Dunn

County Board. The community grew around a sawmill built in 1896 by William Starr, a lumberman from Eau Claire. See Comfort. (Dunn County Historical Society, 81)

Weston. Marathon. Town (organized as Eau Claire in 1856; changed to Weston in 1859) and Village (1996). Named for the Weston Mills, established by William Weston in the early 1850s. Otis Kelly was the first postmaster in 1858. The name of the post office was changed to Kelly's Mill in 1864.

Westport. Dane. Town (1849). Named by Michael O'Malley, the first township chair, for Westport, his former home in County Mayo on the west coast of Ireland, itself named for the eighteenth-century Westport House, the estate of the Marquess of Sligo. (Cassidy, *Dane County Place-Names*)

West Salem. La Crosse. Village (1893). Platted in 1856 for site owners Thomas Leonard, Mills Tourtellotte, and Oscar Elwell. Elwell reportedly suggested the name Rupert, for his former home in Bennington County, Vermont, but the Baptist minister, William Card, proposed Salem, claiming that Salem "means peace and will be a good omen." West was added with establishment of the post office in 1860 to distinguish this community from Salem in Kenosha County. (Kindschy, 15–16)

West Sweden. Polk. Town (1875) and ppl. Many of the early settlers in the late 1860s were from Dalecarlia, Värmland, and Dalsland, Sweden. As reported by Landelius and Jarvi (253), these are western Swedish provinces; thus, West Sweden was an appropriate name. The post office was established in January 1873, Gustaf Bloomgren, postmaster.

Weyauwega [weye uh WEE guh]. Waupaca. Town (1852) and City (1939). Probably from Menominee but the source and derivation are unknown. Proposed explanations of Weyauwega include 'here we rest,' 'today,' 'where we wait for deer,' 'he embodies it,' 'pale water,' and 'tomorrow.' James Duane Doty took credit for proposing the name of the Weyauwaya [*sic*] post office, claiming it was the name of his Menominee guide and meant 'whirling wind.' It has also been suggested that Wey-au-we-ga was the leader of a local Menominee band, and that the name is an adaptation or mistranscription of Menominee *weyawekeh* 'old woman.' The post office was established in July 1850, Benjamin Birdsall, postmaster. (Bright; Vogel, *Indian Names*, 44)

Weyerhaeuser [WEHR how zer]. Rusk. Village (1906). Founded about 1884 by Frederick Weyerhaeuser, president of the Chippewa Logging Company, a conglomerate of logging and lumber interests and one of the business ventures that would make Weyerhaeuser one of the richest men in the world by 1900. Apollonia (q.v.) is named for Weyerhaeuser's daughter. (*Rusk County History*, 35)

Wheeler. Dunn. Village (1922). Laid out in 1884 as Welton, named for site owner Marie Welton. The St. Croix & Chippewa Falls railroad station was Lochiel, named from the Lochiel post office, established in August 1876 by Duncan McPherson from Lochiel, Ontario. The community subsequently took the name of the Wheeler post office established in 1885 by Homer D. Wheeler. (Dunn County Historical Society, 29)

Whitcomb [WIT kuhm]. Shawano. Named for Henry F. Whitcomb of Milwaukee, president of the Wisconsin Central railroad in the late nineteenth century. (Stennett, 138)

White Creek. Adams. The community was laid out as Cascade by Seth Thompson, who built a gristmill at the site in 1853. The name was changed in August 1855 when Thompson established the White Creek post office. Apparently the stream was so called because of its frothy surface. (Goc, *From Past to Present*, 29)

Whitefish Bay. Milwaukee. Village (1892). Named from Whitefish Bay, "so named . . . because it was the favorite feeding ground for whitefish, and fishing ground for fishermen" (Stennett, 138).

Whitehall. Trempealeau. City (1941). Ole Knudtson, who emigrated from Norway in 1844, opened a hotel and blacksmith shop at the site in 1860. The community was laid out in 1862 by site owner Benjamin Franklin Wing, who had established the White Hall post office the year before. The source of the name is uncertain. White Hall is a popular place name, occurring in more than half of the continental states, and one of these may have been transferred to Wisconsin. Likely sources are White Hall, Illinois, where Wing is reported to have lived before settling in Trempealeau County, and Whitehall, New York. (Curtiss-Wedge and Pierce, 272)

White Lake. Langlade. Village (1926). The community grew around a sawmill established on White Lake by the mammoth Yawkey-Bissell Lumber Company in 1916. The lumber company itself was organized by a group of Wausau businessmen that included Cyrus Carpenter Yawkey and Walter Henry Bissell. (Dessureau, 203)

Whitelaw. Manitowoc. Village (1958). Formerly known as Pine Grove. The namesake is probably Whitelaw Reid, American diplomat and editor of the *New York Tribune*. In August 1892, when Anton Ziglinsky established the Whitelaw post office, Reid was a candidate for vice president on the Republican ticket with Benjamin Harrison.

Whitestown. Vernon. Town (1856). Named for Giles White, the founder of Ontario (q.v.) and the first township chair. (*History of Vernon County*, 744)

Whitewater. Walworth. Town (1840) and City (1885). Founded about 1837 by settlers from Milwaukee. The community was named for its location on

Whitewater Creek, itself a translation of Menominee *wapeskiw* 'it is white' and *nepew* 'water.' The stream was the source of white clay used by early settlers to make pottery and bricks. The post office was established in February 1840, David J. Powers, postmaster. (Bright)

Whiting [WEYET ing]. Portage. Village (1947). About 1837 Gilbert Conant and his business partner, Daniel Campbell, established a sawmill east of present Whiting and laid out the community of Conant Rapids. About 1873 Conant and Campbell's sawmill was bought by the brothers Thomas H. and Alexander S. McDill, who laid out McDillville alongside Conant Rapids. In 1892 George A. Whiting, founder of the George A. Whiting Paper Company of Menasha, established the Whiting-Plover Paper Company at the site, primarily to manufacture high quality writing paper. Present Whiting includes both McDillville and Conant Rapids. The McDill post office opened in February 1874 and closed in February 1904. (Rosholt, *Our County, Our Story*, 27, 368)

Whittlesey. Taylor. Platted in 1882 for site owner and first postmaster, George W. Norton. Probably named for Asaph Whittlesey, one of the founders of Ashland and an early state representative from northern Wisconsin. According to legend, Whittlesey snowshoed from Ashland to Sparta (some two hundred miles), where he caught a train to Madison in order to take his seat in the 1860 Wisconsin Assembly. See Ashland. (Whittlesey Homemakers, 4)

Wien [WEEN, VEEN]. Marathon. Town (1867) and ppl. Named for Vienna, Austria, by the first permanent settler, Mathias Halkowitz, who was instrumental in attracting colonists to the area in the early 1860s. Wien is the German form of Vienna. This is the only Wien in the United States. (Marchetti, 10)

Wild Rose. Waushara. Village (1904). The name has generated the expected popular etymologies. By one, the community was named for an abundance of wild roses; by another, workmen digging a foundation for the first store discovered a wild rose bush blooming out of season and considered this a favorable omen; and by another, settlers from Rose, New York, saw their surroundings as a "wild" reminder of their former home. More likely, Wild Rose was simply named from Rose township (q.v.) by James H. Jones, who established the Wild Rose post office in November 1873. (Ramlow, 6, 10)

Wilkinson. Rusk. Town (1923). Probably named for Zeno Wilkinson, an early settler and the first town chair. Possibly named for Alonzo H. Wilkinson, from Bayfield. Alanzo Wilkinson was a state senator in the late 1910s and worked with the American Immigration Company to settle the cutover lands of northern Wisconsin. (Chappelle, *Around the Four Corners*, 28)

Willard. Clark. Founded in 1911 by the Foster Lumber Company. Named from the Willard post office, established in June 1908. The office was named for Willard Foster, the youngest son of Nathaniel C. Foster, founder of the Foster Lumber Company of Fairchild. See Foster. (Curtiss-Wedge, *History of Clark County*, 662)

Willard. Rusk. Town (1907). The name was suggested by Frank W. Tubbs, a Chicago livestock dealer with business interests in Rusk County. Tubbs proposed the name for either a family member or business associate. (M. Meyer, p.c.)

Williams Bay. Walworth. Village (1919). Named for the Williams family. In 1836 Royal Joy Williams, along with brothers Austin, Moses, and Israel, emigrated from Conway, Massachusetts, to Walworth County, eventually settling around the inlet on the northwest shore of Lake Geneva that bears their name. The post office was established in April 1892, Marie R. Williams, postmaster. (Beckwith, 1416)

Williamstown. Dodge. Town (1846). Probably named for William Foster, who, along with Alvin Foster and Chester May, built a dam on the Rock River and established a sawmill about 1845. See Mayville, Dodge County.

Willow. Richland. Town (1854). Named from Big and Little Willow Creeks. Early settlers included John Hake and his sons, who arrived from New York State in the summer of 1852. (Butterfield, *History of Crawford and Richland Counties*, 1281)

Wills. Bayfield. Named for and by Jacob C. Wills, who established the Wills post office in July 1902.

Wilmot [WIL maht]. Kenosha. Founded in 1844 by Asahel W. Benham as Gilead, reportedly named for his family home, Gilead, Connecticut. Formally laid out about 1848 and named for the Wilmot Proviso, a bill introduced in the House of Representatives by David Wilmot of Pennsylvania in 1846 that prohibited slavery in any territory acquired as a result of the Mexican War. Several local accounts claim the name was proposed facetiously, but the names of other communities with similar origins (Proviso in Illinois, for example) were suggested quite seriously. The Wilmot post office was established in July 1849. (Butterfield, *History of Racine and Kenosha Counties*, 553)

Wilson. The towns of Wilson in Eau Claire (1915), Lincoln (1913), and Rusk (1913) Counties were named for Woodrow Wilson (1856–1924), twenty-eighth president of the United States, in office 1913–21.

Wilson. St. Croix. Village (1911). Named for "Captain" William Wilson, one of the major investors and organizers of the Tomah & Lake St. Croix (later the West Wisconsin) railroad in the late 1860s. (Stennett, 196)

Wilson. Sheboygan. Town (1849). Named for David Wilson, an early settler from Ohio in 1840. (Buchen, 341)

Wilton. Monroe. Probably named by settlers from Wilton, Saratoga County, New York, itself named for Wilton, Hillsborough County, New Hampshire, itself named for one of the Wiltons in England. The post office was established in July 1857, Albert S. Ingalls, postmaster.

Winchester. Vilas. Town (1921) and ppl. Winchester has its origins in the Divide Resort, a vacation retreat and fishing camp established by George Buck and his son, Fayette, at the narrows between North and South Turtle Lakes in 1893. In 1902 a consortium of Michigan investors formed the Turtle Lake Lumber Company and after several years began logging operations and changed the name from Divide to Winchester, for Walter Winchester, the company president. In its early years the community was known informally as Tartown, for the tar paper used to construct the company housing units. The Divide post office was established in May 1905, Fayette L. Buck, postmaster, and discontinued in January 1908. (M. Engel, 37)

Winchester. Winnebago. Town (1851) and ppl. The origin of the name is unknown. Winchester is a popular place name, occurring in more than half of the continental states. Any of the Winchesters in New England or Ohio may have been transferred to Wisconsin. The original Winchester is in Hampshire, southern England. The post office was established in October 1852, Sherman R. Hopkins, postmaster.

Windsor [WIN zer]. Dane. Town (1847) and ppl. The first name suggested for the town was Allen, for Vermont's Revolutionary War hero Ethan Allen. This proposal was rejected in favor of Windsor, another Vermont name, proposed by settlers from Windsor County, Vermont. The Windsor post office was established in July 1847, Nathan P. Spaulding, postmaster. (Butterfield, *History of Dane County*, 2:878)

Winfield. Sauk. Town. Named in the fall of 1852 for General Winfield Scott, the Whig candidate for president of the United States at the time. Scott was a national hero following the Mexican War, and several dozen communities and townships, especially in the Midwest, are named in his honor. (Cole, *Baraboo*)

Winnebago [wi nuh BAY go]. County (1840). Named for the Winnebago, a Siouan people whose territory at one time extended from northwest Illinois (where there is also a Winnebago County) through south central Wisconsin to Green Bay, where the Winnebago met Jean Nicolet, the first European to enter Wisconsin, in 1634. Winnebago is from an Algonquian language (probably Potawatomi or Ojibwa), recorded by early French explorers as *Ouininpigou* 'people of the dirty water' or 'people of the stinking water.' *Winne* is a general Algonquian word for 'water'; *bago* has been interpreted as 'strong-smelling,' 'salty,' 'dirty,' perhaps referring to the fact that many Winnebagos lived along the Fox River, which became polluted with rotting fish each summer. Winnipeg is a variant. The Winnebagos' name for themselves was Hochungara. Since 1994 the standard form of the name has been Ho-Chunk 'big voice.' The Town of Fort Winnebago in Columbia County (organized as Winnebago Portage in 1849) takes its name from Fort Winnebago, which was constructed by the U.S. Army in 1828 to ensure freedom of movement along the Fox-Wisconsin portage. The fort was abandoned in 1845.

Winneboujou [win uh BOO zhoo]. Douglas. Winneboujou is a legendary cultural hero of a number of Native American groups living near the Great Lakes. In some stories Winneboujou is a blacksmith, fashioning copper into weapons; in others, he is the creator of landscapes, especially the Apostle Islands. Winneboujou is renamed Hiawatha in Longfellow's epic poem. The post office was established in January 1898, Jacob M. George, postmaster. (D. Brown, 28; Vogel, *Indian Names*)

Winneconne [WIN uh kah nee, win uh KAH nee]. Winnebago. Town (1848) and Village (1887). Winneconne grew around a trading post established by William Bruce on the southern shore of Lake Poygan in 1838. The current spelling was formalized in 1851, replacing Winneconah, Wanekona, Winnicounce, and several other forms. The source of the name is uncertain. A number of origins have been proposed: from Ojibwa *winikaning* 'dirty water'; from an unidentified language meaning 'deer bones,' recalling the site of a venison feast where the long bones were split and the marrow eaten; and from a Menominee leader named Waunau-Ko. There may be some truth to the local legend that Winneconne is derived from Menominee *menekan* 'skull,' referring to the bones remaining after a battle between Native American tribes near Butte des Morts. (Bright; Goc, *One Man, One Village*, 23; Vogel, *Indian Names*, 138)

Winter. Sawyer. Town (1905) and Village (1973). Founded about 1902 and named for Wallace C. Winter, general superintendent of the Chicago, St. Paul, Minneapolis & Omaha railroad at the time. The post office was established in December 1904, Frank Bishop, postmaster. (Stennett, 197)

Wiota [weye OT uh]. Lafayette. Town (1849) and ppl. In 1828 William S. Hamilton, son of Alexander Hamilton, and several others opened lead mines in an area that became known as Hamilton, Hamilton's Diggings, and Wyota Diggings. Hamilton apparently chose the name and formalized the spelling as Wiota when he established the post office in the mid-1830s. The origin and meaning of the name are unclear. Wiota in Cass County, Iowa, the only other Wiota in the United States, is from Dakota (Siouan) for 'many moons, many months.' Wiota, Wisconsin, may be from the same source, but Vogel (xv) suggests that the name may have literary origins or may have been fabricated by settlers from presumed native materials. (Bright; *Lafayette County Bicentennial Book*, 187)

Wisconsin Dells. The city is in parts of four Wisconsin counties: Adams, Columbia, Juneau, and Sauk. In American French *dalles* 'paving stones, flagstones' developed the meaning 'trough, gutter,' and its semantic range was extended first to a gorge or narrow rocky channel in a river, especially one that created rapids or waterfalls, and further to a narrow valley, in particular one between steep rock walls. The Dalles in Wasco County, Oregon, is probably the best known example. Through popular etymology, dalle(s) became dell(s). The Dalles on the St. Croix River south of Osceola retains the earlier form. As early as 1846 the rapids on the Wisconsin River were known as the Delles, and by the mid-1880s the Dells had become a fashionable summer resort. The city of Wisconsin Dells was founded as Kilbourn City by the Wisconsin River Hydraulic Company in 1855, named for Byron Kilbourn, who organized the Milwaukee–La Crosse railroad in the early 1850s and chose this site for a station and a community because it was thought to be equidistant between the termini. Wisconsin Dells was known as Kilbourn until 1931. (Butterfield, *History of Columbia County*, 809)

Wisconsin Rapids. Wood. City (1869). The west side of Wisconsin Rapids was known as Centralia, named from the now-vacated Town of Centralia. Grand Rapids, named for the rapids of the Wisconsin River, developed on the east side. The communities merged as Grand Rapids in 1900. Perhaps because of confusion with Grand Rapids, Michigan, the name was changed to Wisconsin Rapids in 1920. The Centralia post office was established in May 1858 and discontinued in May 1904. (R. Rudolph)

Withee [WITH ee]. Clark. Town (1879) and Village (1901). Named from the Withee post office, established in September 1880 by Niram Withee. In the early 1850s Withee gave up his teaching position in Maine and became a logging entrepreneur in the Black River Valley of Wisconsin. He later served as Clark County treasurer and represented the district in the state assembly in the 1879 and 1880 sessions. (Scholtz)

Wittenburg [WIT uhn berg]. Shawano. Town (1880) and Village (1893). Founded by the Reverend Evan Johnson Homme, a minister of the

Norwegian Lutheran Church of American, who, with help from the synod, established the Martin Luther Norwegian Orphans Home and a facility for the care of the homeless elderly, which opened in 1882. About the same time a group of German Lutheran clergy organized the Martin Luther German Academy. At Rev. Homme's request, the Milwaukee, Lake Shore & Western railroad changed the name of its station from Carbonero, Spanish for 'coal mine,' to Wittenberg, for the theologically famous German city where the Protestant Reformation was begun by Martin Luther in the sixteenth century. (*Commemorative Biographical Record of the Upper Wisconsin Counties*, 132–33)

Witwen [WIT wen]. Sauk. About 1856 Gaudenz Witwen emigrated from the canton of Graubünden, Switzerland, and established a flour and feed mill on Honey Creek. His son, John, was the first postmaster in 1892. (Derleth, 21)

Wolf River. Winnebago. Town (organized as Orihula in 1855; changed to Wolf River in 1861). See Black Wolf.

Wonewoc [WAHN uh wahk]. Juneau. Town (1856) and Village (1878). Logging began in the area in the early 1840s. Delando Pratt, from Madison County, New York, built a gristmill and had the site platted in 1855. The name is from Ojibwa *wonowin* 'howling' (the howling of wolves). The post office was established in February 1856, Jabish T. Clement, postmaster. (Stennett, 140)

Wood. County (1856) and Town (1874). Named for Joseph Wood (1811–90). Born in Seneca County, New York, Wood moved to Little Fort, Illinois (now Waukegan), in 1836, where he served as postmaster, county coroner, and clerk of the court. About 1847 he brought his family to Grand Rapids, Wisconsin (now Wisconsin Rapids), where he built the Magnolia House, a combination hotel, general store, and meeting hall. While serving in the state legislature in 1857, Wood proposed the organization of a new county from Portage and suggested the name Greenwood. The legislature authorized the county but with the name of Wood. Joseph Wood also served as the first county judge and as mayor of Grand Rapids in the 1870s. (*Reflections of 150 Years*, 11–12)

Woodboro. Oneida. Town (1893) and ppl. Founded in 1890 by George E. Wood of Chicago, owner of the Wood Lumber Company. (Doucette et al., 157)

Woodford. Lafayette. Probably named by John Kerns, who established the Woodford post office in August 1888. The reasons for the choice of the name are unknown. By a local popular etymology, Woodford was coined from the cordwood that was cut in the area and the ford in the Pecatonica River at the site. (Stetler, 3–4)

Woodhull. Fond du Lac. Named from the Woodhull post office, established in March 1864 by postmaster David R. Williams, for John Woodhull, the deputy postmaster at Fond du Lac. (Worthing)

Woodman. Grant. Town (1865) and Village (1917). Local historians may be correct in claiming that the namesake is Cyrus Woodman, a lawyer, banker, and purchasing agent for the Boston and Western Land Company, which had the site surveyed in 1863. However, William Stennett, a railroad official, may be right when he claims that the name recognizes Edwin E. Woodman of Hudson, Wisconsin, who served in the state senate in the early 1880s and was later secretary of the Chicago, St. Paul, Minneapolis & Omaha railroad. This may be a case of one name reinforcing the other to the advantage of both. (Butterfield, *History of Grant County*, 872; Stennett, 140)

Woodmohr [WUD mor]. Chippewa. Town (1917). A blend of the names of Western Woodard, who represented the district in the Wisconsin Assembly in the 1910s, and early settler Lawrence Mohr.

Woodruff. Oneida, Vilas. Town (1905) and ppl. Woodruff was platted in December 1888 for Alfred L. Cary, general solicitor for the Milwaukee, Lake Shore & Western railroad, who oversaw extension of the line north from Rhinelander. The name, probably chosen by Cary, is for Charles H. Woodruff of New York, who, along with his law partner Benjamin Aymar Sands, were major stockholders in this and several other Wisconsin railroads. (Stennett, 141)

Woodstock. Richland. Formerly known as Siresville (Syresville) for pioneer settler Alexander Sires, who emigrated from Indiana with his sons, Alexander and William, in 1854. The following year the site was formally laid out by plat owners Quinton Nicks and Milton Satterlee. The name is probably a transfer. The original Woodstock is in Oxfordshire, England. The name was brought to Massachusetts in the late seventeenth century and there are now Woodstocks in some thirty states, including Vermont and New York, each of which contributed substantial numbers of settlers to Wisconsin. The Siresville post office was established in January 1885, Milton Satterlee, postmaster, and changed to Woodstock later that year. (Butterfield, *History of Crawford and Richland Counties*, 1051, 1056, 1057)

Woodville. St. Croix. Village (1911). From about 1872 the site was a changing station on the West Wisconsin railroad known as Kelley's Switch. The name was formalized as Woodville about 1875, reportedly chosen for Woodville, Jefferson County, New York. The post office was established in December 1875, Jonas S. Anderson, postmaster. (Stennett, 197)

Woodworth. Kenosha. Simon Lovett was the original owner of the site of Woodworth, staking a claim about 1839. The first name was apparently

Bristol, for Ira Bristol, until the Kenosha & Beloit railroad established a station about 1862, which was named for Linus Woodworth, from New York State, who had purchased the property in the late 1840s. See Bristol. (Engberg, 74)

Worcester [WOO ster, WUS ster]. Price. Town (1876) and ppl. Founded by the Wisconsin Central railroad about 1872. Named by Charles or Gardner Colby for Worcester, Massachusetts, one of a number of names from the Boston area on the Wisconsin Central line. See Colby. (*Historical Sketches of Dorchester*, 4)

Worden [WORD uhn]. Clark. Town (1893). Named for Zephaniah Worden, originally from New York, an early settler, Civil War veteran, and mail carrier. The post office was established in December 1900, Mitchel Hamman, postmaster. (Scholtz)

Wrights Corners. Trempealeau. Named for landowner and Trempealeau County treasurer Hollister Wright, a Canadian by birth, who arrived in the area about 1854. (*History of Northern Wisconsin*, 2:1051)

Wrightstown. Brown. Town (1851) and Village (1901). In 1836 Hoel Wright, originally from Vermont, established a ferry across the Fox River, giving rise to the name Wright's Ferry. After the county board of supervisors in 1856 authorized Wright to construct a toll bridge at the site, he began calling the settlement Bridgeport. Wright became one of Bridgeport's leading citizens and namesake of the town and village. (D. Martin, 310)

Wuertsburg [WERTS berg]. Marathon. Named in 1887 for his birthplace, Würzburg, Bavaria, by the first postmaster, Franz (Frank) Pancratius Weigand. This is the only Wuertsburg (so spelled) in the United States.

Wyalusing [weye uh LOO sing]. Grant. Town (1854) and ppl. Laid out in the early 1840s by Enos P. Finn, the founder of Patch Grove (q.v.). For the first few years the community was known as Wyoming, probably named from Wyoming Valley in Pennsylvania. The name officially became Wyalusing with establishment of the post office in 1851. Either Finn or first postmaster James M. Otis chose the name for Wyalusing, the township and community in Bradford County, Pennsylvania. Wyalusing is from Munsee Delaware *machiwihilusing* 'place of the old man,' often translated figuratively as 'home of the old warrior.' See Wyoming. (Butterfield, *History of Grant County*, 865)

Wyeville [WEYE vil]. Monroe. Village (1923). Founded by the Chicago & North Western railroad in 1883 as Necedah Junction and renamed from the Wyeville post office in 1911 by site owner Christian Stenholdt. The source of the name is unknown. Stennett, usually quite reliable in these matters, suggests that the post office name was respelled from Wythe or

Wytheville, of which there are several in the eastern states (141). The post office was established in October 1890, Charles Brooks, postmaster.

Wyocena [weye uh SEE nuh]. Columbia. Town (1849) and Village (1909). After failing to establish a viable business at Columbus, Major Elbert Dickason moved to Duck Creek, where he built a combination home and tavern in 1843. Several years later Dickason and Benjamin Dey laid out Wyocena. What looks and sounds like a Native American name has no such roots and is in fact essentially meaningless. Dickason apparently dreamed up the name—quite literally. According to J. Jones, Dickason "said he had been on a journey the night before to a metropolis where all was business and bustle and the name of the city was Wyocena" (359). This is the only Wyocena in the United States.

Wyoming. Waupaca. Town (1890). A transfer from one of the several Wyomings in eastern Pennsylvania, themselves named from Wyoming Valley near Wilkes-Barre. Wyoming is from Munsee Delaware, an Algonquian language, meaning 'at the big flat.' In 1809 Thomas Campbell published *Gertrude of Wyoming: A Pennsylvanian Tale*, a long narrative poem telling the highly romanticized story of a conflict between the Iroquois and the British. Campbell's poem popularized the name and influenced its spread to more than a dozen states, including the state of Wyoming. (McDevitt, 269)

Yellow Lake. Burnett. In the 1830s Joseph Nicollet recorded the name of the lake as Wassawa Gomig, from Ojibwa *Osawa* 'yellow' (241). The post office was established in December 1903, Andrew Melland, postmaster.

Yellowstone. Lafayette. Named from Yellowstone Creek, itself probably named for the color of the local limestone. Also known as Scottstown, for early settler Benjamin Scott, first master of the Yellow Stone post office in 1852. (*Lafayette County Bicentennial Book*, 112)

York. The towns of York in Clark (1873), Dane (1848), Sauk (1850), and Green (1849) Counties were named for and by the many early settlers from New York State. Emigrants from New York were so numerous that they were often referred to generally as Yorkers.

Yorkville. Racine. Town (1842) and ppl. Settlers began to arrive in the 1830s. The name was probably chosen by Chatfield H. Parsons for his home state of New York. Parsons established the Yorkville post office in January 1840.

Young America. Washington. Founded in 1851 by sawmill operator Morris Wait. The community flourished for a time but began to decline when railroad stations were opened at Barton and at West Bend. Wait apparently chose the name from the Young America political and social movement established in the eastern states in the mid-1840s. The movement, which advocated free trade and increased settlement of western lands, was supported by President James K. Polk and U.S. Senator Stephen A. Douglas, both of whom have Wisconsin counties named in their honor. Young America was a popular place name in the middle of the nineteenth century; there are Young Americas in Illinois, Minnesota, Ohio, Indiana, and several other states. (Quickert, 48)

Yuba [YOO buh]. Richland. Village (1935). Site owner Edward Pinick laid out Yuba on Christmas Day, 1855. The source of the name, as Braithwaite (2–3) suggests, is Yuba, the river, city, and county in north central California. By 1855 a number of Wisconson miners had tried their luck in the California gold fields and some had returned with place names and little else. Yuba, California, was named after a village occupied by a Maidu tribe on what became the Yuba River. Whatever meaning the name may have had is unknown, but it does not mean 'river of grapes,' as often reported. For a time, Cuba City (q.v.) was known as Yuba. (Bright)

Zachow [ZAH ko]. Shawano. Named for William C. Zachow, a leading area businessman of the 1880s and 1890s. The post office was established in December 1907, John M. Miller, postmaster. (Stennett, 142)

Zander. Manitowoc. Named for Helmuth Zander, who emigrated from Mecklenburg, Germany, in 1855 and kept the local grocery store. He established the post office in 1900.

Zenda [ZEND uh]. Walworth. Founded with construction of the Chicago, Milwaukee & St. Paul railroad in 1901. Probably named from the popular adventure novel *The Prisoner of Zenda* by Anthony Hope, published in 1894. The post office was established in April 1902, Walter A. Palmer, postmaster. This is one of five Zendas in the United States.

Zittau [ZI to]. Winnebago. Named by settlers from Zittau, Saxony, Germany. The post office was established in February 1881, Benjamin Metzig, postmaster.

Zoar [ZO ar]. Winnebago. As a place name Zoar occurs in about a dozen states. Zoar, Wisconsin, is probably a transfer, likely by settlers from Ohio. The name is ultimately from the biblical city, where Zoar is a place of refuge. Lot fled from Sodom to the relative safety of Zoar. The post office was established in May 1871 by William Spiegelberg, an officer in the Prussian army who immigrated to Wisconsin in 1857.

References

Adams, Kathy. *History of Marion*. Marion, WI: Marion Advertiser, 1988.

"Adams County, Wisconsin, Place Name History." www.wiroots.org/wiadams /admsplaces.html [accessed April 7, 2016].

Almen, Alphonse Peter. *Clayton: Two Historical Sketches*. Clear Lake, WI: Village Press, 1930.

"Along the Galician Grapevine." http://www.galiziengermandescendants.org /Mennonite/newsletter2006Apr.pdf [accessed March 23, 2016].

Amidon, Hazel B. *Township of Dover, Buffalo County, Wisconsin*. Mondovi, WI: 1982.

"Andrew Meggers." http://chrismeek.org/Genealogy/Rothfolk/Meggers1.html [accessed March 23, 2016].

"Area History of Rodell, Wisconsin." www.rodellwi.com/history/history.html [accessed March 23, 2016].

Armour, Robert E. *Superior, Wisconsin, 1857–1885*. Superior, WI: 1994.

Arndt, R. E. *From Forest, to Farming, to Forgotten: A History of Tripoli, Wisconsin (1900–2000)*. Wausau, WI: DigiCopy, 2009.

Bagley through the Years. 1970.

Bailey, W. F. *History of Eau Claire County, Wisconsin, Past and Present*. Chicago: C. F. Cooper, 1914.

Balliet, Sarto. "Townships Emerge." In *Land of the Fox: Saga of Outagamie County*, edited by Gordon Bubolz, 69–92. Appleton, WI: State Centennial Committee, 1949.

Bant, Joyce I. *Culture and Continuity of Knox Mills, Wisconsin, 1864–1931*. Prentice, WI: 1985.

Baraga, Bishop Frederic. *A Dictionary of the Otchipwe Language*. 1878. Reprint (2 vols. in 1). Minneapolis: Ross and Haines, 1966.

Barker, Delores, and Greg Tennies. *History of Kekoskee, Wisconsin and the Surrounding Area*. Fond du Lac, WI: Action Printing, 2008.

Barland, Lois. *Sawdust City: A History of Eau Claire, Wisconsin from the Earliest Times to 1910*. Stevens Point, WI: Worzalla, 1960.

"Barnum Family Genealogy." barnum.org/nti01924.htm [accessed March 23, 2016].

Barquist, Barbara, and David Barquist. *The Summit of Oconomowoc: 150 Years of Summit Town*. Oconomowoc, WI: Summit History Group, 1987.

"Barron County Communities." http://resources.rootsweb.ancestry.com/USA/WI/Barron/ [accessed March 23, 2016].

"Bateman-L Archives." archiver.rootsweb.ancestry.com/th/read/BATEMAN/1999-07/0931621277 [accessed May 16, 2016].

Becker, Ethel. *Know Rock County, 1848–1948*. [Janesville, WI]: Published by authority of the Rock County Board of Supervisors, 1948.

Beckwith, Albert C. *History of Walworth County, Wisconsin*. Indianapolis: Bowen, 1912.

Behling, Agnes A. "The Early History of Price County, Wisconsin." Thesis, University of Colorado, 1941.

Belleville, "Beautiful Village," 1851–1976. Belleville, WI: Belleville Community Club, Richland Observer, 1977.

Bicentennial History of Milton. Milton, WI: Milton Bicentennial Committee, 1977.

Bicha, Karel D. "From Where Come the Badgers?" *Wisconsin Magazine of History* 76, no. 2 (1992–93): 121–31.

Bingham, Helen M. *History of Green County, Wisconsin*. Milwaukee: Burdick & Armitage, 1877.

Biographical History of Clark and Jackson Counties, Wisconsin. Chicago: Lewis, 1891.

Biographical History of La Crosse, Trempealeau and Buffalo Counties, Wisconsin. Chicago: Lewis, 1892.

"Biography of Gideon Truesdell." freepages.genealogy.rootsweb.ancestry.com/~sewis/truesdell.htm [accessed March 23, 2016].

Blang, Dennis. *The Fairchild Story, 1872–1972*. Fairchild, WI: Fairchild Centennial Organization, 1972.

Blau, Irene, and William Gay. *Germantown the Early Years, 1838–1915*. Germantown, WI: The Society, 2008.

Boettcher, Carol D. "History of the Kaehlers Mill Settlement." www.town.cedarburg.wi.us/cm/pdfs/Kaehlers_Mill_History.pdf [accessed March 23, 2016].

Bohn, Belle Cushman. "The Village of Ironton." *Wisconsin Magazine of History* 27 (1944): 310–20.

"Bottkol-L Archives." http://archiver.rootsweb.ancestry.com/th/read/BOTTKOL/2004-10/1098094965 [accessed April 20, 2016].

Braithwaite, Phillip C. *Yuba: A History of a Wisconsin Czech Community*. Marshall, WI: 1998.

"Brazeau." www.rootsweb.ancestry.com/~wioconto/brazeau.htm [accessed March 23, 2016].

Bright, William. *Native American Placenames of the United States*. Norman: University of Oklahoma Press, 2004.

Brown, Dorothy Moulding. "Indian Lover's Leaps in Wisconsin." *Wisconsin Archeologist* 17, no. 4 (1937): 84–87.

———. *Wisconsin Indian Place-Name Legends*. Madison, WI: Folklore Section, Federal Writers' Project, 1936.

Brown, William Fiske. *Rock County, Wisconsin; a New History of Its Cities, Villages, Towns, Citizens and Varied Interests, from the Earliest Times, up to Date*. Chicago: C. F. Cooper, 1908.

Brunson, Alfred. "Wisconsin Geographical Names." *Collections of the State Historical Society of Wisconsin* 1 (1903): 110–15.

Bryant, Benjamin F. *Memoirs of La Crosse County from Earliest Historical Times down to the Present.* Madison, WI: Western Historical Association, 1907.

Buchen, Gustave William. *Index to Historic Sheboygan County.* Sheboygan, WI: The Library, 1953.

Buchmeier, Robin, and Sally Stapleton. *Erin Township, Washington County, Wisconsin: 150th Anniversary Commemorative.* Erin, WI: Erin Anniversary Committee, 1996.

Buehler, J. M. *The Nekoosa Story: A Commemorative History of Nekoosa Papers Inc.* Port Edwards, WI: Nekoosa Papers, 1987.

"Burnett County Communities." www.rootsweb.ancestry.com/~wiburnet/communities .htm [accessed March 24, 2016].

Burton, Paul, and Frances Burton. *Ephraim's Founding Father: The Story of Reverend A. M. Iverson.* Ephraim, WI: Stonehill, 1996.

Butterfield, Consul Willshire. *History of Columbia County, Wisconsin.* Chicago: Western Historical, 1880.

———. *History of Crawford and Richland Counties, Wisconsin.* Springfield, IL: Union, 1884.

———. *History of Dane County, Wisconsin.* Chicago: Western Historical, 1880.

———. *History of Fond du Lac County, Wisconsin.* Chicago: Western Historical, 1880.

———. *History of Grant County, Wisconsin.* Chicago: Western Historical, 1881.

———. *History of Green County, Wisconsin.* Springfield, IL: Union, 1884.

———. *History of La Crosse County, Wisconsin.* Chicago: Western Historical, 1881.

———. *History of Lafayette County, Wisconsin.* Chicago: Western Historical, 1881.

———. *History of Racine and Kenosha Counties, Wisconsin.* Chicago: Western Historical, 1879.

Butteris, Virgil A. *History of Names; Etymology of Crawford County, Wisconsin.* 1971.

Cadott Community Centennial, 1865–1965. [Cadott, WI]: 1965.

Carver, Jonathan. *Three Years Travels through the Interior Parts of North-America for More Than Five Thousand Miles.* Philadelphia: J. Crukshank, 1784.

Cassidy, Frederic G. *Brown County.* Special Collections Department (Coltharp Onomastics Collection), University of Texas at El Paso Library. El Paso: University of Texas at El Paso, c. 1890.

———. *Dane County Place-Names.* Madison: University of Wisconsin Press, (1968) 2009.

———. "From Indian to French to English: Some Wisconsin Place-Names." *Names* 33 (1985): 51–57.

———. "'Koshkonong,' a Misunderstood Place-Name." *Wisconsin Magazine of History* 31 (1948): 429–40.

———. "Miscousing—Wisconsin." *Names* 39 (1991): 191–98.

———. "The Names of Green Bay, Wisconsin." *Names* 21 (1973): 168–78.

———. "The Naming of the Four Lakes." *Wisconsin Magazine of History* 29, 1 (1945): 7–24.

Cauffman, Betty Lou, Gilda A. Finnegan, and Harold Stauffacher. *Fennimore—Then and Now, 1830 to 1980.* [Fennimore, WI]: Dwight T. Parker Library, 1980.

Cech, Jim. *Oak Creek: Fifty Years of Progress.* Charleston, SC: Arcadia, 2005.

Celebrating Hustisford's 150 Year Heritage. Portage, WI: Hustisford Sesquicentennial Committee, 1987.

Centennial Memories: Celebrating the Village of Westfield, 1902–2002. Westfield, WI: Centennial Book Committee, 2002.

Centuria's Fiftieth Anniversary, 1900–1950, September 1–2. Centuria, WI: Centuria Commercial Club, 1950.

Chappelle, Ethel Elliot. *Around the Four Corners.* Rice Lake, WI: Chronotype, 1971.

———. *The "Why of Names" in Washburn County, Wisconsin.* Birchwood, WI: 1965.

"Charles Rollin Tyler." http://www.findagrave.com/cgi-bin/fg.cgi?page=gr&GRid= 44889729 [accessed April 20, 2016].

Chippewa County, Wisconsin: Past and Present. Chicago: S. J. Clarke, 1913.

Christiansen, Ruth Bunker. *Polk County Place Names and Fact Book.* Frederic, WI: 1975.

"City of Darlington." www.wisconsinhistory.org/Content.aspx?dsNav=N:4294963828- 4294963788&dsRecordDetails=R:BA15985 [accessed April 6, 2016].

"City of Greenfield, Wisconsin." www.ci.greenfield.wi.us [accessed April 6, 2016].

City of Owen, Wisconsin, Golden Jubilee, 1925–1975. Owen, WI: Jubilee Committee, 1976.

City of Wauwatosa. Oklahoma City, OK: Mosher-Adams, 1991.

Clark, William L. *Panorama of Progress.* Boyceville, WI: Press-Reporter, 1960.

Clinton Bicentennial, 1776–1976: 1837–1976 History. Clinton, WI: Clinton Community Bicentennial Committee, 1976.

Cole, Henry Ellsworth. *Baraboo and Other Place Names in Sauk County, Wisconsin.* Baraboo, WI: Baraboo News, 1912.

———. *A Standard History of Sauk County, Wisconsin.* Chicago: Lewis, 1918.

Coloma Area Sesquicentennial: "Voices of the Past, Visions of the Future." Coloma, WI: Coloma Area Historical Society, 2008.

Columbia County Historical Society. *Columbia County History Book, 1982: Columbia County, Wisconsin.* Dallas, TX: Taylor, 1982.

Commemorative Biographical Record of Racine and Kenosha Counties, Wisconsin. Chicago: J. H. Beers, 1906.

Commemorative Biographical Record of the Counties of Brown, Kewaunee and Door, Wisconsin. Chicago: J. H. Beers, 1895.

Commemorative Biographical Record of the Counties of Rock, Green, Grant, Iowa and Lafayette, Wisconsin. Chicago: J. H. Beers, 1901.

Commemorative Biographical Record of the Fox River Valley Counties of Brown, Outagamie and Winnebago. Chicago: J. H. Beers, 1895.

Commemorative Biographical Record of the Upper Lake Region. Chicago: J. H. Beers, 1905.

Commemorative Biographical Record of the Upper Wisconsin Counties of Waupaca, Portage, Wood, Marathon, Lincoln, Oneida, Vilas, Langlade and Shawano. Chicago: J. H. Beers, 1895.

Commemorative Biographical Record of the West Shore of Green Bay, Wisconsin, Including the Counties of Brown, Oconto, Marinette and Florence. Chicago: J. H. Beers, 1896.

Common Threads: A History of Four Wisconsin Communities in Green Lake County, Marquette, Kingston, Manchester, Dalton. Kingston, WI: Friends of the Mill Pond Library, 1998.

"Communities Draw Names from Men, Places, Events." 2000. www.usgennet.org/usa /wi/county/eauclaire/history/ourstory/vol5/names.html [accessed March 24, 2016].

"Community of Lake Five." www.slahs.org/history/local/lake_five.htm [accessed March 24, 2016].

"Conrad E. Nystrum Obituary, d. October 5, 1923." boards.ancestry.com/localities
.northam.usa.states.wisconsin.counties.taylor/376/mb.ashx [accessed March 24,
2016].

Conrath, Anthony F., and John M. Terrill. *Conrath Remembered: A Short History of
the Village of Conrath.* 1975.

"Constant Jean Baptiste Thiry, Sr." www.findagrave.com/cgi-bin/fg.cgi?page=gr&
GRid=69802114 [accessed March 24, 2016].

Cooney, Eleanore V. *Little Wolf River Country: An Early History of the Area.* 1976.

Cotter, Mary. *Prescott: Past and Present.* Prescott, WI: Prescott Journal, 1949.

Coulet du Gard, René. *Dictionary of French Place Names in the U.S.A.* Newark, DE:
Editions des Deux Mondes et Slavuta, 1986.

Crotteau, Carolyn R. *Historical Album: Recollections of Times Gone By: Cameron
Centennial, 1879–1979.* [Cameron, WI]: 1978.

Crownhart, Maurice. *Strolling through a Century: The Story of Grantsburg, Burnett
County, Wisconsin from 1865–1965.* Grantsburg, WI: 1965.

Cuba City Centennial: 100 Years, 1875 to 1975. Cuba City, WI: The Committee, 1975.

Curtiss 75th Anniversary Celebration, July 26, 27, 28, 1957. Curtiss, WI: 1957.

Curtiss-Wedge, Franklyn. *History of Buffalo and Pepin Counties, Wisconsin.* Winona,
MN: H. C. Cooper, 1919.

———. *History of Clark County.* Chicago and Winona, MN: H. C. Cooper, 1918.

Curtiss-Wedge, Franklyn, and George O. Jones. *History of Dunn County, Wisconsin.*
Minneapolis: H. C. Cooper, 1925.

Curtiss-Wedge, Franklyn, and Eben Douglas Pierce. *History of Trempealeau County,
Wisconsin.* Chicago and Winona: H. C. Cooper, 1917.

Dallas Centennial, 1870–1970: August 15–16, 1970. http://digital.library.wisc.edu/1711.dl
/WI.IHDallasCent [accessed May 16, 2016].

Damaske, Charles H. *Along the Right-of-Way to Burlington.* 1994.

———. *Along the Right-of-Way to East Troy.* 1995.

———. *Along the Right-of-Way to Sheboygan.* 2001.

———. *Along the Right-of-Way to Waukesha.* 2000.

"Dancy, Wisconsin." http://homepages.rootsweb.ancestry.com/~haywood/towns
/danwi.htm [accessed April 20, 2016].

De Cicco, Peter D. "History of Stoddard." stoddardwi.tripod.com/id5.html [accessed
March 24, 2016].

Derleth, August. *Sauk County, a Centennial History.* Baraboo, WI: Sauk County
Centennial Committee, 1948.

DeRozier, Tim, and Debbie Dohr Halbach. *Journal of a Village: Hilbert, Wisconsin
1873–1998.* Hilbert, WI: Hilbert Centennial Committee, 1998.

Derrick, Beatrice Durand. *Great Scott! A History of Northern Wisconsin's Earlier Days.*
Rev. ed. Webster, WI: 1977.

"Descendants of Unknown Mattausch." freepages.genealogy.rootsweb.ancestry.com
/~shardon/mattausch/d1.htm [accessed March 24, 2016].

Dessureau, Robert M. *History of Langlade County, Wisconsin.* Antigo, WI: Berner
Brothers, 1922.

Dictionary of Wisconsin Biography. Madison: State Historical Society of Wisconsin, 1960.

Dictionary of Wisconsin History. www.wisconsinhistory.org/dictionary [accessed April
6, 2016].

Diedrich, Nicholas, and John Britten Gehl. *History of Clintonville, Wisconsin.* Milwaukee: Cannon Printing, 1937.

Dopke, Jill. "History of Bruemmerville." *Kewaunee Historical Society: Historical Notes* 20, no. 2 (April 2008): 2–3.

Dopke, Jill, and Susan K. Slikkers. *Early History of Carlton Town: Kewaunee County, WI.* Kewaunee, WI: Kewaunee County Historical Society, 2009.

Doucette, Pauline, Lelah Bruso, Patricia Friebert, and Dorothy Guilday. *Oneida County: Centennial History Edition, 1887–1987.* Oneida County, WI: 1987.

"Douglas County." sassmaster.tripod.com/list.html [accessed March 24, 2016].

Drewiske, David P. *Village of Almond Community Resources.* [Stevens Point, WI]: Portage County UW-Extension, 1980.

Driessel, Richard Henry. *A History of the Village of Barton.* Fern Park, FL: 1991.

Dunbar Remembered. Dunbar, WI: Dunbar Centennial Committee, 1987.

Dunlavy, Esther. *History of the Townships, Waupaca County, 1975.* New London, WI: 1975.

Dunn, James Taylor. *The St. Croix: Midwest Border River.* [St. Paul]: Minnesota Historical Society Press, 1979.

Dunn County Historical Society. *Dunn County History.* Dallas, TX: Taylor, 1984.

Durbin, Richard D. *The Wisconsin River: An Odyssey through Time and Space.* Cross Plains, WI: Spring Freshet Press, 1997.

Early History of Grant County Villages, Towns. [Wisconsin]: 1900.

Easton, Augustus B. *History of the Saint Croix Valley.* Chicago: H. C. Cooper, 1909.

Eaton, Conan Bryant. *Death's Door: The Pursuit of a Legend.* Washington Island, WI: Jackson Harbor Press, 1996.

Eccles, Sylvia Miller. *Ozaukee Place Names.* Thiensville, WI: Ozaukee County Historical Society, 1963.

Edgerton Story: A History of Edgerton, Wisconsin. Edgerton, WI: Edgerton Centennial, 1953.

"Edmund Pennington Obit., May 2, 1926." boards.ancestry.com/surnames.pennington /3176/mb.ashx [accessed May 16, 2016].

Ehrlinger, Elda, comp. *Plymouth Township Centennial, Rock County, Wis.* Plymouth, WI: The Commission, 1948.

Ela, Ida L. *The Early History of Rochester, Wisconsin.* [Rochester, WI]: 1935.

"Elroy." www.rootsweb.ancestry.com/~wijuneau/Elroy.htm [accessed March 24, 2016].

Engberg, Mable Glasman. *Bristol Heritage.* Bristol, WI: Bristol Bicentennial Committee, 1976.

Engel, Dave. *Cranmoor: The Cranberry Eldorado.* Rudolph, WI: River City Memoirs, 2004.

Engel, Dave, and Herbert A. Bunde. *Shanagolden: An Industrial Romance: Ashland County History.* Rudolph, WI: River City Memoirs, 1990.

Engel, Marge. "History of the Town of Winchester." co.vilas.wi.us/landuse/wi-app .pdf [accessed April 6, 2016].

Ericson, Timothy L. *A Most Beautiful and Handy Name: Wisconsin Place Names in the St. Croix Valley.* River Falls: University of Wisconsin–River Falls Press, 1997.

Evans, Howard V. *A History of Redgranite-Lohrville and Its High School.* Mt. Pleasant, MI: Central Michigan University Printing Services, 1996.

Falge, Louis. *History of Manitowoc County, Wisconsin.* Chicago: Goodspeed, 1912.

"Family Agnes-Walker-Amble-Benson-Austerman-Grassel-Gruber." http://wc .rootsweb.ancestry.com/cgi-bin/igm.cgi?db=:1617238 [accessed March 24, 2016].

Fimreite, Clifford. *Eleva: Seventy-Fifth Anniversary, 1902–1977.* Eleva, WI: 1977.

Fisher, Lucius G. "Pioneer Recollections of Beloit and Southern Wisconsin." *Wisconsin Magazine of History* 1 (1917): 266–86.

Fitchburg Bicentennial. Fitchburg, WI: Countryside Publications, 1976.

"Florence, Wisconsin." genealogytrails.com/wis/florence/spreadeagle.htm [accessed March 24, 2016].

Folkedahl, Beulah. "Forgotten Villages, Helena." *Wisconsin Magazine of History* 42 (1959): 288–92.

Folsom, William H. C., and E. E. Edwards. *Fifty Years in the Northwest.* St. Paul: Pioneer Press, 1888.

Footsteps of La Crosse: A Journey through Time and Architecture. [La Crosse, WI]: La Crosse Public Library, 2008.

Ford, Alice M., and Millie Dougherty. *Downing, Wisconsin.* Glenwood City, WI: Glenwood City Tribune, 1988.

Forrester, George. *Historical and Biographical Album of the Chippewa Valley, Wisconsin.* Chicago: A. Warner, 1892.

"Foster Township." wiclarkcountyhistory.org/foster/index.htm [accessed April 6, 2016].

Fouks, Gordon, and Doris Fouks. *Deer Park, Wisconsin, the History of the Beginning and the Growth of the Village of Deer Park, Wisconsin and the Surrounding Area.* Deer Park, WI: 1998.

———. *Marion Johnson and L. J. Adgate: Memories of Cylon, Wisconsin and Surrounding Area.* New Richmond, WI: 2003.

Freda, Edward W., and Bernie Miller. *Algoma (West Algoma): History Review Story.* Oshkosh, WI: 1994.

Frederick, George C. "A Study of the 'Iron Ridge' Mine." *Field Station Bulletin.* 27, no. 1 (Spring 1994): 1–36.

———. *When Iron Was King in Dodge County, Wisconsin, 1845–1928.* Mayville, WI: Mayville Historical Society, 1993.

"Fred Piehl." http://www.worldheritage.org/articles/Fred_Piehl [accessed April 20, 2016].

Gagnon, Evan. *Neshotah: The Story of Two Rivers, Wisconsin.* Stevens Point, WI: Worzalla, 1969.

Galesville Centennial: In the Garden of Eden: 1854–1954. Galesville, WI: Centennial Committee, 1954.

Gamroth, Clarence J. *Historical Album: 100 Years, Independence, Wisc.* Independence, WI: 1976.

Gannett, Henry. *The Origin of Certain Place Names in the United States.* Washington: Government Printing Office, 1905.

Gard, Robert, and L. G. Sorden. *The Romance of Wisconsin Place Names.* New York: October House, 1968.

Gempler, Jackie, Leotta Ley, Tonia James Anderson, and Cindy Reynolds Doyle. *A History of the Village of Jonesdale.* [Dodgeville, WI]: Centennial Book Committee, 1985.

"George Stangel." boards.ancestry.com/localities.northam.usa.states.wisconsin
.counties.kewaunee/1631.2.1/mb.ashx [accessed May 16, 2016].

Gerber, Emil. *Memories of Cobban.* [Jim Falls, WI]: 1986.

———. *Making of Jim's Falls and Area.* [Jim Falls, WI]: 1989.

"Ghost" Towns of Waupaca County. Royalton, WI: Waupaca County Historical Society,
1991.

Gnacinski, Janneyne Longley, and Louise Baneck Longley. *Sullivan, Town 6 North: A
History of the Town of Sullivan, Jefferson County, Wisconsin.* Waukesha, WI:
Freeman, 1970.

Goc, Michael J. *From Past to Present.* Friendship, WI: Adams County Historical Society,
1999.

———. *Land Rich Enough.* Northridge, CA: Windsor Publications, 1988.

———. *Many a Fine Harvest.* Baraboo, WI: Sauk County Historical Society, 1990.

———. *100 Years on the Flambeau.* Friendship, WI: New Past Press, 1989.

———. *One Man, One Village.* Friendship, WI: New Past Press, 1985.

"Good Old Days." wiclarkcountyhistory.org/clark/news/OldDays/1999_4_7.htm
[accessed May 16, 2016].

Gordon, Linda, and Kathy Grant. *Osceola: A Village Chronicle: 1844–1994.* Osceola,
WI: Osceola Historical Society, 1994.

Gordon, Newton S., and Franklyn Curtiss-Wedge. *History of Barron County, Wisconsin.*
Minneapolis: H. C. Cooper, 1922.

Grant County History, 1900–1976. [Lancaster, WI]: Resource Committee of Grant
County, 1976.

Grawey, Frances Felch. *History of the Town of Porterfield.* Peshtigo, WI: Peshtigo
Times, 1988.

"Green Bay & Western Lines." www.greenbayroute.com/people.htm [accessed May
16, 2016].

Greene, Helen Mary Schancer. *Lugerville, Town of Flambeau, 1904–1954.* Park Falls,
WI: Price County Historical Society, 1992.

"Green Grove Township History." www.usgennet.org/usa/wi/county/clark/greengrove
/history/index.htm [accessed March 25, 2016].

Haese, Robert. *Three Score Years and Fifteen: Being a Review of Seventy-Five Years of
Progress of the Forest Junction Congregation on the Appleton District of the Wisconsin
Conference of the Evangelical Church, 1866–1941.* Forest Junction, WI: Zion
Evangelical Church, 1941.

Hagen, Gerald A. *History of Altoona.* Altoona, WI: 1987.

Haight, Theron W. *Memoirs of Waukesha County: From the Earliest Historical Times
down to the Present.* Madison, WI: Western Historical Association, 1907.

Hale, James B. *Going for the Mail: A History of Door County Post Offices.* Green Bay,
WI: Brown County Historical Society, 1996.

Hamilton, Edmund C. *The Story of Monroe: Its Past and Its Progress toward the Present.*
Monroe, WI: Monroe Public Schools Print Shop, 1976.

"Hamilton M. Peyton." zenithcity.com/zenith-city-history-archives/biography/peyton-
hamilton [accessed April 6, 2016].

Harney, Richard J. *History of Winnebago County, Wisconsin, and Early History of the
Northwest.* Oshkosh, WI: Allen & Hicks, 1880.

Hartung, Richard P. *Cooksville: A Guide.* Janesville, WI: Rock County Historical
Society, 1982.

Hathaway, Joshua. "Indian Names." *Collections of the State Historical Society of Wisconsin*, 1 (1903): 116–18.

"Hayes, Oconto County, Wisconsin." www.rootsweb.ancestry.com/~wioconto/tvhayes .htm [accessed March 25, 2016].

Hayward, Alice McCaul. *Story of Tomah*. Tomah, WI: Journal Print, 1955.

Heltemes, Kim J. *Poy Sippi and Eastern Waushara County*. Charleston, SC: Arcadia, 2005.

Heritage of Hartford. Hartford, WI: Hartford Centennial Committee, 1983.

Heritage of Iron & Timber, 1880–1980. Florence County, WI: Published for Florence County, Wisconsin, under the direction of the Florence County Centennial Committee, 1980.

Hildebrand, Janice. *Heart of Sheboygan County: Sheboygan Falls, Plymouth, Lima, and Lyndon Townships*. Dallas, TX: Curtis Media Corp, 1992.

Hiles, William, and Sheryl Hiles. *Yellow River Pioneers*. Pittsville, WI: Pittsville Historical Society, 1987.

Hintz, Martin, and Daniel Hintz. *Day Trips from Milwaukee*. Guilford, CT: Globe Pequot Press, 2003.

Historical/Architectural Resources Survey. Neenah, WI: Heritage Research and Wisconsin Historical Society, 2004.

Historical Sketches of Dorchester. Dorchester, WI: Dorchester Days, 1973.

Historical Sketches of the Town of Oulu, Bayfield County, Wisconsin, 1889–1956. Oulu, WI: The Club, 1956.

"Historic Dates, Places, and People of Tomahawk." www.wlhn.org/counties/histtom3 .html [accessed April 5, 2016].

Historic Genesee Township. Genesee Depot, WI: The Society, 1985.

Historic Hatfield. Hatfield, WI: Hatfield Fire Department and the Hatfield Chamber of Commerce, 1992.

Historic Perry. Daleyville, WI: Perry Historical Center, 1994.

History of Amberg. Amberg, WI: The High School, 1947.

History of Augusta. Augusta, WI: Augusta Centennial Committee, 1956.

History of Bruce. Bruce, WI: Bruce Historical Committee, 1984.

History of Dodge County. Chicago: Western Historical, 1880.

History of Fence. Fence, WI: The Town, 1996.

History of Iowa County, Wisconsin Containing an Account of Its Settlement, Growth, Development and Resources. Chicago: Western Historical Company and Wisconsin Historical Society, 1881.

History of Jackson. Germantown, WI: Germantown Press, 1976.

History of Jefferson County. Chicago: Western Historical, 1879.

History of Northern Wisconsin. Chicago: Western Historical, 1881.

"History of Racine, Wisconsin." www.racinehistory.com/srw.htm [accessed April 7, 2016].

History of Rock County, Wisconsin. Chicago: Western Historical, 1879.

History of Sauk County, Wisconsin. Chicago: Western Historical, 1887.

History of Taylor County, Wisconsin. Gilman, WI: 1923.

History of the Glidden Four-Town Area. Glidden WI: Glidden Area Historical Society and Museum, 1984.

"History of the Nenno Family." math.uww.edu/~mcfarlat/pictures/nennohis.htm [accessed April 7, 2016].

History of the Settlement of Darien, Allens Grove, and Fairfield. [Darien, WI]: The Committee, 1976.

"History of the Wisconsin Veterans Home at King." http://dva.state.wi.us/Documents /newsMediaDocuments/WDVA%20Toolkit/Brochures/WDVA_B3402_History _of_the_Wisconsin_Veterans_Home.pdf [accessed March 25, 2016].

History of Town of Clayton, Winnebago County, Wisconsin. Larsen, WI: Winchester Area Historical Society, 1999.

History of Vernon County, Wisconsin. Springfield, IL: Union, 1884.

History of Washington and Ozaukee Counties, Wisconsin. Chicago: Western Historical, 1881.

History of Waukesha County, Wisconsin. Chicago: Western Historical, 1880.

Hladish, Kathryn, Agnes Wudel, and Louis Hladish. *Harmony Happenings: Late 1800s to 1993.* Park Falls, WI: Weber & Sons, 1994.

Holand, Hjalmar Rued. *History of Door County, Wisconsin, the County Beautiful.* Chicago: S. J. Clarke, 1917.

Holford, Castello N. *History of Grant County, Wisconsin.* Marceline, MO: Walsworth, 1900.

Holton's Heritage, 1875–1975. Abbotsford, WI: Abbotsford Printing, 1976. http://digital .library.wisc.edu/1711.dl/WI.Holton [accessed April 7, 2016].

Houghton, Barbara H., Jane Licht, and Margaret F. Nielsen. *City of the Second Lake: A History of McFarland, Wisconsin.* McFarland, WI: Community Publications, 1976.

Howell, Liz, Pearl Foshion, and Dorothy Ackerman. *Land of the Great Gray Wolf.* Sister Bay, WI: Dragonsbreath Press, 1988.

Hubbell, Homer Bishop. *Dodge County, Wisconsin.* Chicago: S. J. Clarke, 1913.

Hudson, John C. "The Creation of Towns in Wisconsin." In *Wisconsin Land and Life*, edited by Robert C. Ostergren and Thomas R. Vale, 197–220. Madison: University of Wisconsin Press, 1997.

Huebsch, Allen, and Jane Huebsch. *Edgar: An Illustrated History.* Edgar, WI: Edgar Centennial Committee, 1998.

Hunt, John Warren. *Wisconsin Gazetteer.* Madison, WI: B. Brown, 1853.

"Iron Range Route." user.pids.net/vindalu/W&M/prototype2.htm [accessed March 25, 2016].

Iron River. Iron River, WI: Book Committee, 1992.

"Isaar." Isaar Booster Club. www.isaar.4t.com/index.html [accessed March 25, 2016].

Ixonia Township through a Century. Ixonia, WI: Ixonia Happy Homemakers, 1956.

Jackson County, a History. Black River Falls, WI: Jackson County Historical Society, 1984.

Jackson County Reader: An Anthology of Articles about Jackson County, Wisconsin. Black River Falls, WI: The Committee, 1975.

Jaeger, Alida, Carl F. Jaeger, Waldmar Nass, and Thomas Reiss. *Heritage of Ixonia: 1846–1996.* Watertown, WI: Watertown Daily Times, 1996.

Jambois, Nancy K. *Genoa History.* 1983.

Janes, Henry F. "Early Reminiscences of Janesville." *Wisconsin Historical Collections* 6 (1872): 426–35.

Janik, Erika. *A Short History of Wisconsin.* Madison: Wisconsin Historical Society Press, 2010.

Jantsch, Jim. *Dorchester, Small in Size, Big in History and Happenings*. Dorchester, WI: 2005.

Jerrard, Leigh P. *The Brule River of Wisconsin*. Chicago: Hall & Son, 1956.

"John J. Doyle obit." boards.ancestry.com/localities.northam.usa.states.wisconsin .counties.barron/918/mb.ashx [accessed May 16, 2016].

Johnson, Duane D., and Hampton L. Wilmot. *A Place-Name Study of River Falls, Wisconsin and the Surrounding Area*. 1966.

Johnson, Dwight A. *Fountain City May Have Talkie Shows: The Story of a Small Town and Its Weekly Newspaper*. Basking Ridge, NJ: Arlan Communications, 1994.

"John Thomas Marsden." records.ancestry.com/John_Thomas_Marsden_records .ashx?pid=23458868 [accessed April 7, 2016].

Jones, George O., and Norman S. McVean. *History of Lincoln, Oneida and Vilas Counties*. Minneapolis: H. C. Cooper, 1924.

———. *History of Wood County*. Minneapolis: H. C. Cooper, 1923.

Jones, James Edwin. *History of Columbia County, Wisconsin*. Chicago: Lewis, 1914.

A Journey into Mellen. 1986.

Juneau County. Friendship, WI: New Past Press, 1988.

"Justin K. Wentworth." bay-journal.com/bay/1he/writings/wentworth-justin-k.html [accessed March 31, 2016].

Kabitzke, Donald J. *North Prairie, an Historic Wisconsin Village, 1834–1950*. Milwaukee: 1983.

Keller, Fred H. "A Colgate Baseball Team?" www.livinglakecountry.com/sussexsun /news/52966277.html [accessed March 31, 2016].

Kellogg, Louise Phelps. *Organization, Boundaries and Names of Wisconsin Counties*. Madison: State Historical Society of Wisconsin, 1910.

"Kenosha County, WI Placenames." www.rootsweb.ancestry.com/~wikenosh /placenames.htm [accessed March 31, 2016].

Kepler, Twylah Shaw, and Jerry Bower. *Sabin: A History*. Richland Center, WI: Brewer Public Library, 1981.

Kessinger, L. *History of Buffalo County, Wisconsin*. Alma, WI: 1888.

Kewaunee, Wisconsin—Where Rail and Water Meet. Kewaunee, WI: American Legion, Kewaunee Post No. 29, 1927.

Keyes, Elisha W. *History of Dane County*. Madison, WI: Western Historical, 1906.

Kientz, Florence. *Alverno: The Story of the Franciscan Sisters of Alverno, Wisconsin, 1866–1919*. Washington, DC: Catholic Education Press, 1919.

Kietzer, Jane. *Lomira through the Years: 1899–1999*. Fond du Lac, WI: Action Publications, 1999.

Kindschy, Errol. *West Salem: The Story of Its Development*. West Salem, WI: Board of Education, 1963.

Kittleson, Dorothy E. *Brown Deer Then and Now: Commemorating Wisconsin's Sesquicentennial, 1848–1998*. Brown Deer, WI: Brown Deer Historical Society, 1998.

Kleiman, Jeff. *The Marshfield Story*. [Marshfield, WI]: Marshfield History Project, 1997.

Kobylarz, Dave. *Armstrong Creek Memories: Armstrong Creek, Wisconsin Diamond Jubilee, 1922–1997*. Armstrong Creek, WI: Armstrong Creek Diamond Jubilee Committee, 1997.

Koehler, Lyle. *History of Cataract, Wisconsin*. Evansville, IN: Unigraphic, 1977.

————. *Sparta, Wisconsin: The History of One Rural Community in the Nineteenth Century.* Evansville, IN: Unigraphic, 1977.

Kort, Ellen. *The Fox Heritage: A History of Wisconsin's Fox Cities.* Woodland Hills, CA: Windsor Publications, 1984.

Kortenhof, Kurt Daniel. *Sugar Camp, 1891–1941.* Eau Claire, WI: Heins Publications, 1996.

Kretche, Robert J. *West Lima Area History from 1850.* 2000.

Krier, Beatrice Wester. *Tapestry of Luxembourgers: The Making of Belgium.* Belgium, WI: 1987.

Krog, Carl Edward. "Marinette: Biography of a Nineteenth Century Lumbering Town." Thesis, University of Wisconsin–Madison, 1971.

Krogstad, Roland, and Donna M. O'Keefe. *Hartland Heritage: A History of Hartland Township, Pierce County, Wisconsin.* Madison, WI: 2010.

Kronenwetter, Michael. *Wisconsin Heartland: The Story of Wausau and Marathon County.* Midland, MI: Pendell, 1984.

Krueger, Lillian. "Waukesha, 'The Saratoga of the West.'" *Wisconsin Magazine of History* 24 (1941): 395–424.

Krug, Merton E. *History of Reedsburg and the Upper Baraboo Valley.* Madison, WI: 1929.

Lacher, J. Henry A. *The Taverns and Stages of Early Wisconsin.* Madison, WI: Published for the Society, 1915.

Laessig, Patti. *Town of Day, 101 Years: 1881–1982, Centennial Book.* [Rozelville, WI]: [Centennial Committee, Town of Day], 1982.

"LaFarge, Wisconsin." www.lafarge-wisconsin.com/history.html [accessed April 7, 2016].

Lafayette County Bicentennial Book, 1776–1976. Mt. Vernon, IN: Windmill Publications. 1991.

Lamm, W. Thomas, and James D. Janke. *Village of Somerset Community Resources.* Madison, WI: UW Environmental Awareness Center, 1977.

"Land Divisions within Waukesha County." www.slahs.org/history/local/historic_places/land_divisions.htm [accessed March 31, 2016].

Landelius, Otto Robert, and Raymond Jarvi. *Swedish Place-Names in North America.* Carbondale: Southern Illinois University Press, 1985.

Lang, Milton E. "Discourse on How Wabeno Got It's [*sic*] Name: Also Others." 1980.

Lapham, Increase Allen. *Wisconsin: Its Geography and Topography.* Milwaukee: Hopkins, 1846.

Larsen, Gina S., and Kathleen Caylor. *Putting Pulaski on the Map: Pulaski, Wisconsin Centennial, 1910–2010.* Pulaski, WI: Nsight Telservices, 2010.

Larson, Eric M. E. *Cornucopia, Wisconsin: A Concise History.* Cornucopia, WI: 1990.

Latton, Arthur J. *Reminiscences and Anecdotes of Early Taylor County.* [La Crosse, WI]: [Brookhaven Press], (1947) 2001.

Lauper, Lucile, Ethelyn Thompson, and Mary Thompson. *The Hollandale Review.* Blanchardville, WI: Ski Printers, 1987.

Lawson, Publius V. *History, Winnebago County, Wisconsin.* Chicago: C. F. Cooper, 1948.

"Lehman-L Archives." archiver.rootsweb.ancestry.com/th/read/LEHMAN/1999-09/0937288554 [accessed April 7, 2016].

Lehner, George A. *A Backward Glance: A Narrative History of Palmyra and the Surrounding Area*. Palmyra, WI: Palmyra Historical Society, 1991.

Lessard, Elva. *Fifield, 1876–1976*. Fifield, WI: 1976.

Lewis, Craig Allen. *Early Hurley, the 1880s*. Hudson, WI: Iron County Historical Society, 1984.

Liebenow, Roland R. *London, Wisconsin "Railroad Town."* Cambridge, WI: Back to the Woods, 2003.

Local History, Suring School District. 1979.

Lofgren, C. *Historical Album: Stone Lake, Wisconsin*. Stone Lake, WI: 1977.

Lovesy, Carla. *The Early Days of Briggsville, Marquette County, Wisconsin, 1850–1950*. [Briggsville, WI]: 1950.

Lucas, Henry Stephen. "The Founding of New Amsterdam in La Crosse County." *Wisconsin Magazine of History* 31 (1947): 42–60.

Luebke, Arthur L. *Pioneer Beloit*. Beloit, WI: Beloit Historical Society, 1977.

"Luxembourgers in America." www.loc.gov/rr/european/imlu/luxem.html [accessed March 31, 2016].

"Mabel Tainter Memorial Theater." www.washburn.edu/cas/art/cyoho/archive/MidwestTravel/tainter/index.html [accessed March 31, 2016].

Manitowoc County WI Archives History. "District 2 Cooperstown—Greenstreet." files.usgwarchives.net/wi/manitowoc/history/schools/district8ogms.txt [accessed March 31, 2016].

Marchetti, Louis. *History of Marathon County, Wisconsin and Representative Citizens*. Chicago: Richmond-Arnold, 1913.

Marinette County Centennial, 1879–1979. [Marinette, WI]: Marinette County Historical Society, 1979.

"Marinette County, Wisconsin: Genealogy and Local History." www.rootsweb.ancestry.com/~wimarine/townships.html [accessed March 31, 2016].

Marple, Eldon M. *The Visitor Who Came to Stay: Legacy of the Hayward Area*. Hayward, WI: Country Print Shop, 1971.

Martin, Chas. I. *History of Door County, Wisconsin*. Sturgeon Bay, WI: Expositor Job Print, 1881.

Martin, Deborah Beaumont. *History of Brown County, Wisconsin*. Chicago: S. J. Clarke, 1913.

Martin, Roy L. *History of the Wisconsin Central*. Boston: Railway and Locomotive Historical Society, 1941.

Martinson, Earl. *Lodi Sesquicentennial, 1811–1961*. [Lodi, WI]: The Committee, 1961.

McBride, Sarah D. *History Just Ahead: A Guide to Wisconsin's Historical Markers*. Madison: State Historical Society of Wisconsin, 1999.

McCafferty, Michael. "On Wisconsin: The Derivation and Referent of an Old Puzzle in American Placenames." *Onoma* 8 (2003): 39–56.

McDevitt, Robert. *From Sawmills to Villages: The Early History of Big Falls, Caroline, Leopolis & Pella and Buckbee, Granite City, Hunting & Split Rock*. Marion, WI: Marion Advertiser, 1992.

McKenna, Maurice. *Fond du Lac County, Wisconsin, Past and Present*. Chicago: S. J. Clarke, 1912.

McKenney, Lucille Dombrock. *History Notes of the Lamar Community*. 1967.

McLean, Douglas. *Maple Bluff: A History of the Village and the Community.* [Madison, WI]: 1974.

McLenegan, Annie S. *Centennial History of the Town of Turtle, Rock County, Wisconsin.* 1936.

Memorial and Biographical Record . . . of Columbia, Sauk, and Adams Counties. Chicago: Geo. A. Ogle, 1901.

"Memories of Forest Co." content.wisconsinhistory.org/cdm/ref/collection/wch/id /66729 [accessed April 7, 2016].

Mendl, Blanche, and Jerry Mendl. *Pioneer History of the Township of Ackley.* [Antigo, WI]: 1976.

Meyer, Orrin W. "Se Souvenir (To Remember)." 1964. calumet.uwex.edu/files/2010/05 /SouvenirBookletWebVersion.pdf [accessed March 31, 2016].

Meyer, Shirlene, and Carol Wuennecke. *The History of Delta, Wisconsin.* Mason, WI: S. Viskoe, 1974.

Meyers, Harold B. "Sweet, Secret World of Forrest Mars." features.blogs.fortune.cnn .com/2013/03/31/the-sweet-secret-world-of-forrest-mars-fortune-1967 [accessed April 7, 2016].

Miazga, Vicki. *The First 100 Years: Minocqua-Woodruff, 1888–1988.* Minocqua, WI: Lakeland Times, 1988.

Michael, Pat Adams. "Origin of Town Names." wigenweb.org/shawano/townnames .html [accessed April 7, 2016].

Mikoš, Susan G. *Poles in Wisconsin.* Madison: Wisconsin Historical Society Press, 2012.

Minaghan, William B., and Tim J. Vanderhoef. *The History of Calumet County, Wisconsin.* Kenosha, WI: Tim J. Vanderhoef, 1984.

Mining & Rollo Jamison Museum, Platteville, Wisconsin. "Early Remembrances of J.H. Rountree Lead Mines & Platteville Written 1870." http://mining.jamison .museum/Websites/MiningJamisonMuseum/images/John_Rountree.pdf [accessed April 7, 2016].

"Miscellaneous Laona Area News Items." www.laonahistory.com/MiscLaonaNews Items.html [accessed March 31, 2016].

Moede, Ila Hill. *Grandma's Footprints: A History of Shawano from 1843–1918.* Shawano, WI: 1991.

Monroe County. Sparta, WI: Monroe County Local History Room, 1984.

Montgomery, Ruth Ann. *Evansville Glimpses of the Grove.* [Evansville, WI]: 1990.

Morris, Robert R. *Glendale, Wisconsin: Rich Past, Bright Future, 1950–2000.* Glendale, WI: Glendale, Wisconsin, 50th Anniversary Committee, 2000.

Morrissey, Deb, and Jim Moore. *Centennial Memories: A Century of Gates-Rusk County History, 1901–2001.* [Ladysmith, WI]: Rusk County Centennial Book Committee, 2002.

Mortimer, Gilbert. "History of Valton." www.mortimergen.com/alliesgen/history1 .html [accessed March 31, 2016].

Mosinee Centennial, August 9, 10, 11: 1857–1957. Mosinee, WI: Centennial Brochure Committee, 1957.

"M. R. Baldwin Obituary." www.mainstreet-marketplace.com/pages/2008Feb08/Peopel %20Deaths/Baldwin%20Milton01.htm [accessed March 31, 2016].

Muchka, Albert. *West Allis.* Charleston, SC: Arcadia, 2003.

Mundstock, Jeanette, and Tom Stoker. *Footsteps through the Past: A Short History of Monona, Town of Bloomington Grove and East Madison.* Monona: Community Herald Newspapers, 1976.

Nagle, John. *John Nagle's History of Manitowoc County, Wisconsin, 1878.* Manitowoc, WI: Manitowoc Historical Society, 1974.

Nagel, Paul. *I Remember, I Remember: History and Lore of Jump River, Wisconsin.* Eau Claire, WI: 1986.

Nagel, Paul R., and Curtis Deuel. *The Villages of Ruby and Arnold and the Wisconsin, Ruby & Silhawn Ry.* Eau Claire, WI: 1987.

Nehring, Barbara. *Vilas County, Headwaters to Wisconsin.* Vilas County, WI: Vilas County Chamber of Commerce, 1998.

"Nelson Ottman." familytreemaker.genealogy.com/users/h/e/l/Patricia-Hellerud-/WEBSITE-0001/UHP-0212.html [accessed fall 2013].

New Richmond Centennial. New Richmond, WI: Centennial Book Committee, 1957.

Nicollet, Joseph N. *The Journals of Joseph N. Nicollet: A Scientist on the Mississippi Headwaters, with Notes on Indian Life, 1836–37.* St. Paul: Minnesota Historical Society, 1970.

Nowicki, Adela, and Pearl Kolpack. *Rietbrock Centennial, 1880–1980.* [Wisconsin]: 1980.

Nyberg, Jacqueline. *St. Croix Falls, 1838–1988.* St. Croix Falls, WI: St. Croix Falls Historical Society, 1988.

"Obituary of Edward A. Goodnough." *Wisconsin Daily State Gazette*, February 1, 1890. www.public.coe.edu/~theller/soj/unc/tame-indians/goodnough-bio.html [accessed April 5, 2016].

"Oconto County, Wisconsin: Town of How." www.rootsweb.ancestry.com/~wioconto/tvhow.htm [accessed April 5, 2016].

Olafson, Marion, and Marjory Livingston. *Livingston, Wisconsin, 1880–1980.* 1980.

Olsen, Theodore V. *The Rhinelander Story.* Rhinelander, WI: 1960.

———. *Roots of the North.* Rhinelander, WI: Pineview, 1979.

Osseo Area Bicentennial Book. [Osseo, WI]: 1976.

Ott, John Henry. *Jefferson County, Wisconsin and Its People.* Chicago: S. J. Clarke, 1917.

Our Heritage. Waupaca, WI: Waupaca County Heritage Committee, 1976.

"Outagamie County." files.usgwarchives.net/wi/outagamie/news/nl/V/5readfd.txt [accessed April 5, 2016].

Palmer, Barbara, and Jim Pederson. *The Town of Norway, Then and Now.* Norway, WI: Town of Norway Bicentennial Committee, 1983.

Paprock, John-Brian, and Teresa Peneguy Paprock. *Sacred Sites of Wisconsin.* Black Earth, WI: Trails Books, 2001.

Pattison, Mary Ann. *Buffalo County: A Pictorial History.* Virginia Beach, VA: Donning, 1993.

Pedrick, Samuel M. *A History of Ripon, Wisconsin.* Ripon, WI: Ripon Historical Society, 1964.

Pellman, James C. *Wisconsin Far Northwest: Brief Histories of the Rural Communities in Northern Douglas County.* Maple, WI: Old-Brule Heritage Society, 2004.

Pepin County History. Pepin County, WI: Pepin County History Book Committee, 1985.

Perret, Maurice E. *Portage County, of Place and Time*. Stevens Point, WI: Cornerstone Press, 1992.

Petranovich, Helen Hathaway. *History of Hersey*. Glenwood City, WI: Glenwood City Tribune, 1980.

Phillips, Melva. *Along the Military Ridge to Ridgeway*. Ridgeway, WI: 1976.

Phillips, Wisconsin. Park Falls, WI: F. A. Weber, 1976.

Pickering, Verne, and Donald Pickering. *Hatley: History of a Central Wisconsin Village*. Edina, MN: Beaver's Pond Press, 2009.

Pierce County's Heritage. River Falls, WI: Pierce County Historical Society, 1971.

Pintar, Ruth. *Our Part of America: Browntown, Cadiz, Jordan 1890–1990*. Monroe, WI: New Life Press, 1990.

Polleys, A. D. *Stories of Pioneer Days in the Black River Valley*. Black River Falls, WI: Banner-Journal, 1948.

"Portage Canal Society, History." http://www.portagecanalsociety.websitesusa.net /DesktopDefault.aspx_tabid=167.html [accessed April 20, 2016].

Portrait and Biographical Album of Rock County. Chicago: Acme Publishing, 1889.

Portrait and Biographical Record of Sheboygan County. Chicago: Excelsior, 1894.

"Port Wing, Wisconsin." http://portwingwi.com/home/about-us/pw_history/ [accessed April 20, 2016].

"Preserving the Past for the Future." www.saukcountyhistory.org/rockspringsimage .html [accessed April 5, 2016].

Prey, Hal. *Greendale: The Little Village That Could—and Did*. Greendale, WI: Country Books, 2004.

Prueher, Grace Brooks. *Bloomer Centennial, 1855–1955: A History and Program*. Bloomer, WI: 1955.

Pukall, Sue. "History of the Town of Morris." wigenweb.org/shawano/morris.html [accessed April 5, 2016].

"Pulaski Centennial, 1910–2010." athayse.fatcow.com/id21.html [accessed April 5, 2016].

Quickert, Carl. *Washington County, Wisconsin: Past and Present*. Chicago: S. J. Clarke, 1912.

Ramlow, Robert A. *Wild Rose, Wisconsin, Centennial, 1873–1973*. Waushara County, WI: Graphic Associates, 1973.

"Redgranite." www.redgranitewisconsin.com/History.html [accessed April 5, 2016].

Redmann, Nicole M. *Sturtevant, WI, the First 100 Years 1907–2007*. Sturtevant, WI: 2008.

"Re: Embry Is a French Name." http://www.genealogy.com/forum/surnames/topics /embry/742/ [accessed April 19, 2016].

Reetz, Elaine. *Come Back in Time*. Princeton, WI: Fox River Publishing, 1981.

"Re: Rantz." genforum.genealogy.com/rantz/messages/42.html [accessed April 5, 2016].

Reflections of 150 Years. Wisconsin Rapids, WI: Barking Dog Publishing, 1978.

Reinders, Marlene, and Florence Melberg. *Addison, Township No. XI N Range No. XVIII E 4th Mer. Wisconsin, 1846–1976*. Hartford, WI: Hartford Booster, 1976.

Remembering the Past! Rubicon Township Sesquicentennial. Dodge County, WI: 1998.

Rhyner, Jeanne M. *Schofield Then & Now*. Schofield, WI: 1976.

"Rib Lake Historical Society Newspaper Notes." riblakehistory.com/2013/Newpaper
    Notes.pdf [accessed April 5, 2016].

Richards, Randolph A. *History of Monroe County*. Chicago: Cooper, 1912.

Riis, Dick, and Vicki Koenen. *Danbury Diamond Anniversary History 1912–1987*.
    Danbury, WI: Danbury Diamond Anniversary Committee, 1987.

Riley, Michael. "A History of Plover." www.pchswi.org/archives/communities/plover
    /hplover1.html [accessed April 5, 2016].

Rockwell, Houser F, and Carolee Rzepiejewski. *West Central Wisconsin and Mondovi
    Area History*. Eau Claire: University of Wisconsin–Eau Claire, University Copy
    Center, 1988.

Rogers, Fred J. "Early Eastern Jackson County History." In *A Place Called City Point:
    Centennial, 1889–1989*, edited by R. J. Hanson, 44–54. Pittsville, WI: 1989.

Rohe, Randall E. *Ghosts of the Forest: Vanished Lumber Towns of Wisconsin*. Marinette:
    Forest History Association of Wisconsin, 2002.

———. "Names on the Land: A Legacy of the Wisconsin Lumber Era." *Voyageur* 2
    (1985): 17–24.

———. "Place-names: Relics of the Great Lakes Lumber Era." *Journal of Forest History*
    28 (1984): 126–35.

Romenesko, Celine. *Holy Angels, Darboy: 1850–2000, Time Gone by Time Yet to Be*.
    Darboy, WI: Holy Angels Catholic Church, 2002.

Rosholt, Malcolm. *Our County, Our Story: Portage County, Wisconsin*. Stevens Point:
    Portage County Board of Supervisors, 1959.

———. *Town 25 North: A Short History of Alban Township and Village of Rosholt, Portage
    County, Wisconsin*. [Rosholt, WI]: 1949.

Rucker, Della G. *From the McCauslin to Jab Switch*. Oconto, WI: Oconto County
    Economic Development Corp, 1999.

———. *History of Czech Settlements*. Sheboygan Falls: Wisconsin's Ethnic Settlement
    Trail, 1995.

———. "Lumbering Makes Oconto County Cities and Villages." www.rootsweb
    .ancestry.com/~wioconto/logging3.htm [accessed March 31, 2016].

Rudolph, Jack. *Birthplace of a Commonwealth: A Short History of Brown County, Wis-
    consin*. Green Bay, WI: Brown County Historical Society, 1976.

Rudolph, Robert S. *Wood County Place Names*. Madison: University of Wisconsin
    Press, 1970.

"Rudolph Reif." boards.ancestry.com/surnames.reif/7.9.10.11/mb.ashx [accessed April
    5, 2016].

Ruff, Allen. *Black Earth, a History*. Madison: Wisconsin Power and Light, 1992.

Rusk County History. Dallas, TX: Taylor, 1983.

Ryan, Thomas Henry. *History of Outagamie County*. Chicago: Goodspeed, 1911.

Saga of Frederic. Frederic, WI: Golden Jubilee Committee, 1951.

"Saint Cloud History." www.stcloudwi.com/Files/StCloudHistorytextonly.pdf [ac-
    cessed March 24, 2016].

St. Nazianz. St. Nazianz, WI: St. Nazianz Sesquicentennial Committee, 2004.

"Samuel Appleton." http://www.apl.org/node/250 [accessed April 5, 2016].

Schafer, Joseph. *Wisconsin Domesday Book: Town Studies*. Madison: State Historical
    Society of Wisconsin, 1924.

Schmidt, Ruth. "Lannon and Its Quarries." In *Lannon History: Village of Lannon Golden Jubilee 1930–1980*, edited by Fred Keller, 5–9. [Lannon, WI]: Sussex-Lisbon Area Historical Society, 1980.

Schmidt, Walter, and Elise Rockman Schmidt. *Gresham Centennial, 1908–1958 These Hewed the Way to Civilization*. Gresham, WI: Gresham Semi-centennial Committee, 1958.

Schoenick, Gene Edward. "A History of River Falls, Wisconsin, 1848–1885." Thesis, University of Minnesota, 1967.

Scholtz, Kay. "A Brief History of Clark County, Wisconsin." wigenweb.org/clark/history /brief.html [accessed April 5, 2016].

Scott, Margaret Helen. *Place Names of Richland County*. Richland Center, WI: Richland County Publishers, 1973.

Sebenthall, Betty. *Mount Horeb Centennial Book: 1861–1961*. Madison, WI: Mt. Horeb Chamber of Commerce, 1961.

Seefelt, Edward R., and James C. Stoltenberg. *Can Anything Good Come Out of New Hope?* [Wisconsin]: 2007.

Selin, Stanley. "Ole Branstad." http://www.korseberg.com/tekster/branstad.html [accessed April 5, 2016].

Sesquicentennial History of Shullsburg. Shullsburg, WI: Badger Historical Society of Shullsburg, 1977.

Shaw, John. "Shaw's Narrative." *Wisconsin Historical Collections* 2 (1856): 197–231.

Shawano County Centuarawno, 1853–1953. 1953.

Shepard, Gordon H. "History of Iowa County Wisconsin." Thesis, Colorado State College of Education, Division of Social Studies, 1950.

Shepherd, Vera Gerardy, and Ed Weiler. *Hales Corners, Wisconsin: A History in Celebration of 150 Years, 1837–1987*. Hales Corners, WI: Hales Corners Historical Society, 1988.

Silver, Wallace W. *Oxcart Days, 1854–1940*. New Richmond, WI: Leader, 1940.

Simenson, Bob. *Pictorial History Book of Barron County, Wisconsin*. Dallas, TX: Curtis Media, 1993.

Simonar, Carol J., and Neoma Michalski. *History of Luxemburg, Wisconsin*. Luxemburg, WI: Luxemburg Diamond Jubilee and Historical Committee, 1983.

Sjostrom, Marilyn. *Athens, Wisconsin Centennial*. Athens, WI: Centennial Committee, 1990. http://digital.library.wisc.edu/1711.dl/WI.Athens [accessed April 5, 2016].

Smith, Alice E. *Baraboo: An Inquiry into the Origin of the Name*. Baraboo, WI: 1953.

Smith, Mariam. *History of Omro*. [Wisconsin]: 1976.

Smith, Samuel E. *History of Markesan and Vicinity*. Markesan, WI: Markesan Bi-Centennial Celebration, 1976.

"Snider-L Archives." http://archiver.rootsweb.ancestry.com/th/read/SNIDER /2006-01/1138128930 [accessed April 21, 2016].

"SooLine History." https://groups.yahoo.com/neo/groups/SooLineHistory /conversations/messages/13926 [accessed April 5, 2016].

Sorenson, Gordon G. *Drummond Centennial, 1882–1982*. Drummond, WI: 1982.

Souvenir in Print and Pictures of the Fifty Year History of the Town of Tripp. [Tripp, WI]: The Committee, 1961.

Souvenir of Oregon Centennial. Oregon, WI: Oregon Observer, 1941.

Souvenir Program and Centennial History. Reedsburg, WI: Centennial Historical Committee, 1948.

"Spider Chain of Lakes Association." http://spiderchainoflakes.org/ [accessed April 20, 2016].

Stanley, Our Town. Stanley, WI: The Society, 1981.

Stark, William F. *Pine Lake*. Sheboygan, WI: Zimmermann Press, 1971.

Stein, Lois Roepke. *Kenosha, 1835–1983*. Norfolk, VA: Donning, 1983.

Stennett, W. H. *History of the Origin of the Place Names Connected with the Chicago & North Western and Chicago, St. Paul, Minneapolis & Omaha Railways*. Chicago: 1908.

Stetler, Ester Anderson. *Earliest History of Woodford, Wisconsin*. Darlington, WI: Southwest Graphics, 1983.

Stewart, George R. *Names on the Land: A Historical Account of Place-Naming in the United States*. New York: Random House, 1945.

Stingl, Jim. "Welcome to Imalone, a Place to Go with a Friend." *Milwaukee Journal Sentinel*. July 22, 2007.

Stone, Fanny S. *Racine, Belle City of the Lakes, and Racine County, Wisconsin*. Chicago: S. J. Clarke, 1916.

Stone, Harriet Amy. *Racine: A Tricentennial Issue*. Lexington: University of Kentucky, 1998.

Stratford Centennial Book. Stratford, WI: Centennial Book Committee, 1991.

Straub, Alfred G. *The History of Marathon, Wis, 1857–1957*. Marathon, WI: Marathon Times, 1957.

Susedik, Tina. *Nestled among the Lakes and Pines: A Centennial History of Sampson Township, 1898–1998*. Hayward, WI: 1998.

Svob, Mike. *Paddling Southern Wisconsin: 83 Great Trips by Canoe and Kayak*. Madison, WI: Trails Books, 2006.

Swart, Hannah. *Koshkonong Country Revisited: An Anthology*. Muskego, WI: Marek Lithographics, 1981.

Taylor, E. A., and Charles Holme. *Paris: Past and Present*. London: "The Studio," 1915.

Taylor, Mary. *An Intensive Architectural and Historical Survey of Green County*. 1980.

Techtmann, Catherine. *Rooted in Resources*. Friendship, WI: New Past Press, 1993.

Terrill, John M. *Ladysmith Lore: 1885, a Centennial View*. Ladysmith, WI: Ladysmith Centennial Steering Committee, 1985.

Terry, Mary Grace. *The Story of Durward's Glen*. St. Camillus Institute, 1958.

Thomas, Bruce. *Door County: Wisconsin's Peninsular Jewel*. New Berlin, WI: Sells Printing Company, 1993.

"Thomas J. Lessor." boards.ancestry.com/localities.northam.usa.states.wisconsin.counties.shawano/3481/mb.ashx? [accessed April 6, 2016].

Thompson, Ethelyn, Lucile Lauper, and Lenice Disrud. *History of the Town of Moscow*. Hollandale, WI: Holland, 1976.

"Town of Bergen, Marathon County, Wisconsin." genealogytrails.com/wis/marathon/history/bergen.htm [accessed April 6, 2016].

Town of Conover, Vilas County, Wisconsin. http://townofconover.com/wp-content/uploads/2015/09/History-of-Conover.pdf [accessed April 6, 2016].

Town of Emery Centennial. Emery, WI: Centennial Committee, 1989.

Town of Frankfort Centennial, 1890–1990. http://digital.library.wisc.edu/1711.dl/WI
.Frankfort [accessed April 6, 2016].

Town of Hewitt: 1776 Bicentennial 1976. http://digital.library.wisc.edu/1711.dl/WI
.Hewitt [accessed April 6, 2016].

"Town of Morgan." 2008. http://www.townofmorgan.org/ [accessed April 6, 2016].

Town of Morrison, 1855–2005. http://townofmorrison.org/uploads/ckfiles/files/History
/1855-2005.pdf [accessed April 6, 2016].

Town of Trenton, Village of Newburg & Myra, Wisconsin Bicentennial. Bicentennial
Committee, 1976.

Trachte, William D. *The History of Marshall, Wisconsin.* Marshall, WI: 1991.

"Tripoli: Lincoln County, Wis." usgennet.org/usa/wi/county/lincoln/somo/history
/1874_1974HistoryTripoli.htm [accessed April 6, 2016].

"Truman Abraham Warren." users.usinternet.com/dfnels/warren.htm [accessed April
6, 2016].

Truttschel, Mary Agnes. "Cities and Villages." In *Land of the Fox: Saga of Outagamie
County*, edited by Gordon Bubolz, 93–115. Outagamie County State Centennial
Committee, 1949. http://digital.library.wisc.edu/1711.dl/WI.aplFox [accessed
April 6, 2016].

Tully, Dennis P., and Donald J. Vande Sand. *Burlington.* Charleston, SC: Arcadia,
2005.

Uhls, Dean, and Roland Gullickson. *Holmen Area Centennial, 1862–1962: June 22, 23,
24.* Holmen, WI: N. Nelson, 1962.

"Underhill, Wisconsin." http://www.epodunk.com/cgi-bin/genInfo.php?locIndex=
24568 [accessed April 6, 2016].

Unity, Wisconsin: Centennial. http://digital.library.wisc.edu/1711.dl/WI.Unity [accessed
April 6, 2016].

*Van Dyne Centennial, 1866–1966: The History and Anecdotes of a Small Wisconsin
Community.* Van Dyne, WI: Van Dyne Volunteer Fire Department, 1966.

Velte, Charles H. *Historic Lake Poygan.* Neenah, WI: 1976.

Vilas County. Vilas County, WI: Vilas County Chamber of Commerce, 1998.

"Village of Portland." www.dodgejeffgen.com/archive/Portland/Portland13.html [ac-
cessed April 6, 2016].

"Village of Potter." villageofpotter.com [accessed April 6, 2016].

"Village of Valders, Village History." valders.org/valdershistory.htm [accessed April 6,
2016].

Viroqua Centennial. Viroqua: Broadcaster Print, 1946.

Vogel, Virgil J. *Indian Names on Wisconsin's Map.* Madison: University of Wisconsin
Press, 1991.

———. "Wisconsin's Name: A Linguistic Puzzle." *Wisconsin Magazine of History* 48
(1965): 181–86.

Wakefield, J. *History of Waupaca County, Wisconsin.* Waupaca, WI: D. L. Stinchfield,
1890.

Ward, Janice. *Next Stop Dresser Junction.* Osceola, WI: Osceola Sun, 1976.

Ward, William M. *The First 100 Years: A History of Soldiers Grove.* Soldiers Grove, WI:
Edward W. Herbst, 1964.

Ware, John M. *Standard History of Waupaca County, Wisconsin.* Chicago: Lewis,
1917.

"Waukesha County, Online Genealogy and Family History Library." www.linksto thepast.com/waukesha/marFbios.php [accessed April 6, 2016].

Waukesha County, Wisconsin: Selected Histories. Brookfield, WI: The Students, 1980.

Weatherhead, Harold. *Westward to the St. Croix: The Story of St. Croix County, Wisconsin*. Hudson, WI: St. Croix County Historical Society, 1978.

Weber, Nicholas P. *Caledonia: Journey to a Village, 1835–2008*. Caledonia, WI: Weber, 2008.

"Webster, Wisconsin." www.websterwisconsin.com./?110090 [accessed April 6, 2016].

Westover, Ruth. *Waukau Centennial Pageant*. Waukau, WI: Waukau Centennial Association, 1946.

Wheeler, A. C. *Chronicles of Milwaukee*. Milwaukee: Jermain & Brightman, 1861.

Whelan, Lincoln F. "'Them's they': The Story of Monches, Wisconsin." *Wisconsin Magazine of History* 24 (1940–41): 39–55.

Whittlesey Homemakers. *Pioneer Days*. Park Falls, WI: F. A. Weber and Sons, 1980.

Whyte, William Foote. *Settlement of the Town of Lebanon, Dodge County*. Madison, WI: 1916.

Wiff, Patricia M. *The Lefse and Lutefisk Belt: A History of the Village and Township of Martell, 1840–1920*. [Wisconsin]: 1983.

"Willard Wickham Seery." www.werelate.org/wiki/Person:Willard_Seery_(1) [accessed April 6, 2016].

"William Irvine." chippewacounty.com/business/things/william-irvine [accessed April 6, 2016].

Williams, Dorothy E. *The Spirit of West Bend*. 1980.

Winding through the Town of Wayne. [Wisconsin]: 1998.

Wisconsin Atlas and Gazetteer. 10th ed. Yarmouth, ME: DeLorme, 2008.

Wojta, Joseph Frank. *A History of the Town of Two Creeks, Manitowoc County, Wisconsin*. Madison, WI: Littel, 1945.

Worthing, Ruth Shaw. *The History of Fond Du Lac County, as Told by Its Place-Names*. 1976.

Wulff, Eugene C. *The New Holstein Story*. [New Holstein, WI]: 1986.

Wymore, Jeanette, and Edna I. Nelson. *Glen Flora: Gleanings from the Past*. Ladysmith, WI: Cloverland Press, 1988.

Yadon, W. Gordon. *History of Delavan*. Delavan, WI: 1982.

Zamzow, DuWayne. *Berlin's Memories in 1976*. Wausau, WI: Roto-Graphic, 1976.

Zarnoth, Dorothy. *History of Reedsville to 1976*. Brillion, WI: Zander Press, 1976.

Zehner, David J. *The History of Dale (Poker Flat) and Medina (Young's Corner), Wisconsin*. Neenah, WI: John Habermann, 1989.

Ziller, Carl. *History of Sheboygan County*. Chicago: S. J. Clarke, 1912.

Zurawski, Joseph W. *Kewaunee County, Wisconsin*. Chicago: Arcadia, 2000.